PREVIOUSLY ON NINJA SLAYER...

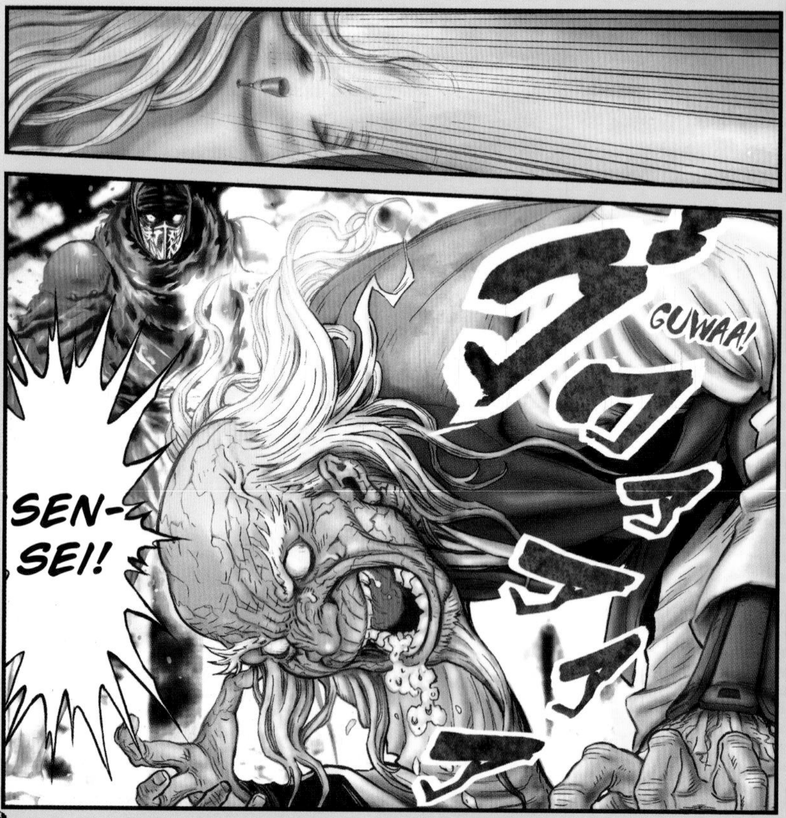
GUWAA!
SEN-SEI!

Ninja Slayer sought the antidote for the anti-ninja virus, “Takeuchi,” which had infected Master Dragon Gendoso. His search brought him to a secret meeting with the self-proclaimed journalist Nancy Lee.

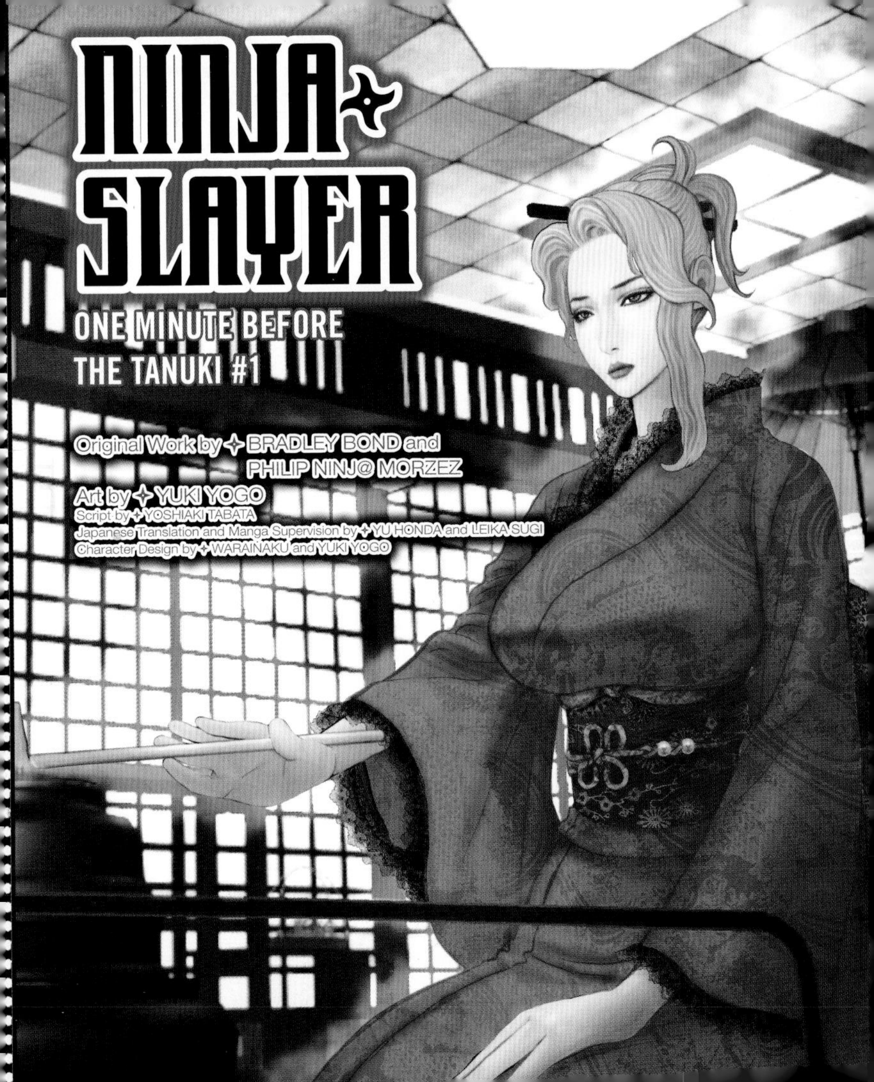
NINJA SLAYER
ONE MINUTE BEFORE THE TANUKI #1
Original Work by ✦ BRADLEY BOND and PHILIP NINJ@ MORZEZ
Art by ✦ YUKI YOGO
Script by ✦ YOSHIAKI TABATA
Japanese Translation and Manga Supervision by ✦ YU HONDA and LEIKA SUGI
Character Design by ✦ WARAINAKU and YUKI YOGO

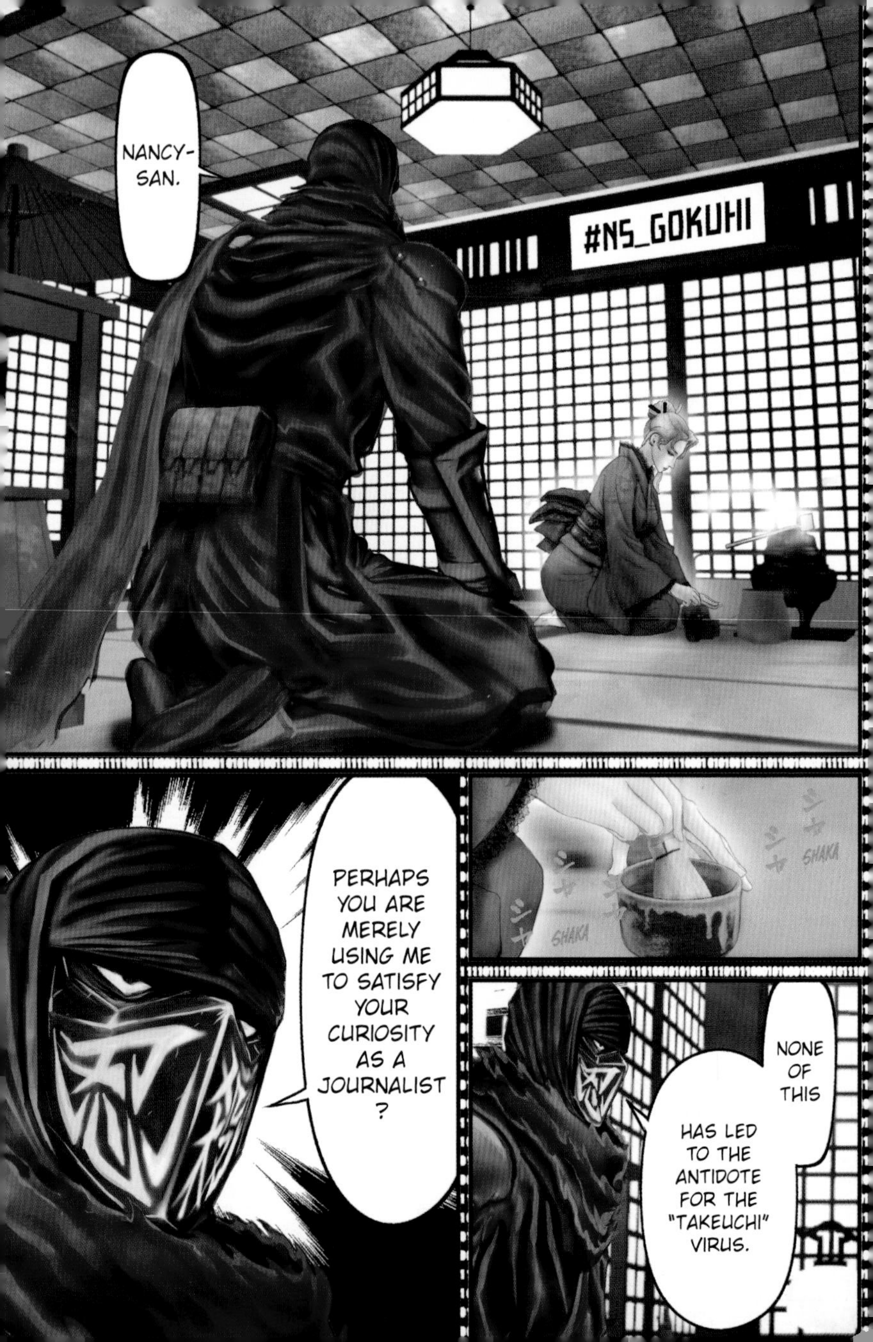
#NS_GOKUHI
NANCY-SAN.
SHAKA
SHAKA
NONE OF THIS HAS LED TO THE ANTIDOTE FOR THE "TAKEUCHI" VIRUS.
PERHAPS YOU ARE MERELY USING ME TO SATISFY YOUR CURIOSITY AS A JOURNALIST?

CONTENTS

ONE MINUTE BEFORE THE TANUKI

Original Work by ✦ BRADLEY BOND and
PHILIP NINJ@ MORZEZ

Art by ✦ YUKI YOGO
Script by ✦ Yoshiaki Tabata
Japanese Translation and Manga Supervision by ✦ Yu Honda and Leika Sugi
Character Design by ✦ Warainaku and Yuki Yogo

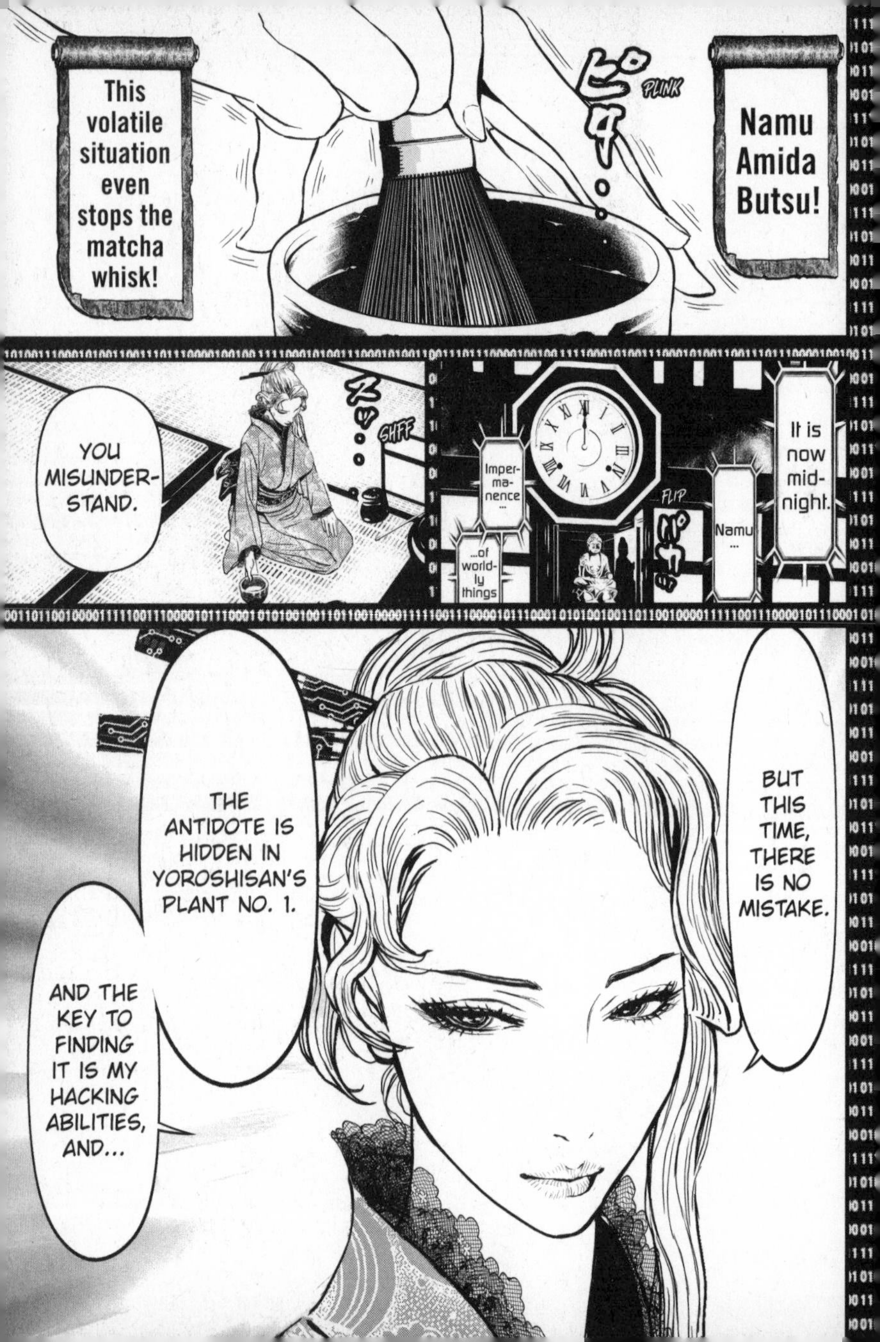
Namu Amida Butsu!
PLINK
This volatile situation even stops the matcha whisk!
It is now mid-night.
Namu ...
FLIP
Imper-ma-nence ...
...of world-ly things
SHFF
YOU MISUNDER-STAND.
BUT THIS TIME, THERE IS NO MISTAKE.
THE ANTIDOTE IS HIDDEN IN YOROSHISAN'S PLANT NO. 1.
AND THE KEY TO FINDING IT IS MY HACKING ABILITIES, AND...

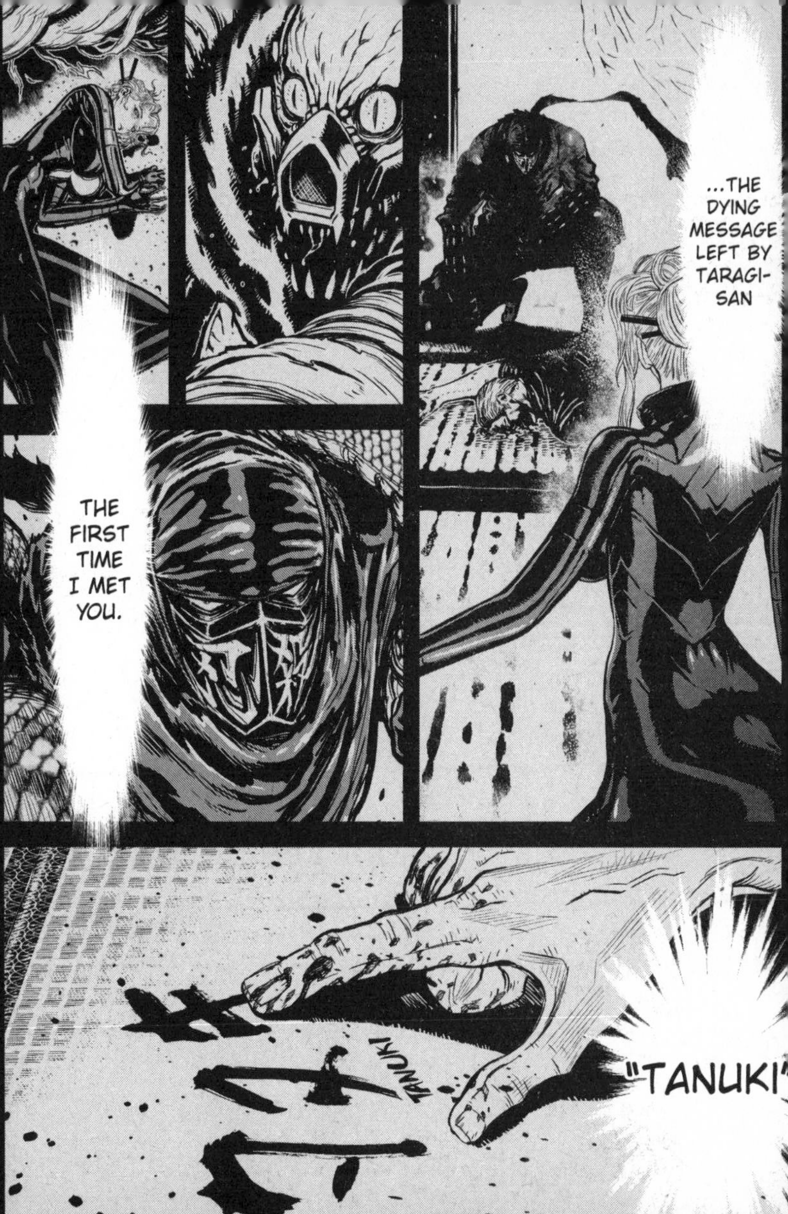
...THE DYING MESSAGE LEFT BY TARAGI-SAN
THE FIRST TIME I MET YOU.
"TANUKI"
TANUKI

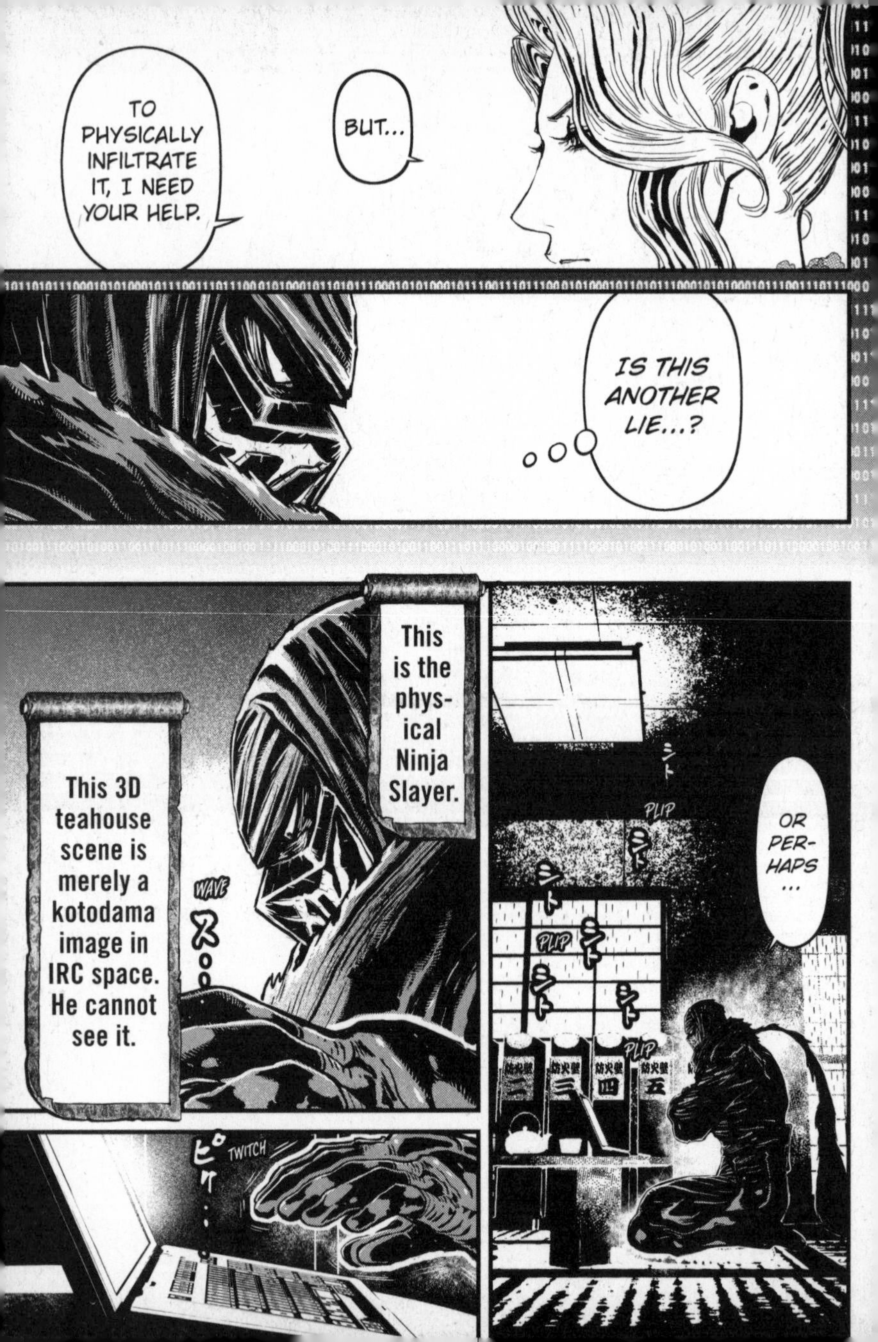
BUT...
TO PHYSICALLY INFILTRATE IT, I NEED YOUR HELP.
IS THIS ANOTHER LIE...?
OR PERHAPS...
シト
PLIP
シト
シト
シト
PLIP
シト
シト
PLIP
防火壁 二
防火壁 三
防火壁 四
防火壁 五
This is the physical Ninja Slayer.
This 3D teahouse scene is merely a kotodama image in IRC space. He cannot see it.
WAVE
ス...
ピク...
TWITCH

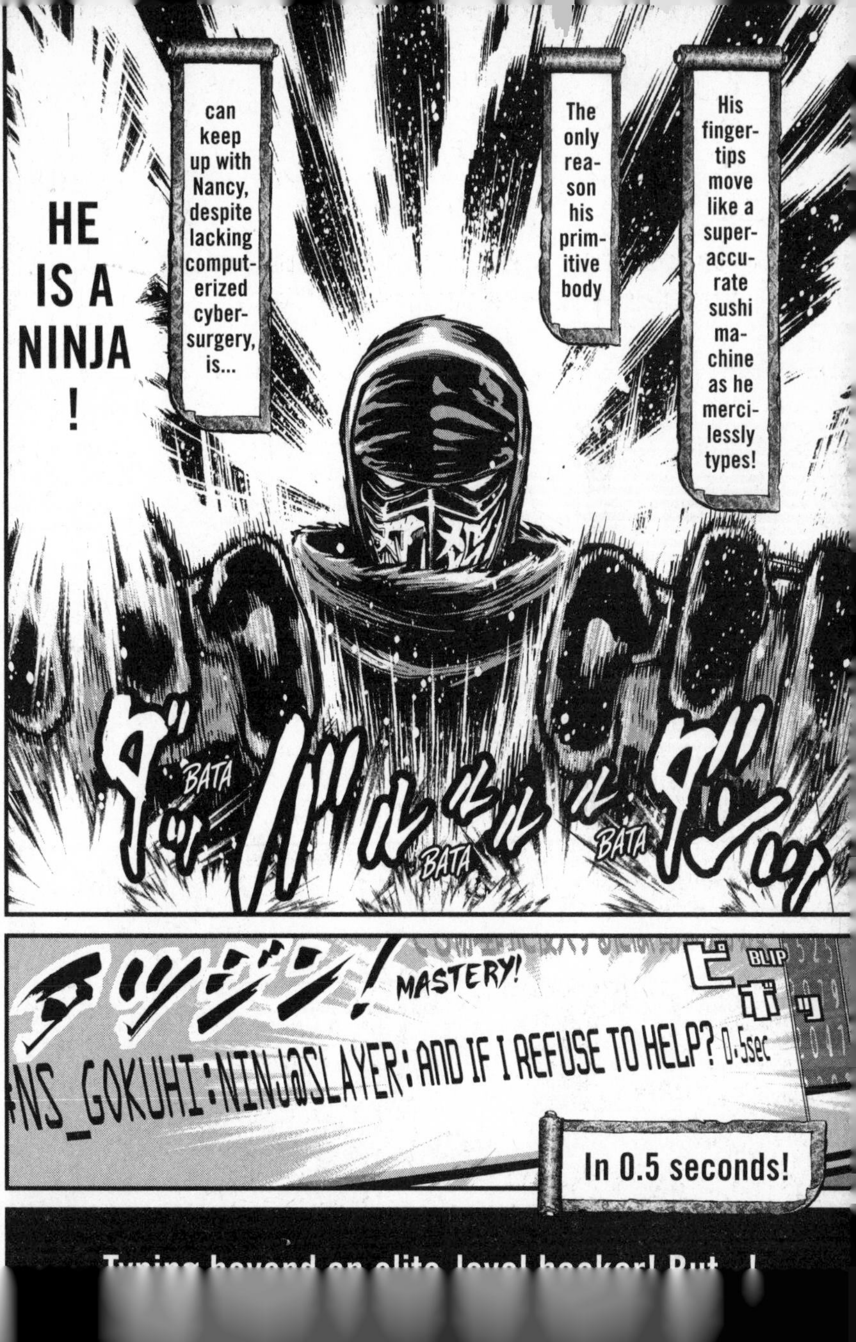
His fingertips move like a super-accurate sushi machine as he mercilessly types!
The only reason his primitive body
can keep up with Nancy, despite lacking computerized cyber-surgery, is...
HE IS A NINJA!
BATA
BATA
BATA
BLIP
MASTERY!
NS_GOKUHI:NINJA@SLAYER: AND IF I REFUSE TO HELP? 0.5sec
In 0.5 seconds!

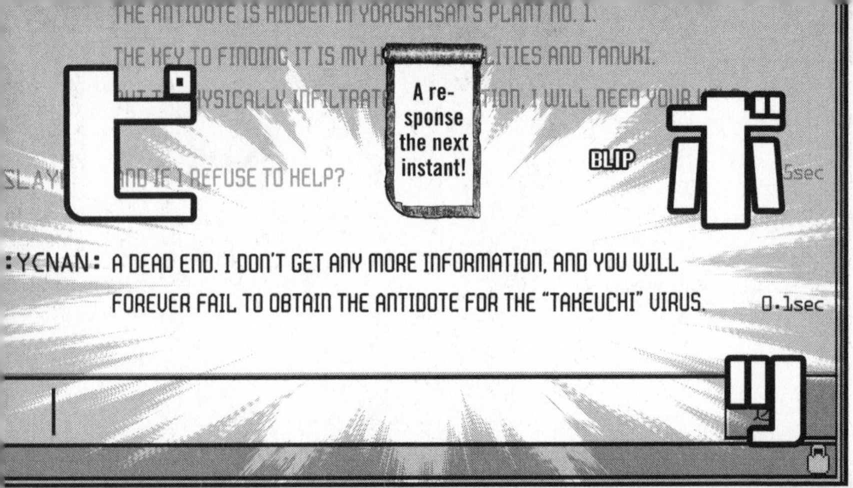
THE ANTIDOTE IS HIDDEN IN YOROSHISAN'S PLANT NO. 1.
LITIES AND TANUKI.
AND IF I REFUSE TO HELP?
5sec
ボ
BLIP
A re-sponse the next instant!
ピ
:YCNAN: A DEAD END. I DON'T GET ANY MORE INFORMATION, AND YOU WILL FOREVER FAIL TO OBTAIN THE ANTIDOTE FOR THE "TAKEUCHI" VIRUS.
0.1sec
ッ

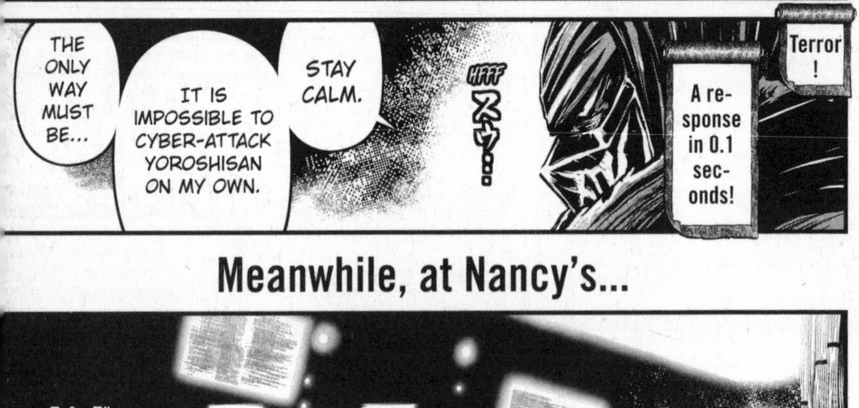
Terror!
A re-sponse in 0.1 sec-onds!
HFFF
スッ…
STAY CALM.
IT IS IMPOSSIBLE TO CYBER-ATTACK YOROSHISAN ON MY OWN.
THE ONLY WAY MUST BE...

Meanwhile, at Nancy's...

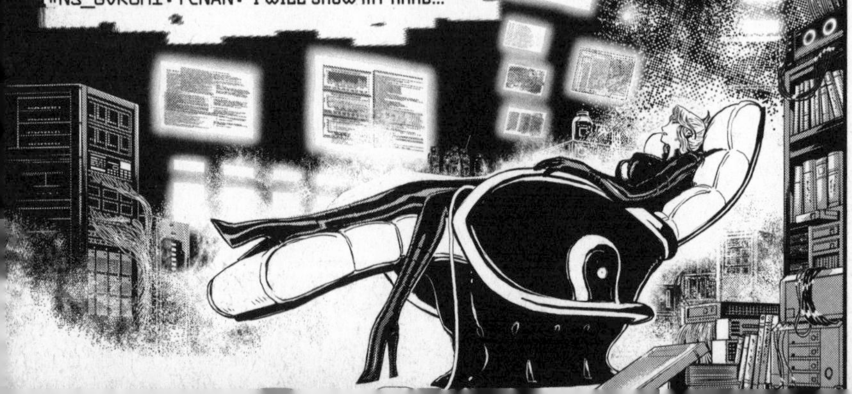
ピボッ BLIP
#NS_GOKUHI:YCNAN: I WILL SHOW MY HAND...

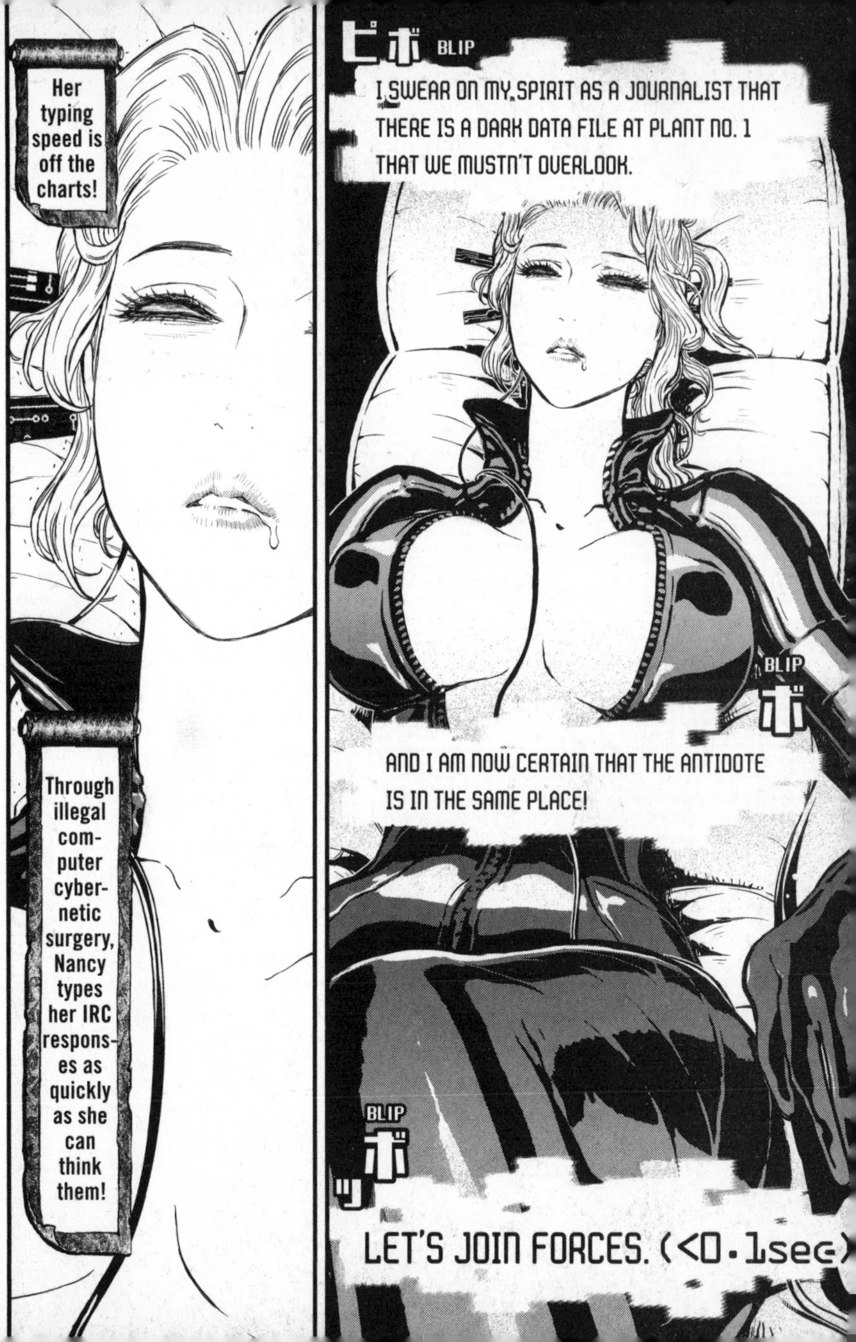
ピポ BLIP
I SWEAR ON MY SPIRIT AS A JOURNALIST THAT THERE IS A DARK DATA FILE AT PLANT NO. 1 THAT WE MUSTN'T OVERLOOK.
BLIP ボ
AND I AM NOW CERTAIN THAT THE ANTIDOTE IS IN THE SAME PLACE!
BLIP ボッ
LET'S JOIN FORCES. (<0.1sec)
Her typing speed is off the charts!
Through illegal computer cybernetic surgery, Nancy types her IRC responses as quickly as she can think them!

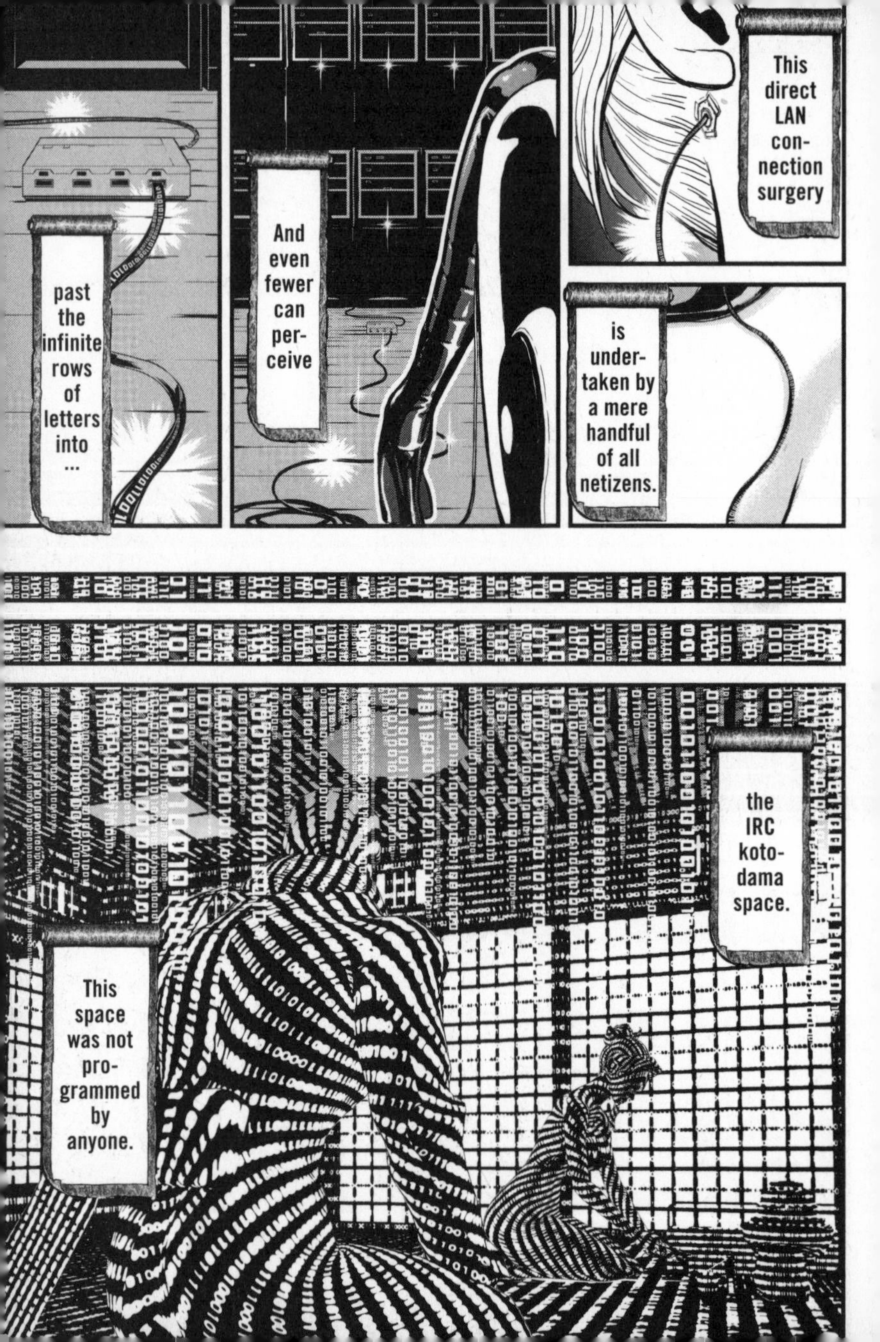
This direct LAN con-nection surgery
is under-taken by a mere handful of all netizens.
And even fewer can per-ceive
past the infinite rows of letters into ...
the IRC koto-dama space.
This space was not pro-grammed by anyone.

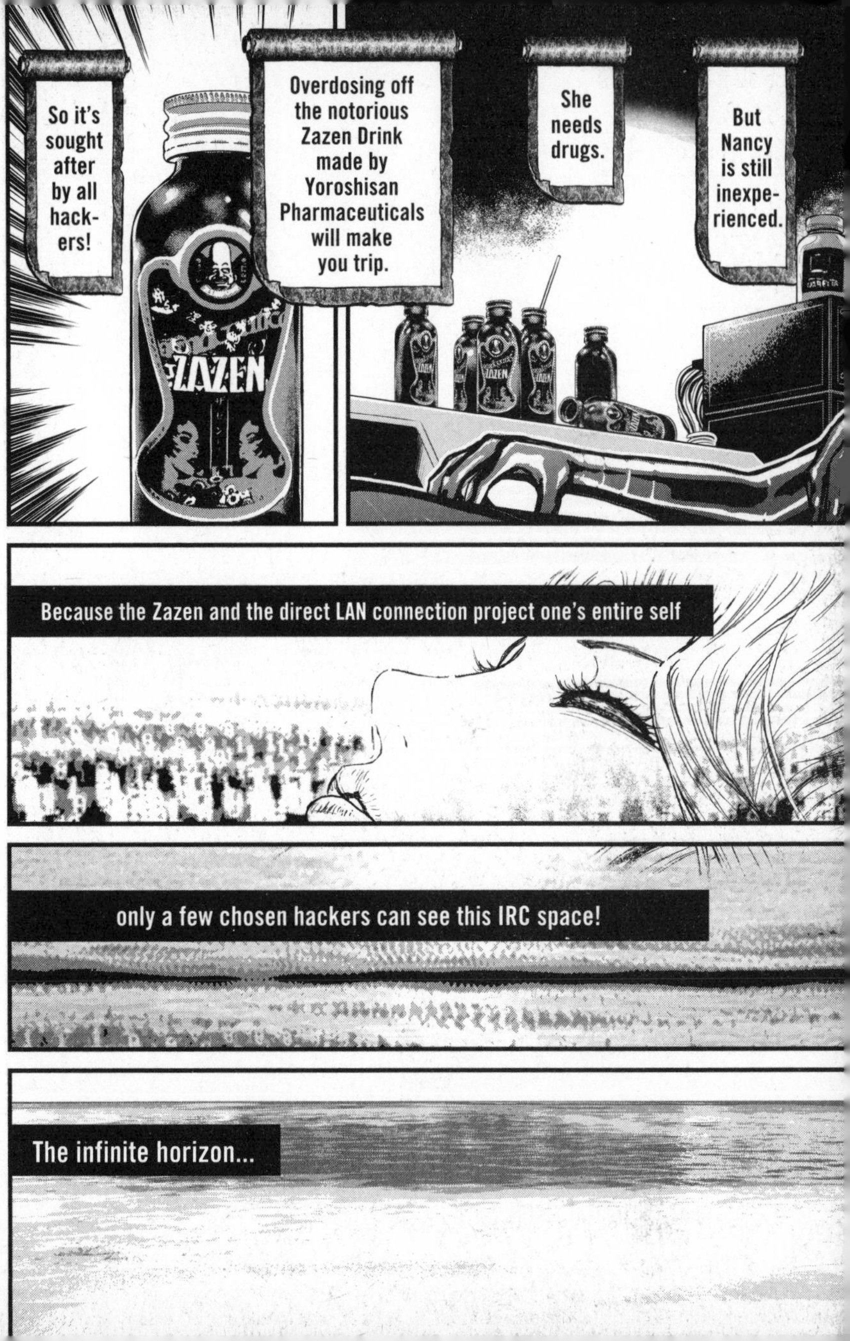
But Nancy is still inexperienced.
She needs drugs.
Overdosing off the notorious Zazen Drink made by Yoroshisan Pharmaceuticals will make you trip.
So it's sought after by all hackers!
ZAZEN
Because the Zazen and the direct LAN connection project one's entire self
only a few chosen hackers can see this IRC space!
The infinite horizon...

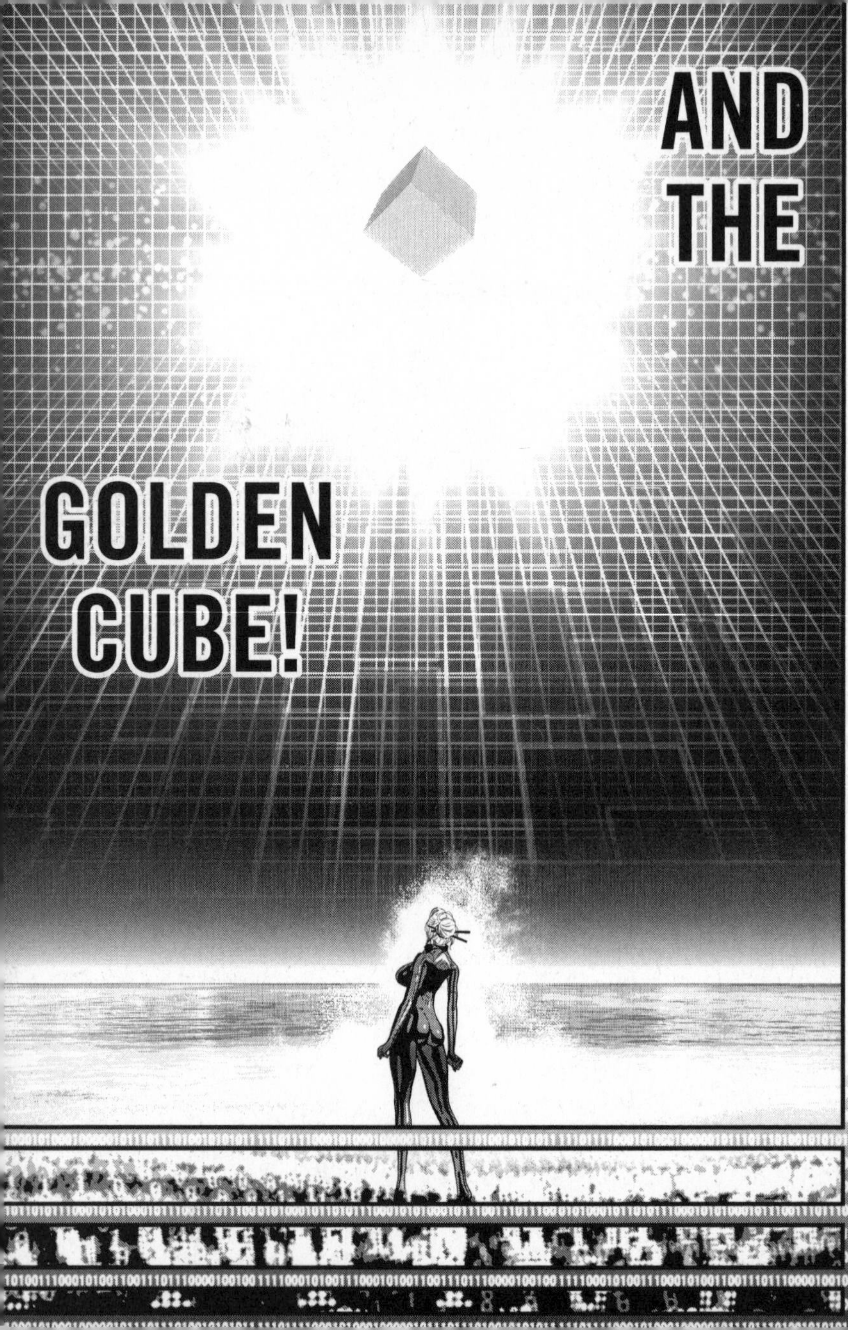
AND THE
GOLDEN CUBE!

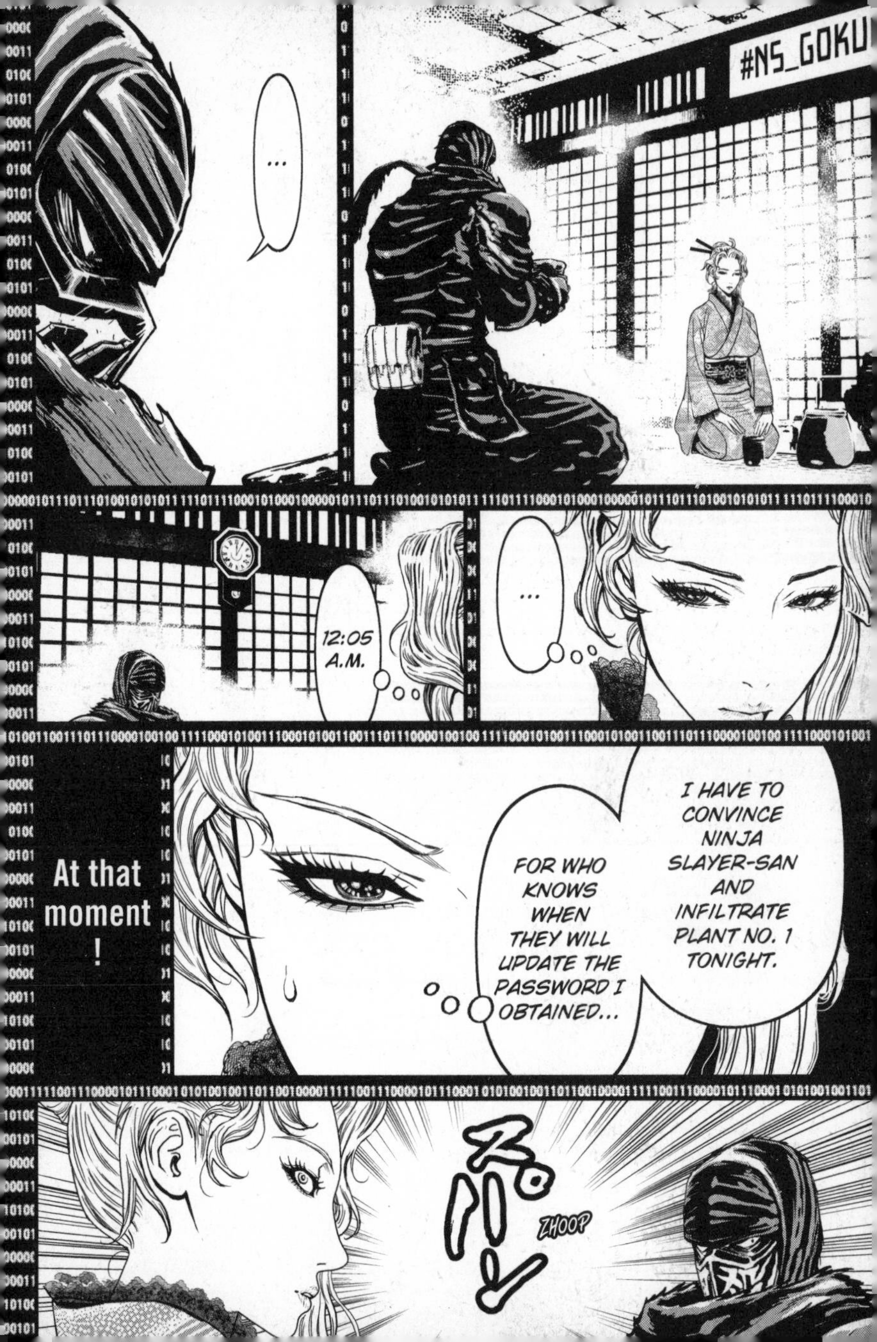
#NS_GOKU
…
…
12:05 A.M.
I HAVE TO CONVINCE NINJA SLAYER-SAN AND INFILTRATE PLANT NO. 1 TONIGHT.
FOR WHO KNOWS WHEN THEY WILL UPDATE THE PASSWORD I OBTAINED…
At that moment!
ZHOOP

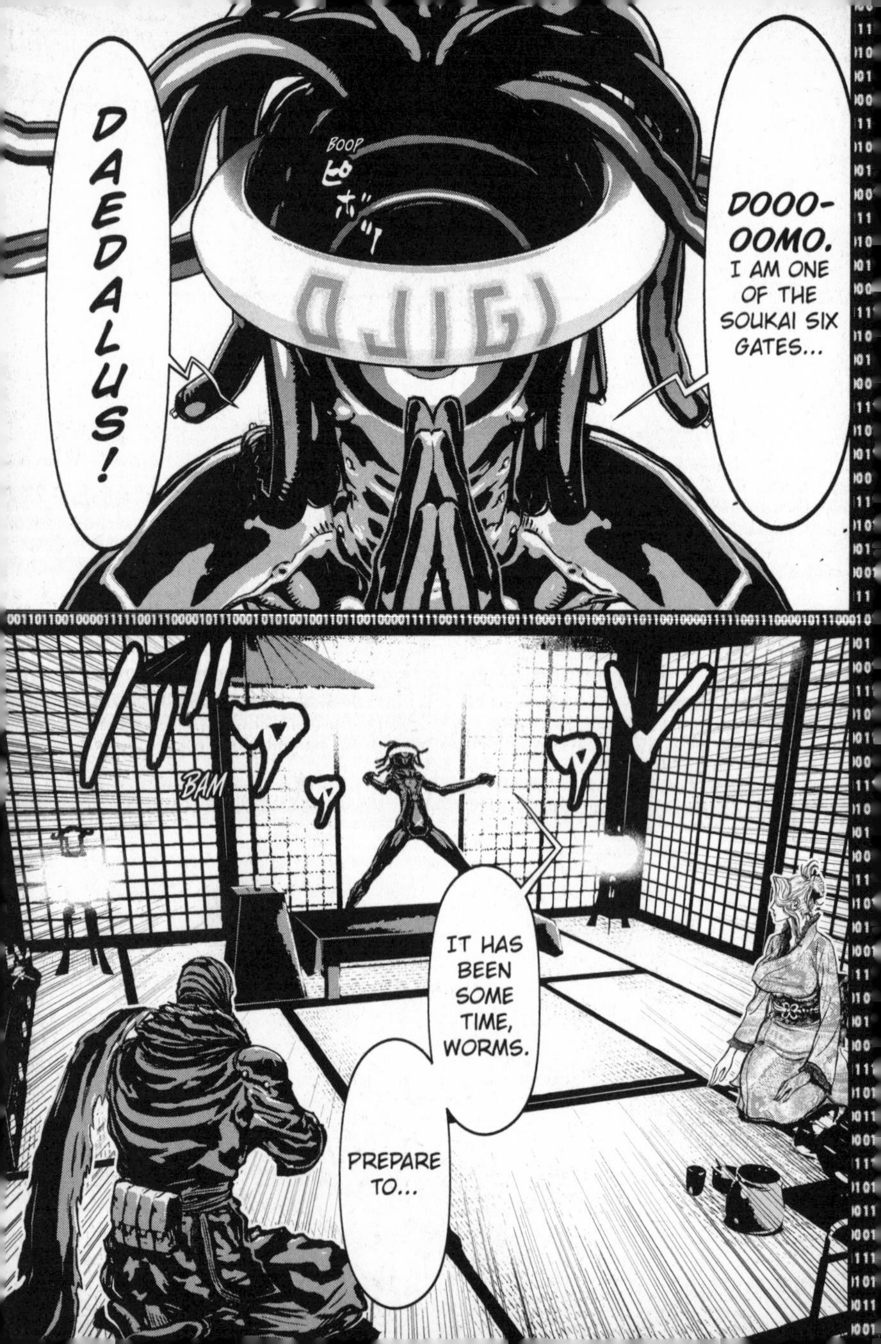
DOOOO-OOMO. I AM ONE OF THE SOUKAI SIX GATES...
DAEDALUS!
BOOP
ピポッ
BAM
IT HAS BEEN SOME TIME, WORMS.
PREPARE TO...

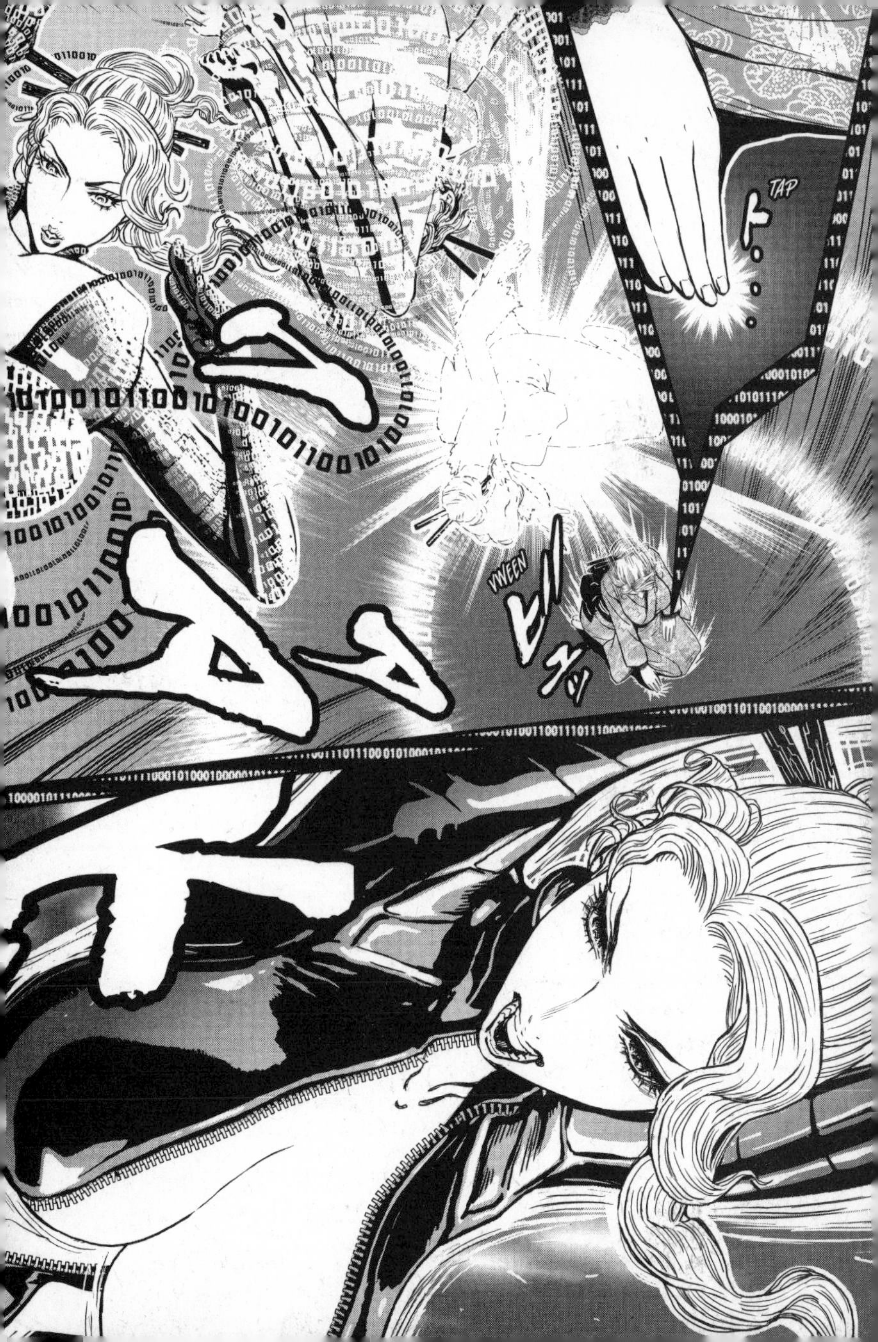
TAP
ト…
VWEEN

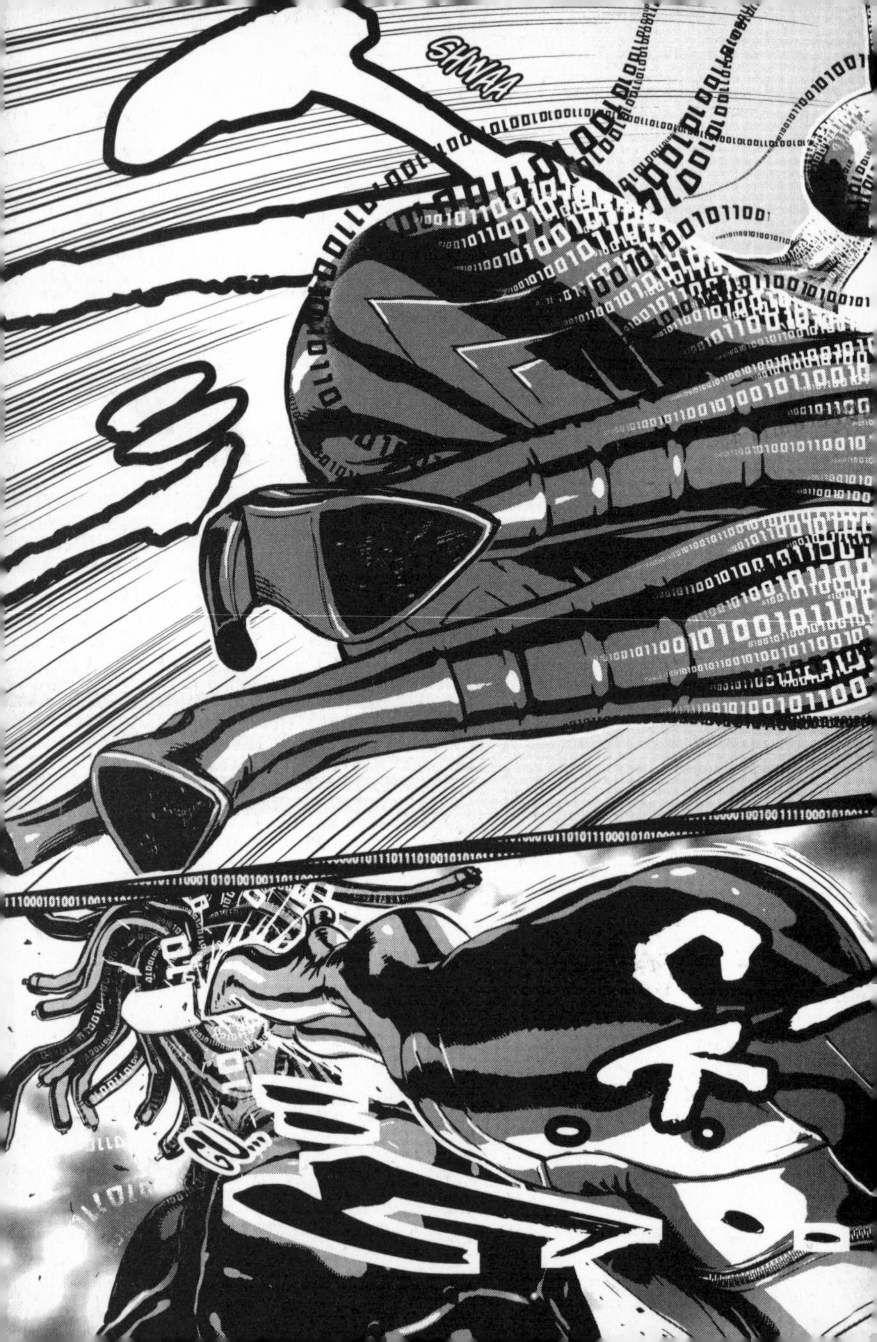
SHWAA

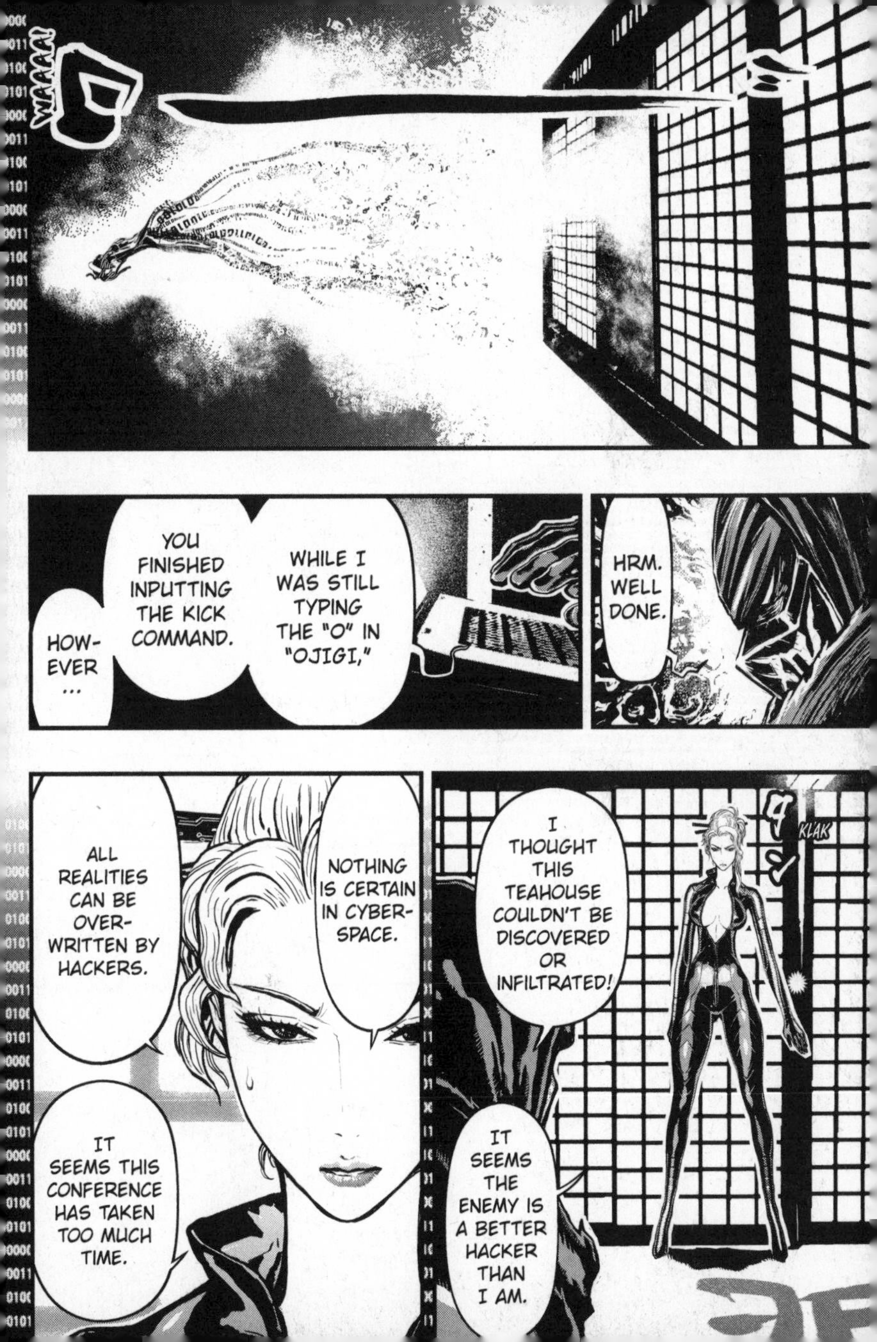
WAAAA!
HRM. WELL DONE.
WHILE I WAS STILL TYPING THE "O" IN "OJIGI,"
YOU FINISHED INPUTTING THE KICK COMMAND.
HOW-EVER ...
KLAK
I THOUGHT THIS TEAHOUSE COULDN'T BE DISCOVERED OR INFILTRATED!
IT SEEMS THE ENEMY IS A BETTER HACKER THAN I AM.
NOTHING IS CERTAIN IN CYBER-SPACE.
ALL REALITIES CAN BE OVER-WRITTEN BY HACKERS.
IT SEEMS THIS CONFERENCE HAS TAKEN TOO MUCH TIME.

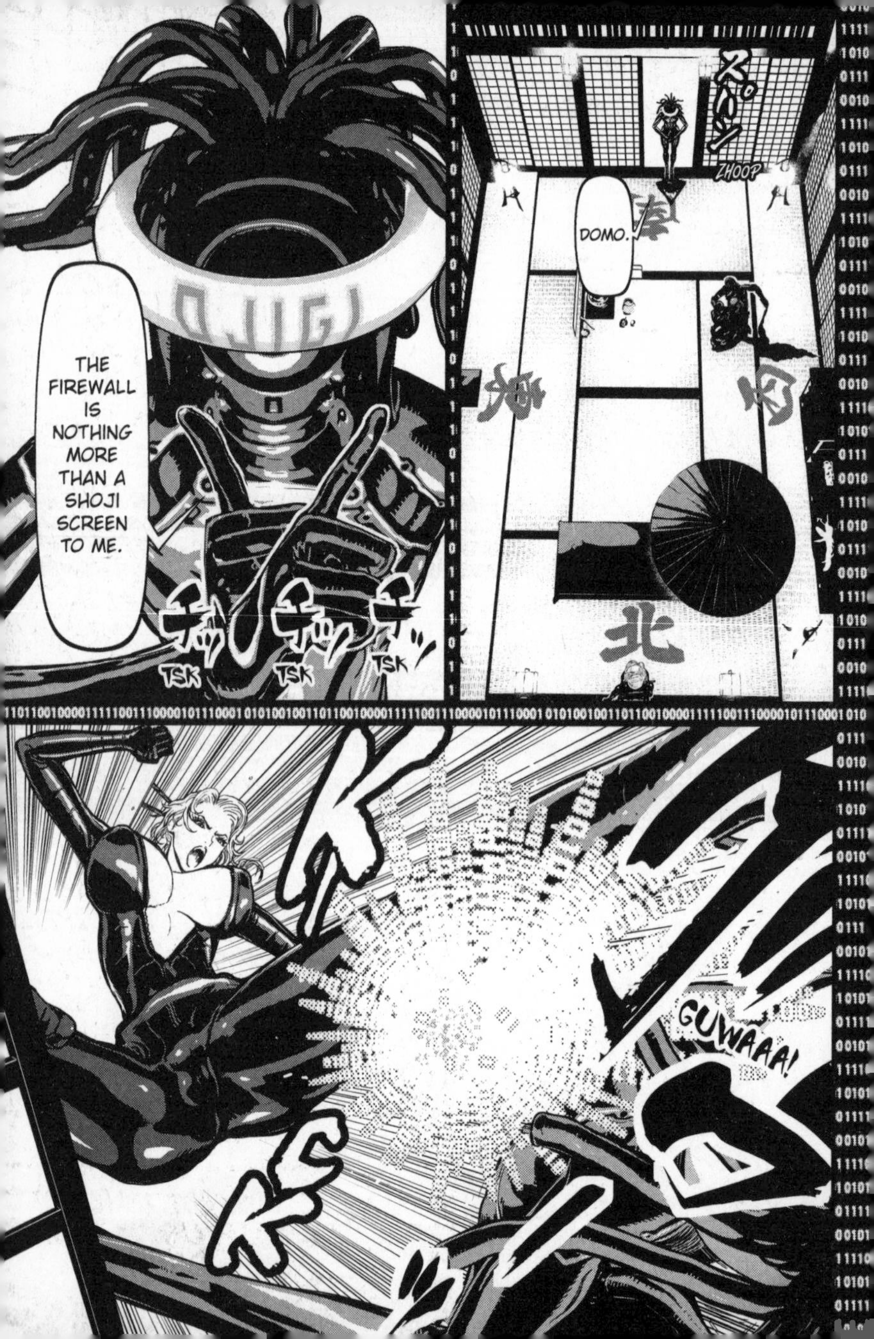
ZHOOP
DOMO.
OJIGI
THE FIREWALL IS NOTHING MORE THAN A SHOJI SCREEN TO ME.
TSK
TSK
TSK
GUWAAA!

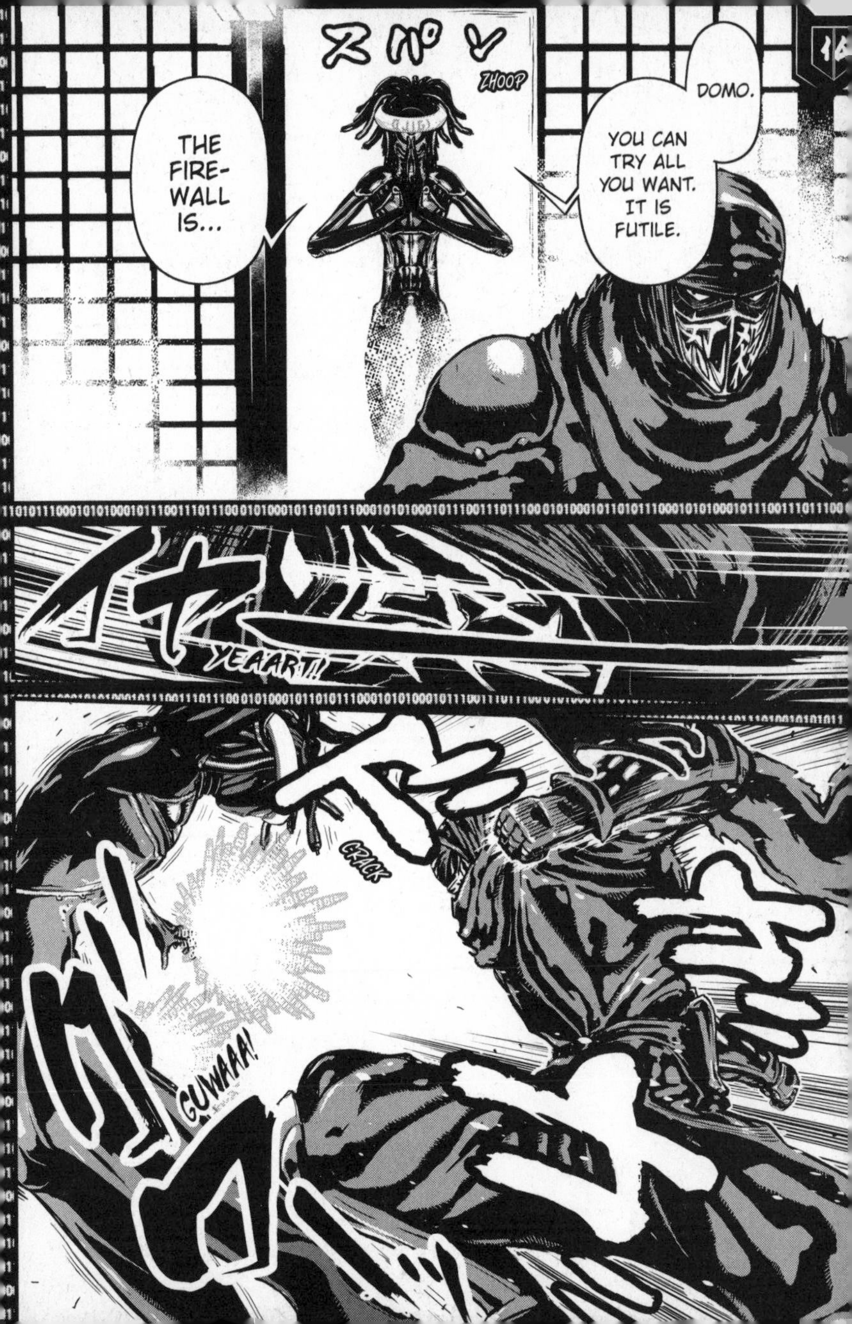
DOMO.
ZHOOP
YOU CAN TRY ALL YOU WANT. IT IS FUTILE.
THE FIRE-WALL IS...
YEAAART!
CRACK
GUWAAA!

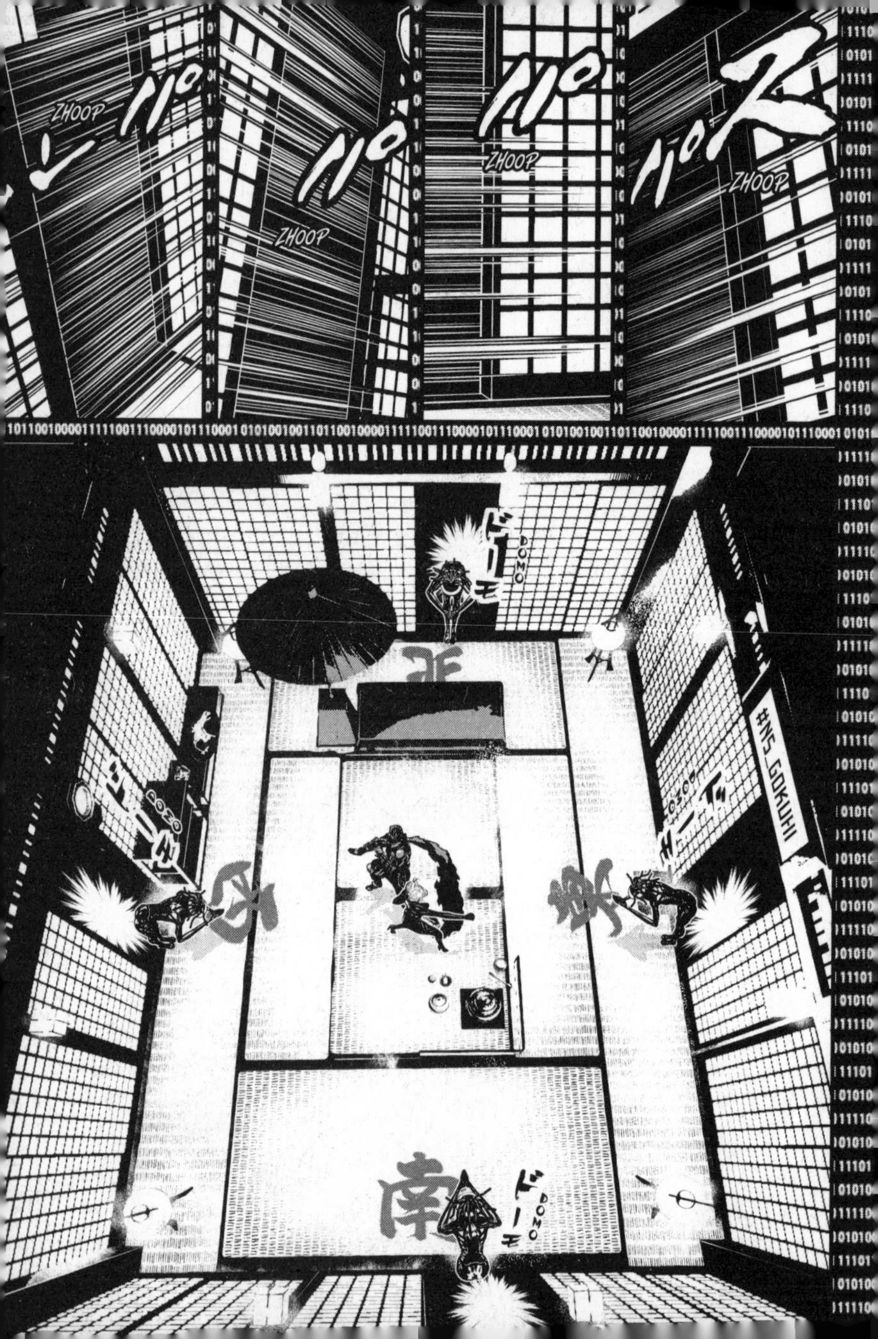
ZHOOP
ZHOOP
ZHOOP
ZHOOP
ドーモ
DOMO
#NS_GOKUHI
ドーモ
DOMO

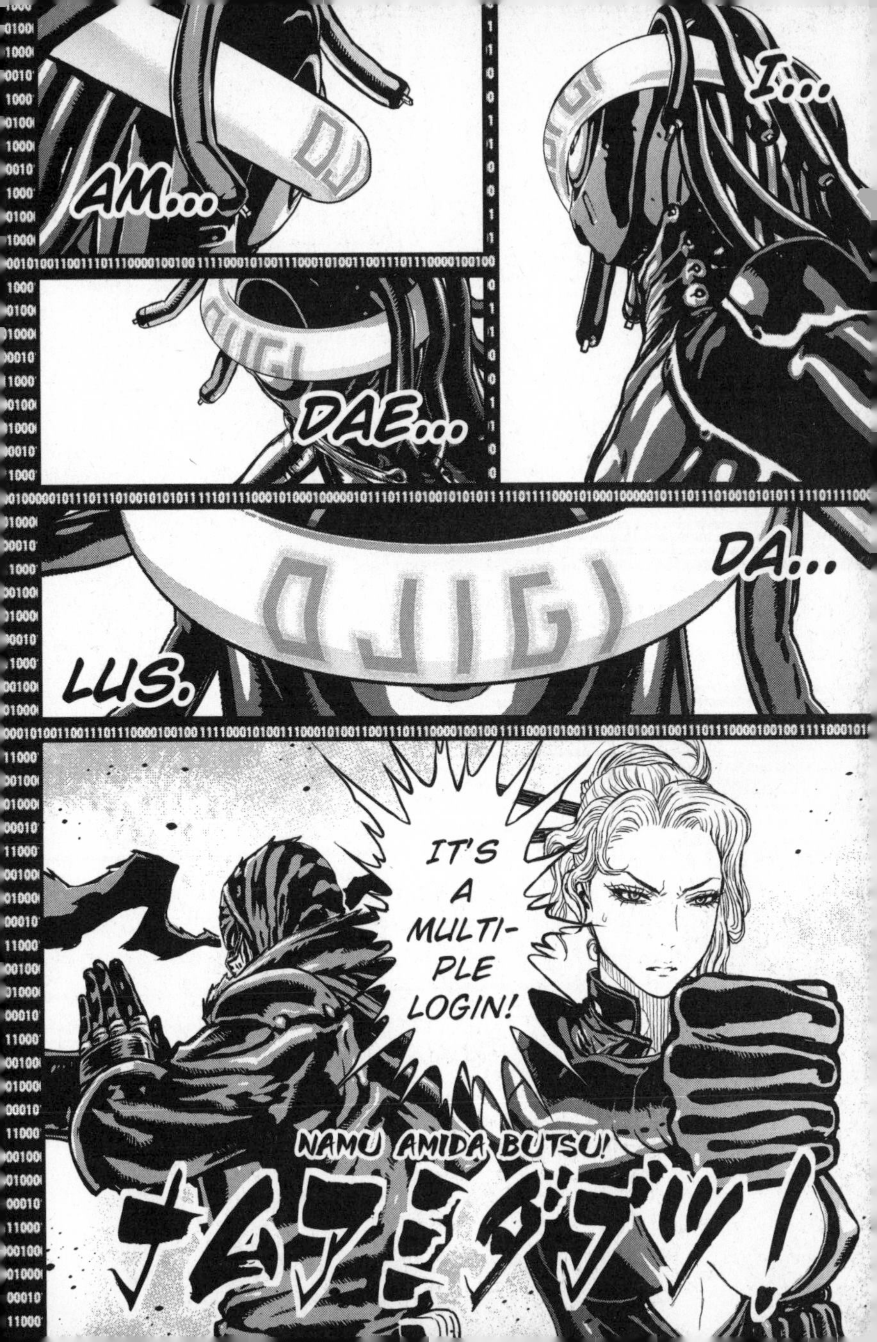
I...
AM...
DAE...
DA...
LUS.
IT'S A MULTI-PLE LOGIN!
NAMU AMIDA BUTSU!
ナムアミダブツ!

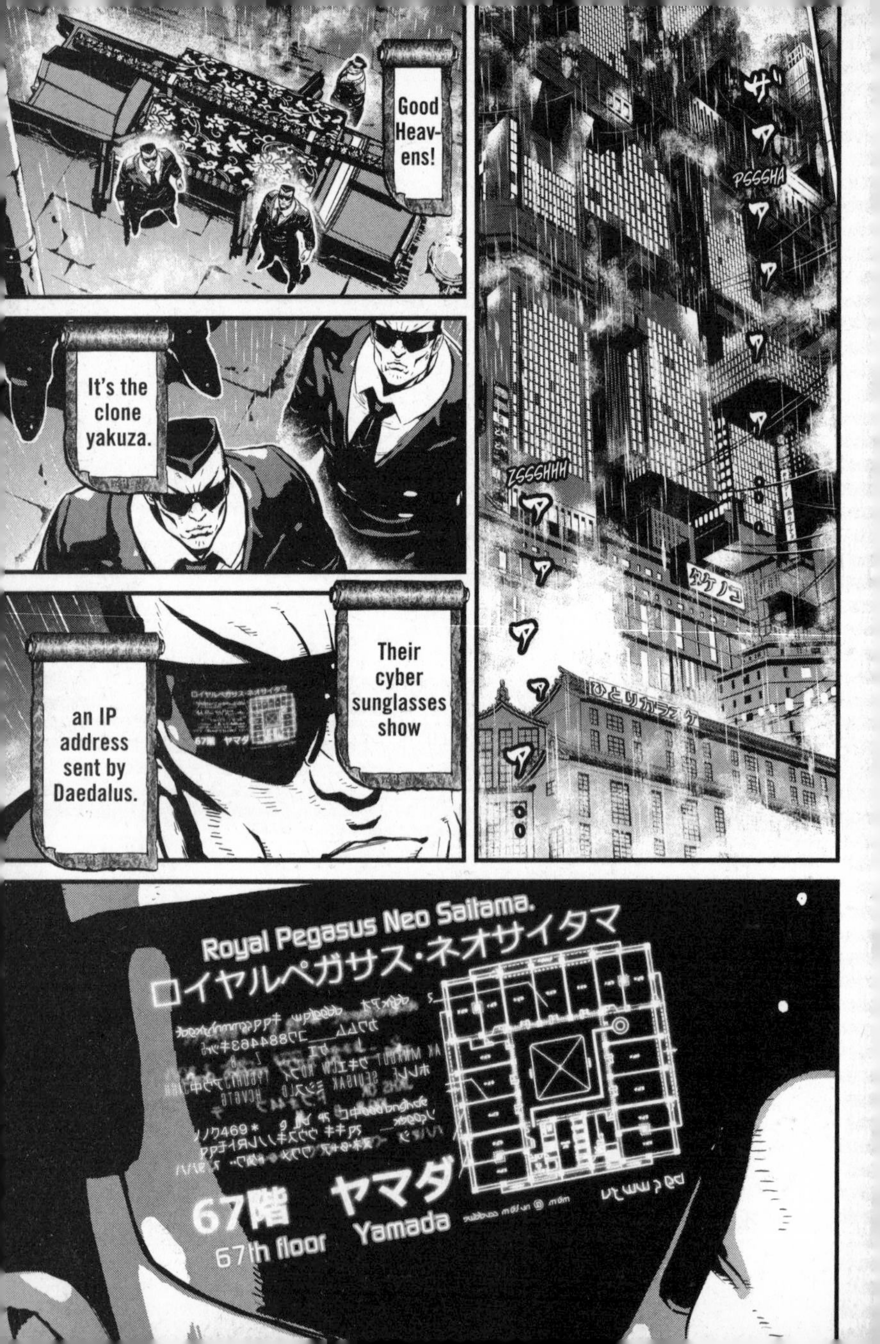
PSSSHA
ZSSSHHH
Good Heav-ens!
It's the clone yakuza.
Their cyber sunglasses show
an IP address sent by Daedalus.
Royal Pegasus Neo Saitama.
ロイヤルペガサス・ネオサイタマ
67階
67th floor
ヤマダ
Yamada

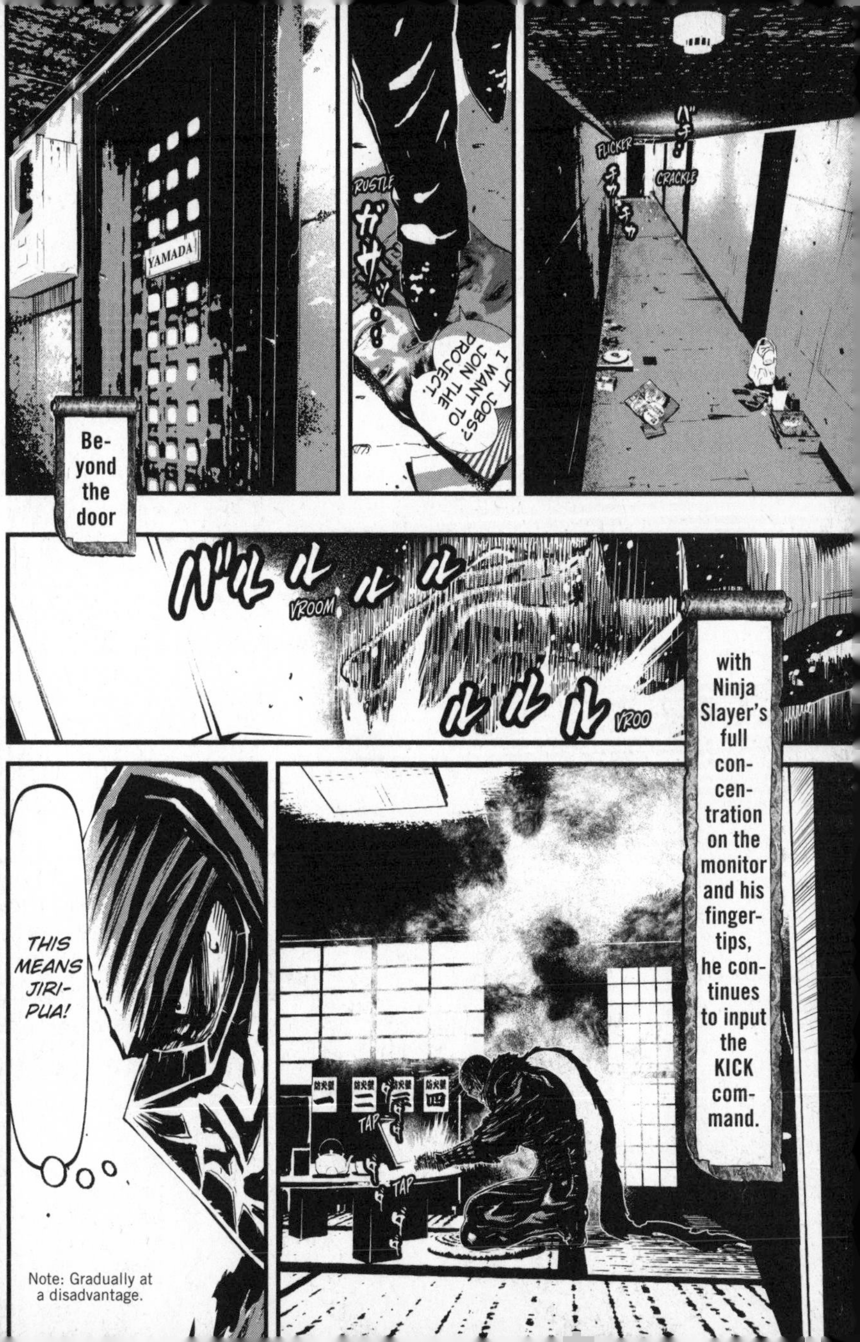
FLICKER
CRACKLE
RUSTLE
OT JOBS? I WANT TO JOIN THE PROJECT.
YAMADA
Be-yond the door
VROOM
VROO
with Ninja Slayer's full con-cen-tration on the monitor and his finger-tips, he con-tinues to input the KICK com-mand.
TAP
TAP
THIS MEANS JIRI-PUA!
Note: Gradually at a disadvantage.

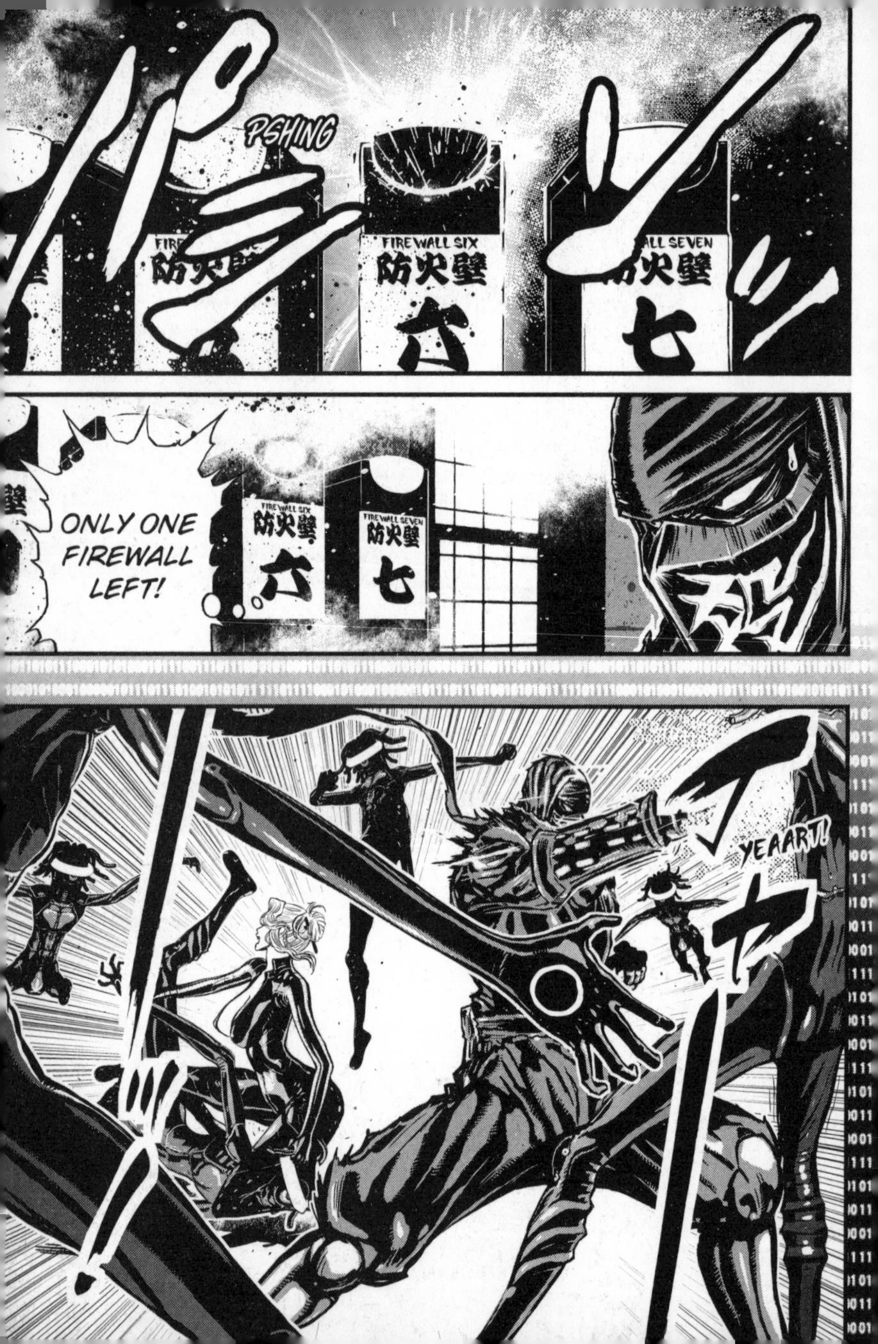
FIREWALL SEVEN
防火壁
七
FIREWALL SIX
防火壁
六
PSHING
FIREWALL SEVEN
防火壁
七
FIREWALL SIX
防火壁
六
ONLY ONE FIREWALL LEFT!
YEAART!

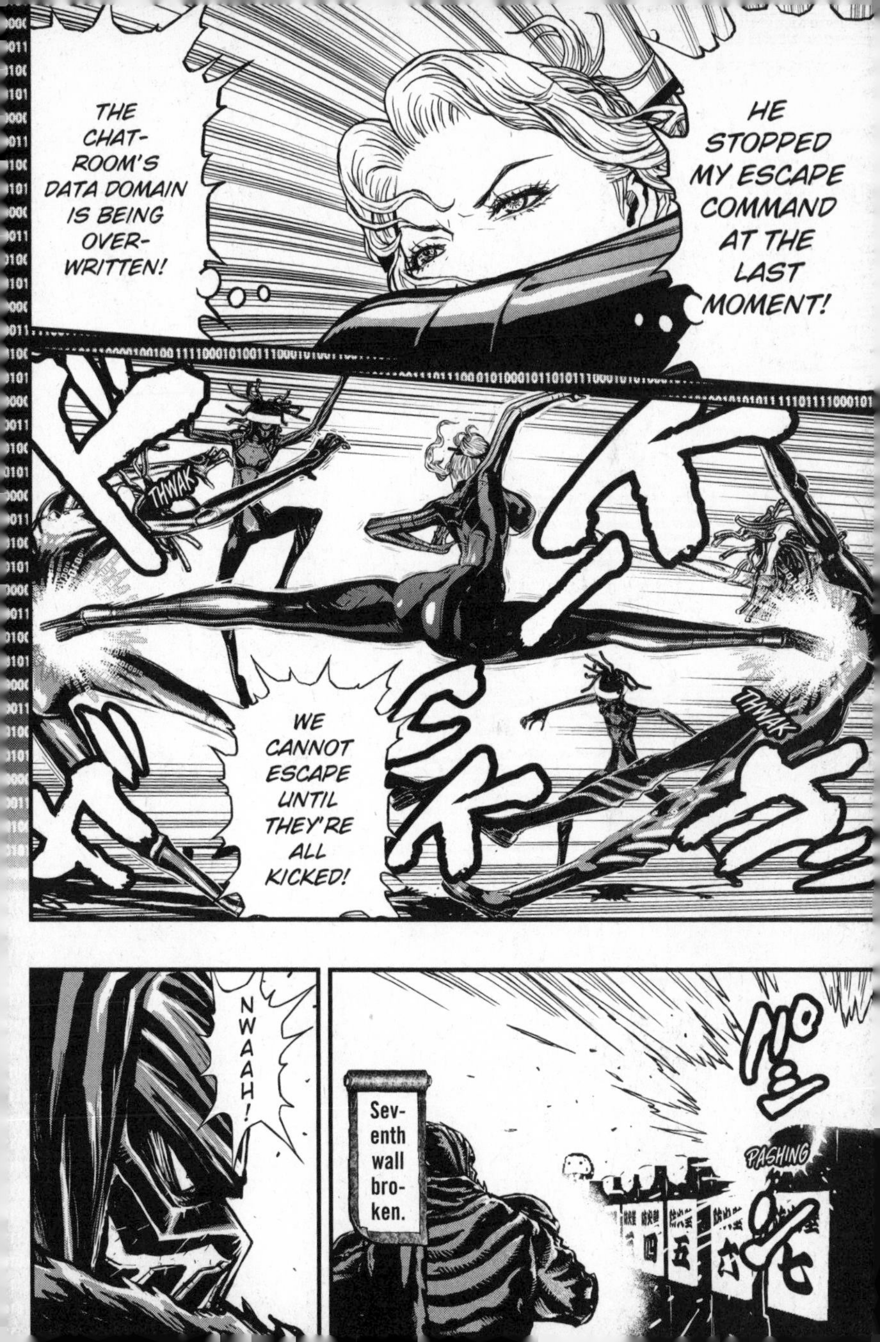
HE STOPPED MY ESCAPE COMMAND AT THE LAST MOMENT!
THE CHAT-ROOM'S DATA DOMAIN IS BEING OVER-WRITTEN!
THWAK
WE CANNOT ESCAPE UNTIL THEY'RE ALL KICKED!
THWAK
PASHING
Seventh wall broken.
NWAAAH!

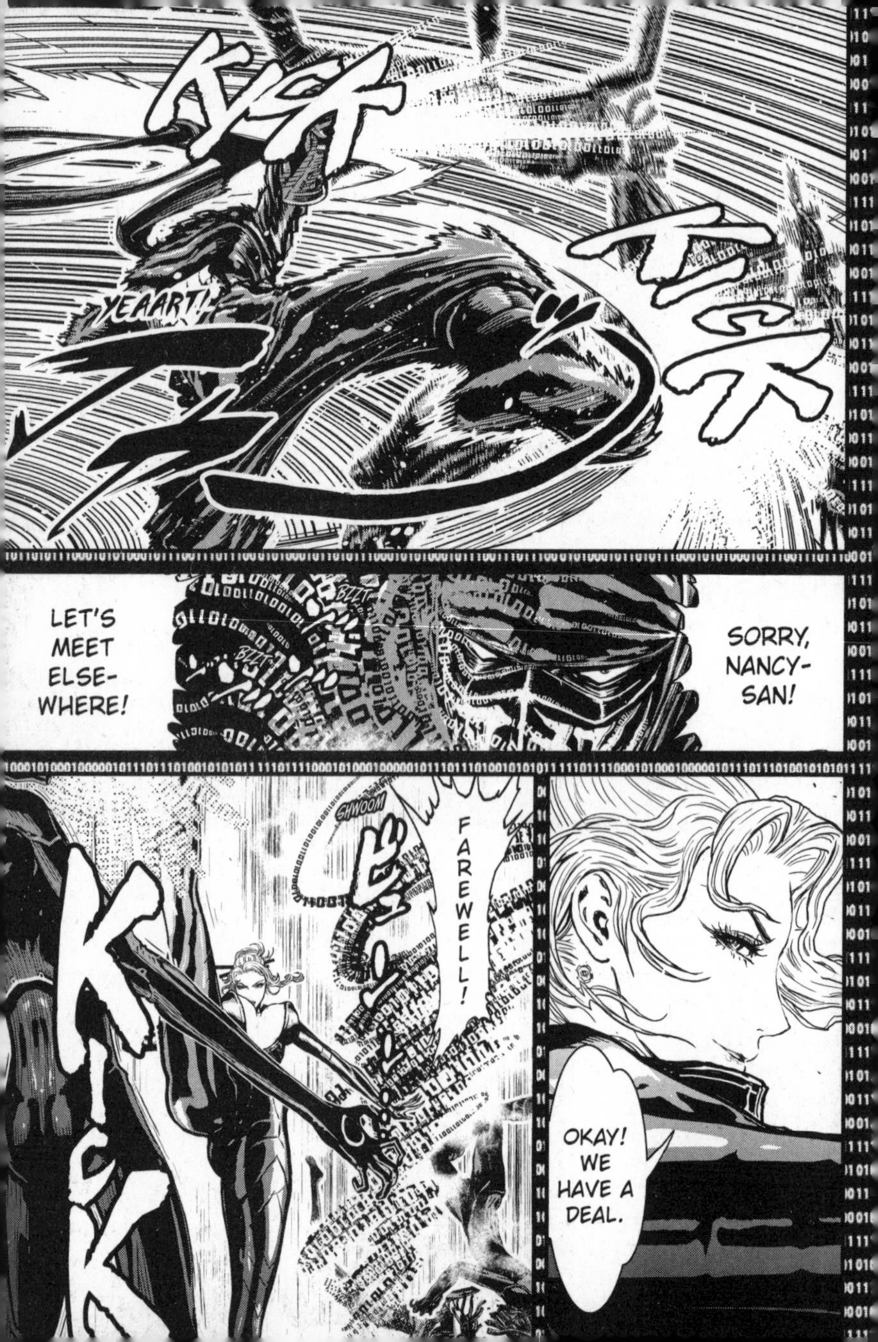
KICK
YEAART!
KICK
SORRY, NANCY-SAN!
BZZT
BZZT
LET'S MEET ELSE-WHERE!
OKAY! WE HAVE A DEAL.
SHWOOM
FAREWELL!
KICK

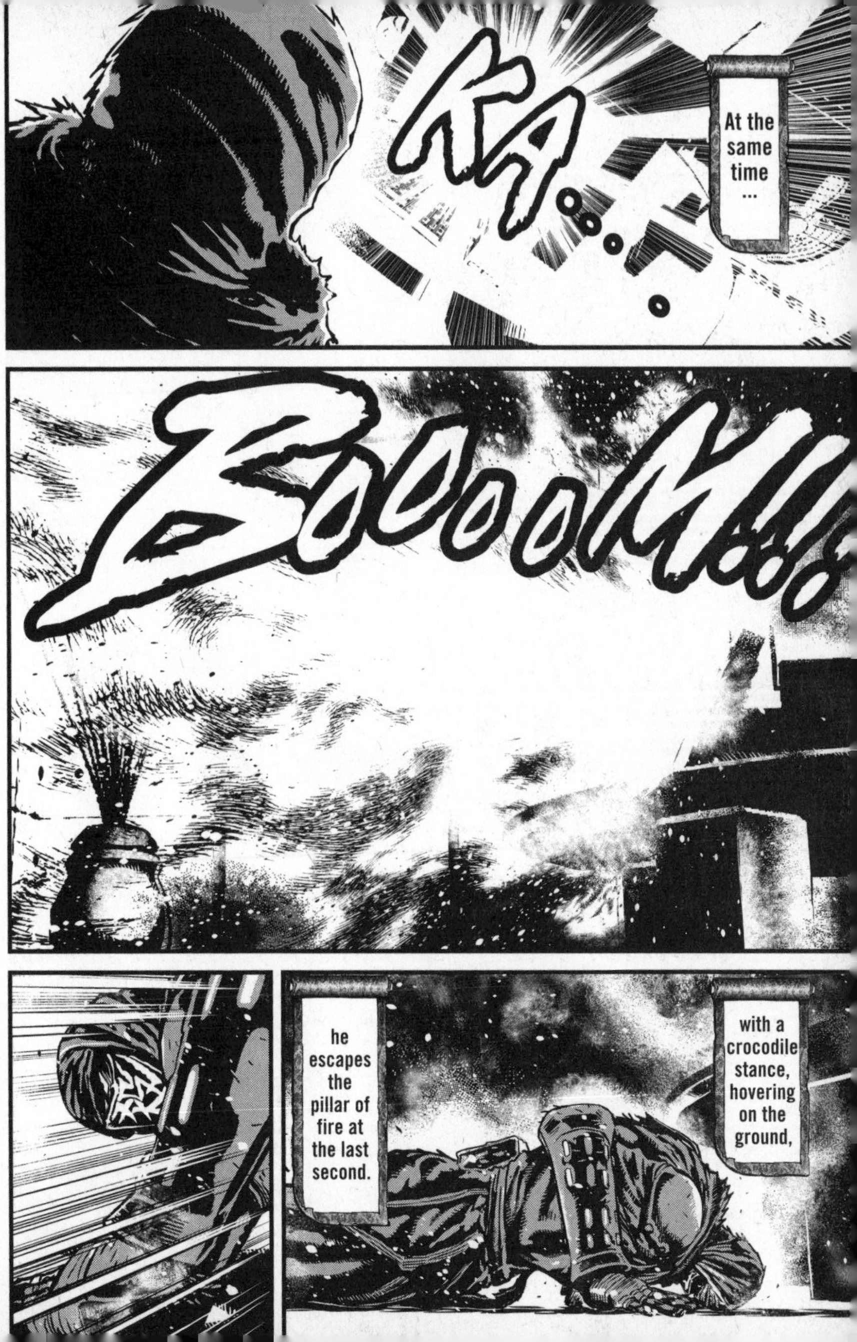
At the same time ...
KA...
BOOOOM!!
with a crocodile stance, hovering on the ground,
he escapes the pillar of fire at the last second.

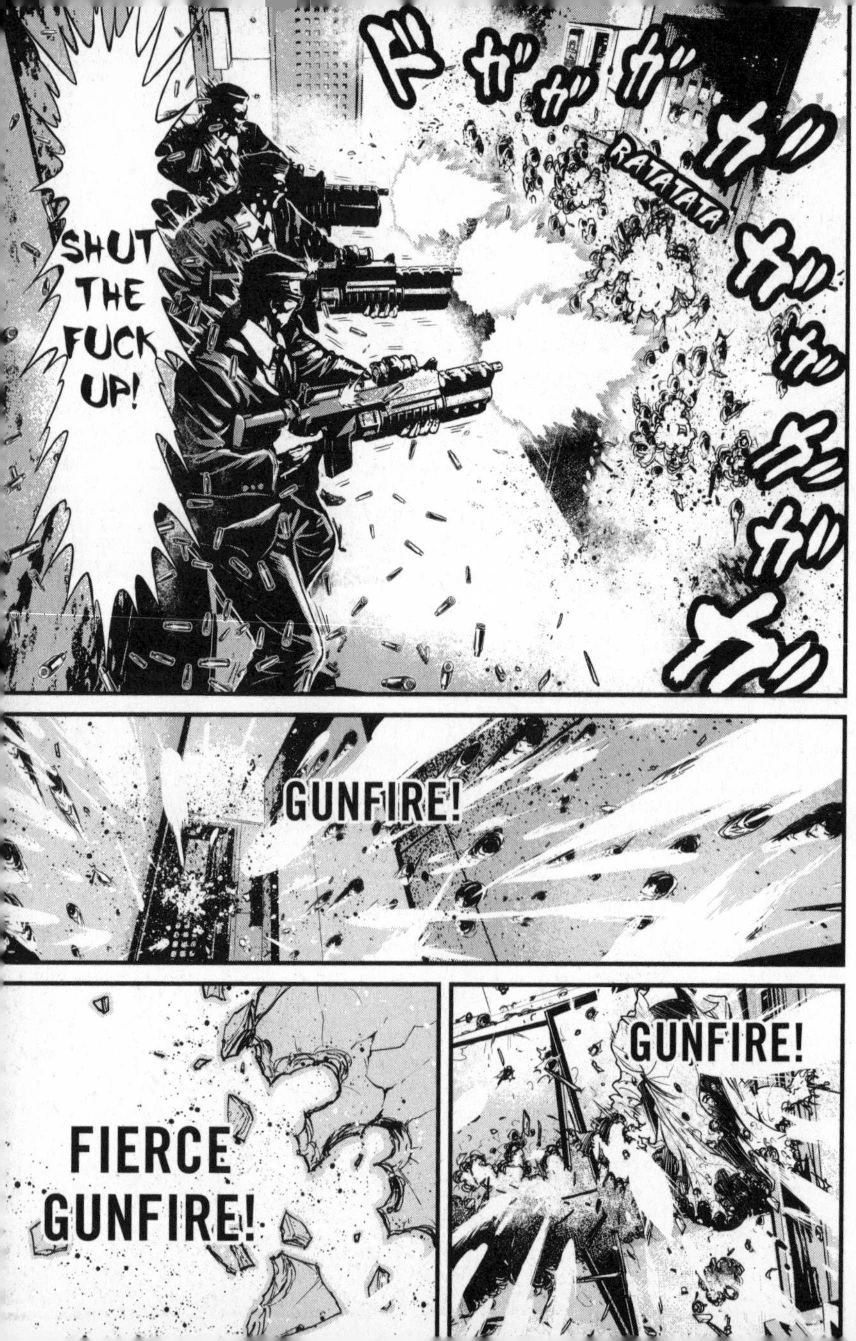
RATATATA
SHUT THE FUCK UP!
GUNFIRE!
GUNFIRE!
FIERCE GUNFIRE!

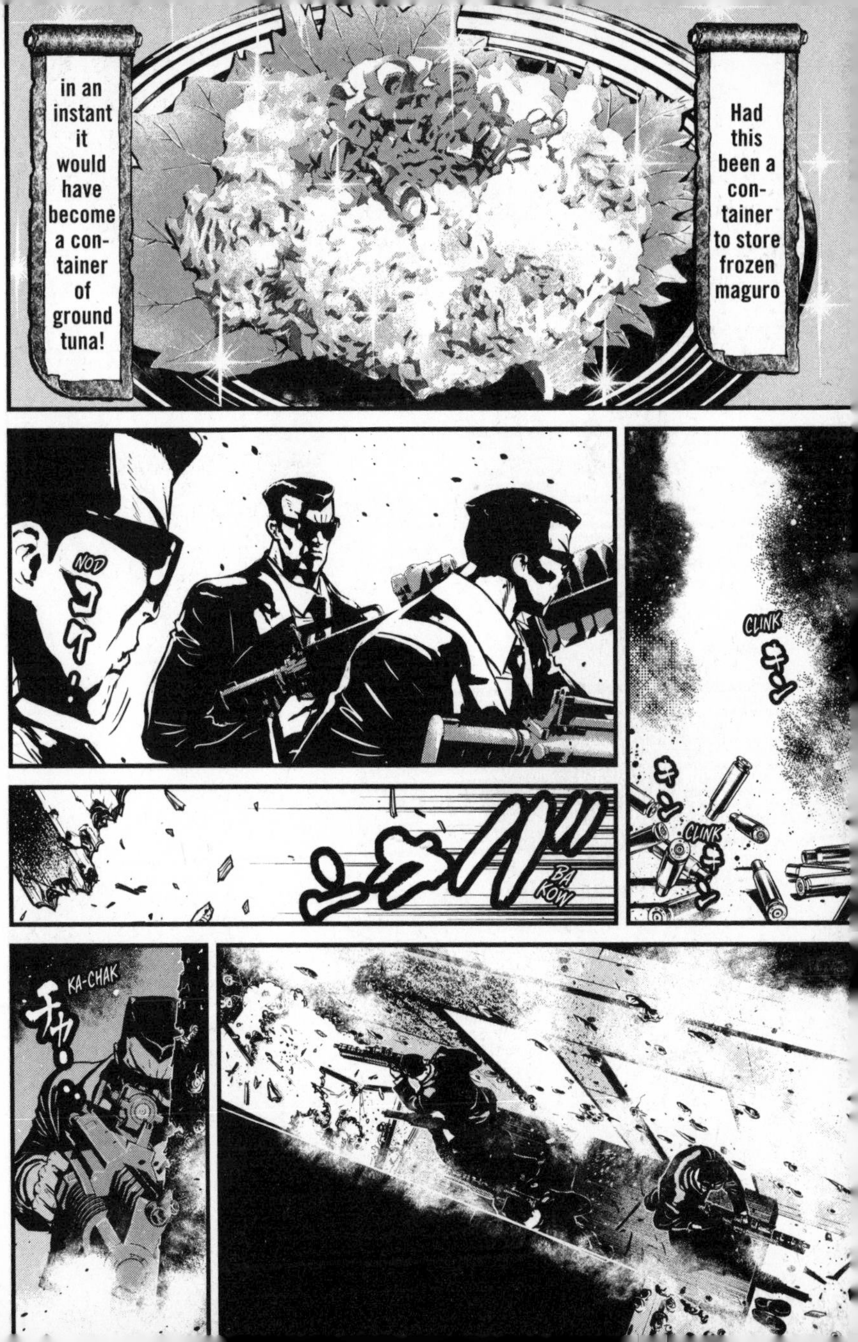
Had this been a container to store frozen maguro
in an instant it would have become a container of ground tuna!
CLINK
CLINK
NOD
BAKOW
KA-CHAK

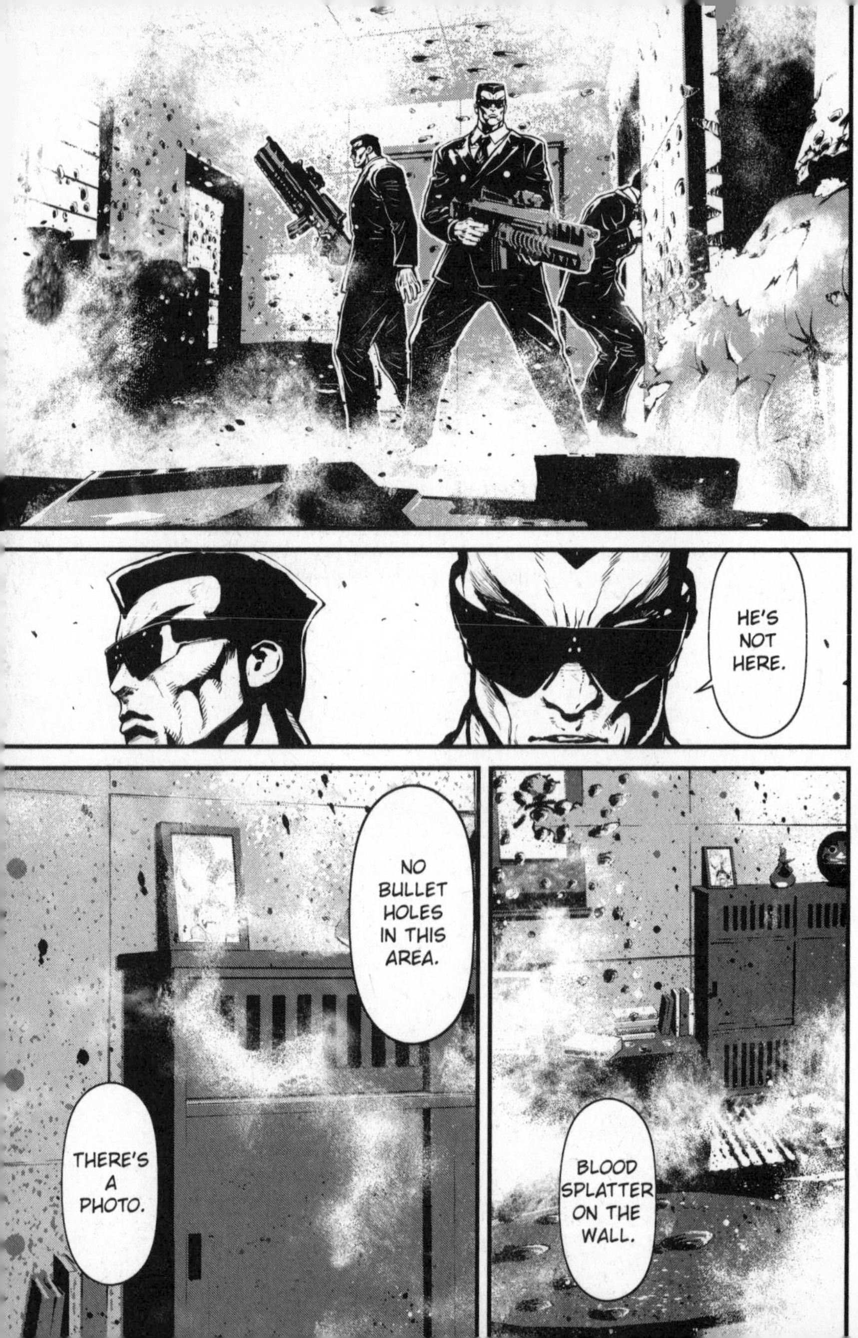
HE'S NOT HERE.
BLOOD SPLATTER ON THE WALL.
NO BULLET HOLES IN THIS AREA.
THERE'S A PHOTO.

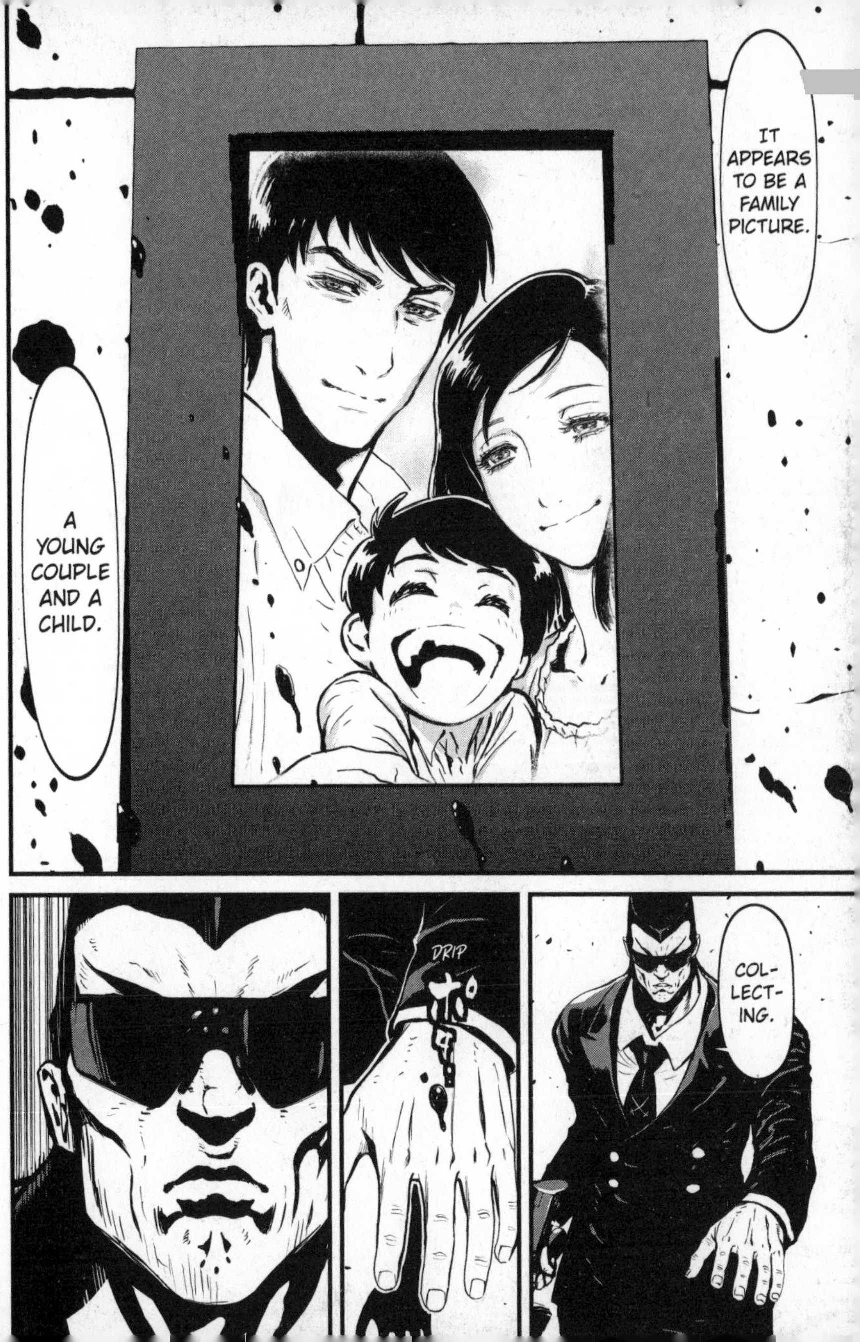
IT APPEARS TO BE A FAMILY PICTURE.
A YOUNG COUPLE AND A CHILD.
COL-LECT-ING.
DRIP

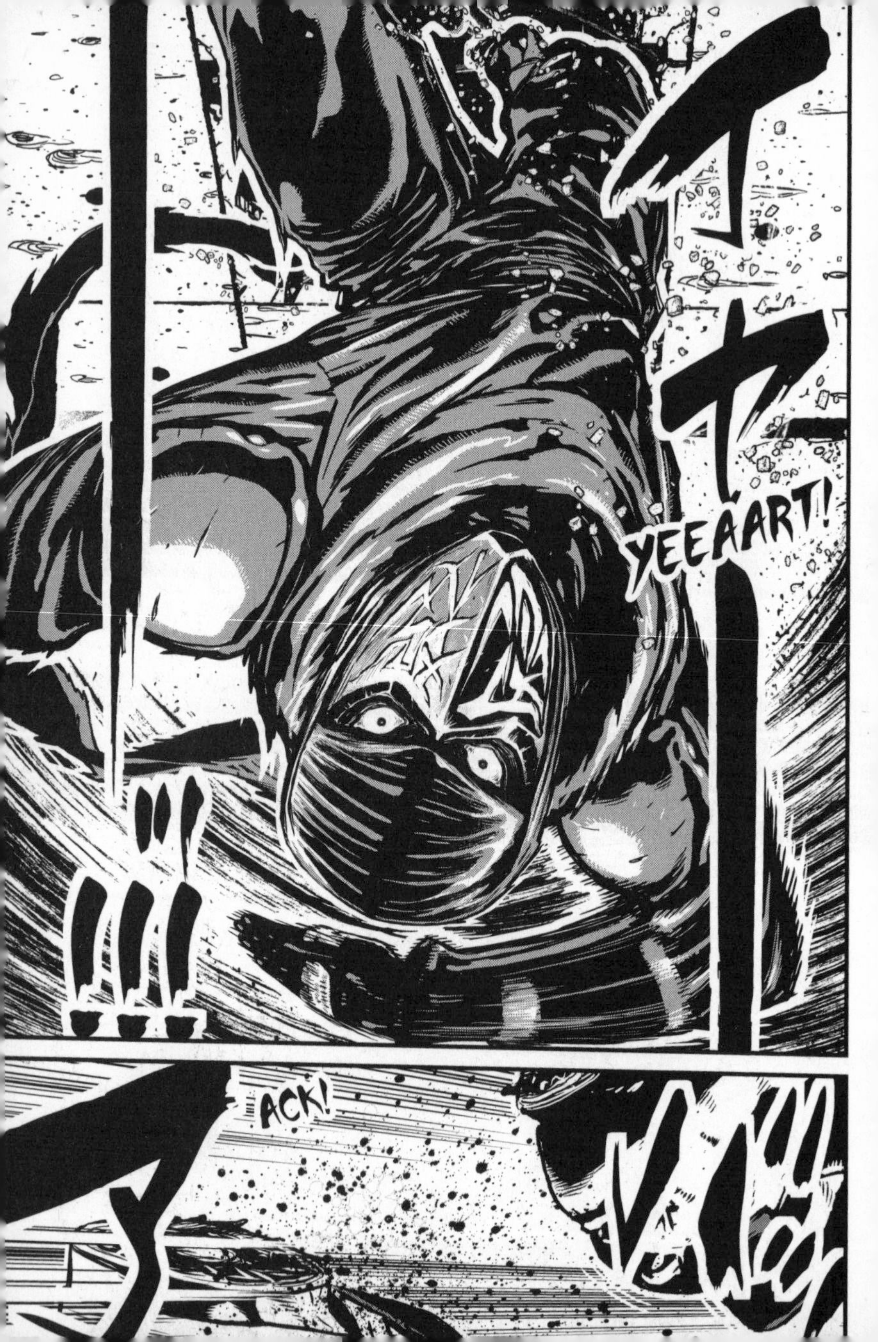
YEEAART!
ACK!

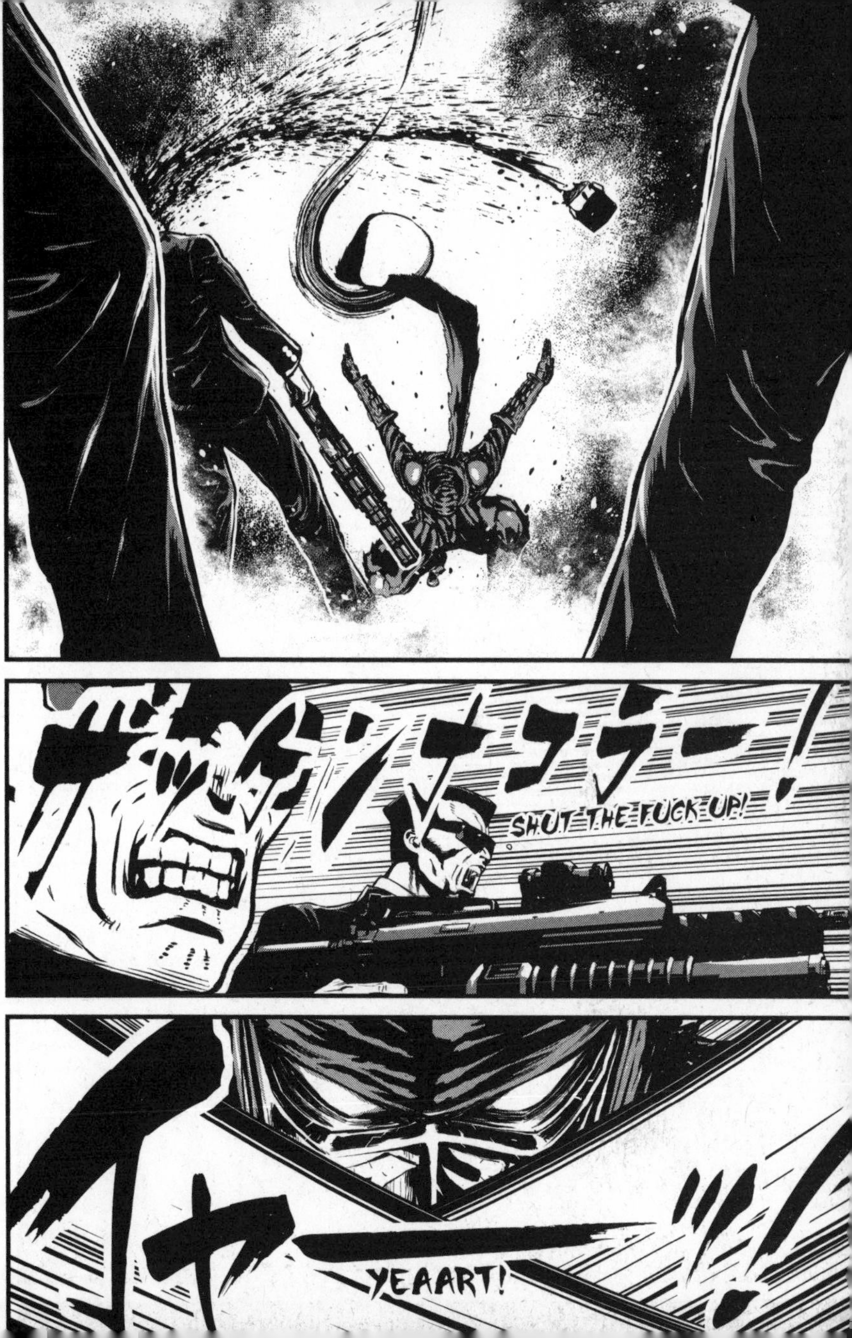
ザッケンナコラー!
SHUT THE FUCK UP!
イヤーッ!
YEAART!

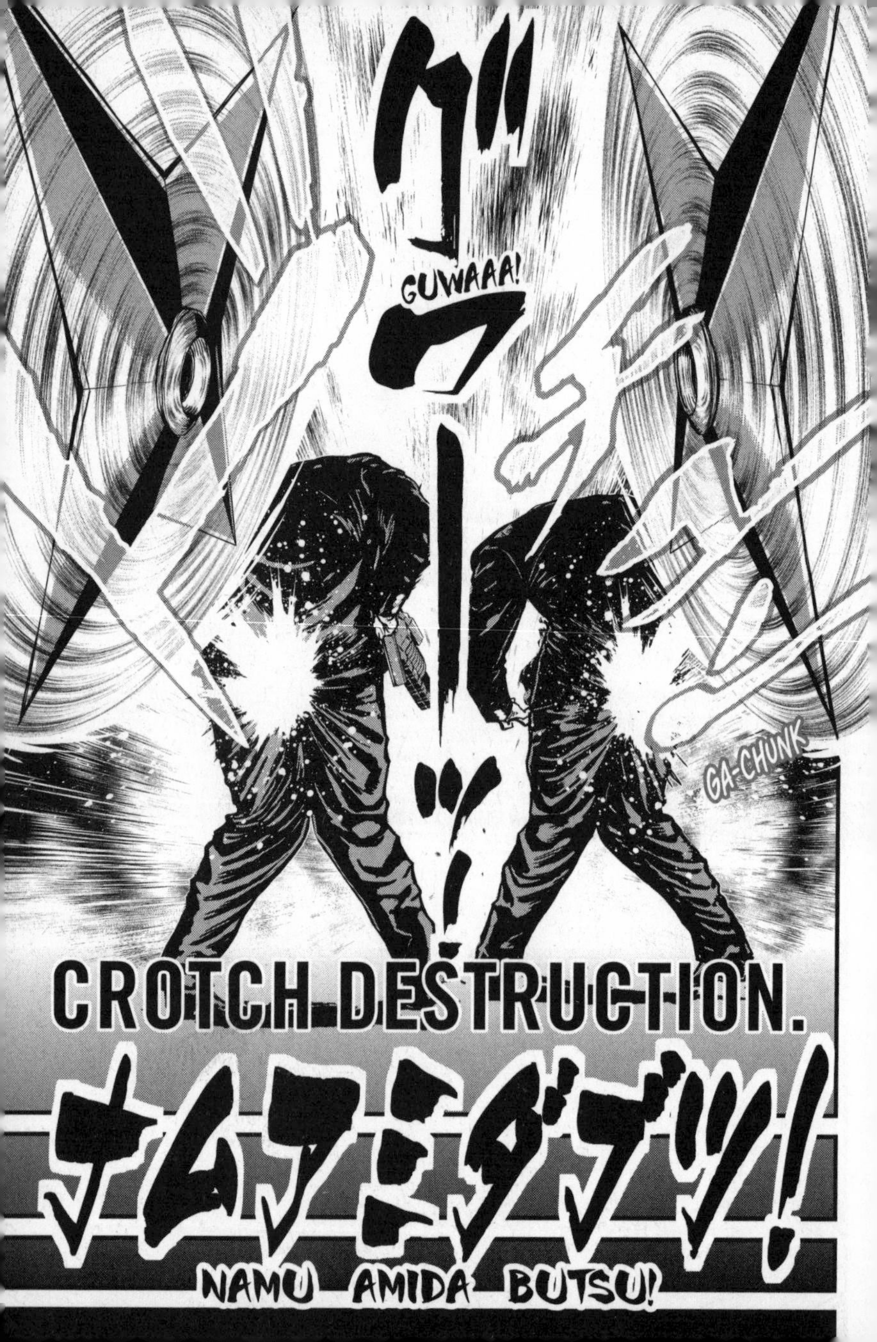
グァーッ!
GUWAAA!
GA-CHUNK
CROTCH DESTRUCTION.
ナムアミダブツ!
NAMU AMIDA BUTSU!

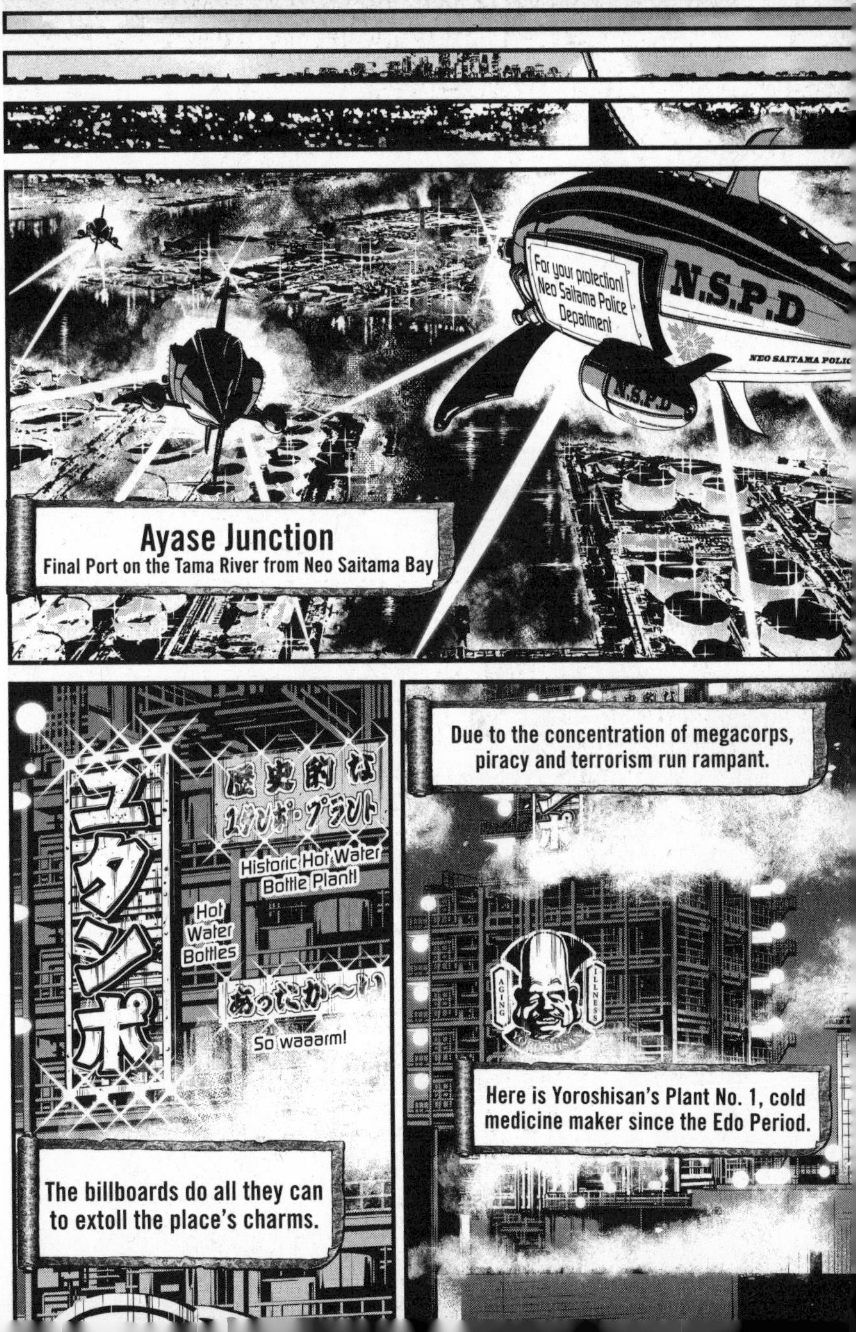
N.S.P.D
For your protection! Neo Saitama Police Department
NEO SAITAMA POLIC
N.S.P.D
Ayase Junction
Final Port on the Tama River from Neo Saitama Bay
Due to the concentration of megacorps, piracy and terrorism run rampant.
AGING
ILLNESS
Here is Yoroshisan's Plant No. 1, cold medicine maker since the Edo Period.
歴史的な
ユタンポ・プラント
Historic Hot Water Bottle Plant!
ユタンポ
Hot Water Bottles
あったか〜い
So waaarm!
The billboards do all they can to extoll the place's charms.

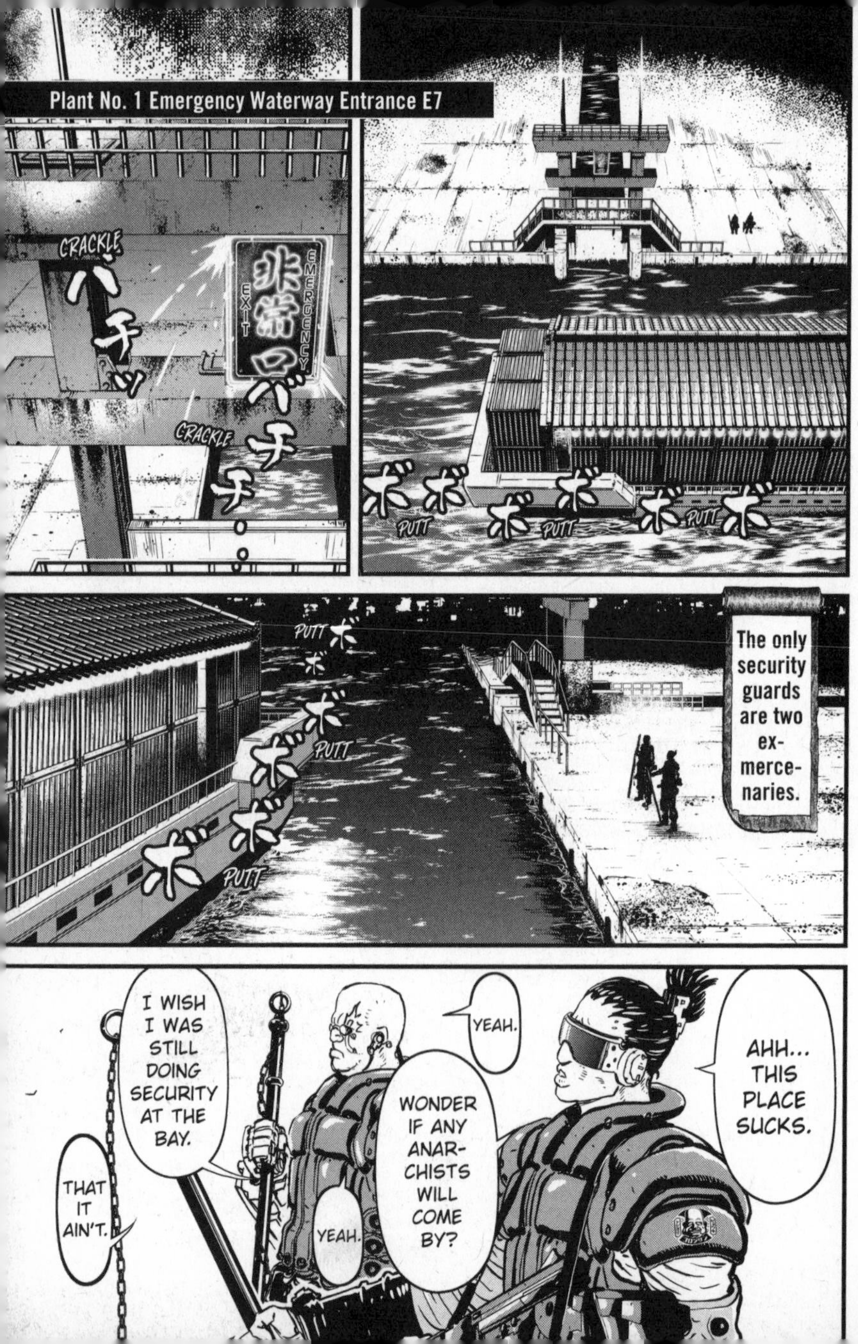
Plant No. 1 Emergency Waterway Entrance E7
ボボボボボボ
PUTT
PUTT
PUTT
CRACKLE
バチッ
非常口
EMERGENCY
EXIT
CRACKLE
バチチチ。。
ボボボボボボボ
PUTT
PUTT
PUTT
The only security guards are two ex-mercenaries.
AHH... THIS PLACE SUCKS.
YEAH.
I WISH I WAS STILL DOING SECURITY AT THE BAY.
WONDER IF ANY ANARCHISTS WILL COME BY?
YEAH.
THAT IT AIN'T.

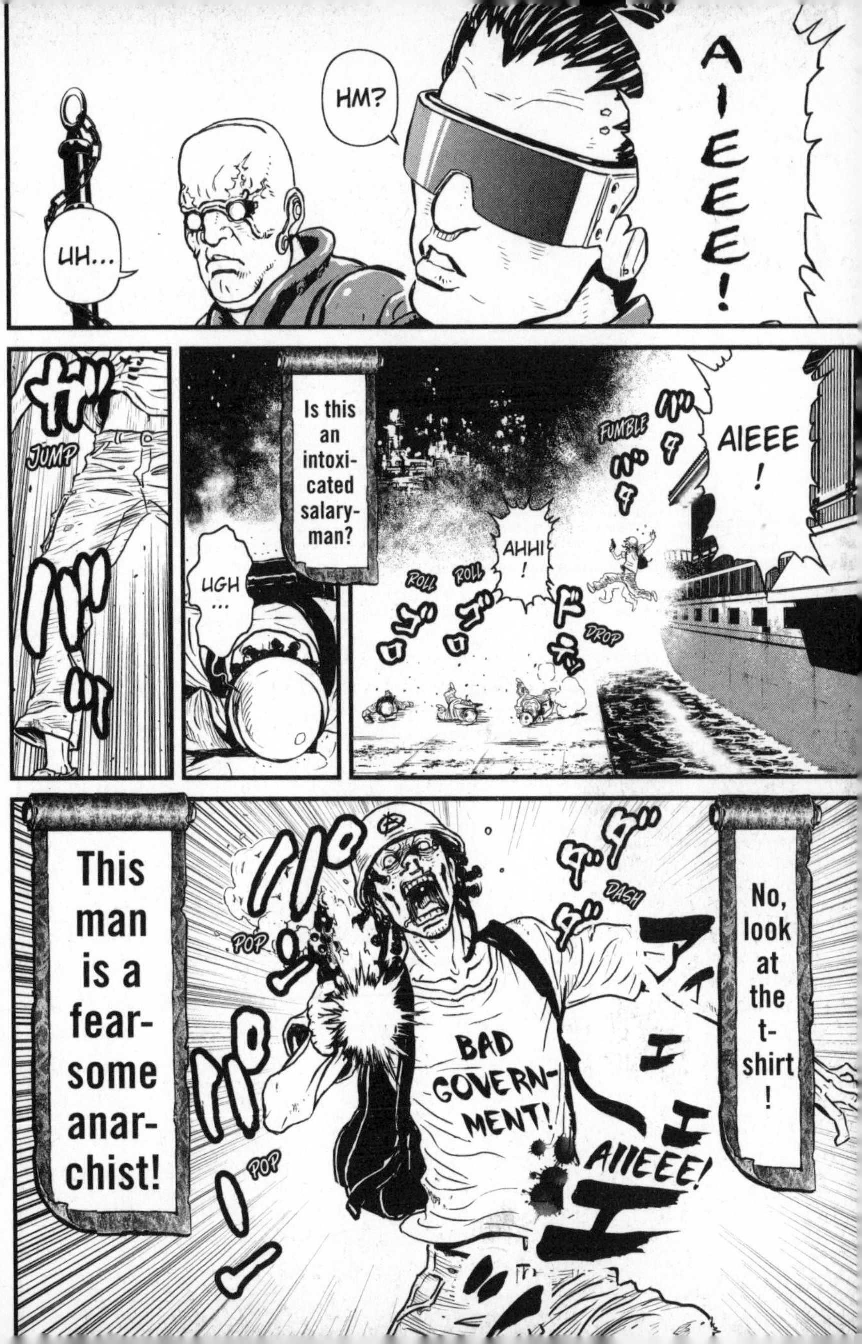
AIEEE!
HM?
UH...
AIEEE!
FUMBLE
AHHI!
ROLL
ROLL
DROP
Is this an intoxicated salaryman?
UGH...
JUMP
No, look at the t-shirt!
DASH
AIIEEE!
BAD GOVERNMENT!
POP
POP
This man is a fearsome anarchist!

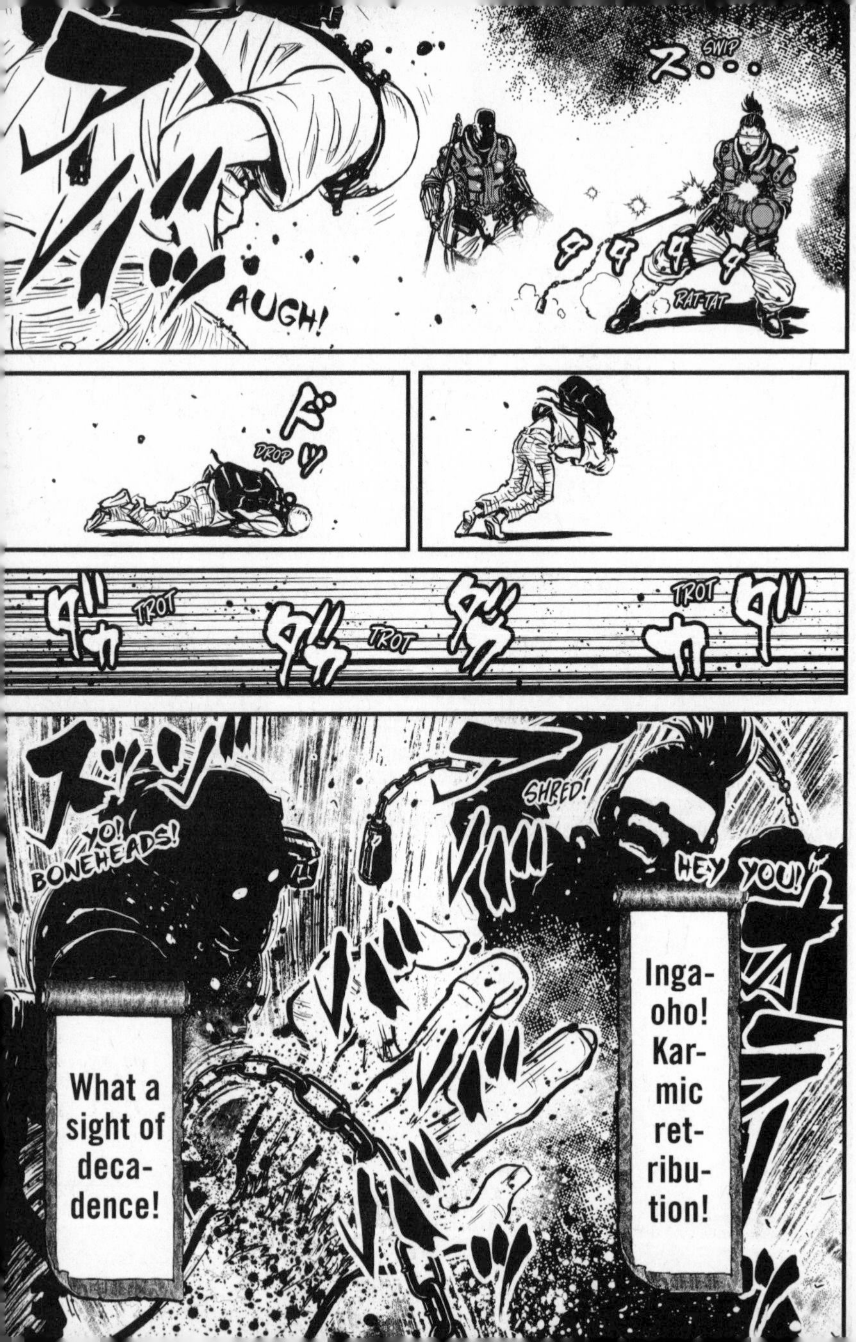
SWIP
RAT-TAT
AUGH!
DROP
TROT
TROT
TROT
HEY YOU!
SHRED!
YO! BONEHEADS!
Inga-oho! Karmic retribution!
What a sight of decadence!

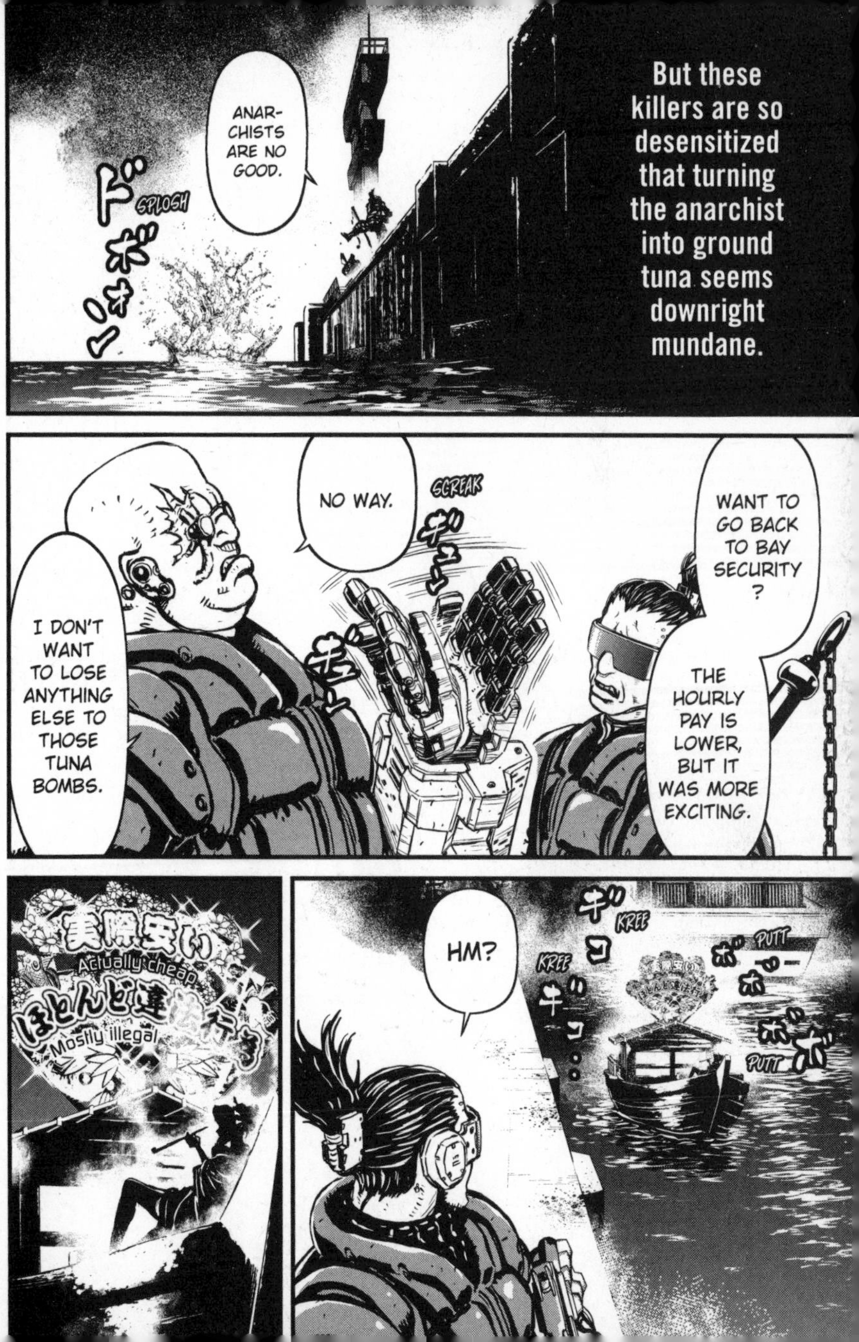

But these killers are so desensitized that turning the anarchist into ground tuna seems downright mundane.
ANAR-CHISTS ARE NO GOOD.
SPLOSH
WANT TO GO BACK TO BAY SECURITY?
THE HOURLY PAY IS LOWER, BUT IT WAS MORE EXCITING.
SCREAK
NO WAY.
I DON'T WANT TO LOSE ANYTHING ELSE TO THOSE TUNA BOMBS.
PUTT
KREE
HM?
KREE
PUTT
実際安い
Actually cheap
ほとんど違法行
Mostly illegal

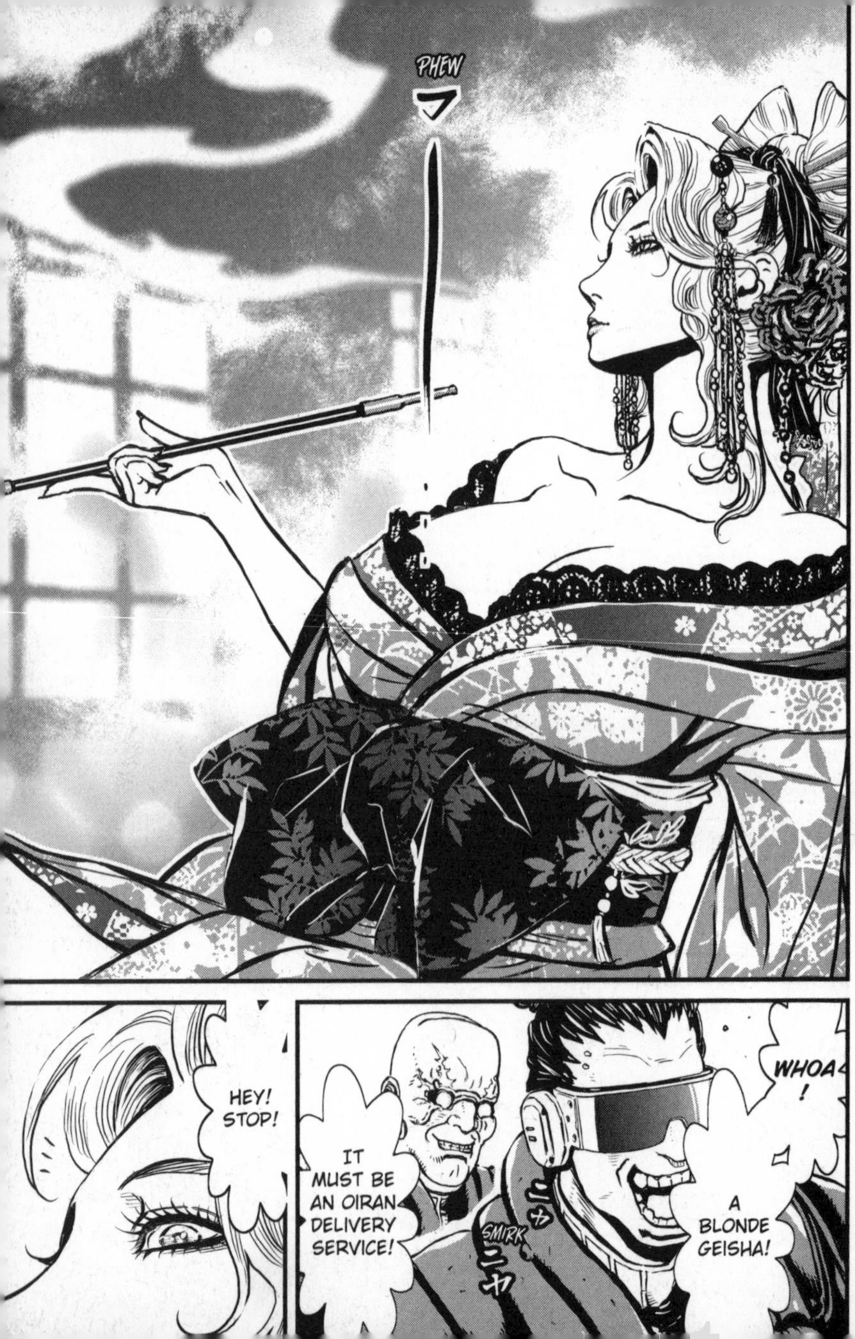
PHEW
WHOA!
A BLONDE GEISHA!
IT MUST BE AN OIRAN DELIVERY SERVICE!
SMIRK
HEY! STOP!

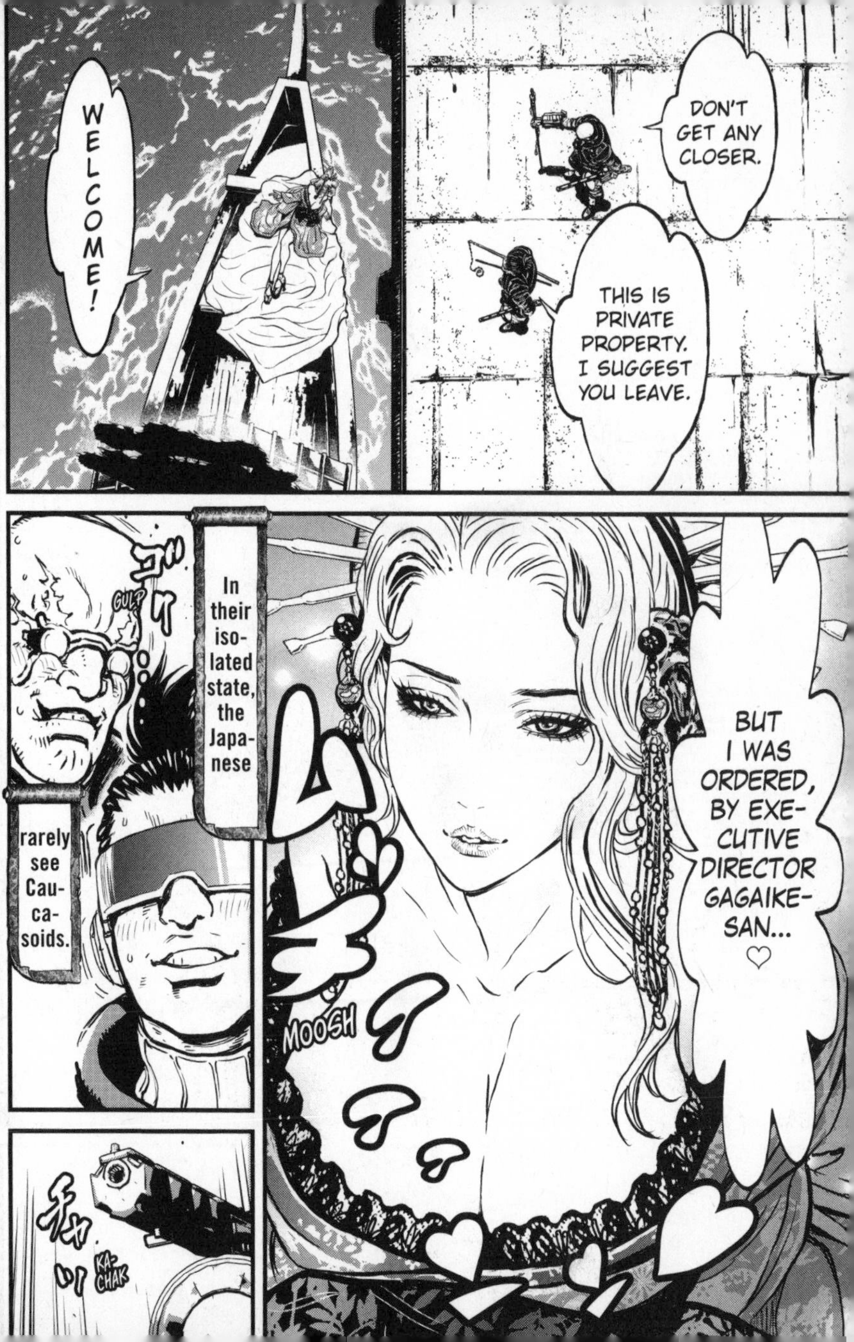
DON'T GET ANY CLOSER.
THIS IS PRIVATE PROPERTY. I SUGGEST YOU LEAVE.
WELCOME!
BUT I WAS ORDERED, BY EXE-CUTIVE DIRECTOR GAGAIKE-SAN... ♡
MOOSH
GULP
In their iso-lated state, the Japa-nese
rarely see Cau-ca-soids.
KA-CHAK

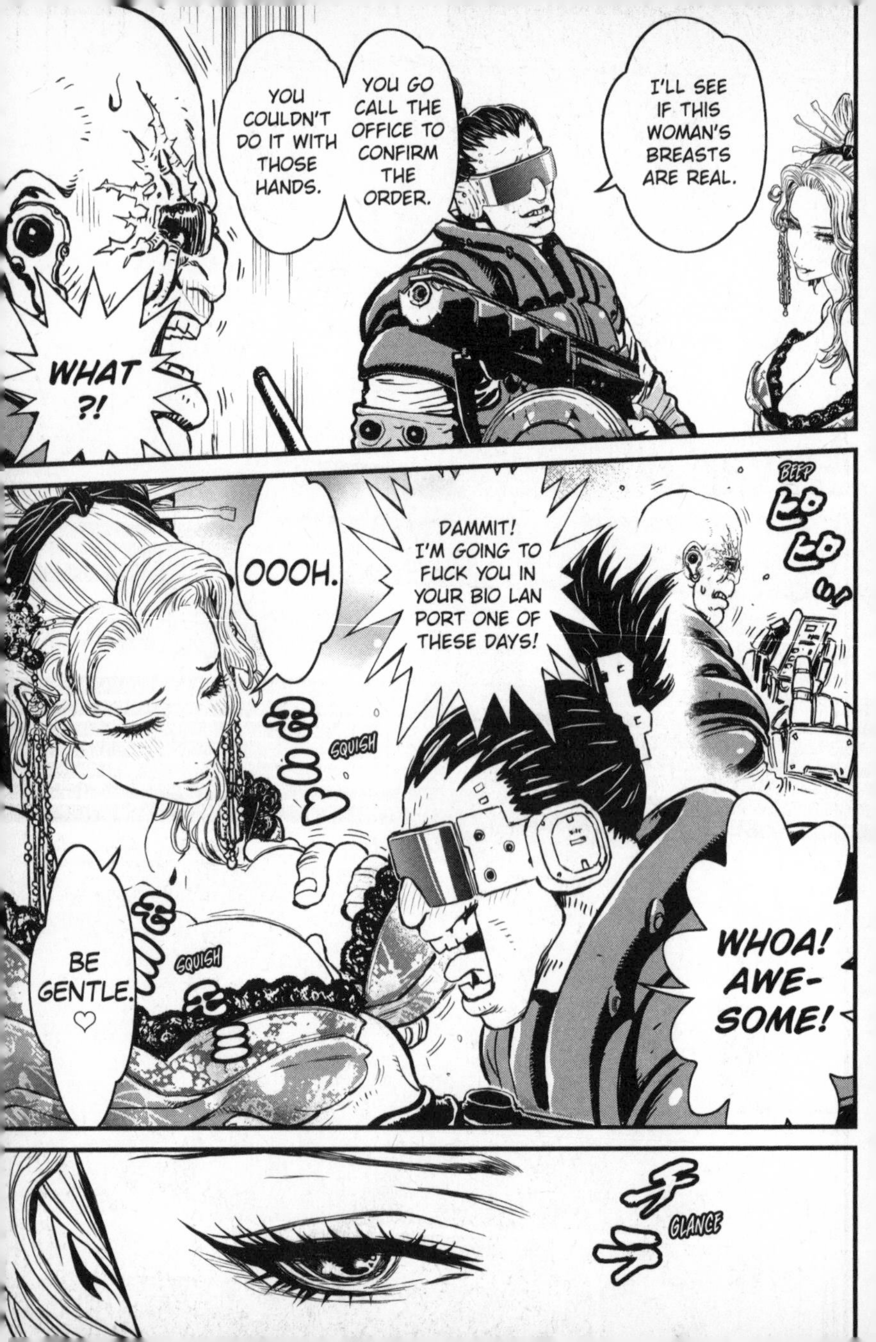
I'LL SEE IF THIS WOMAN'S BREASTS ARE REAL.
YOU GO CALL THE OFFICE TO CONFIRM THE ORDER.
YOU COULDN'T DO IT WITH THOSE HANDS.
WHAT ?!
BEEP
DAMMIT! I'M GOING TO FUCK YOU IN YOUR BIO LAN PORT ONE OF THESE DAYS!
WHOA! AWE-SOME!
OOOH.
SQUISH
BE GENTLE. ♡
SQUISH
GLANCE

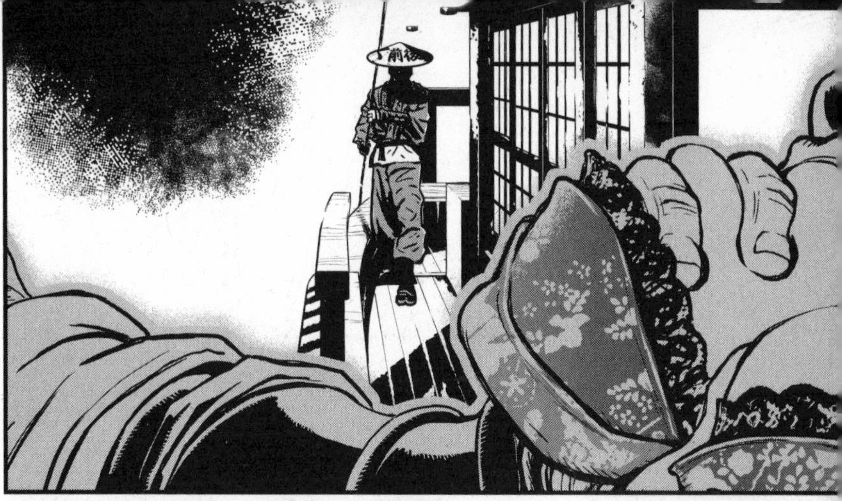
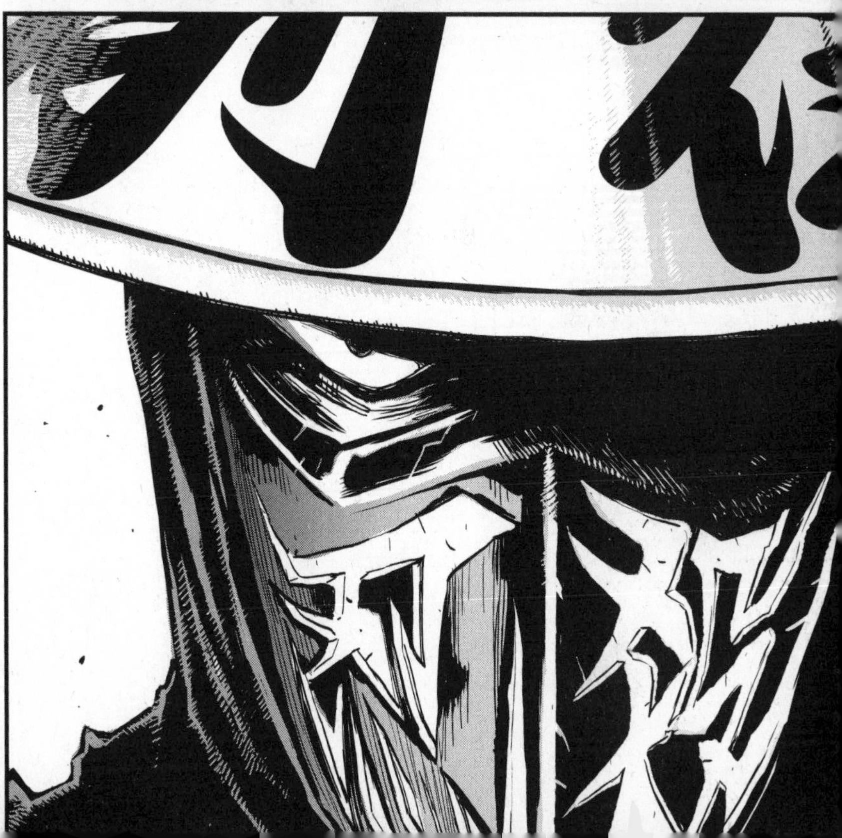

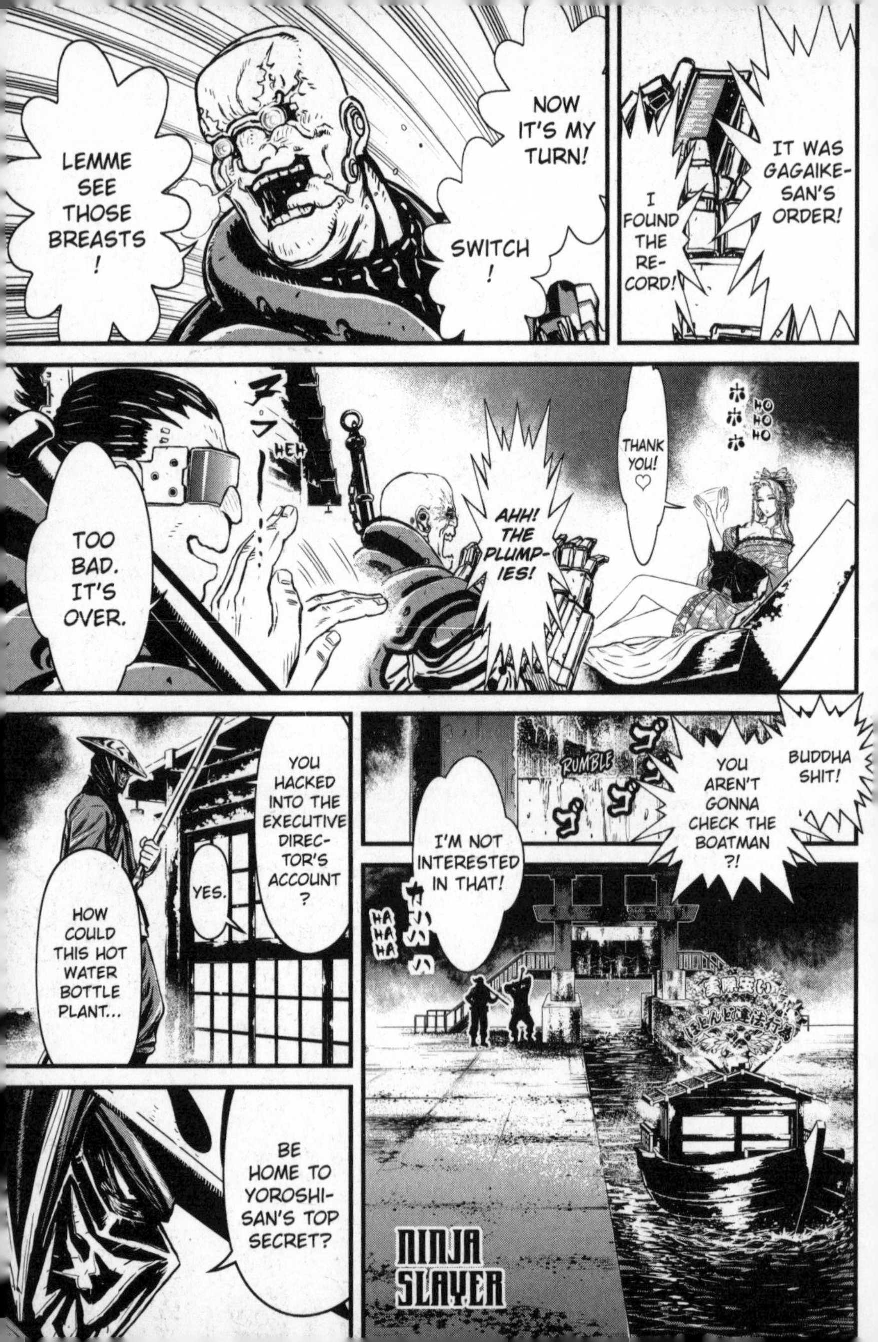

IT WAS GAGAIKE-SAN'S ORDER!
I FOUND THE RECORD!
NOW IT'S MY TURN!
SWITCH!
LEMME SEE THOSE BREASTS!
HO HO HO
THANK YOU! ♡
AHH! THE PLUMPIES!
HEH
TOO BAD. IT'S OVER.
RUMBLE
BUDDHA SHIT!
YOU AREN'T GONNA CHECK THE BOATMAN?!
I'M NOT INTERESTED IN THAT!
HA HA HA
NINJA SLAYER
YOU HACKED INTO THE EXECUTIVE DIRECTOR'S ACCOUNT?
YES.
HOW COULD THIS HOT WATER BOTTLE PLANT...
BE HOME TO YOROSHI-SAN'S TOP SECRET?

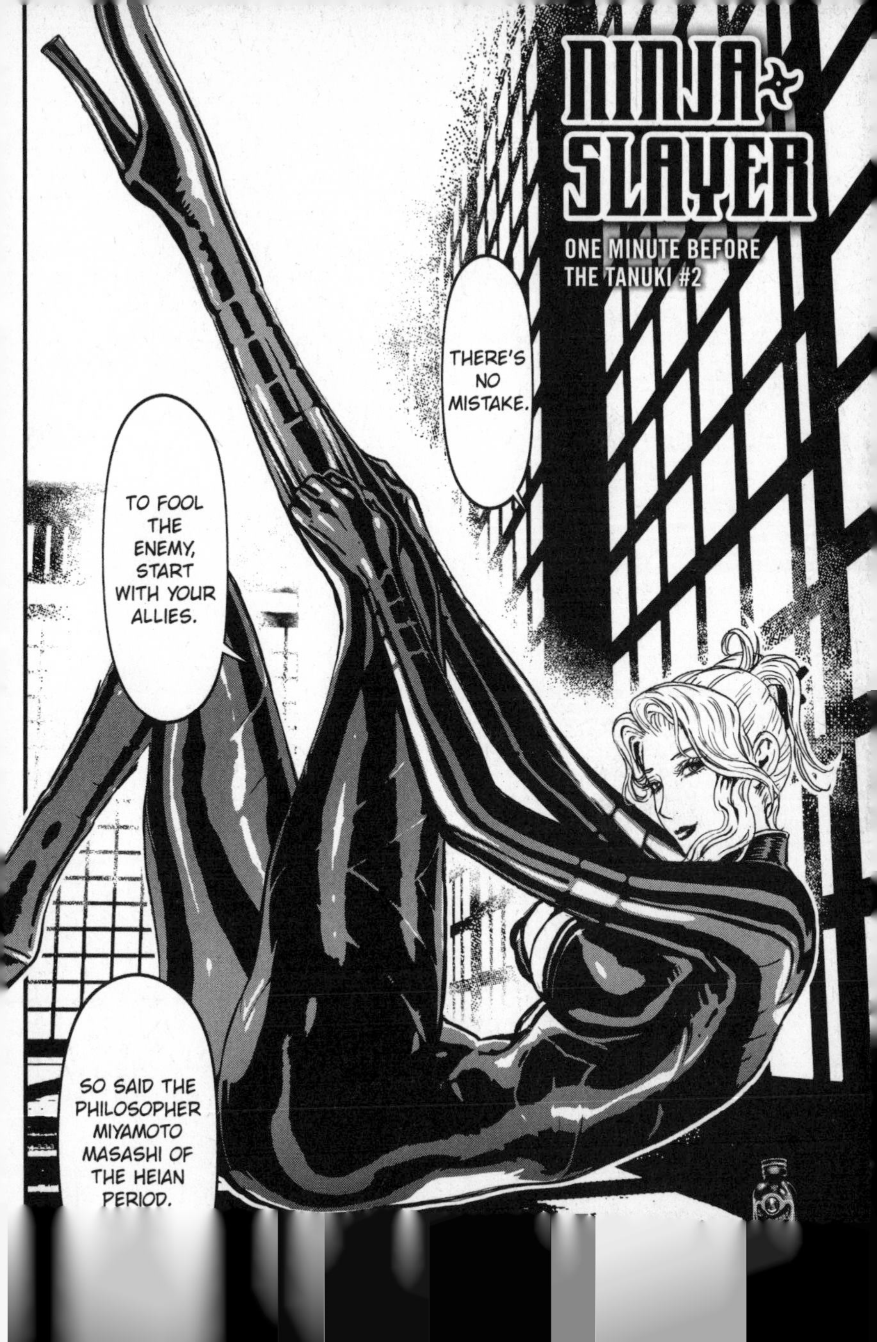
NINJA SLAYER
ONE MINUTE BEFORE THE TANUKI #2
THERE'S NO MISTAKE.
TO FOOL THE ENEMY, START WITH YOUR ALLIES.
SO SAID THE PHILOSOPHER MIYAMOTO MASASHI OF THE HEIAN PERIOD.

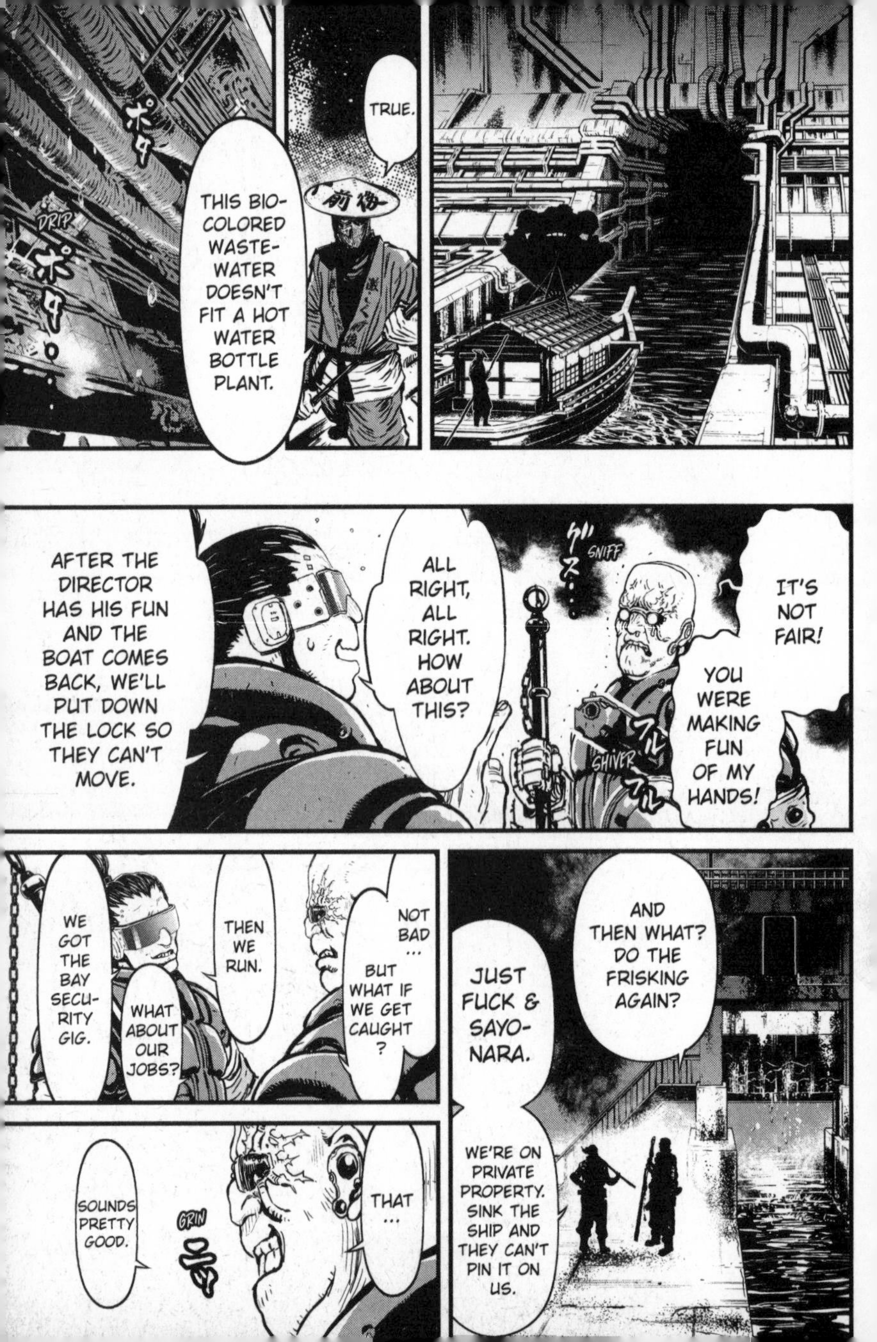
TRUE.
THIS BIO-COLORED WASTE-WATER DOESN'T FIT A HOT WATER BOTTLE PLANT.
ポタ
DRIP
ポタ
IT'S NOT FAIR!
YOU WERE MAKING FUN OF MY HANDS!
SNIFF
SHIVER
ALL RIGHT, ALL RIGHT. HOW ABOUT THIS?
AFTER THE DIRECTOR HAS HIS FUN AND THE BOAT COMES BACK, WE'LL PUT DOWN THE LOCK SO THEY CAN'T MOVE.
AND THEN WHAT? DO THE FRISKING AGAIN?
JUST FUCK & SAYO-NARA.
WE'RE ON PRIVATE PROPERTY. SINK THE SHIP AND THEY CAN'T PIN IT ON US.
NOT BAD...
BUT WHAT IF WE GET CAUGHT?
THEN WE RUN.
WHAT ABOUT OUR JOBS?
WE GOT THE BAY SECU-RITY GIG.
THAT...
GRIN
SOUNDS PRETTY GOOD.

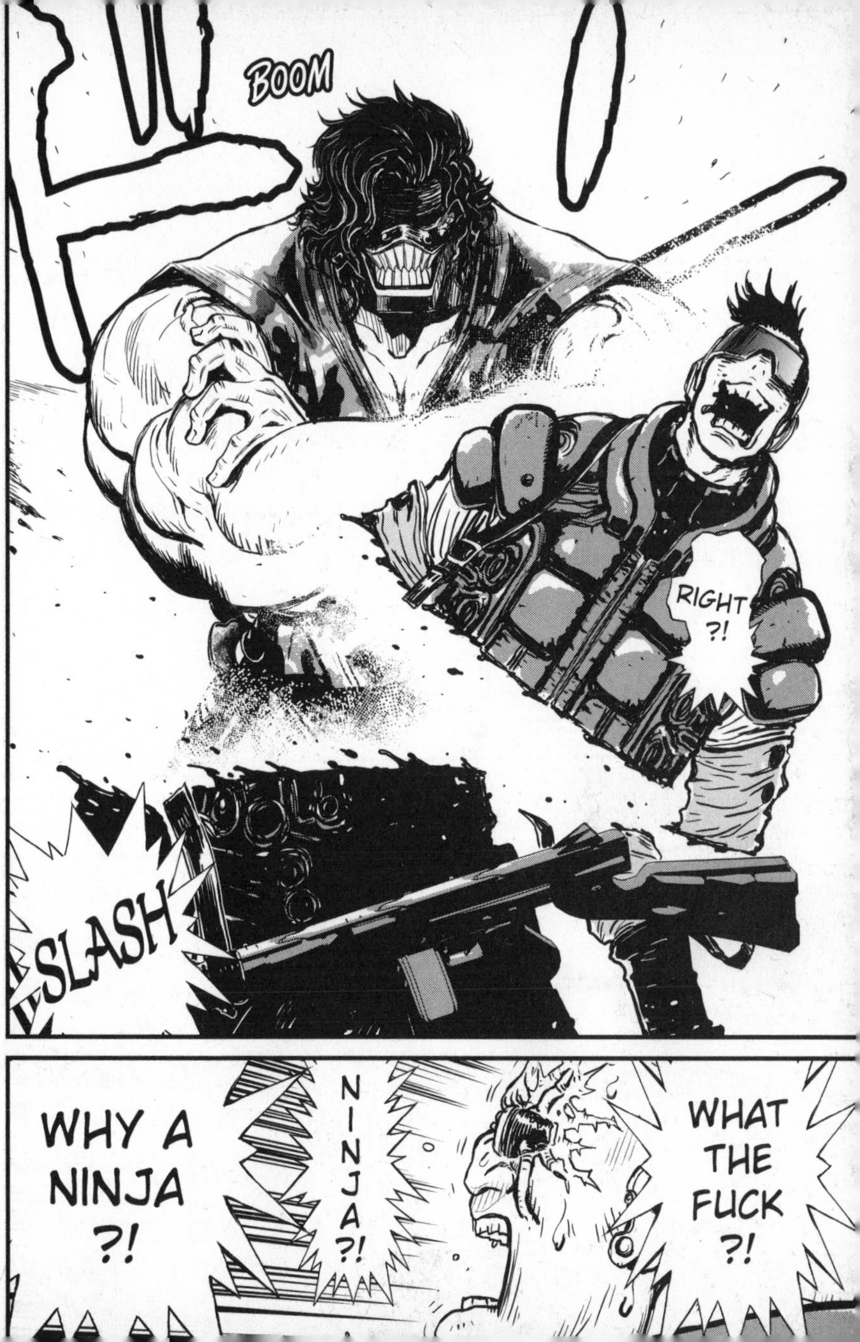
BOOM
RIGHT ?!
SLASH
WHAT THE FUCK ?!
NINJA ?!
WHY A NINJA ?!

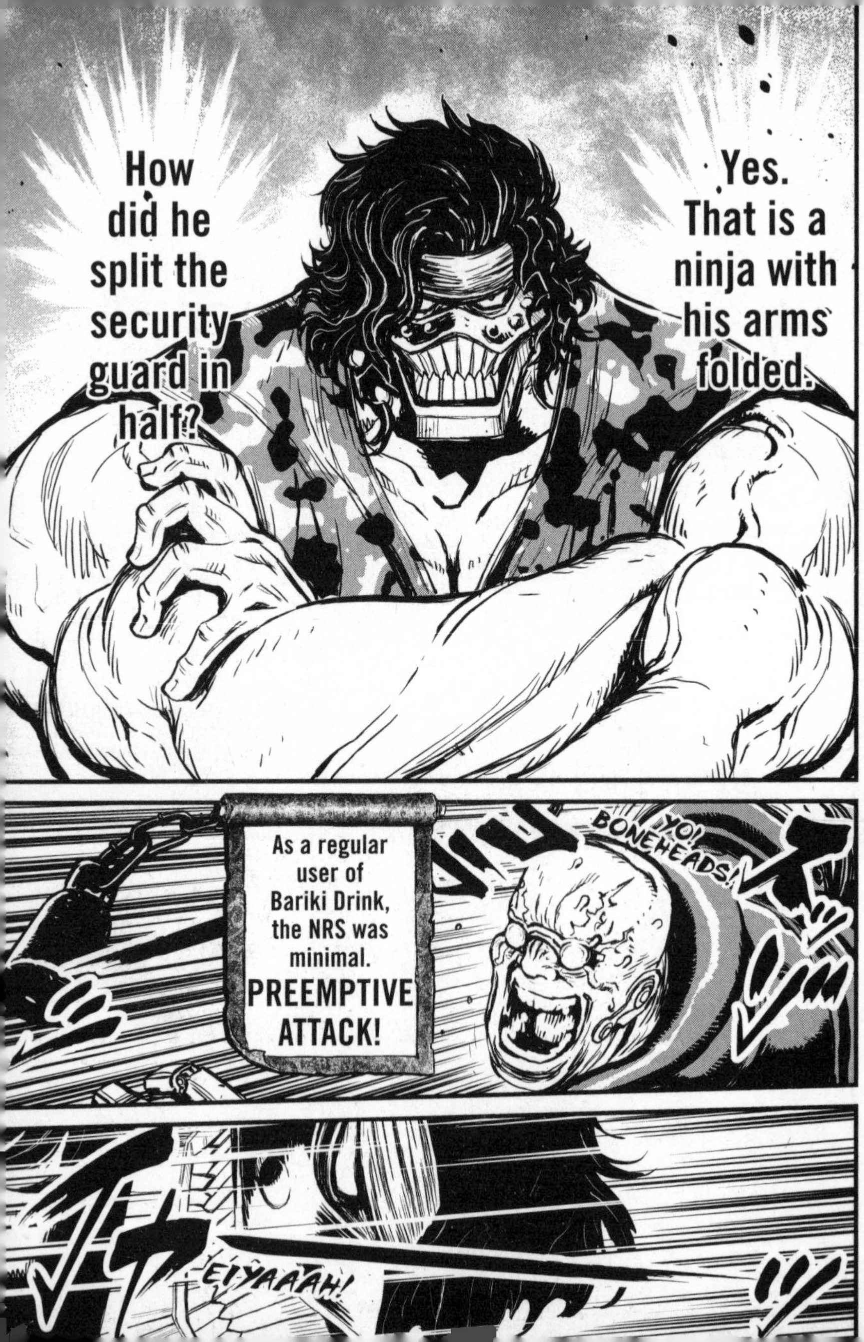
Yes. That is a ninja with his arms folded.
How did he split the security guard in half?
YO! BONEHEADS!
As a regular user of Bariki Drink, the NRS was minimal.
PREEMPTIVE ATTACK!
EI-YAAAAH!

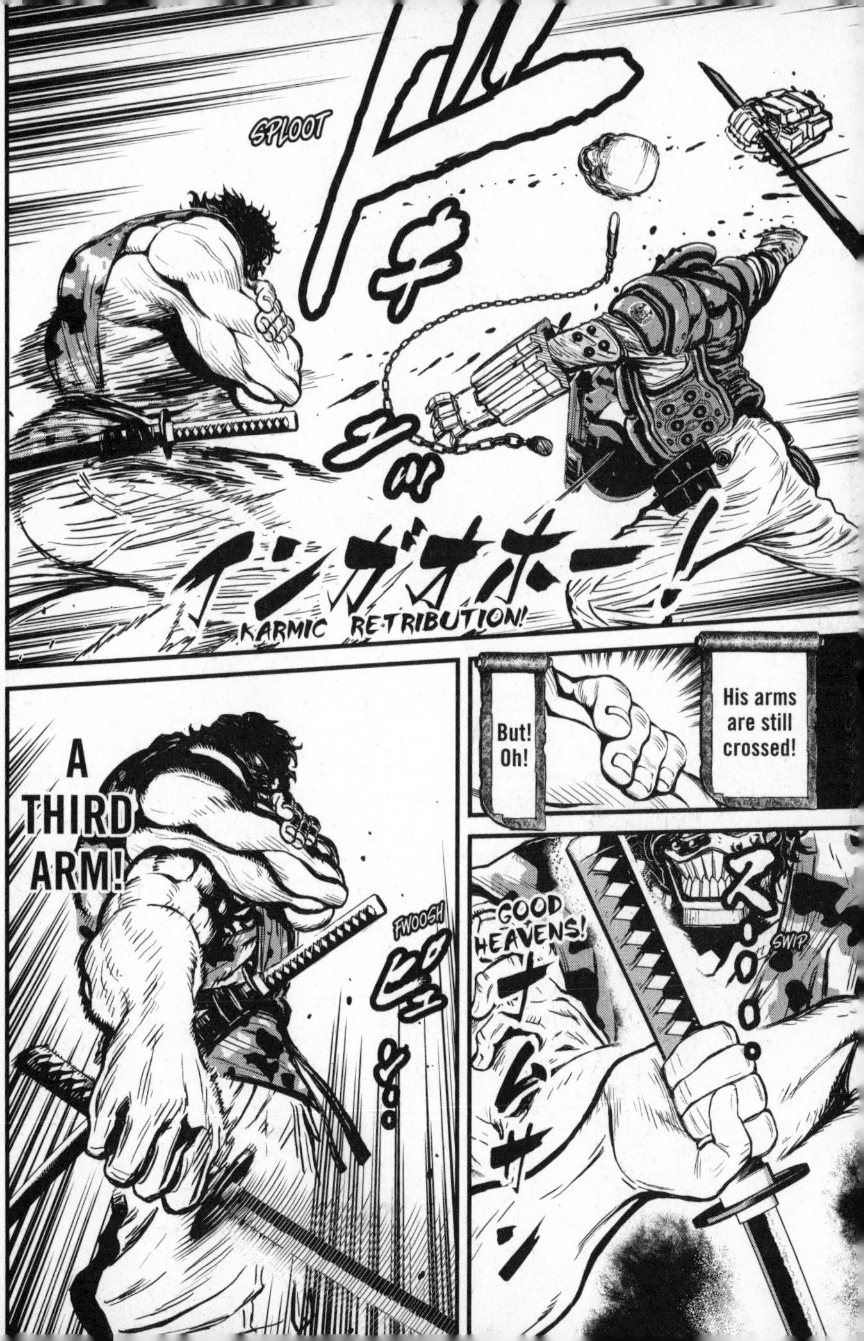
SPLOOT
インガオホー！
KARMIC RETRIBUTION!
His arms are still crossed!
But! Oh!
GOOD HEAVENS!
SWIP
A THIRD ARM!
FWOOSH

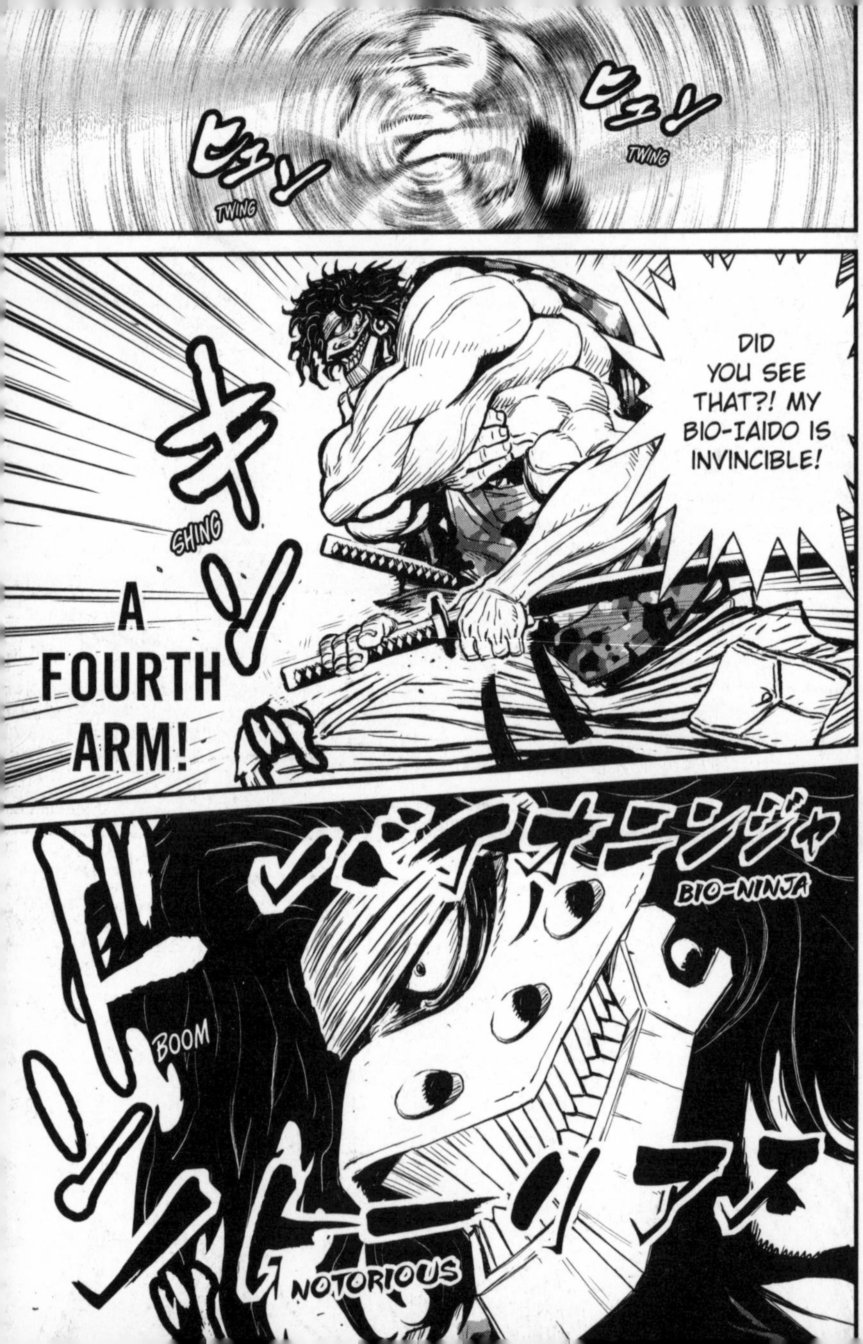
ヒュン
TWING
ヒュン
TWING
DID YOU SEE THAT?! MY BIO-IAIDO IS INVINCIBLE!
キン
SHING
A FOURTH ARM!
バイオニンジャ
BIO-NINJA
ノートリアス
NOTORIOUS
ドーン
BOOM

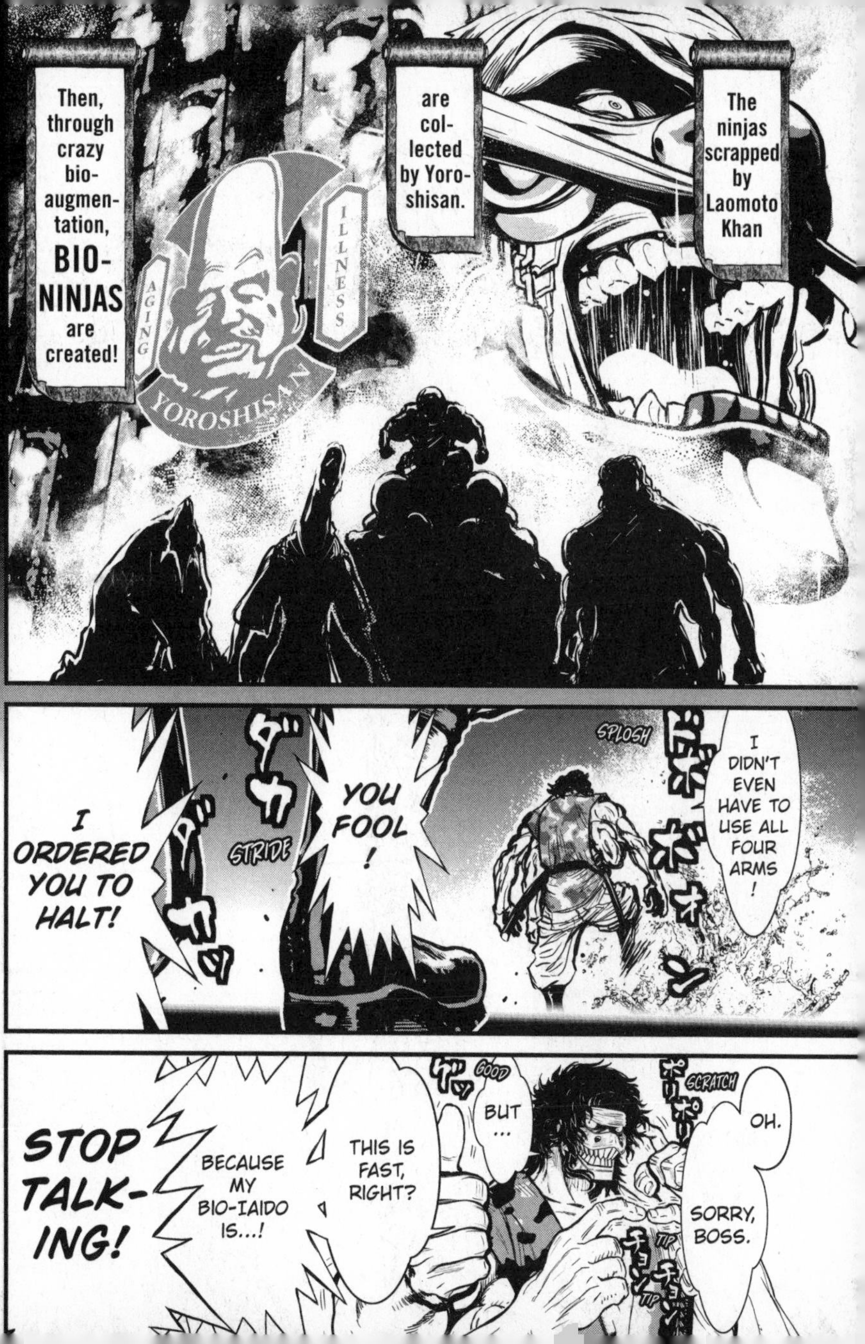
The ninjas scrapped by Laomoto Khan
are collected by Yoroshisan.
ILLNESS
AGING
YOROSHISAN
Then, through crazy bio-augmentation, BIO-NINJAS are created!
I DIDN'T EVEN HAVE TO USE ALL FOUR ARMS!
SPLOSH
YOU FOOL!
STRIDE
I ORDERED YOU TO HALT!
OH.
SORRY, BOSS.
SCRATCH
TIP
TIP
BUT...
GOOD
THIS IS FAST, RIGHT?
BECAUSE MY BIO-IAIDO IS...!
STOP TALKING!

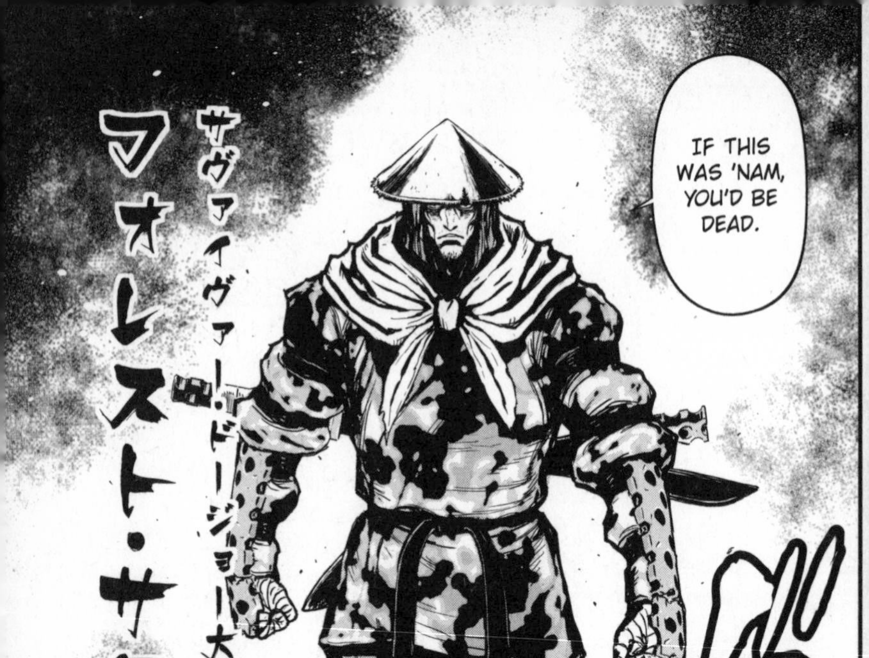
IF THIS WAS 'NAM, YOU'D BE DEAD.
ドーン
BOOM
サヴァイヴァー・ドージョー大将
SURVIVOR DOJO BOSS,
フォレスト・サワタリ
FOREST SAWATARI

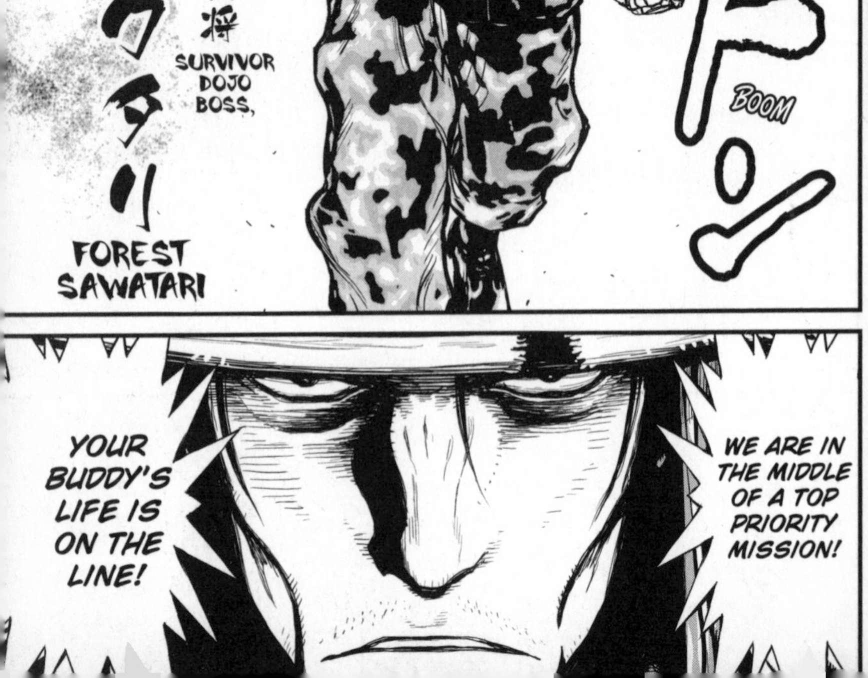
WE ARE IN THE MIDDLE OF A TOP PRIORITY MISSION!
YOUR BUDDY'S LIFE IS ON THE LINE!

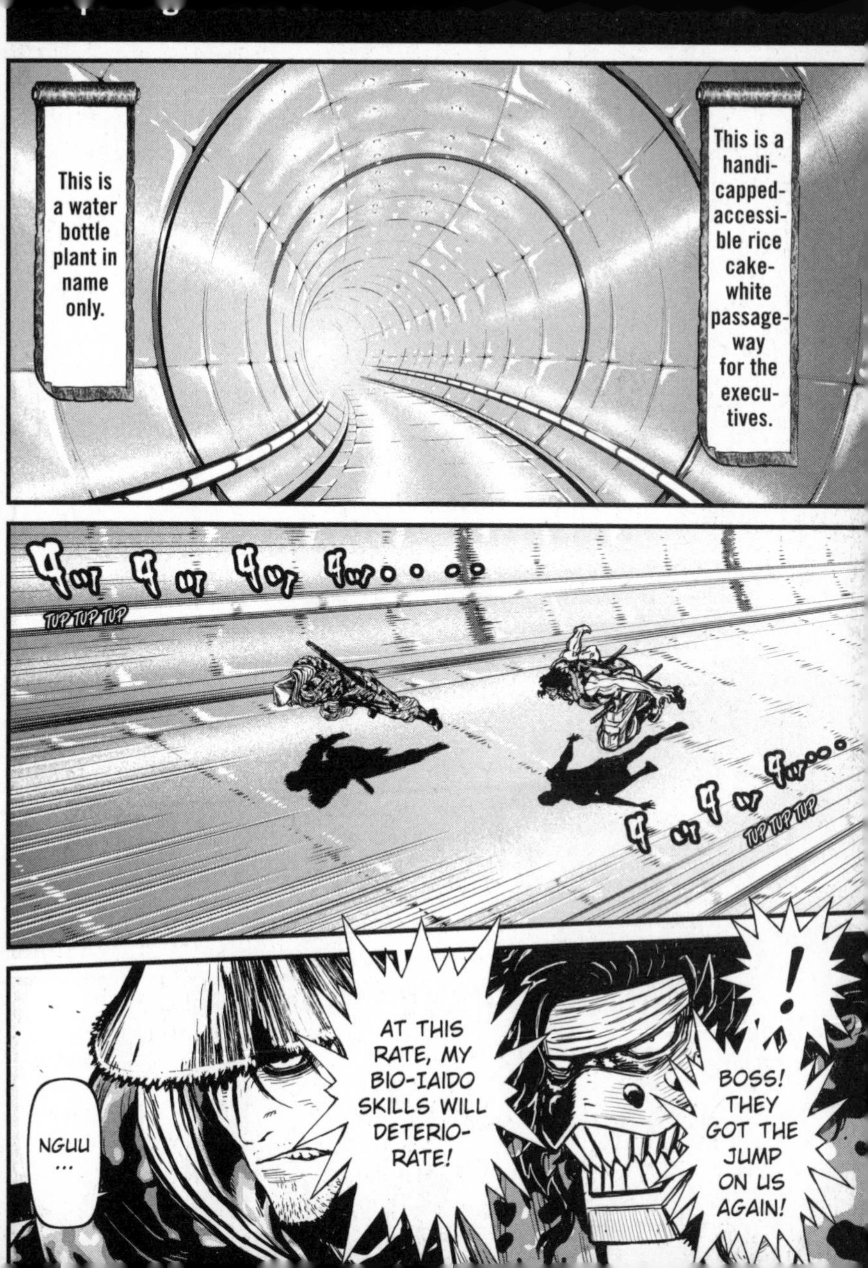
This is a handicapped-accessible rice cake-white passageway for the executives.
This is a water bottle plant in name only.
TUP TUP TUP
TUP TUP TUP
!
BOSS! THEY GOT THE JUMP ON US AGAIN!
AT THIS RATE, MY BIO-IAIDO SKILLS WILL DETERIORATE!
NGUU...

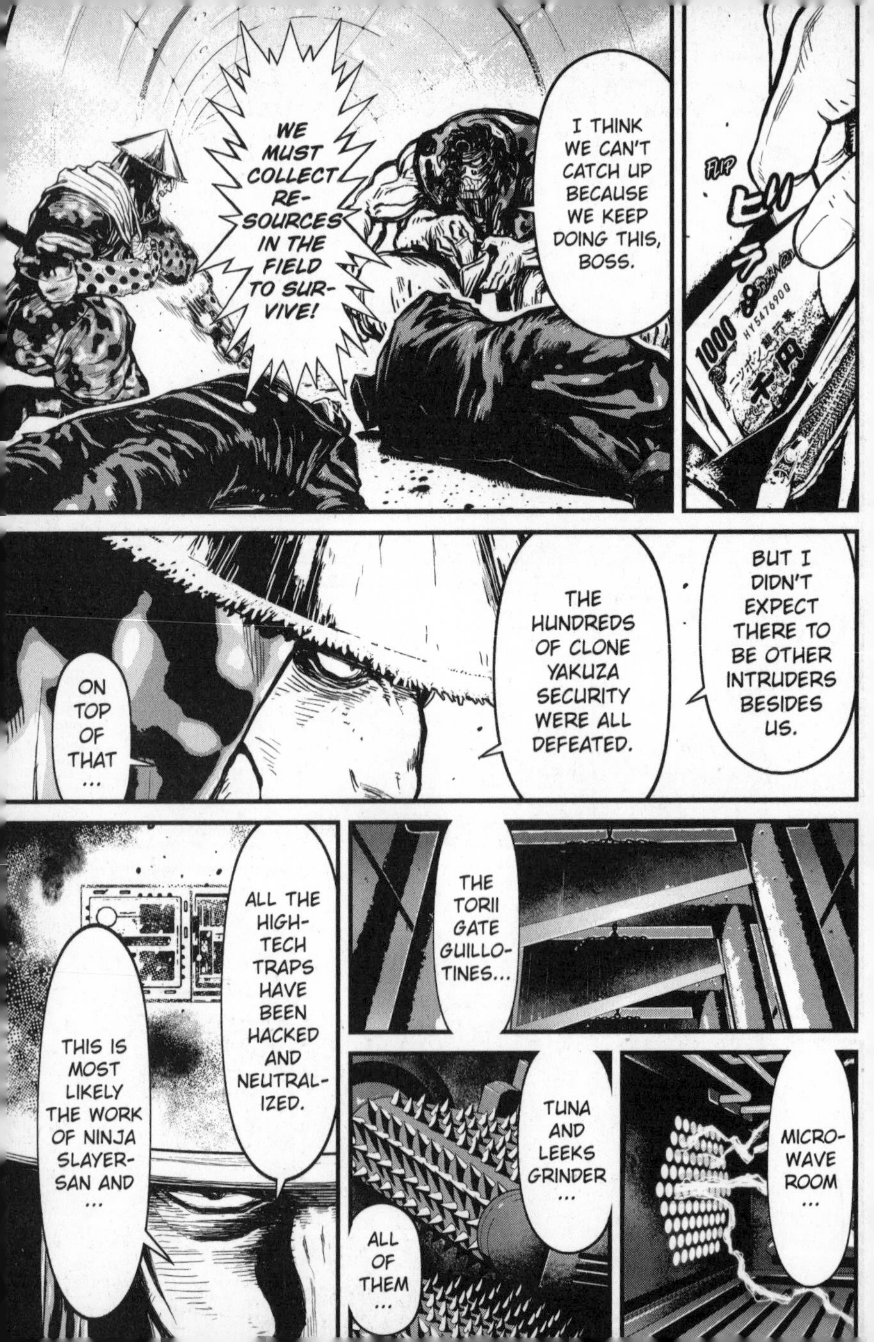
FLIP
I THINK WE CAN'T CATCH UP BECAUSE WE KEEP DOING THIS, BOSS.
WE MUST COLLECT RE-SOURCES IN THE FIELD TO SUR-VIVE!
BUT I DIDN'T EXPECT THERE TO BE OTHER INTRUDERS BESIDES US.
THE HUNDREDS OF CLONE YAKUZA SECURITY WERE ALL DEFEATED.
ON TOP OF THAT ...
THE TORII GATE GUILLO-TINES...
MICRO-WAVE ROOM ...
TUNA AND LEEKS GRINDER ...
ALL OF THEM ...
ALL THE HIGH-TECH TRAPS HAVE BEEN HACKED AND NEUTRAL-IZED.
THIS IS MOST LIKELY THE WORK OF NINJA SLAYER-SAN AND ...

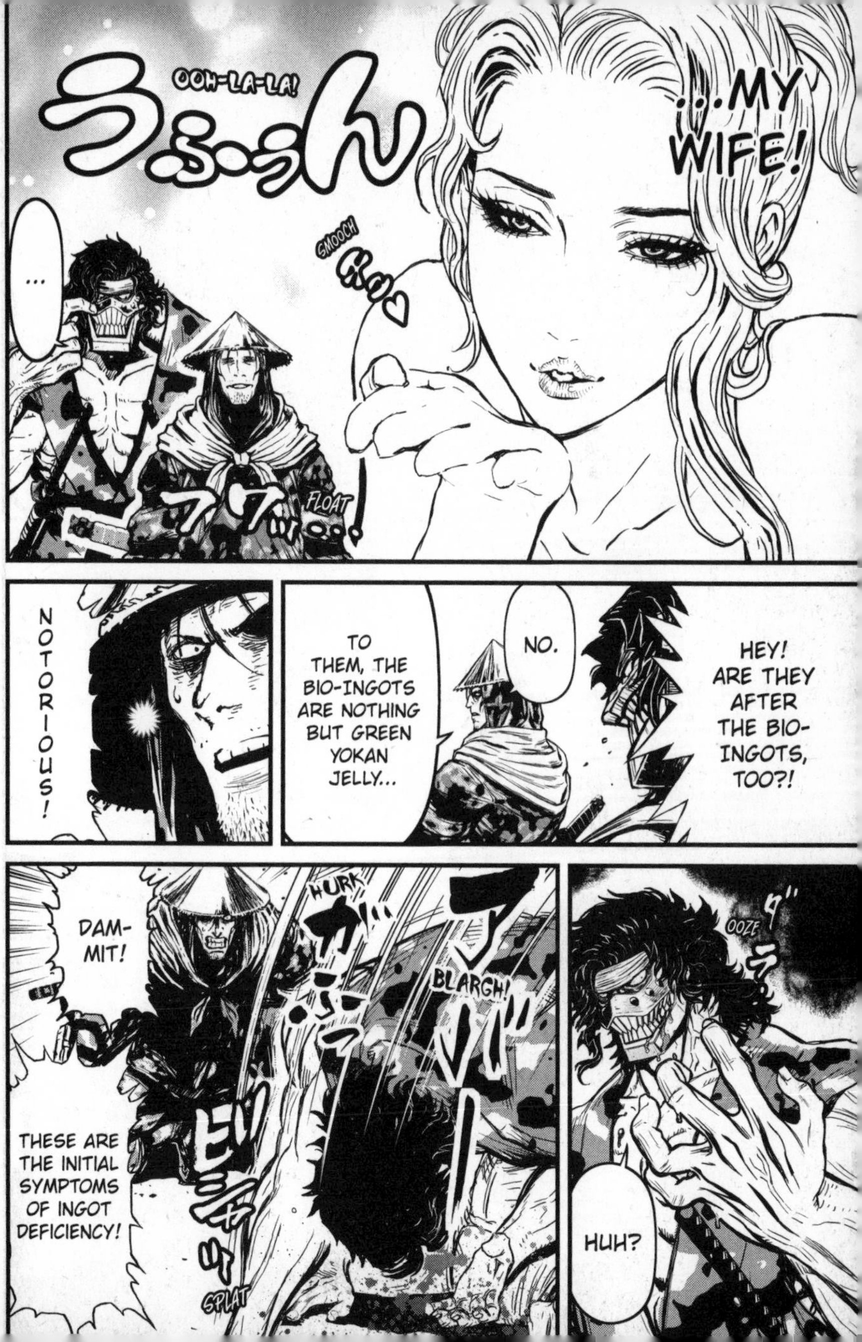
...MY WIFE!
OOH-LA-LA!
SMOOCH
...
FLOAT
HEY! ARE THEY AFTER THE BIO-INGOTS, TOO?!
NO.
TO THEM, THE BIO-INGOTS ARE NOTHING BUT GREEN YOKAN JELLY...
NOTORIOUS!
OOZE
HUH?
HURK
BLARGH!
DAM-MIT!
THESE ARE THE INITIAL SYMPTOMS OF INGOT DEFICIENCY!
SPLAT

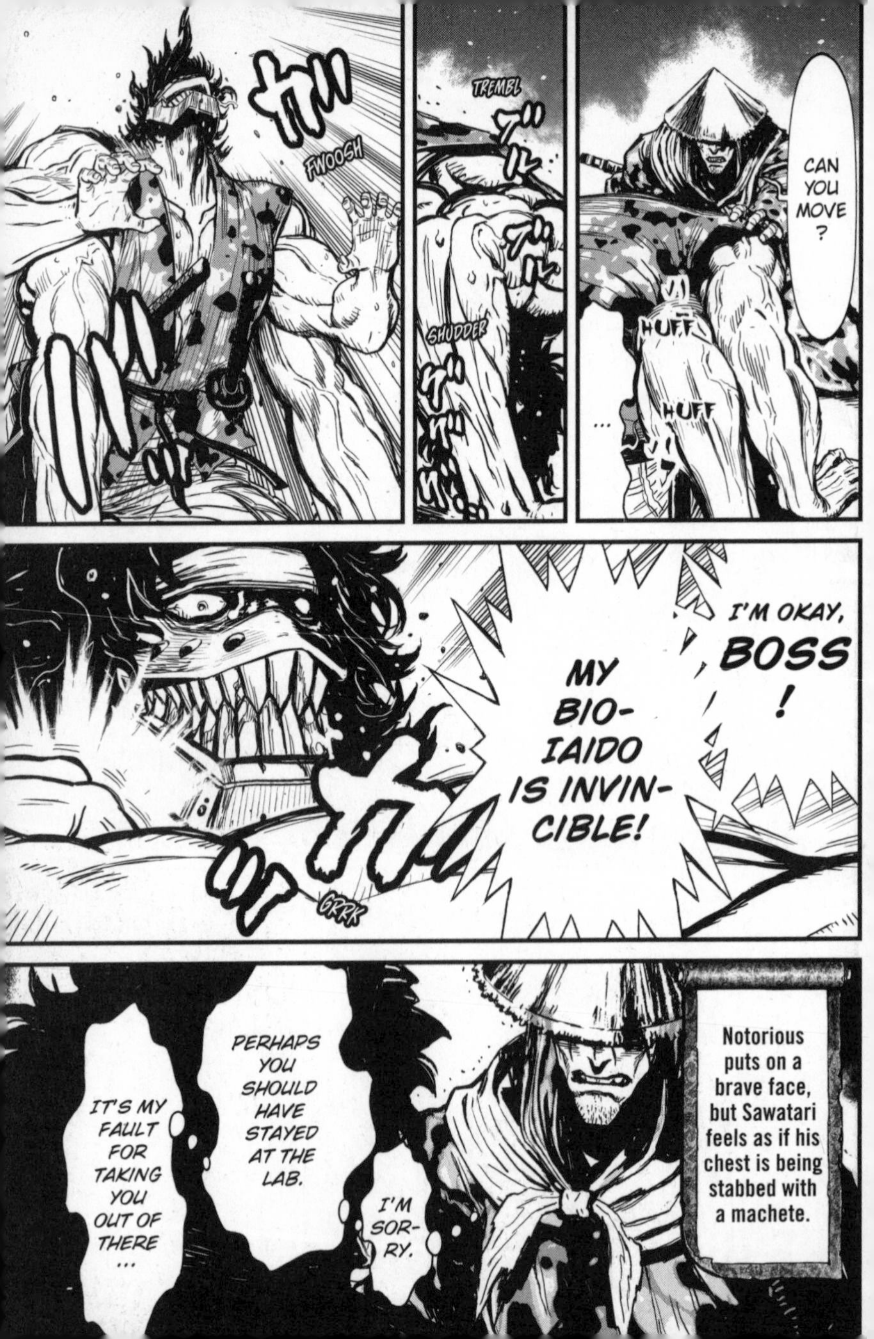
CAN YOU MOVE?
HUFF
HUFF
...
TREMBL
SHUDDER
FWOOSH
I'M OKAY, BOSS!
MY BIO-IAIDO IS INVINCIBLE!
GRRK
Notorious puts on a brave face, but Sawatari feels as if his chest is being stabbed with a machete.
I'M SORRY.
PERHAPS YOU SHOULD HAVE STAYED AT THE LAB.
IT'S MY FAULT FOR TAKING YOU OUT OF THERE...

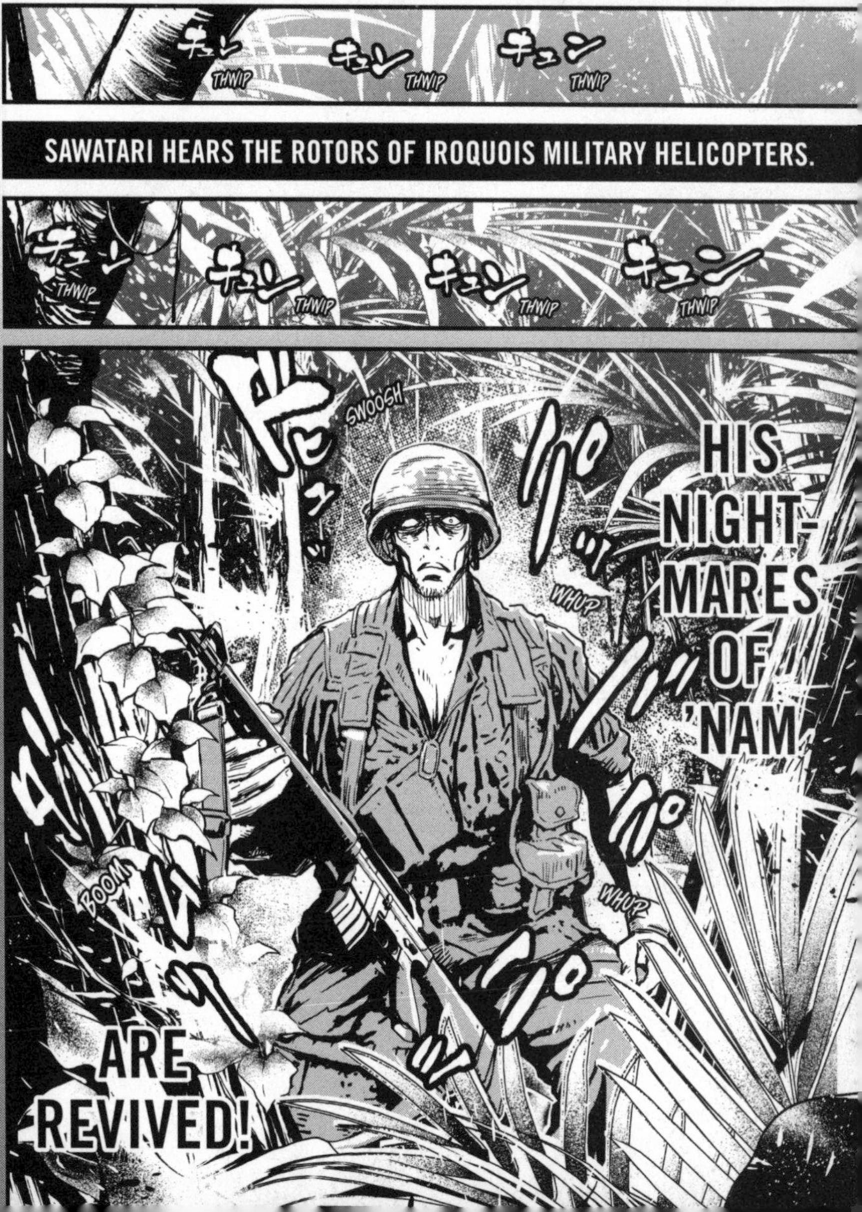

キュン
THWIP
キュン
THWIP
キュン
THWIP
SAWATARI HEARS THE ROTORS OF IROQUOIS MILITARY HELICOPTERS.
キュン
THWIP
キュン
THWIP
キュン
THWIP
キュン
THWIP
HIS NIGHT-MARES OF 'NAM
WHUP
WHUP
SWOOSH
BOOM
ARE REVIVED!

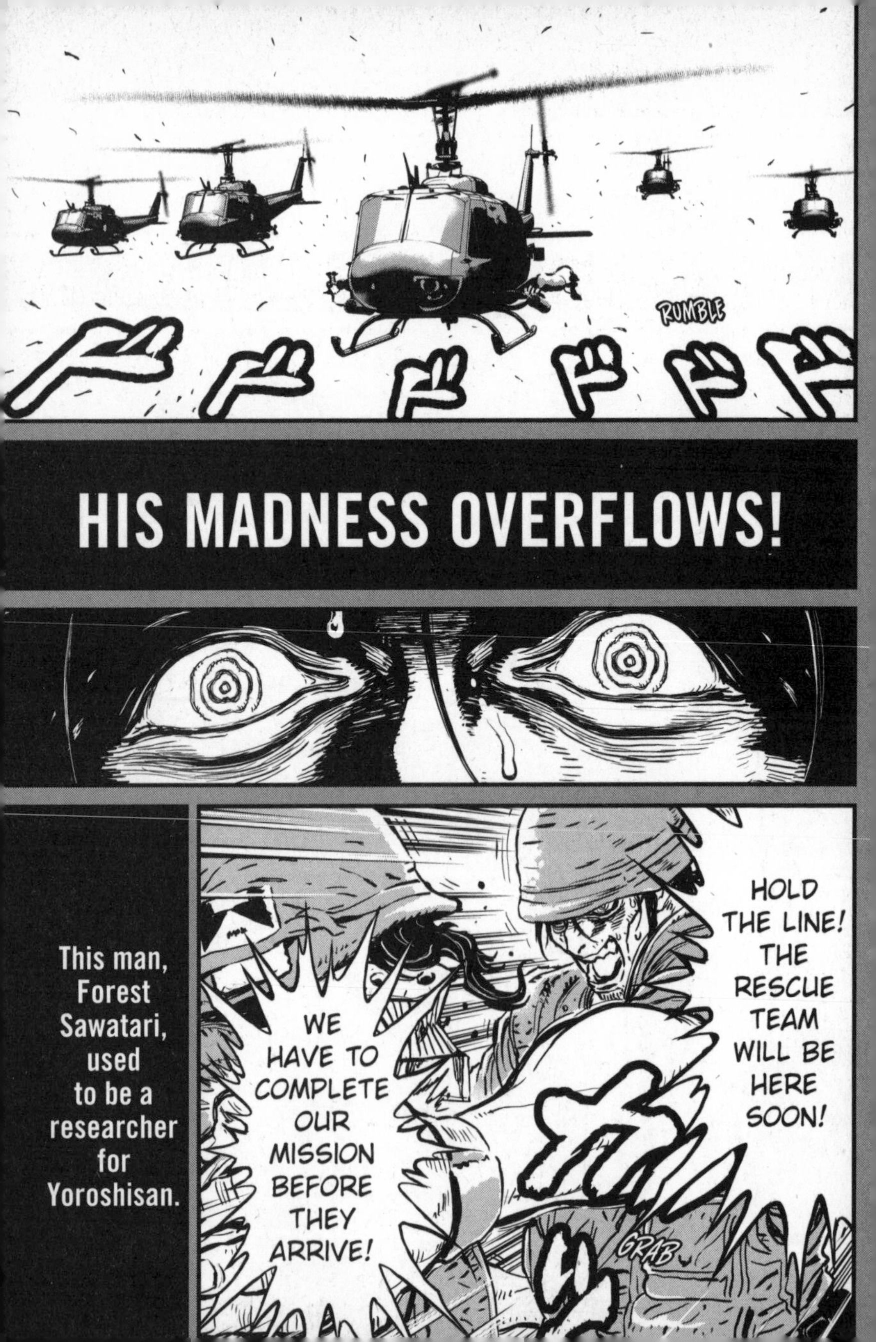
RUMBLE
HIS MADNESS OVERFLOWS!
HOLD THE LINE! THE RESCUE TEAM WILL BE HERE SOON!
WE HAVE TO COMPLETE OUR MISSION BEFORE THEY ARRIVE!
GRAB
This man, Forest Sawatari, used to be a researcher for Yoroshisan.

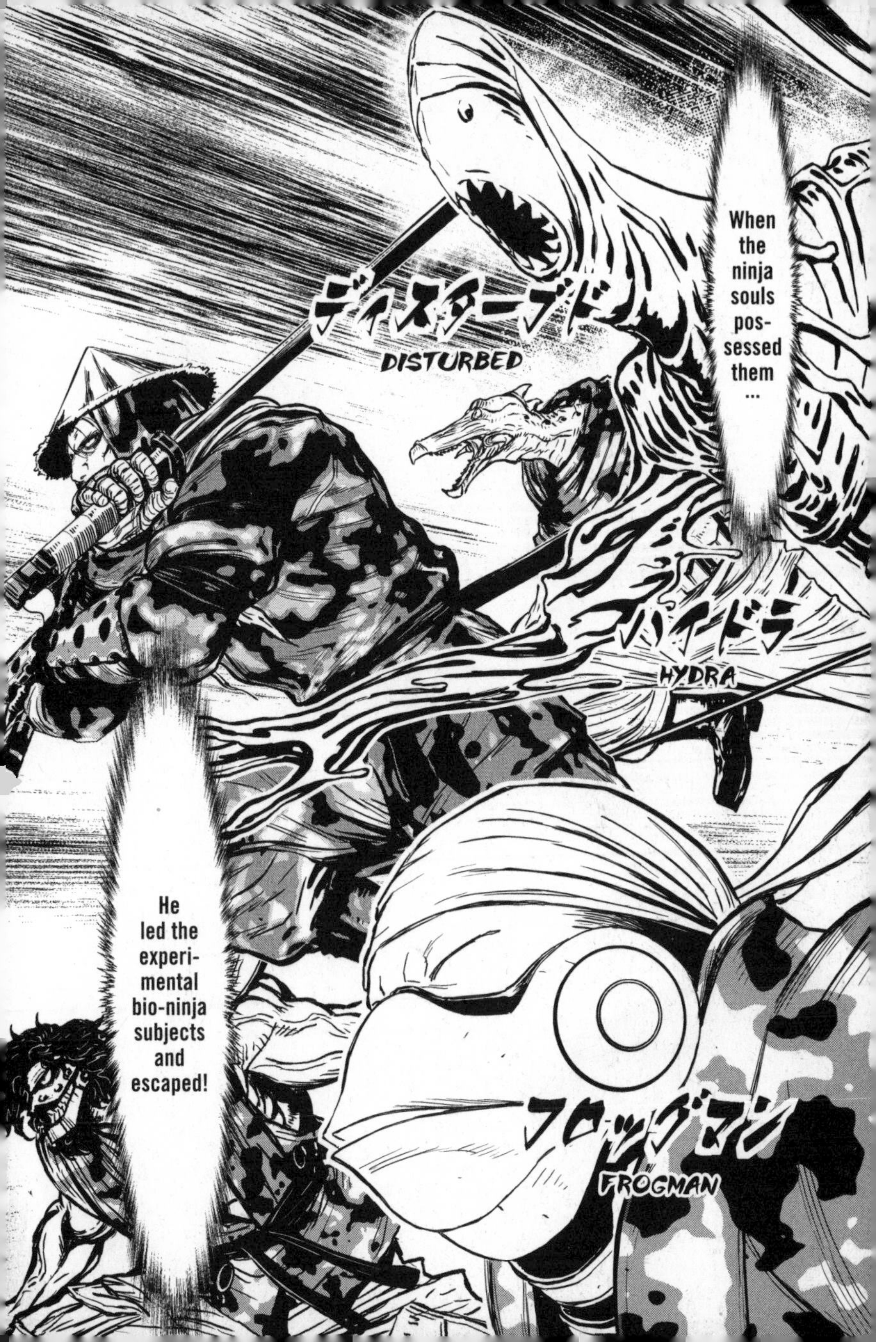

When the ninja souls pos-sessed them ...
ディスターブド
DISTURBED
ハイドラ
HYDRA
He led the experi-mental bio-ninja subjects and escaped!
フロッグマン
FROGMAN

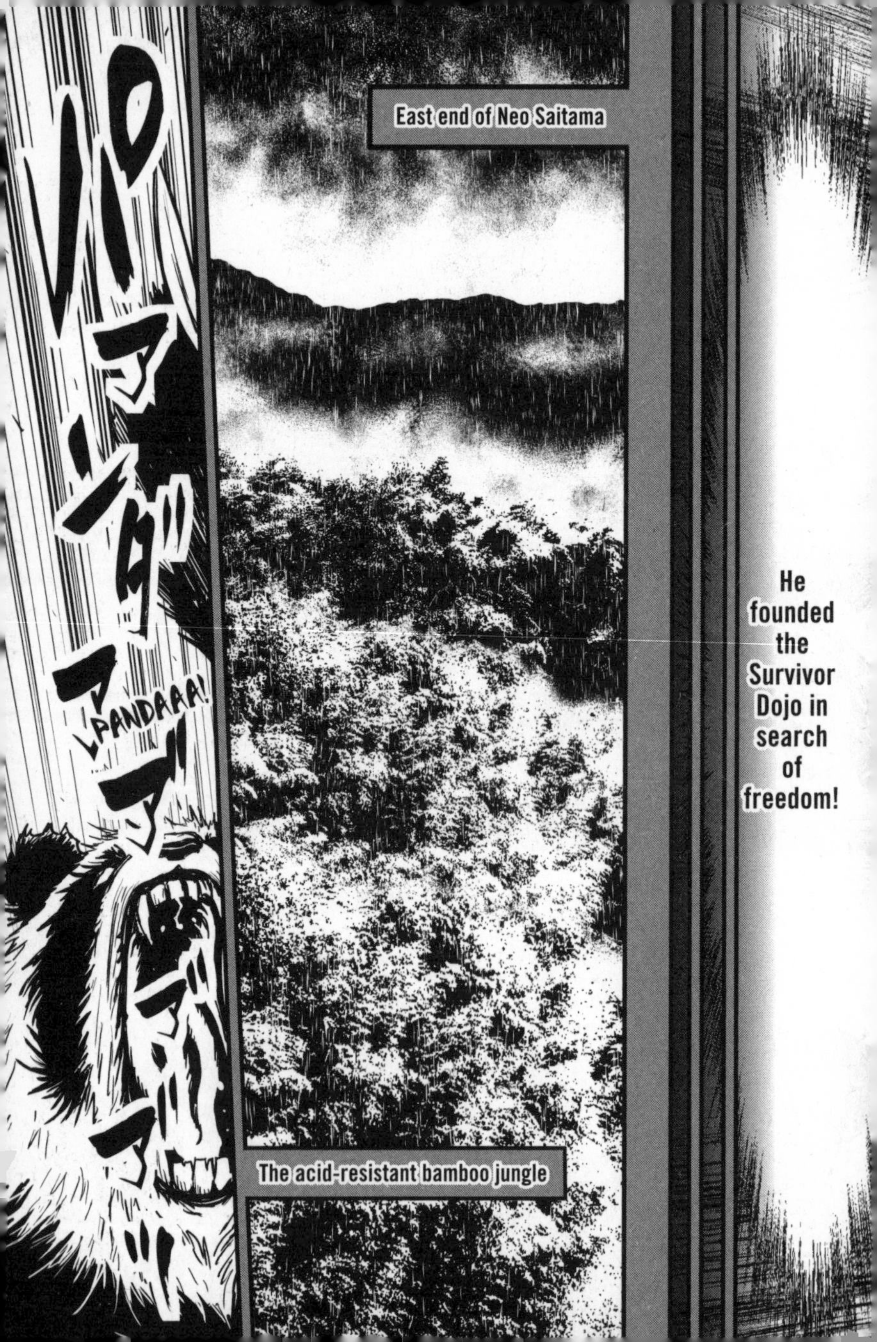
He founded the Survivor Dojo in search of freedom!
East end of Neo Saitama
The acid-resistant bamboo jungle
PANDAAA!

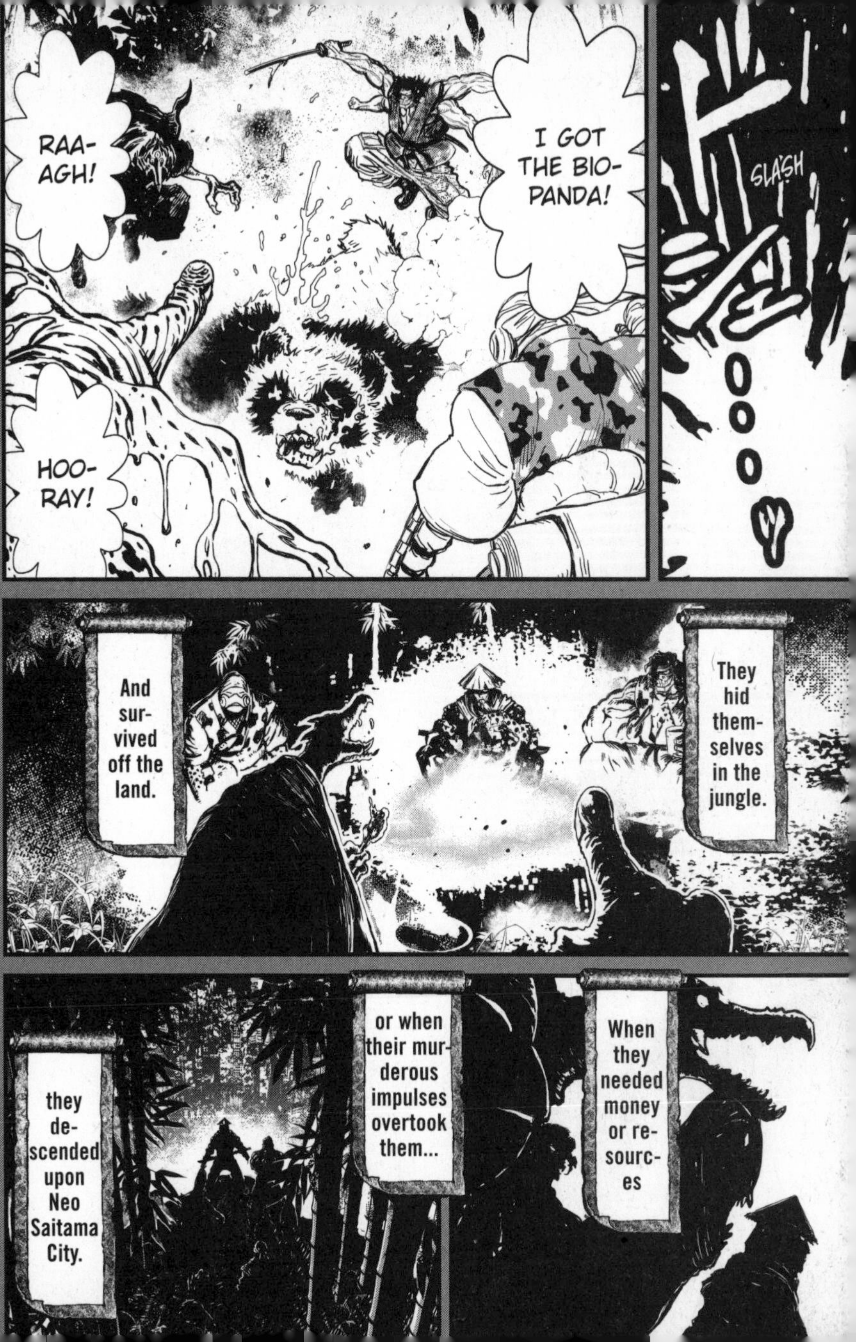
SLASH
I GOT THE BIO-PANDA!
RAA-AGH!
HOORAY!
They hid themselves in the jungle.
And survived off the land.
When they needed money or resources
or when their murderous impulses overtook them...
they descended upon Neo Saitama City.

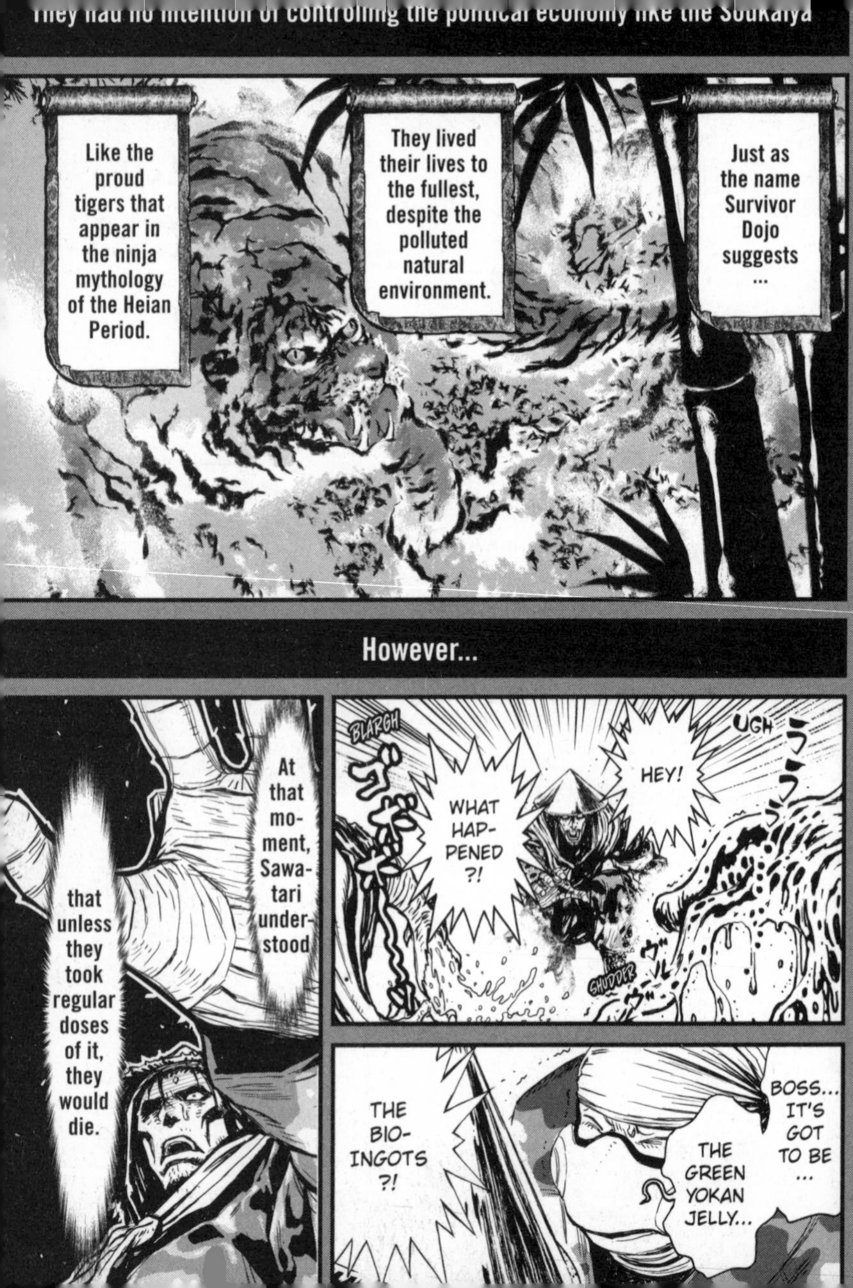
They had no intention of controlling the political economy like the Soukaiya
Just as the name Survivor Dojo suggests ...
They lived their lives to the fullest, despite the polluted natural environment.
Like the proud tigers that appear in the ninja mythology of the Heian Period.
However...
UGH
HEY!
WHAT HAPPENED ?!
BLARGH
SHUDDER
BOSS... IT'S GOT TO BE ...
THE GREEN YOKAN JELLY...
THE BIO-INGOTS ?!
At that moment, Sawatari understood
that unless they took regular doses of it, they would die.

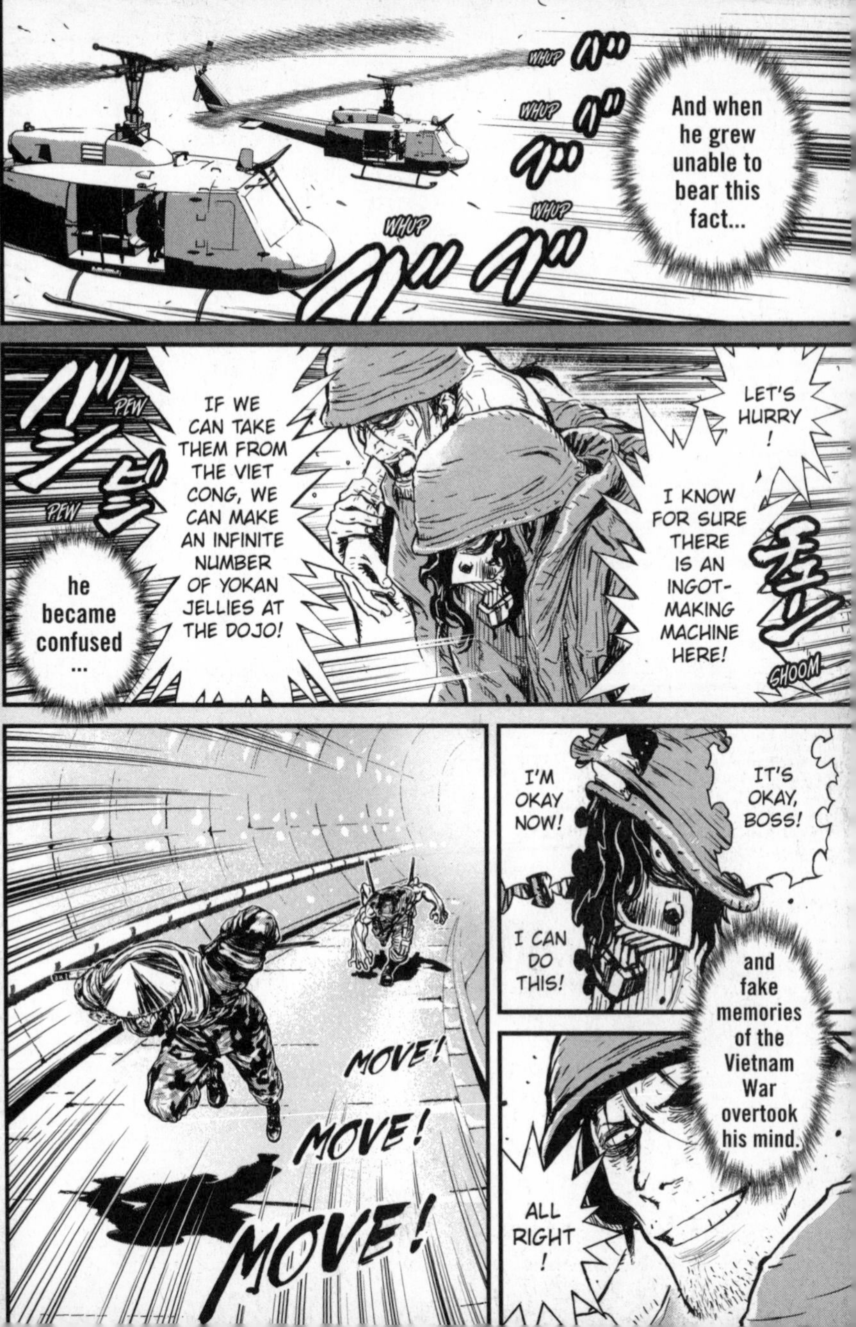
And when he grew unable to bear this fact...
WHUP
WHUP
WHUP
WHUP
LET'S HURRY!
I KNOW FOR SURE THERE IS AN INGOT-MAKING MACHINE HERE!
SHOOM
IF WE CAN TAKE THEM FROM THE VIET CONG, WE CAN MAKE AN INFINITE NUMBER OF YOKAN JELLIES AT THE DOJO!
PEW
PEW
he became confused ...
IT'S OKAY, BOSS!
I'M OKAY NOW!
I CAN DO THIS!
and fake memories of the Vietnam War overtook his mind.
ALL RIGHT!
MOVE!
MOVE!
MOVE!

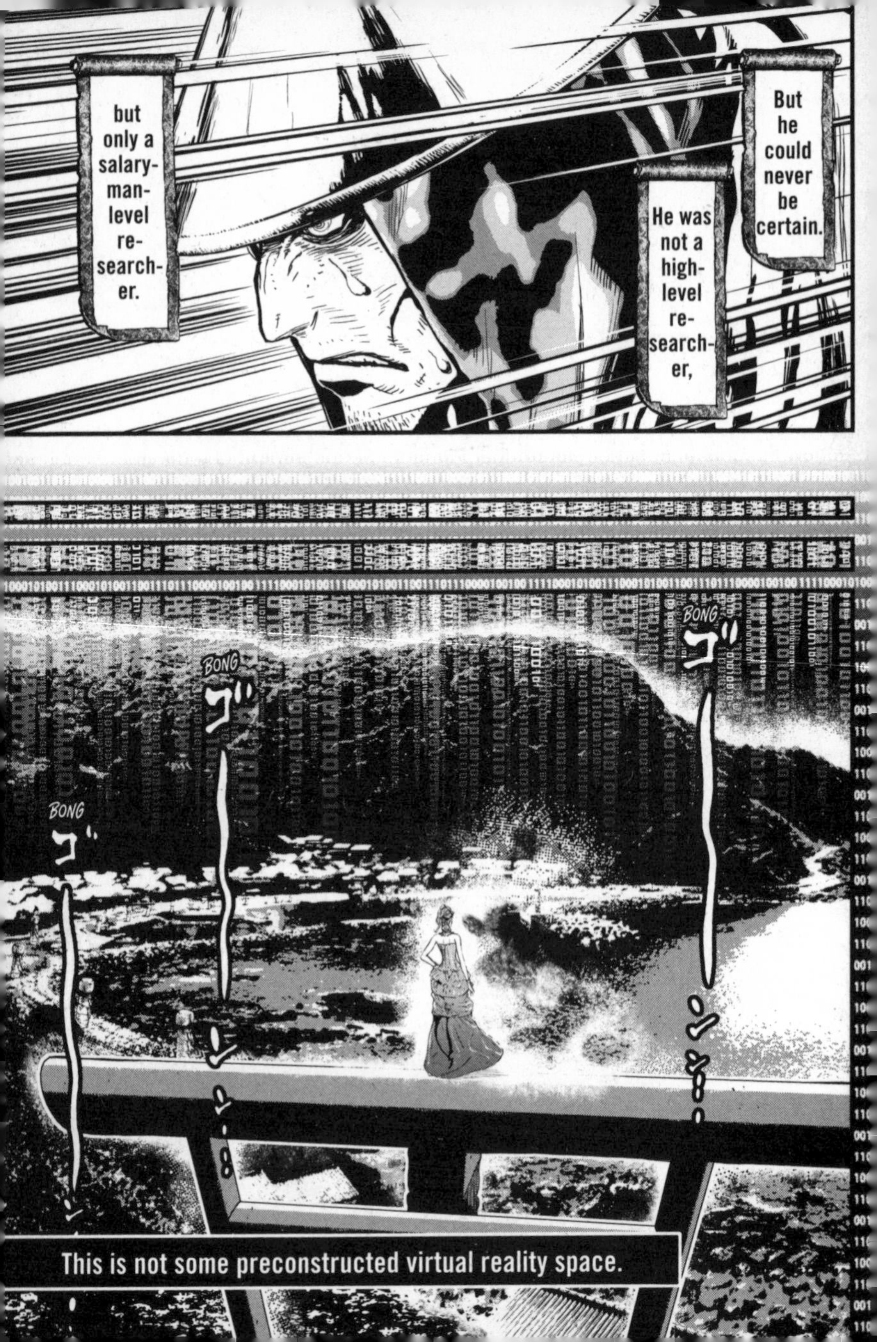
But he could never be certain.
He was not a high-level re-searcher,
but only a salary-man-level re-searcher.
BONG ゴ
BONG ゴ
BONG ゴ
This is not some preconstructed virtual reality space.

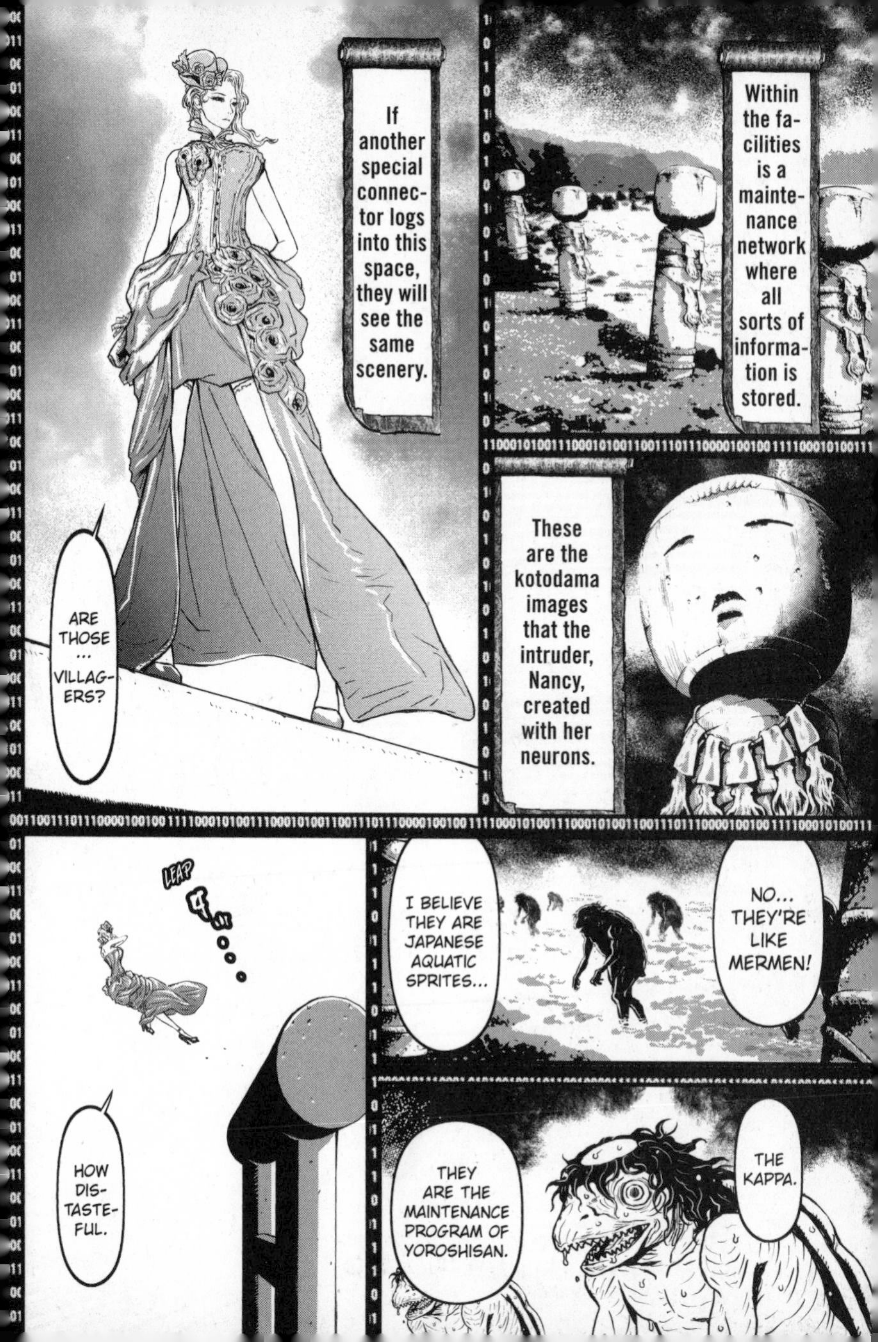
Within the facilities is a maintenance network where all sorts of information is stored.
These are the kotodama images that the intruder, Nancy, created with her neurons.
If another special connector logs into this space, they will see the same scenery.
ARE THOSE... VILLAGERS?
NO... THEY'RE LIKE MERMEN!
I BELIEVE THEY ARE JAPANESE AQUATIC SPRITES...
THE KAPPA.
THEY ARE THE MAINTENANCE PROGRAM OF YOROSHISAN.
LEAP
HOW DISTASTEFUL.

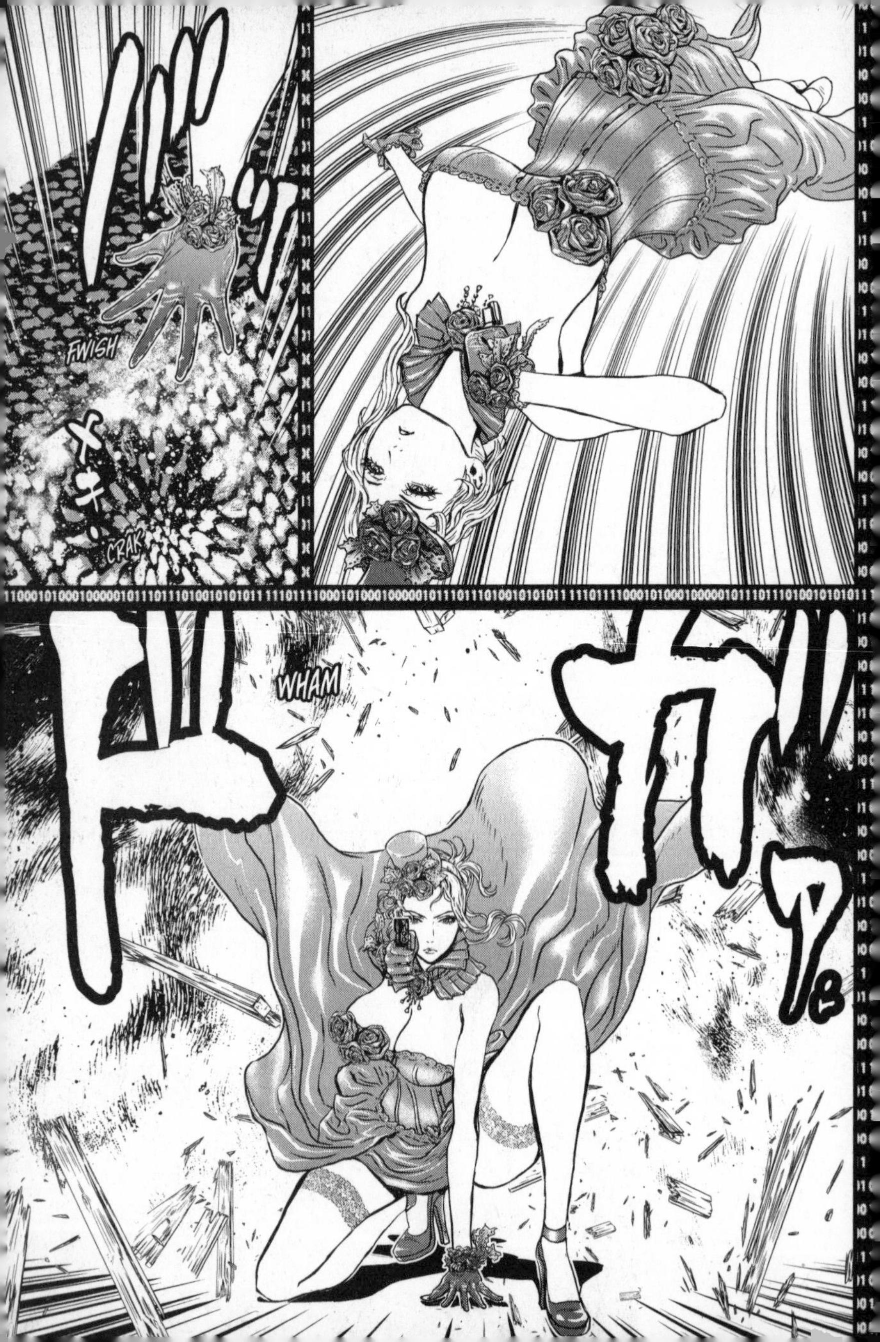
FWISH
CRAK
WHAM

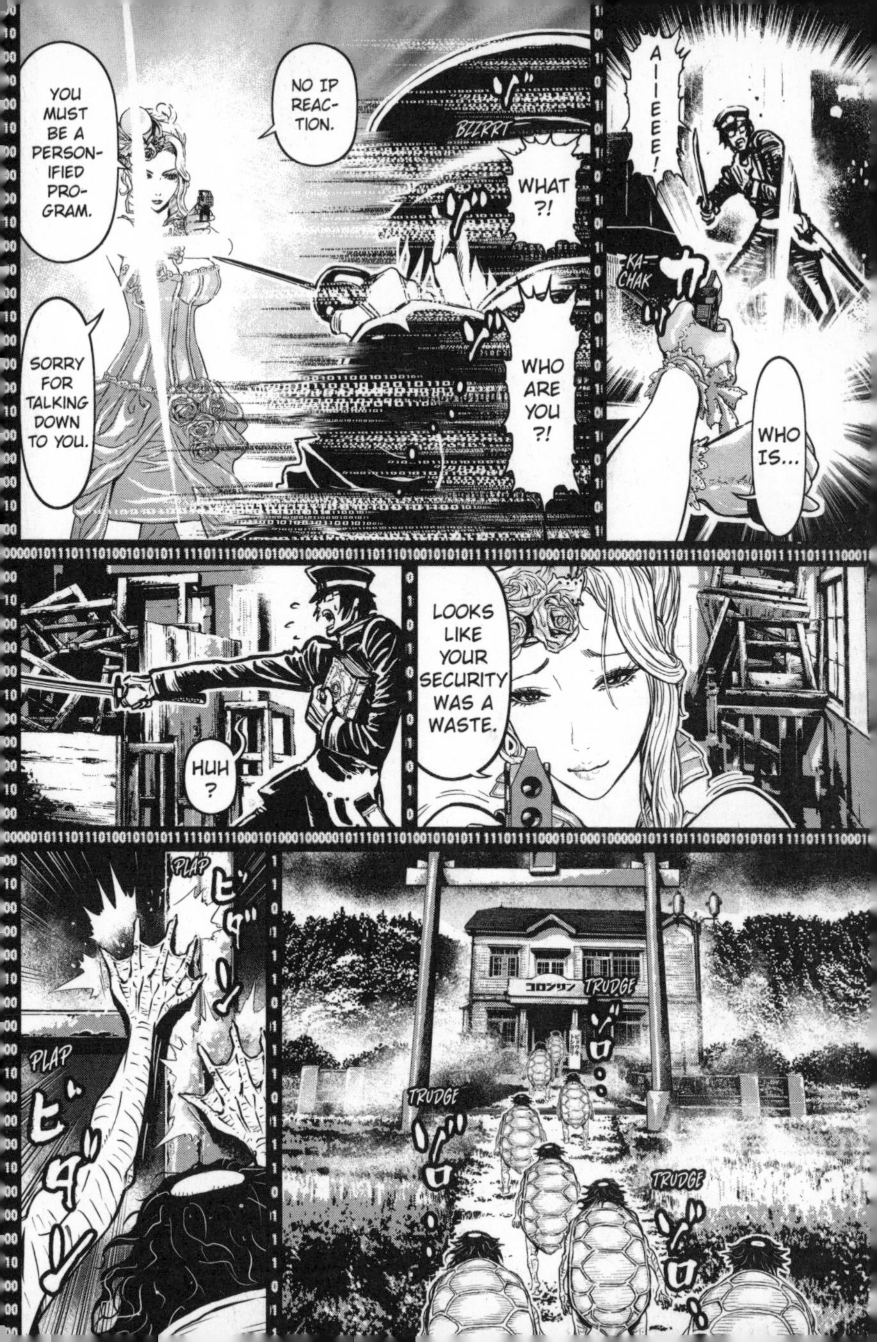
AIIEEE!
KA-CHAK
WHO IS...
BZZRRT
WHAT?!
NO IP REACTION.
YOU MUST BE A PERSONIFIED PROGRAM.
WHO ARE YOU?!
SORRY FOR TALKING DOWN TO YOU.
LOOKS LIKE YOUR SECURITY WAS A WASTE.
HUH?
コロンサン
TRUDGE
TRUDGE
TRUDGE
PLAP
PLAP

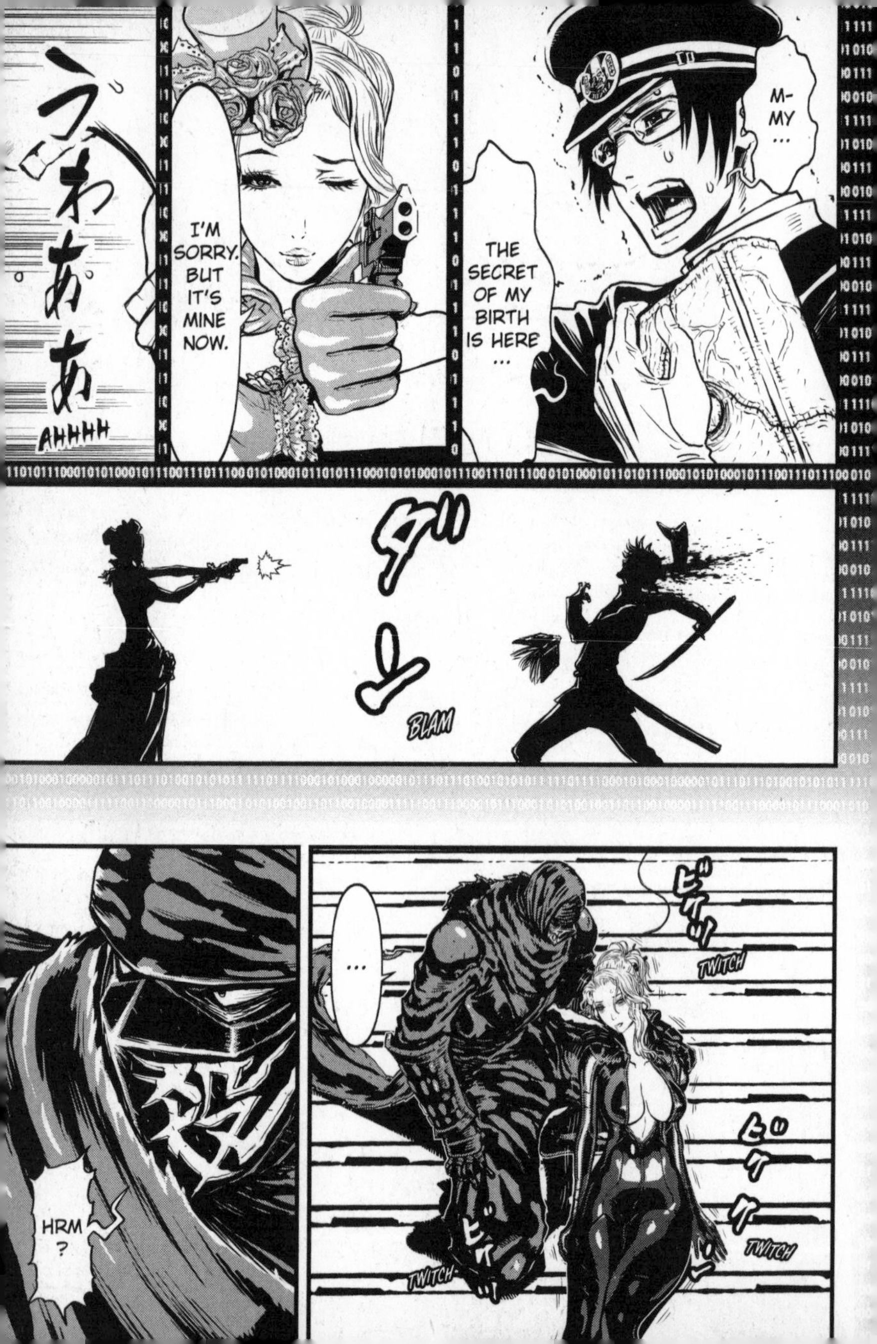
M-MY ...
THE SECRET OF MY BIRTH IS HERE ...
I'M SORRY. BUT IT'S MINE NOW.
うわああ
AHHHH
BLAM
...
TWITCH
TWITCH
TWITCH
HRM?

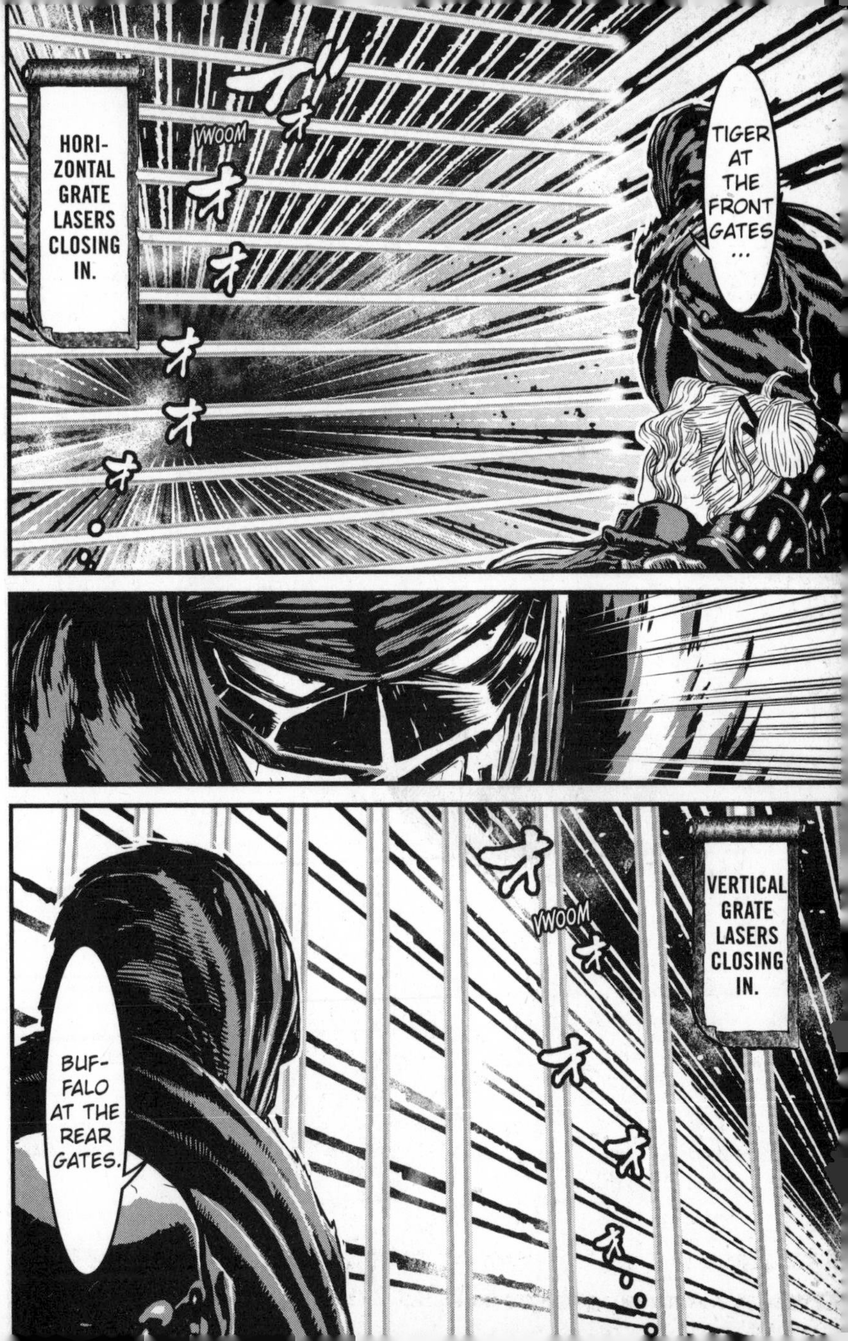
TIGER AT THE FRONT GATES...
HORIZONTAL GRATE LASERS CLOSING IN.
VWOOM
VERTICAL GRATE LASERS CLOSING IN.
VWOOM
BUFFALO AT THE REAR GATES.

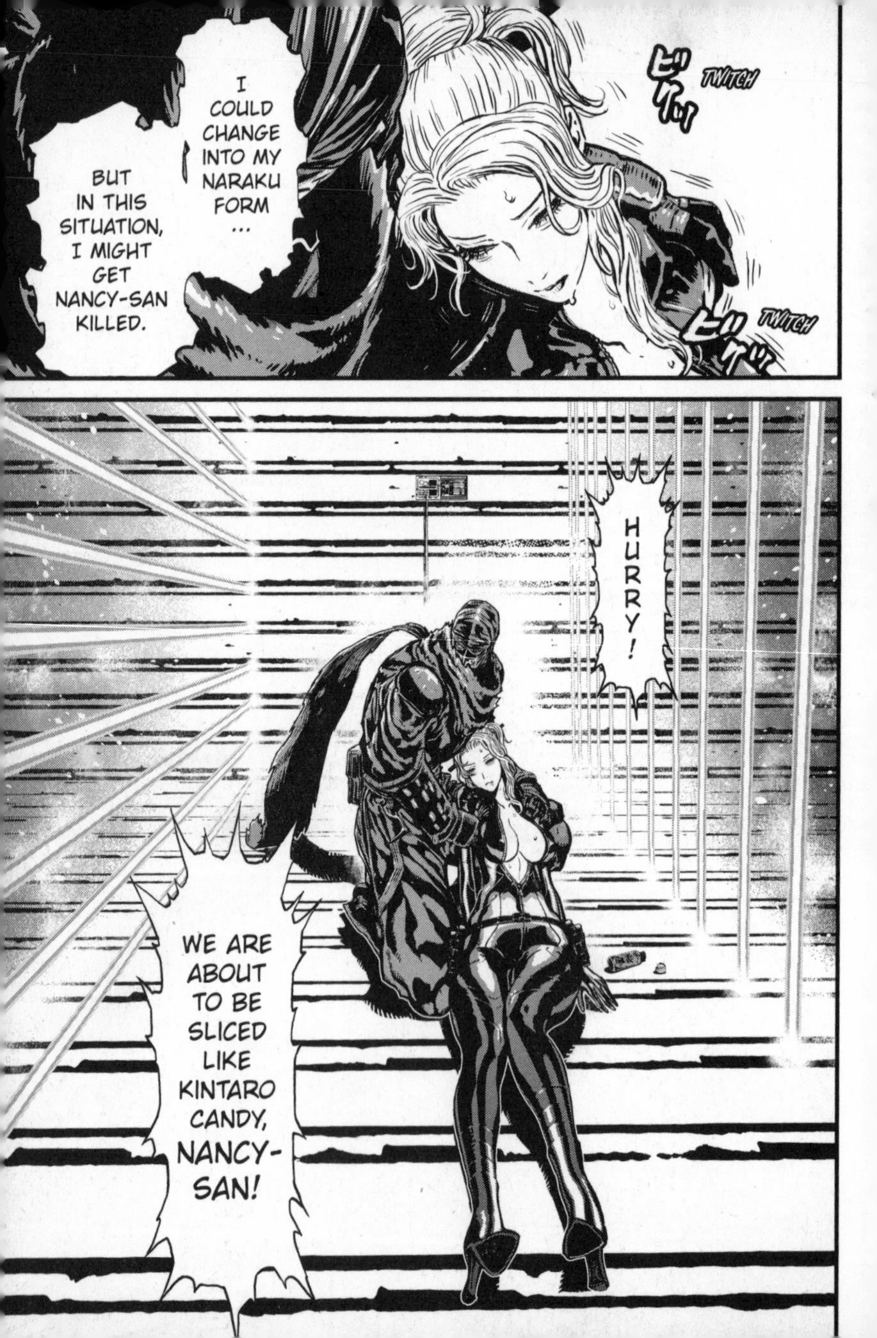
TWITCH
I COULD CHANGE INTO MY NARAKU FORM ...
BUT IN THIS SITUATION, I MIGHT GET NANCY-SAN KILLED.
TWITCH
HURRY!
WE ARE ABOUT TO BE SLICED LIKE KINTARO CANDY, NANCY-SAN!

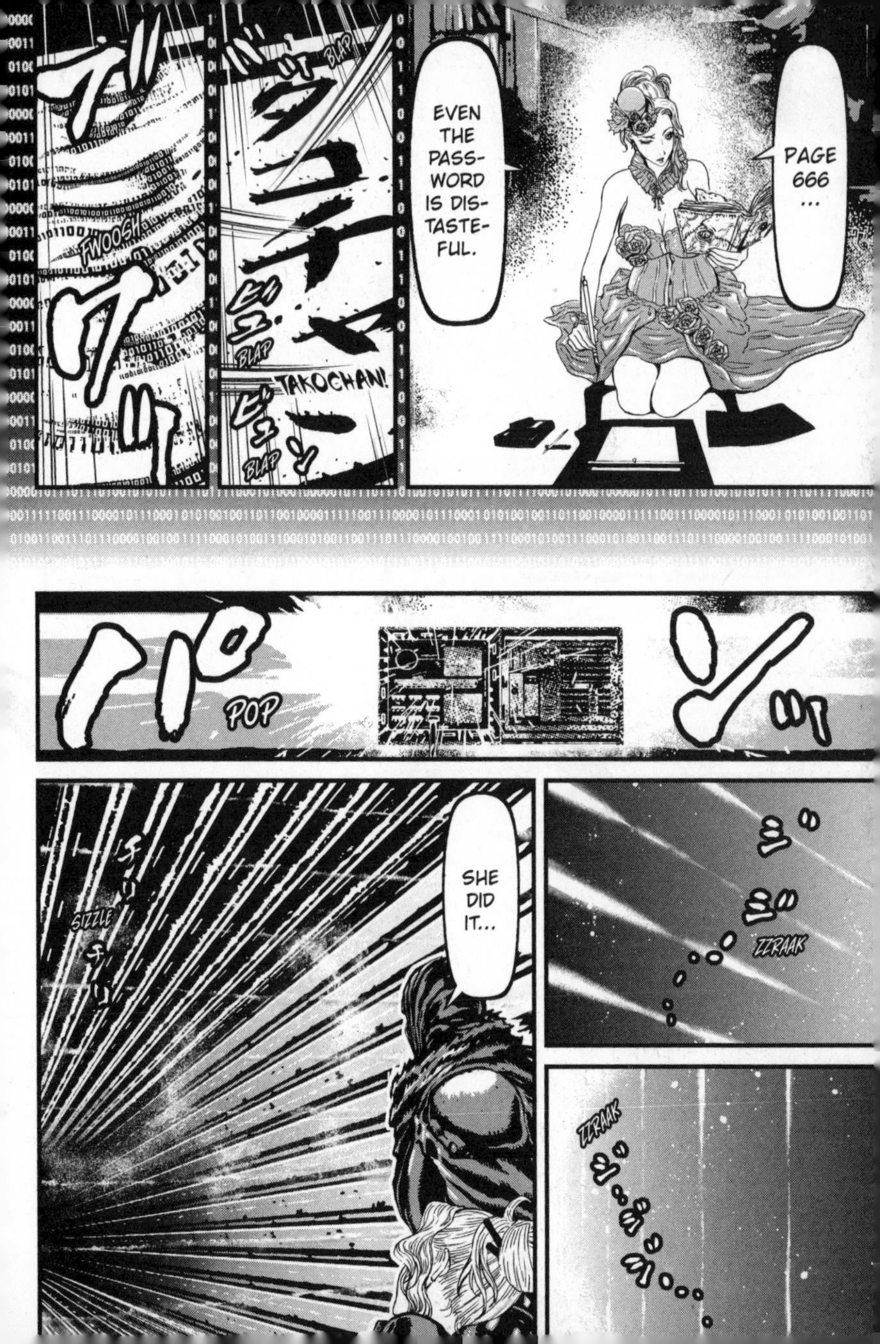
PAGE 666 ...
EVEN THE PASS-WORD IS DIS-TASTE-FUL.
BLAP
BLAP
TAKOCHAN!
BLAP
FWOOSH
POP
ZZRAAK
ZZRAAK
SHE DID IT...
SIZZLE

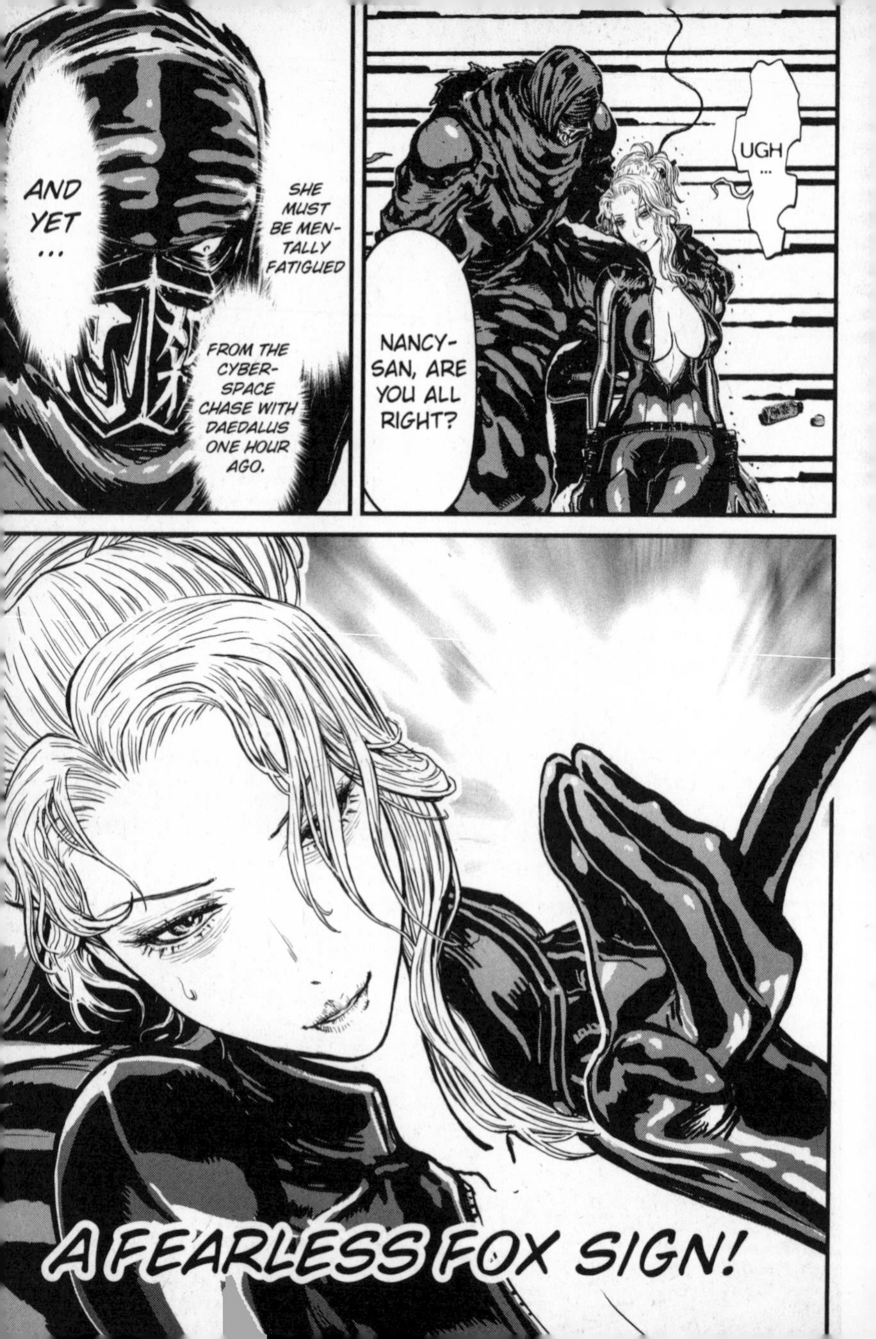
UGH ...
NANCY-SAN, ARE YOU ALL RIGHT?
SHE MUST BE MEN-TALLY FATIGUED
FROM THE CYBER-SPACE CHASE WITH DAEDALUS ONE HOUR AGO.
AND YET ...
A FEARLESS FOX SIGN!

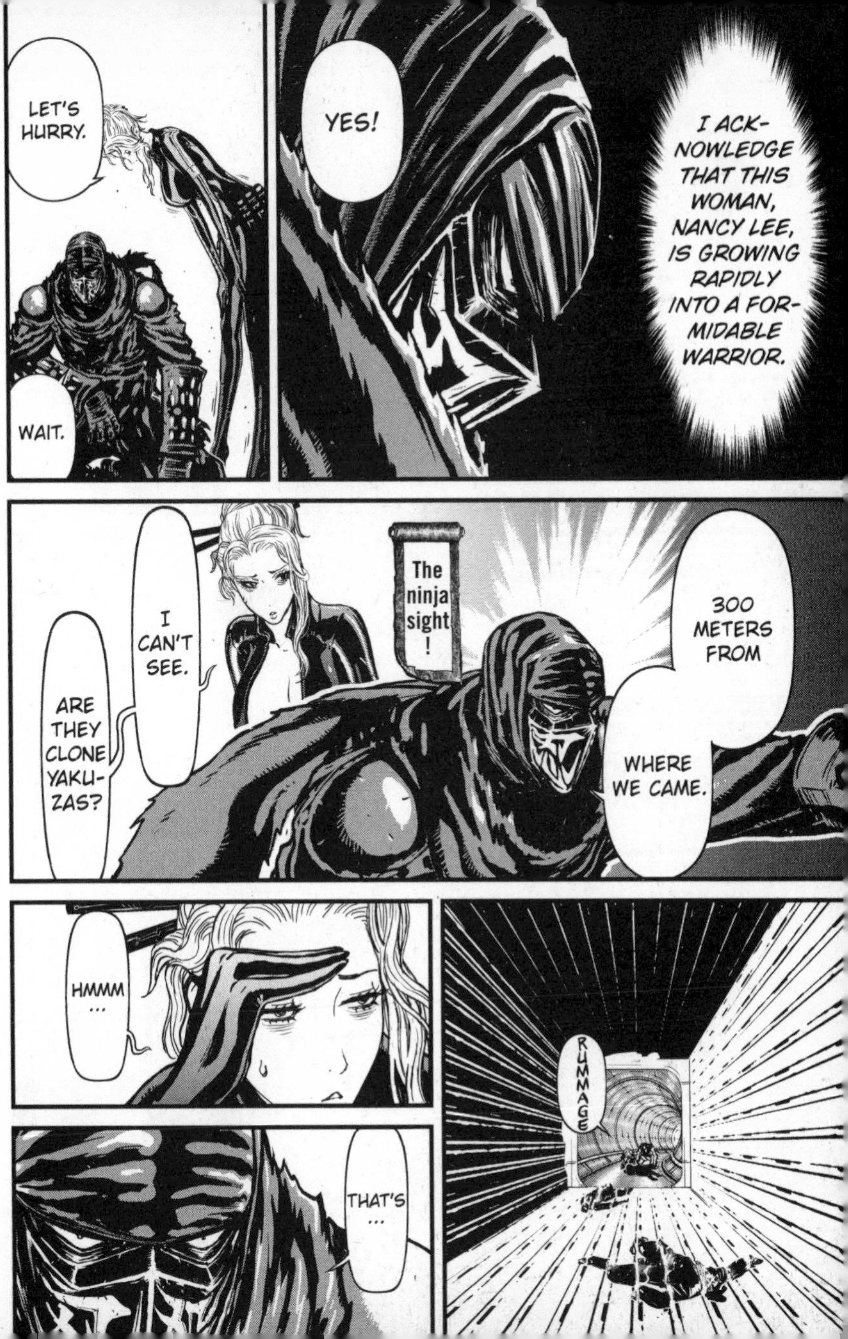
I ACKNOWLEDGE THAT THIS WOMAN, NANCY LEE, IS GROWING RAPIDLY INTO A FORMIDABLE WARRIOR.
YES!
LET'S HURRY.
WAIT.
300 METERS FROM
WHERE WE CAME.
The ninja sight!
I CAN'T SEE.
ARE THEY CLONE YAKUZAS?
RUMMAGE
HMMM...
THAT'S...

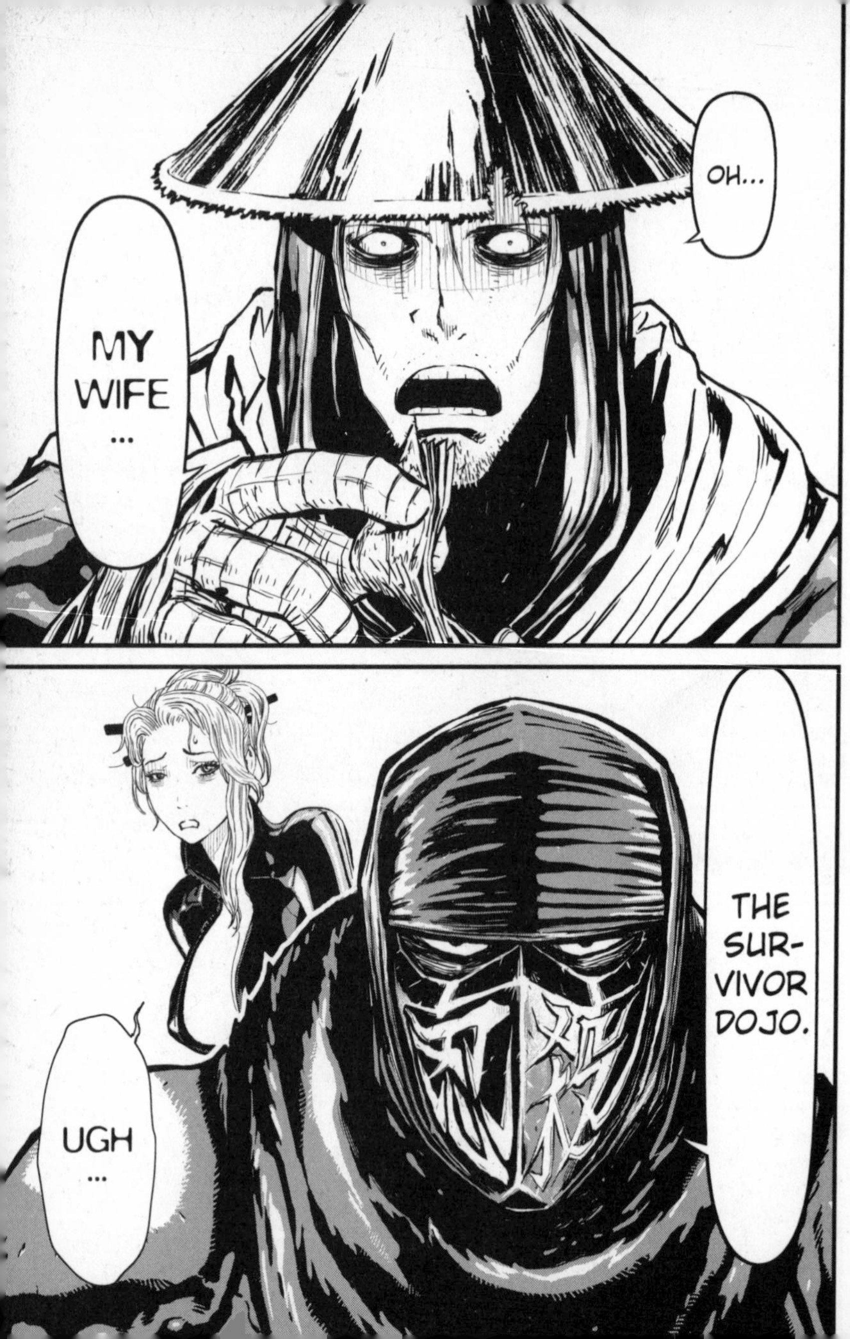
OH...
MY WIFE ...
THE SUR-VIVOR DOJO.
UGH ...

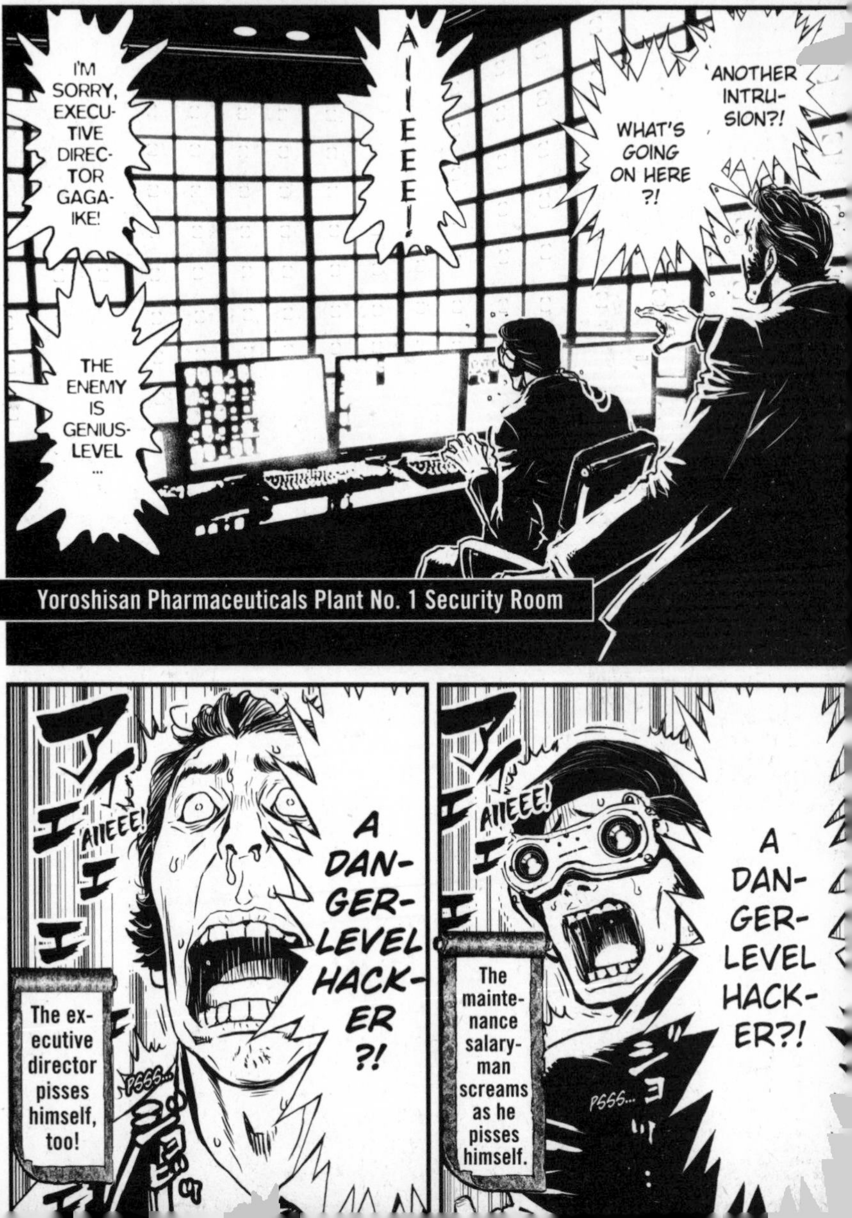
ANOTHER INTRUSION?!
WHAT'S GOING ON HERE?!
AIIEEEE!
I'M SORRY, EXECUTIVE DIRECTOR GAGAIKE!
THE ENEMY IS GENIUS-LEVEL...
Yoroshisan Pharmaceuticals Plant No. 1 Security Room
AIIEEE!
A DANGER-LEVEL HACKER?!
The maintenance salaryman screams as he pisses himself.
PSSS...
AIIEEE!
A DANGER-LEVEL HACKER?!
The executive director pisses himself, too!
PSSS...

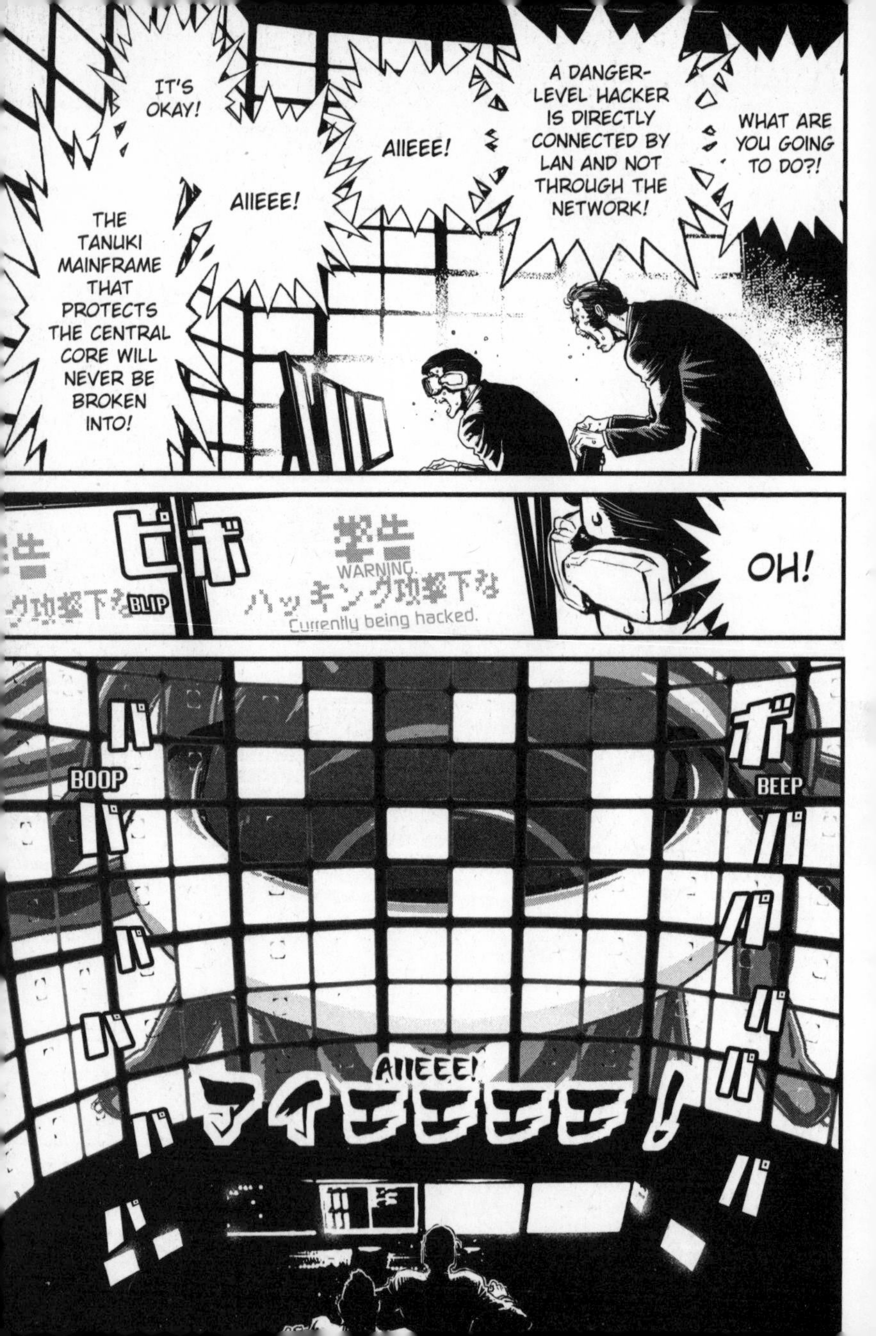
WHAT ARE YOU GOING TO DO?!
A DANGER-LEVEL HACKER IS DIRECTLY CONNECTED BY LAN AND NOT THROUGH THE NETWORK!
AIIEEE!
AIIEEE!
IT'S OKAY!
THE TANUKI MAINFRAME THAT PROTECTS THE CENTRAL CORE WILL NEVER BE BROKEN INTO!
OH!
警告
WARNING
ハッキング攻撃下な
Currently being hacked.
ピボ
BLIP
ボ
BEEP
バ
BOOP
アイエエエエ！
AIIEEE!

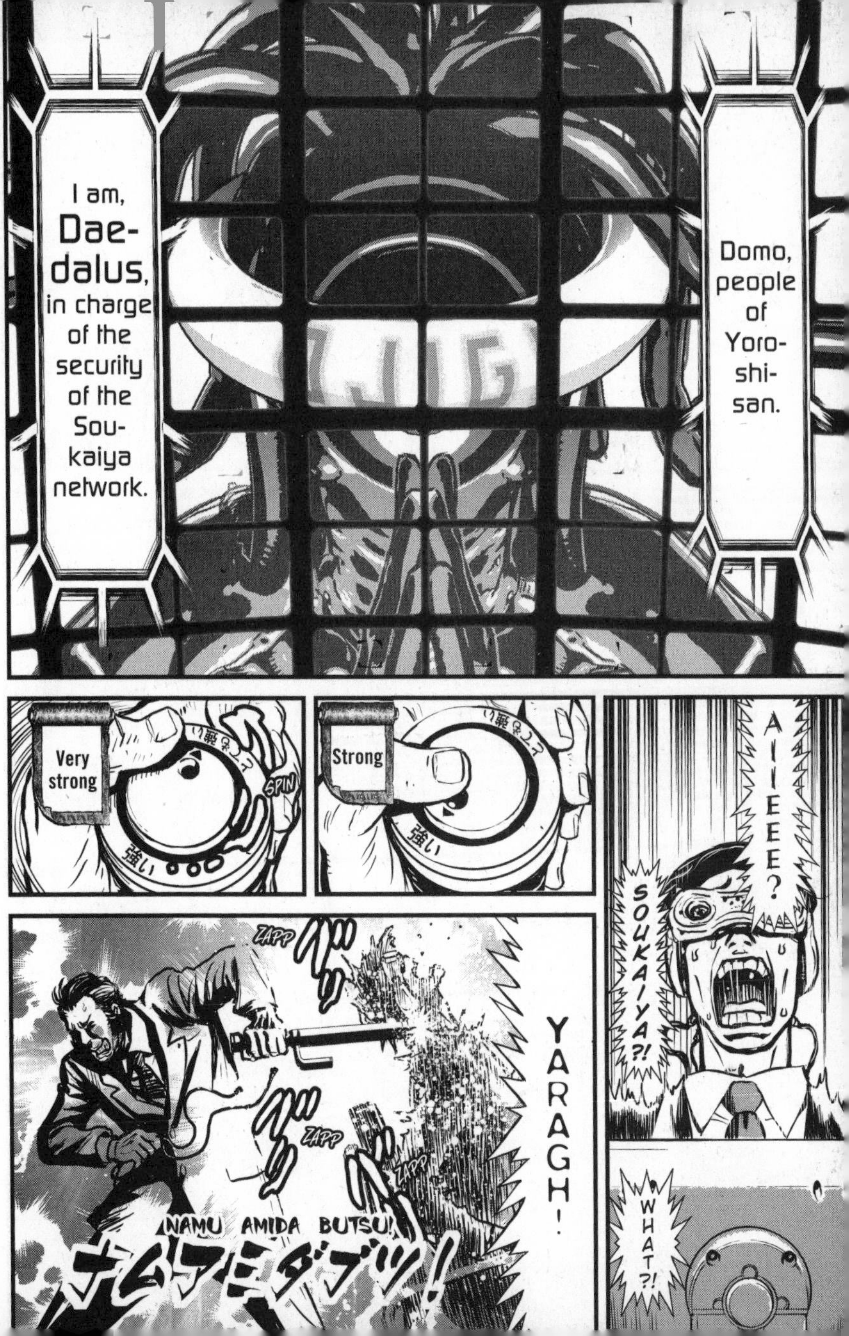

Domo, people of Yoroshi-san.
I am, Daedalus, in charge of the security of the Soukaiya network.
AIIEEE?
SOUKAIYA?!
WHAT?!
Strong
強い
Very strong
SPIN
強い
ZAPP
YARAGH!
ZAPP
ZAPP
NAMU AMIDA BUTSU!
ナムアミダブツ!

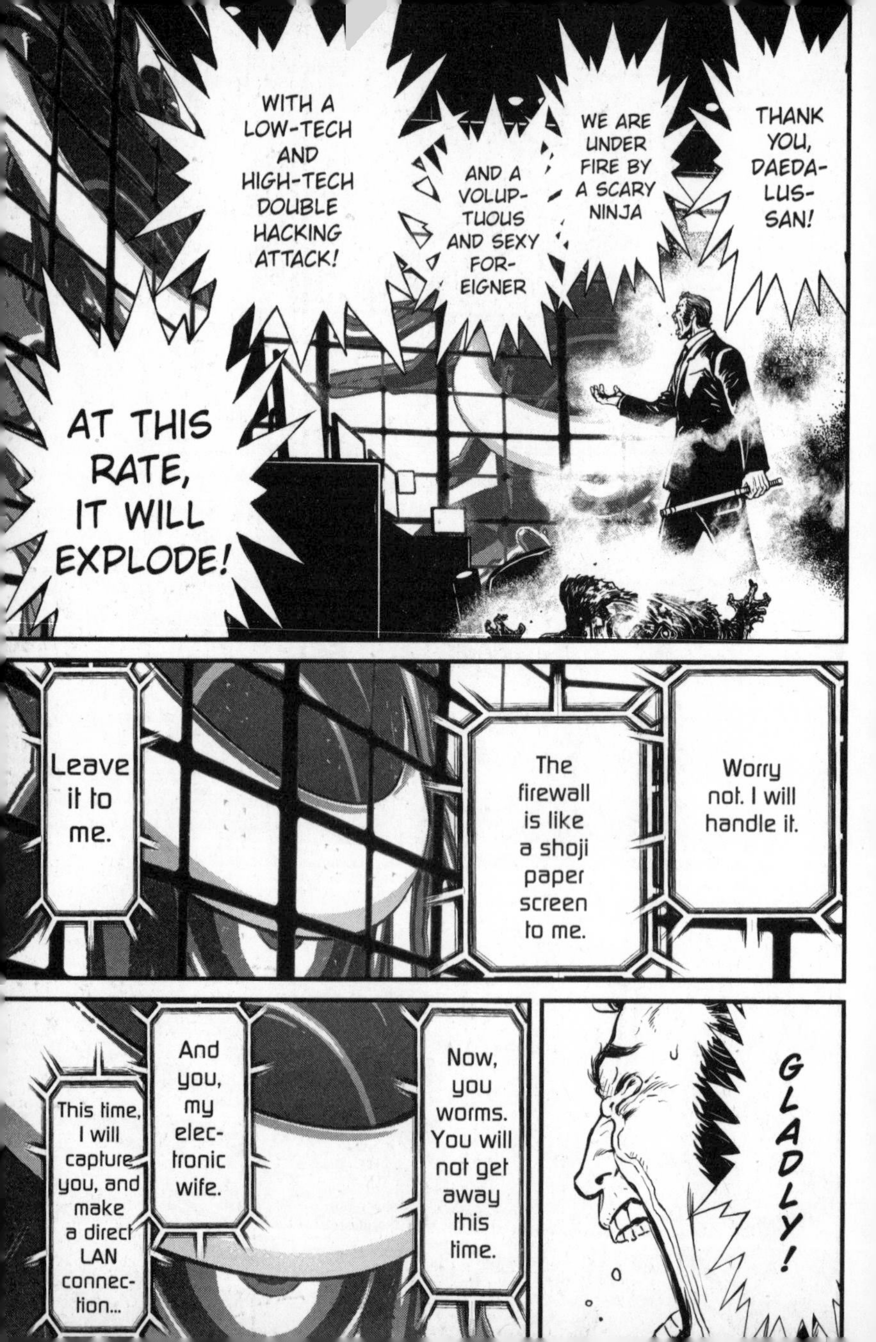
THANK YOU, DAEDALUS-SAN!
WE ARE UNDER FIRE BY A SCARY NINJA
AND A VOLUPTUOUS AND SEXY FOREIGNER
WITH A LOW-TECH AND HIGH-TECH DOUBLE HACKING ATTACK!
AT THIS RATE, IT WILL EXPLODE!
Worry not. I will handle it.
The firewall is like a shoji paper screen to me.
Leave it to me.
GLADLY!
Now, you worms. You will not get away this time.
And you, my electronic wife.
This time, I will capture you, and make a direct LAN connection...

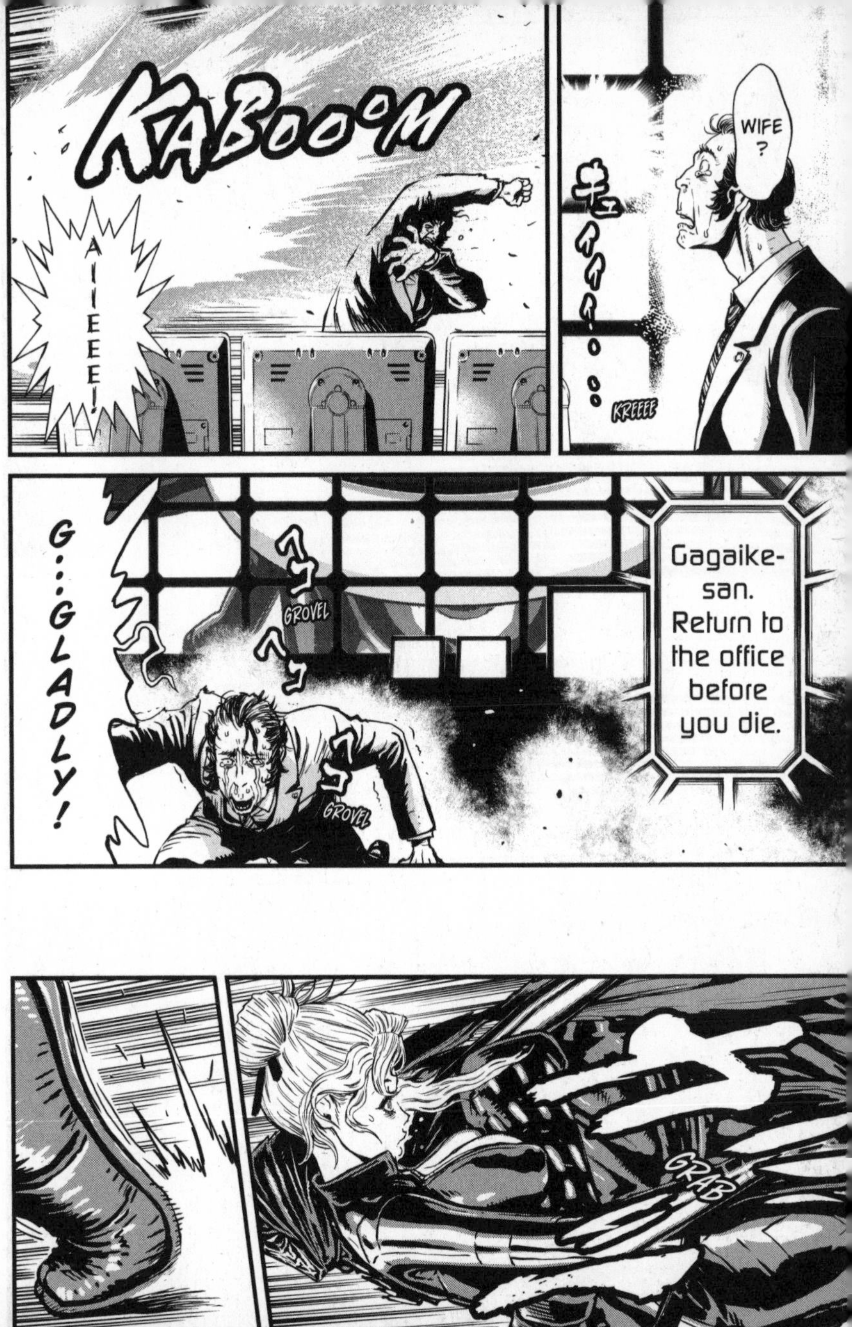

WIFE?
キュイイイ…
KREEEE
KABOOOM
AIIEEE!
Gagaike-san. Return to the office before you die.
G...GLADLY!
GROVEL
GROVEL
GRAB

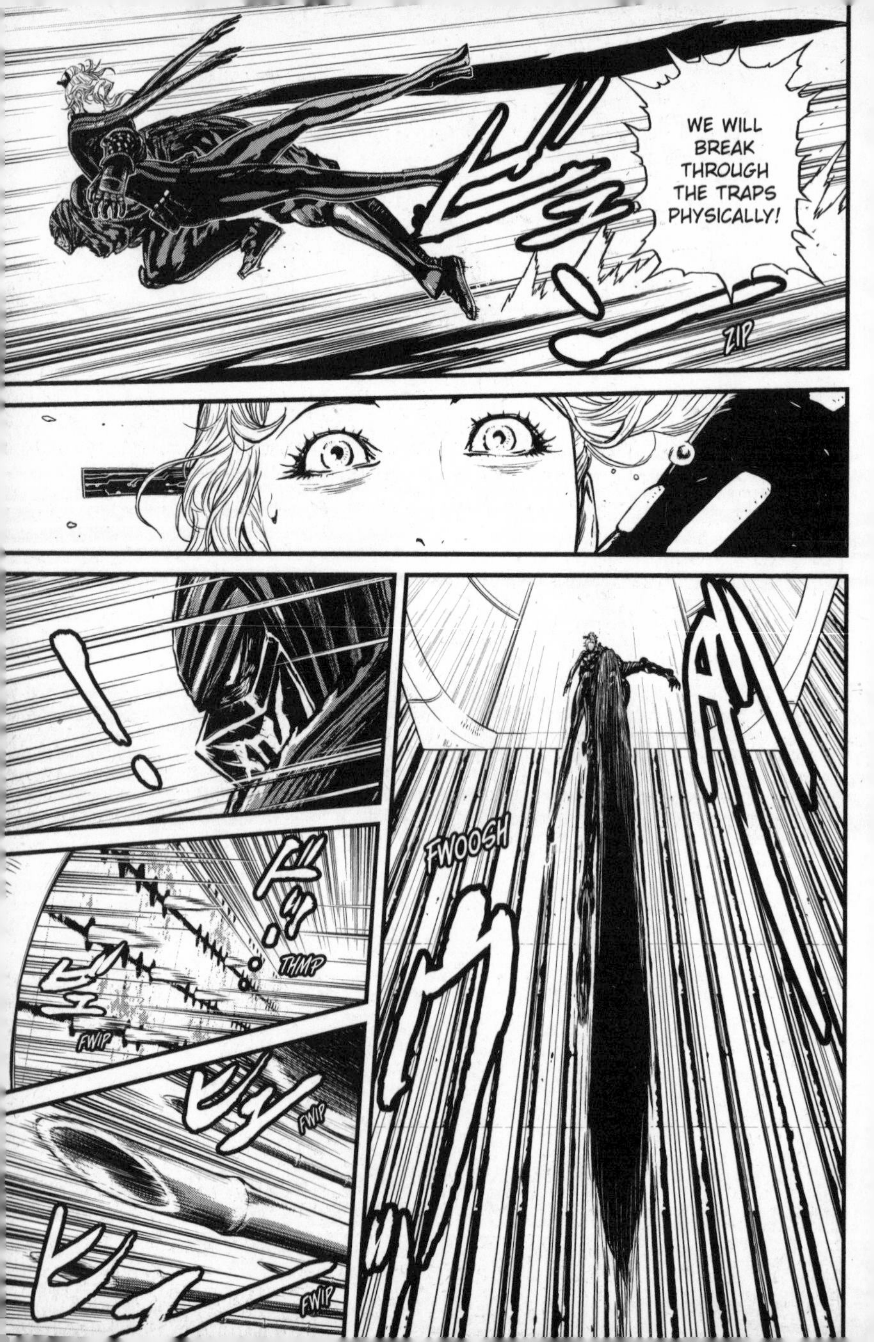

WE WILL BREAK THROUGH THE TRAPS PHYSICALLY!
ZIP
FWOOSH
THMP
FWIP
FWIP
FWIP

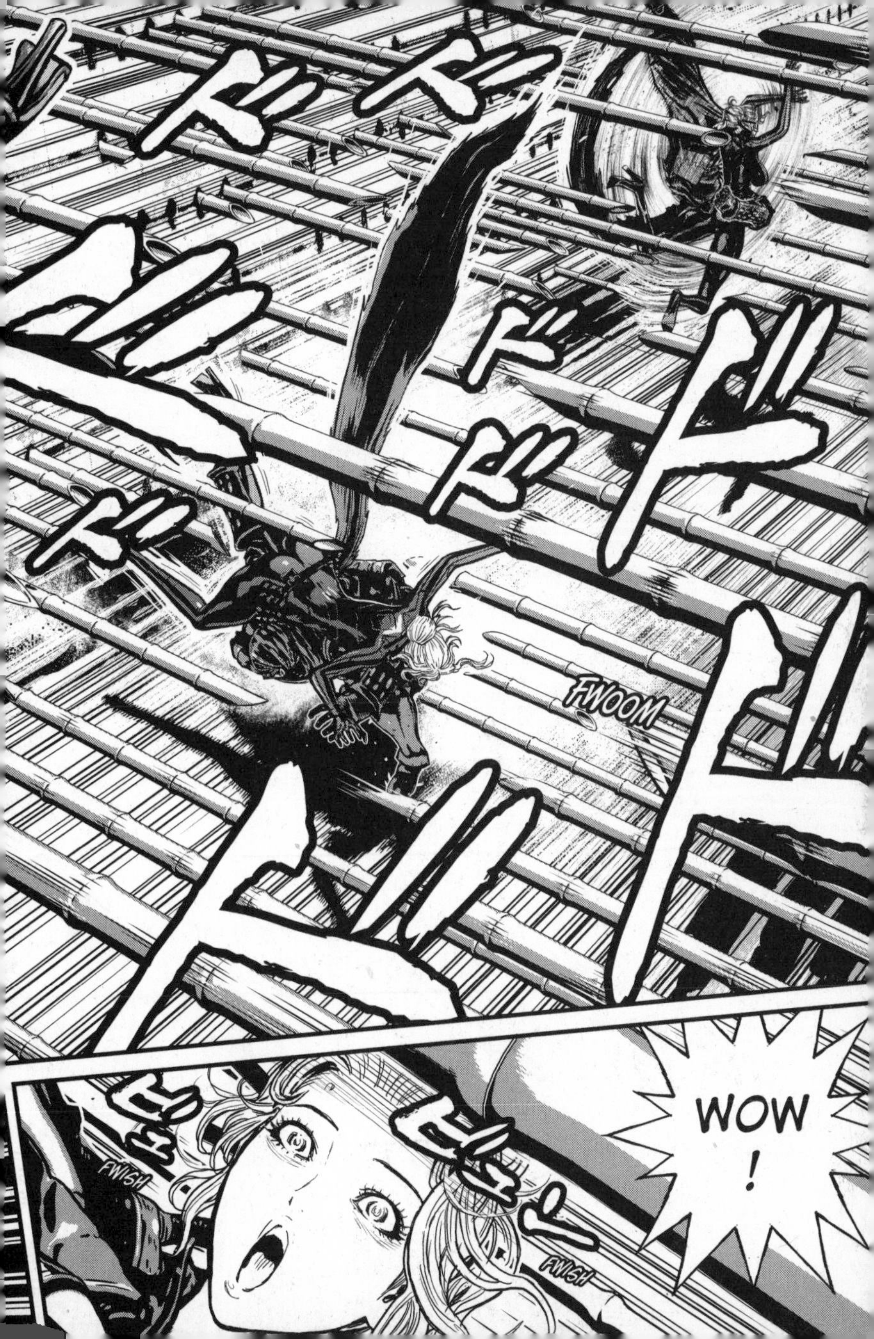
FWOOM
WOW !
FWISH
FWISH

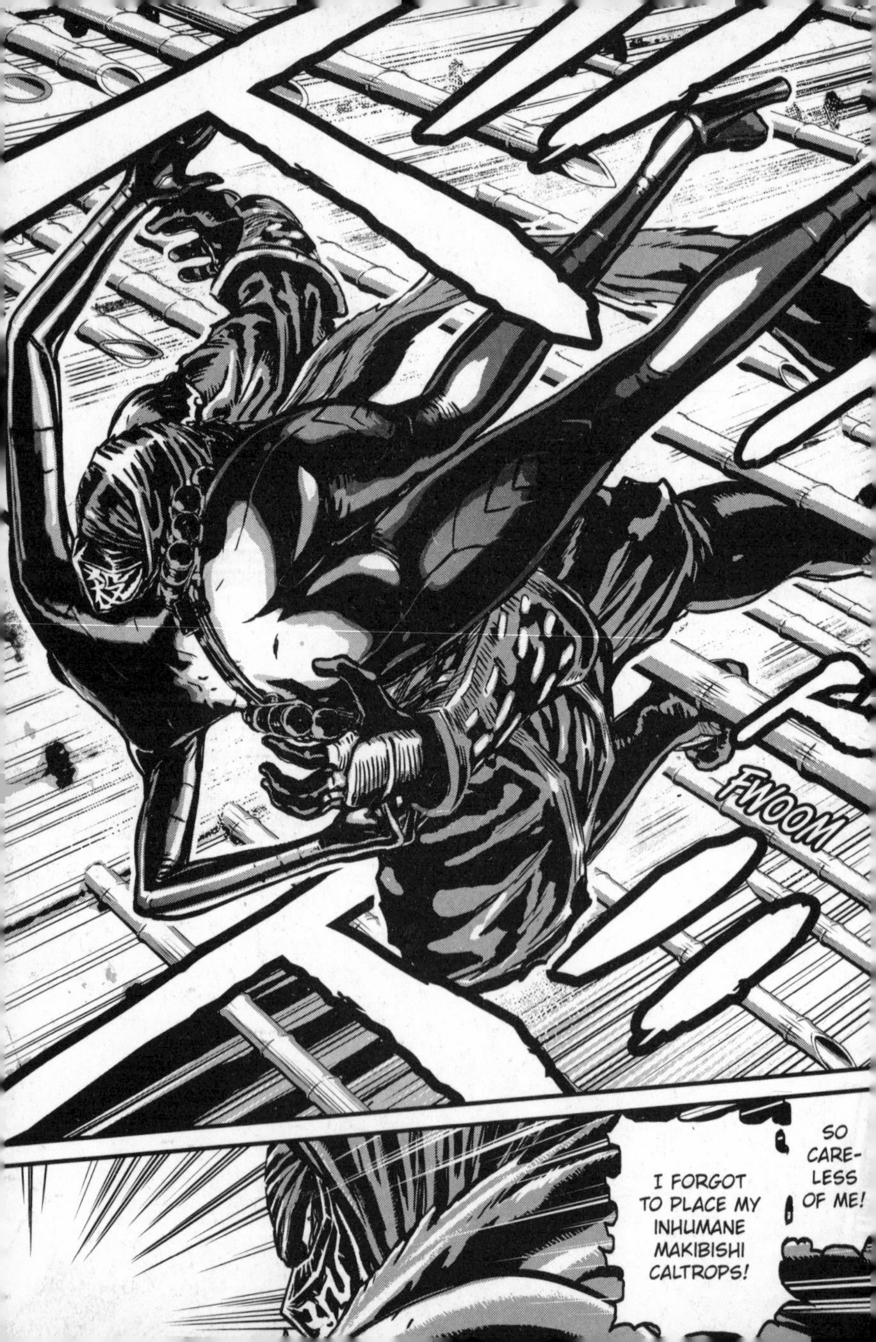
FWOOM
SO CARE-LESS OF ME!
I FORGOT TO PLACE MY INHUMANE MAKIBISHI CALTROPS!

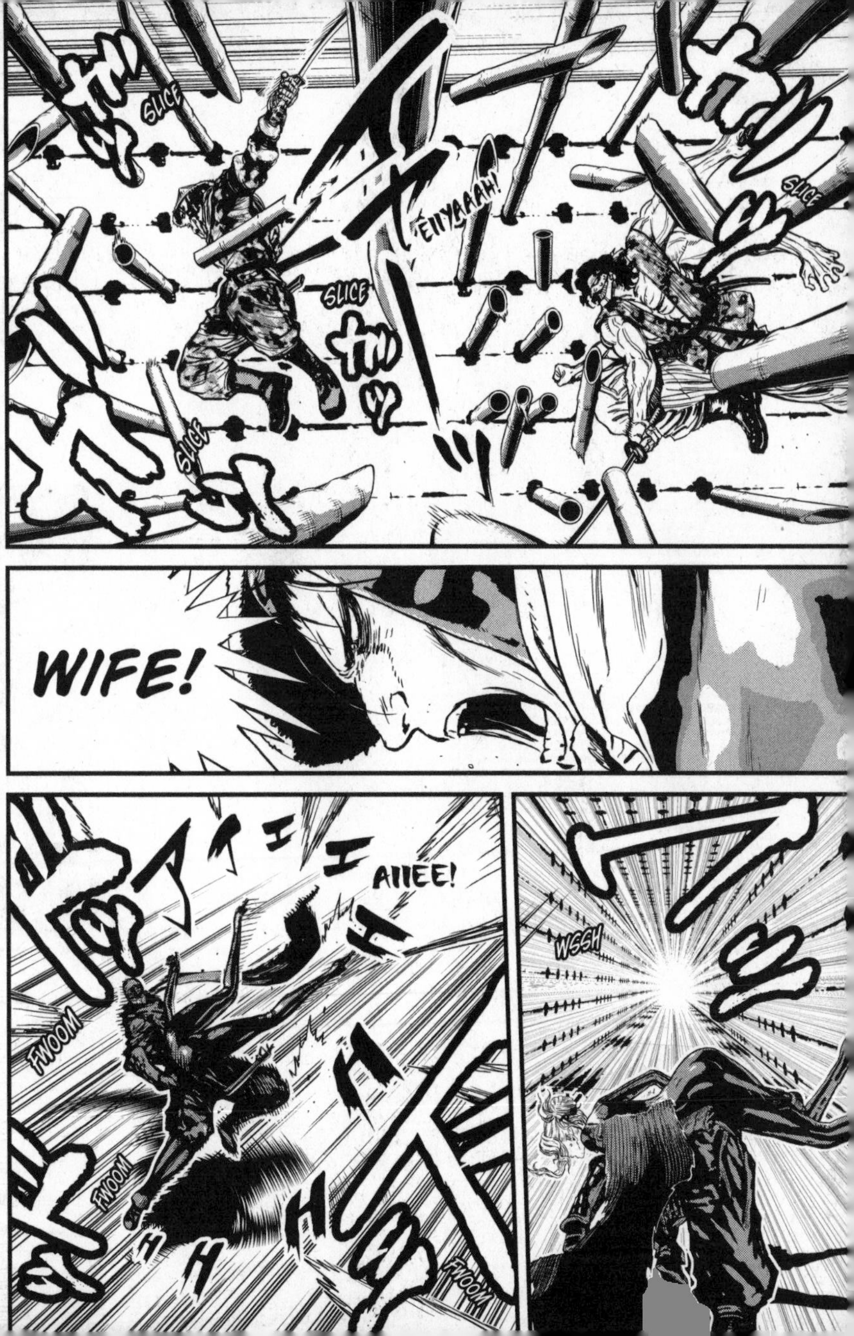
SLICE
EIIYAAAH!
SLICE
SLICE
SLICE
WIFE!
WSSH
AIIEE!
FWOOM
FWOOM
FWOOM

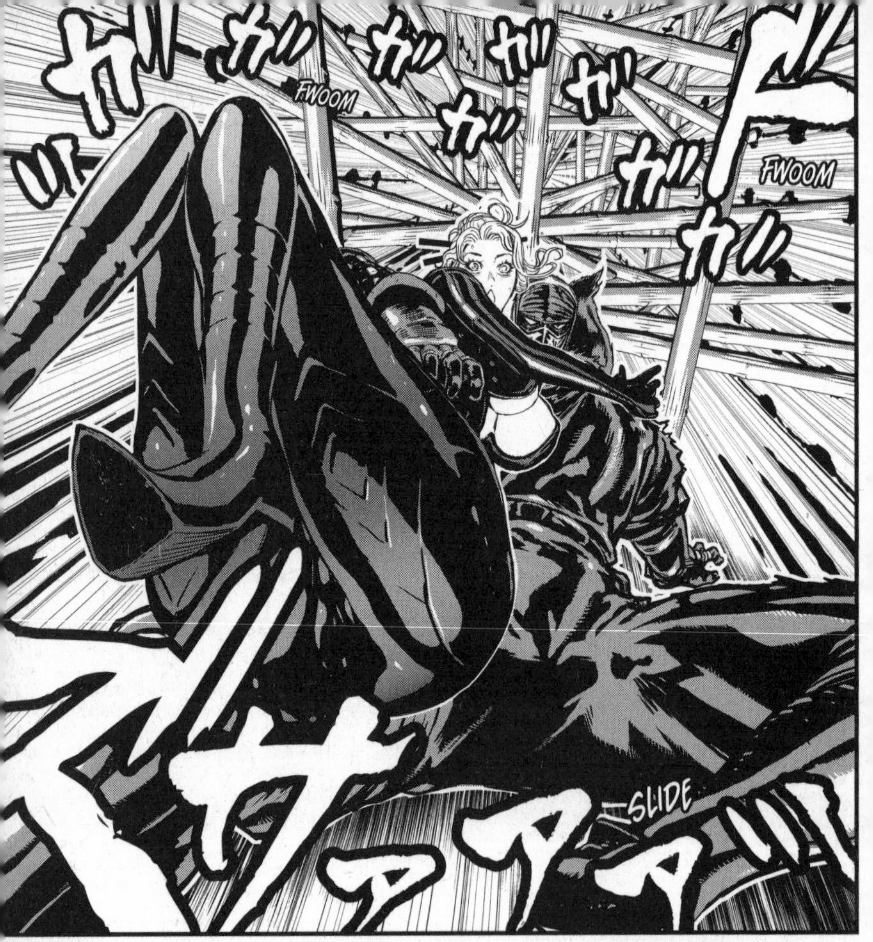
FWOOM
FWOOM
SLIDE

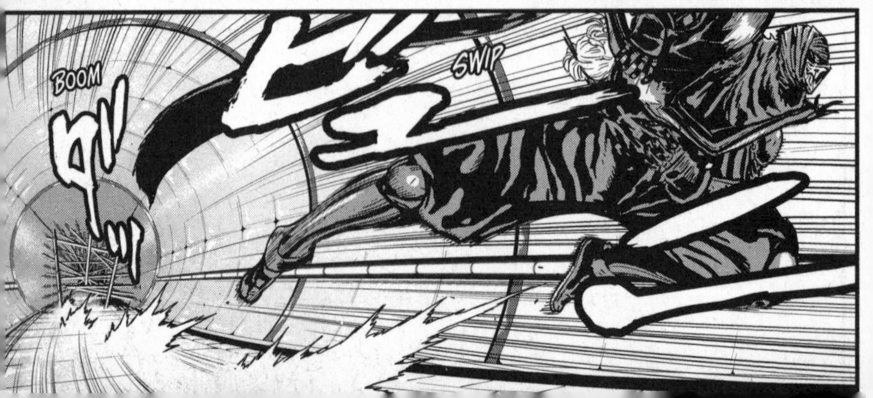
SWIP
BOOM

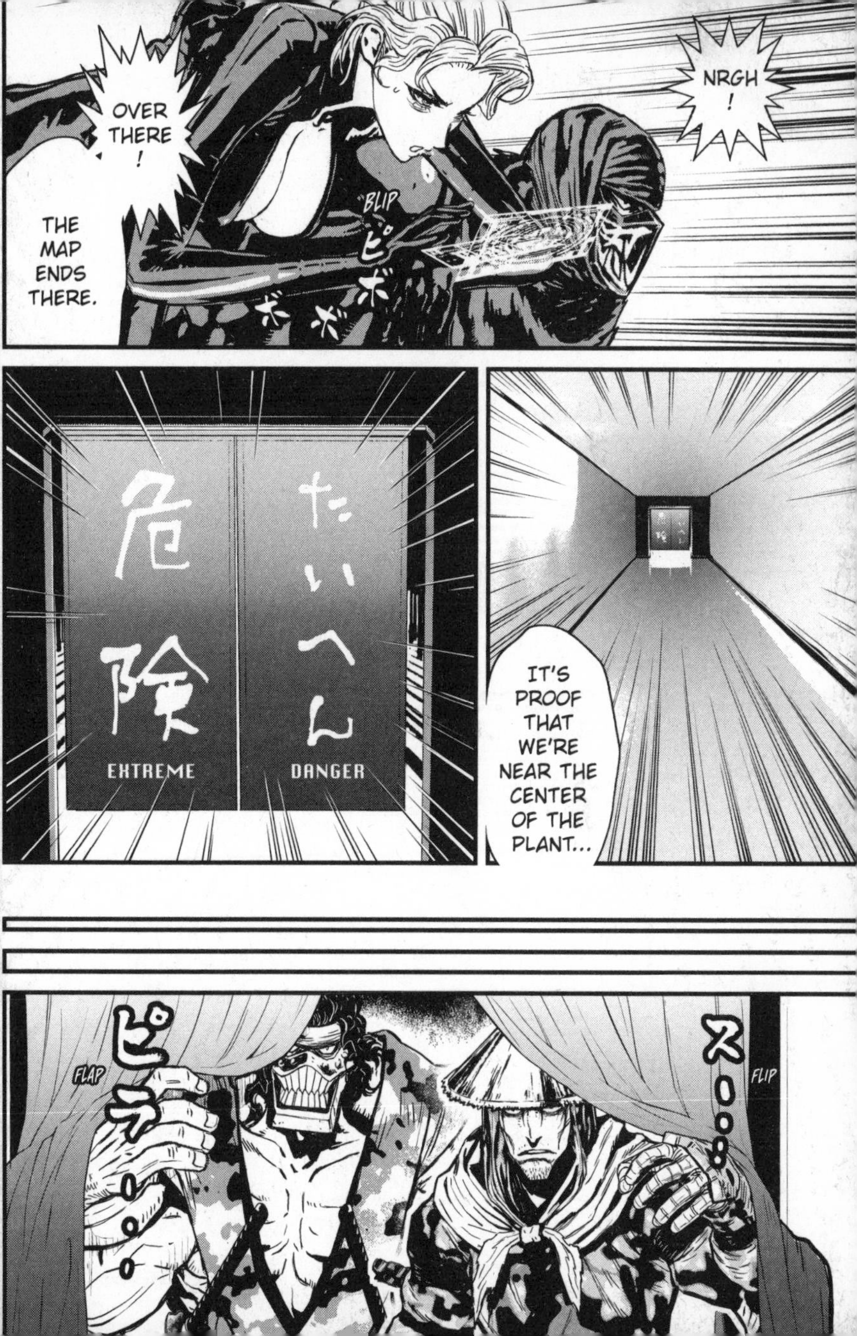

NRGH!
BLIP
OVER THERE!
THE MAP ENDS THERE.
IT'S PROOF THAT WE'RE NEAR THE CENTER OF THE PLANT...
たいへん
DANGER
危険
EXTREME
FLIP
FLAP

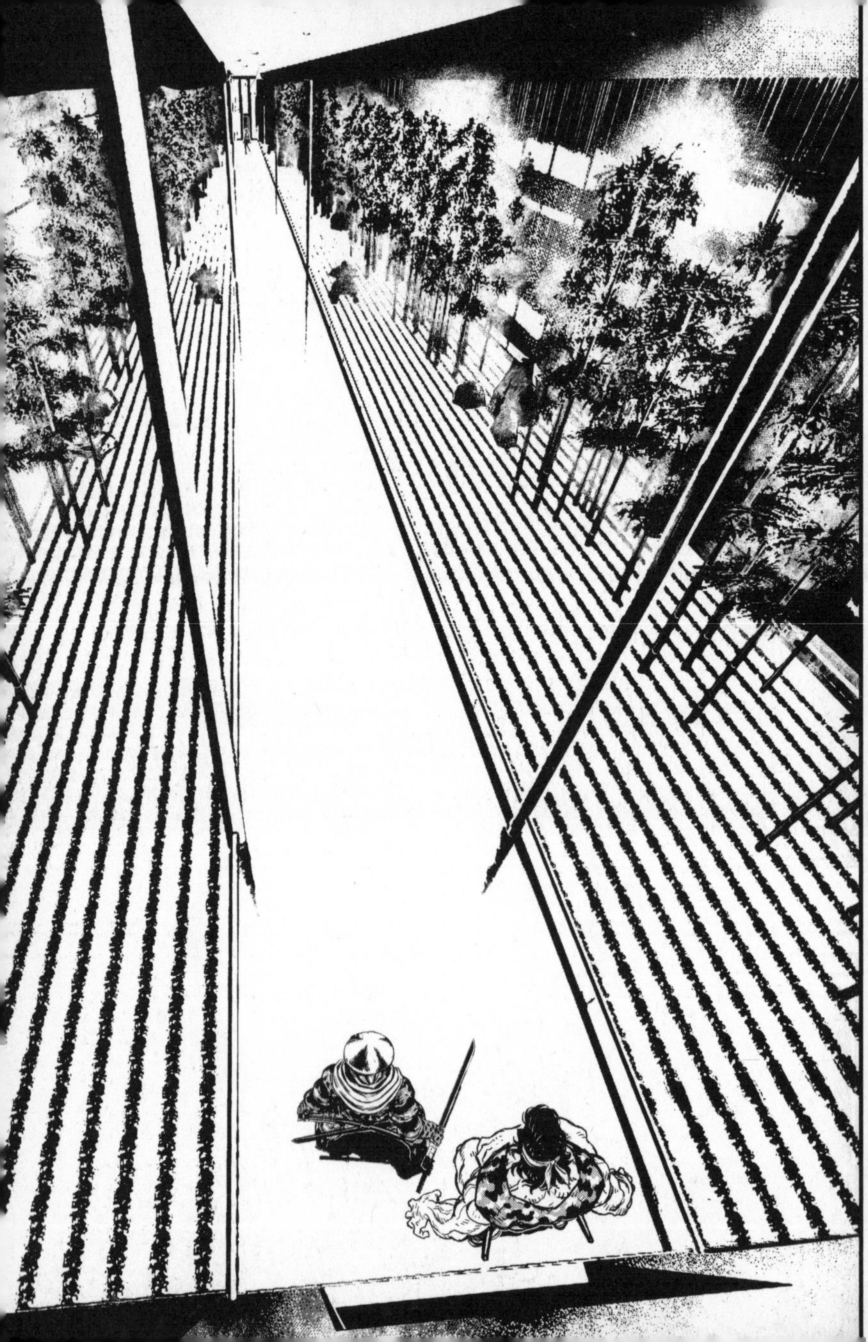

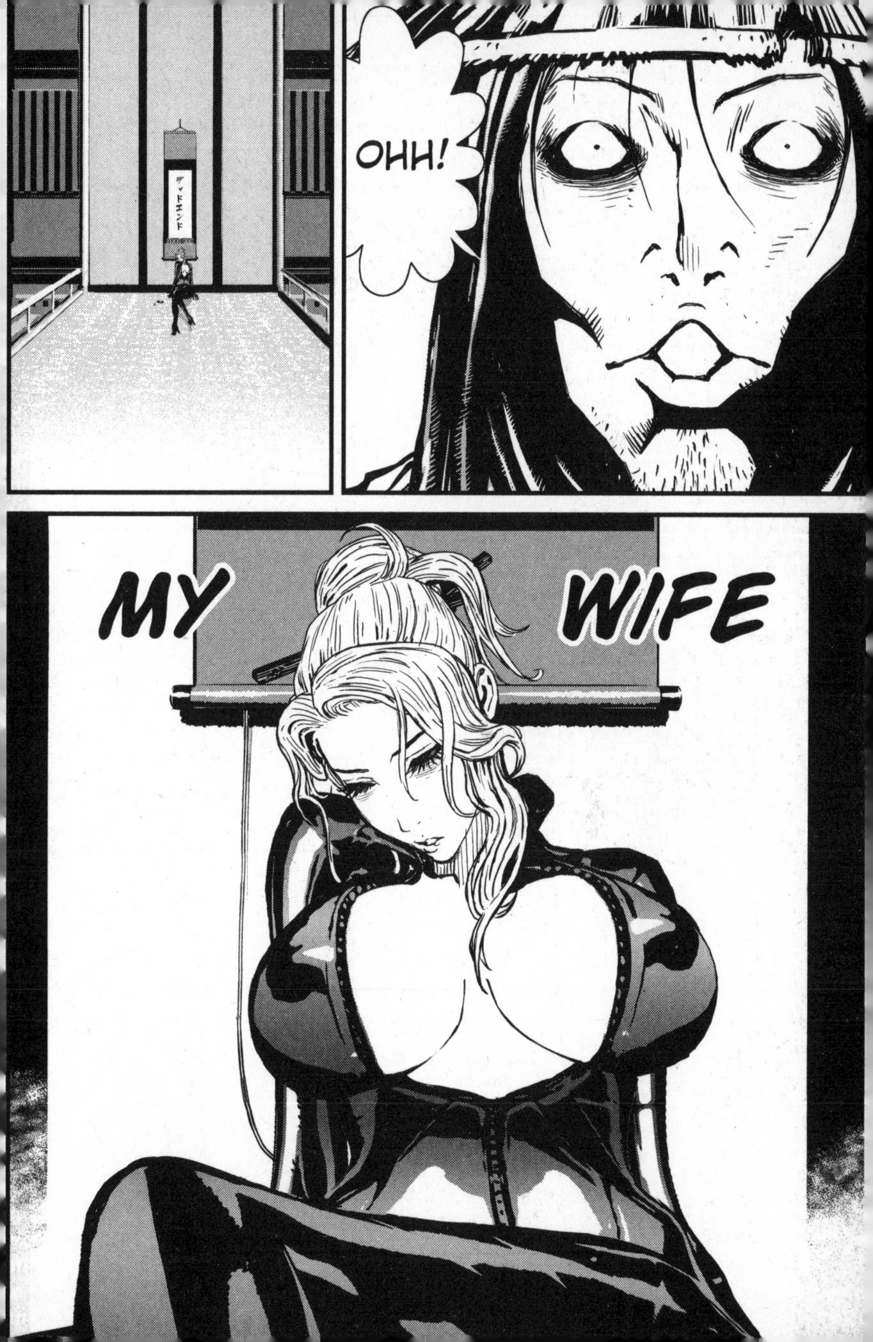
OHH!
デッドエンド
Deadend
MY WIFE

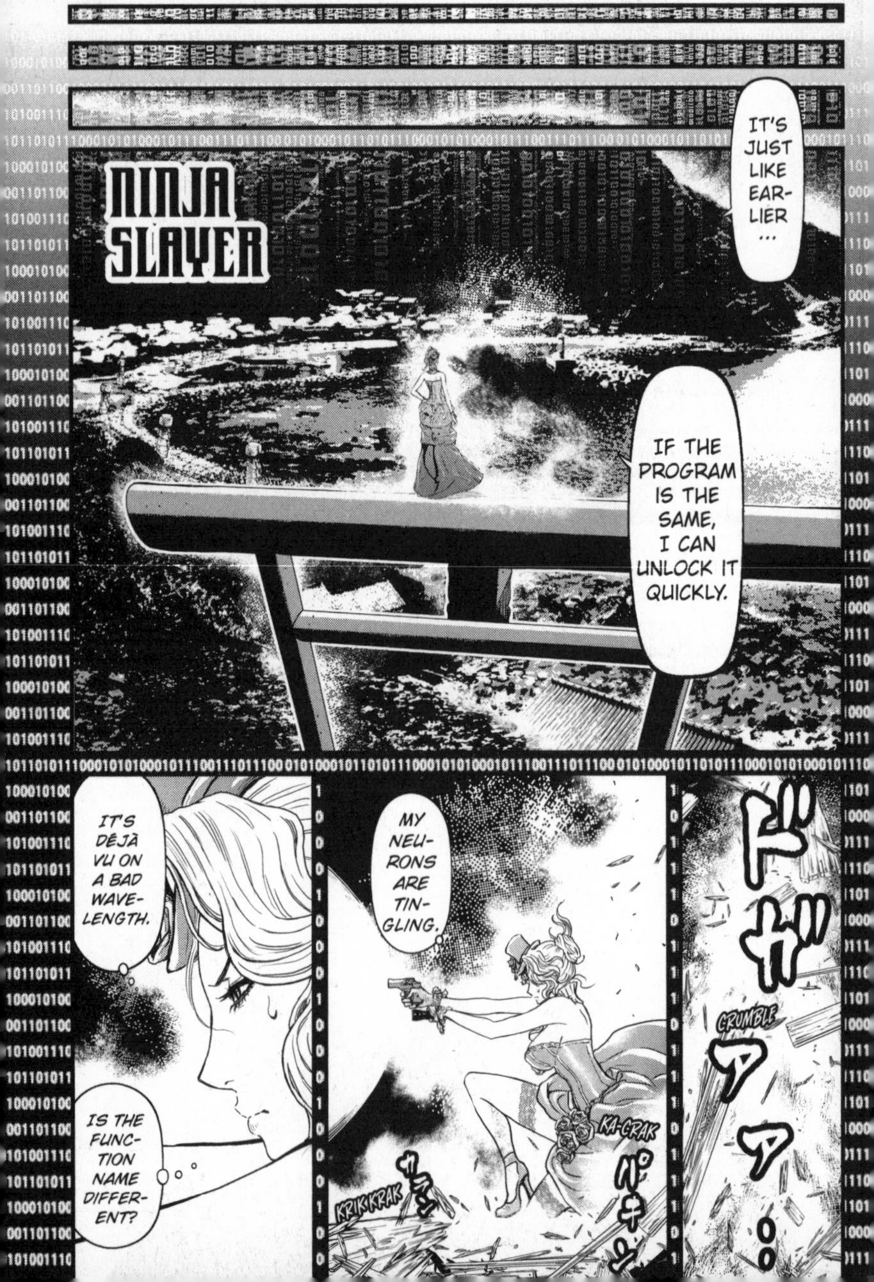
NINJA SLAYER
IT'S JUST LIKE EAR-LIER...
IF THE PROGRAM IS THE SAME, I CAN UNLOCK IT QUICKLY.
ドガ
CRUMBLE
ア
ア...
MY NEU-RONS ARE TIN-GLING.
KA-GRAK
KRIK KRAK
IT'S DÉJÀ VU ON A BAD WAVE-LENGTH.
IS THE FUNC-TION NAME DIFFER-ENT?

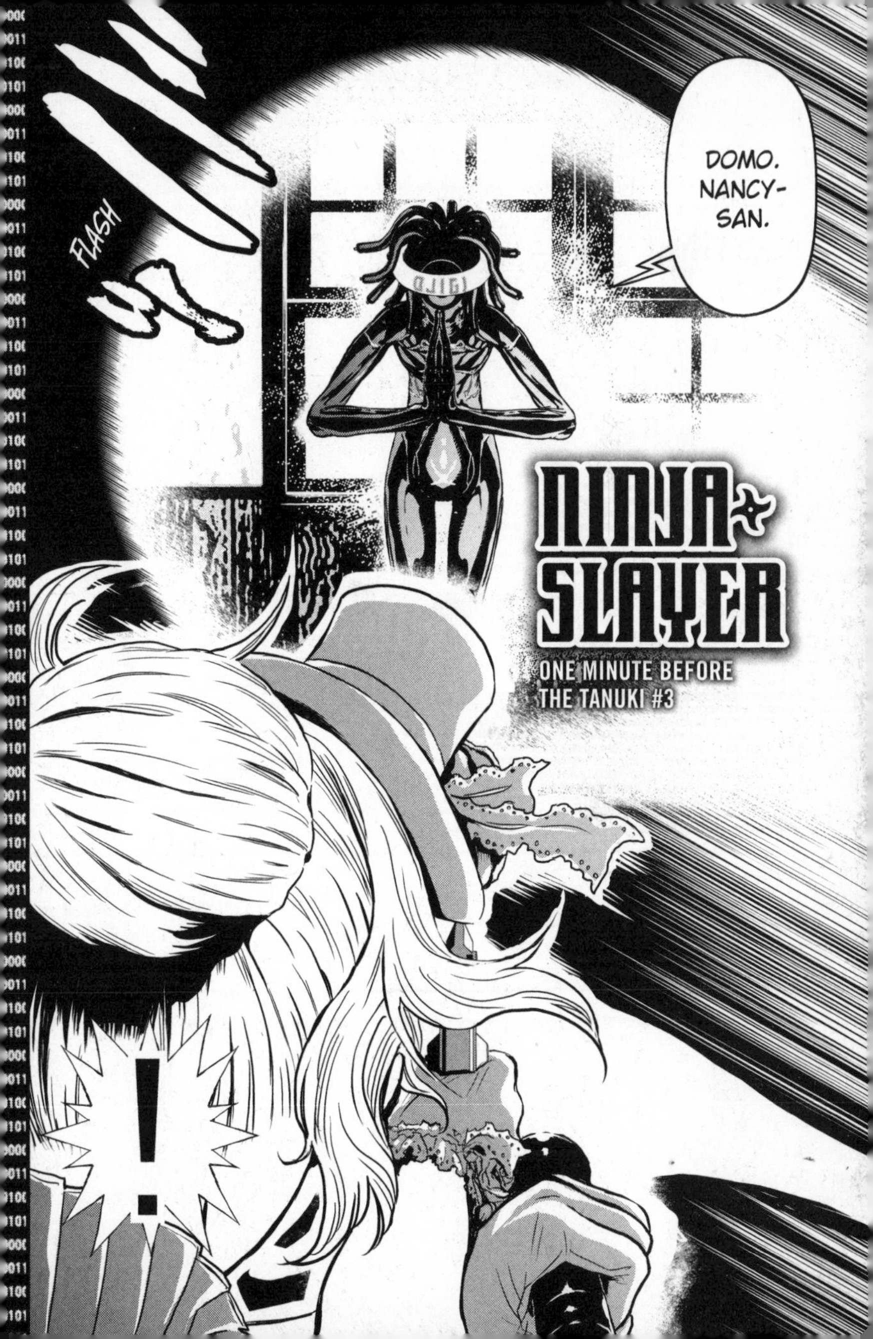
DOMO. NANCY-SAN.
FLASH
NINJA SLAYER
ONE MINUTE BEFORE THE TANUKI #3
!

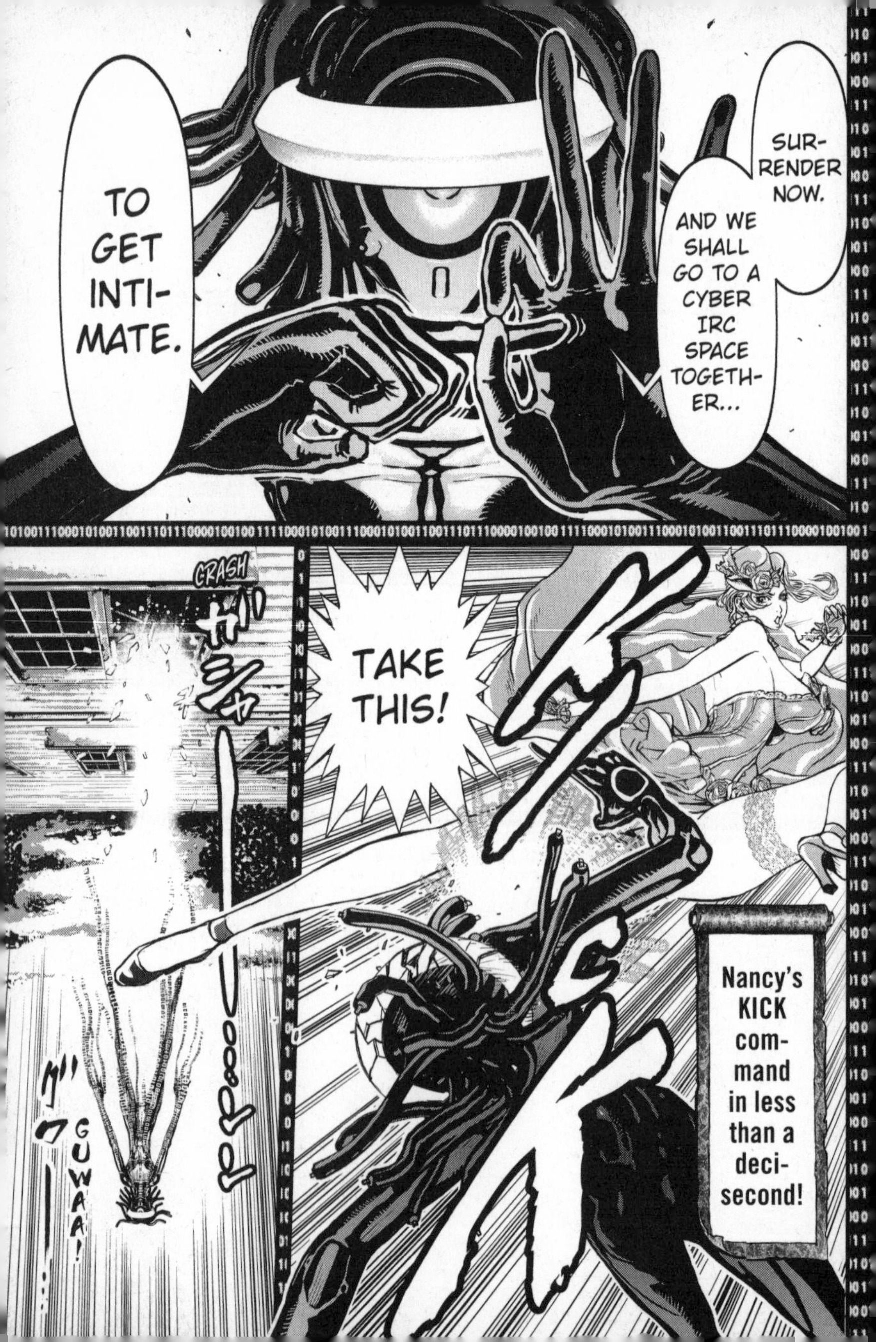
SURRENDER NOW.
AND WE SHALL GO TO A CYBER IRC SPACE TOGETHER...
TO GET INTIMATE.
TAKE THIS!
Nancy's KICK command in less than a decisecond!
CRASH
GUWAA!

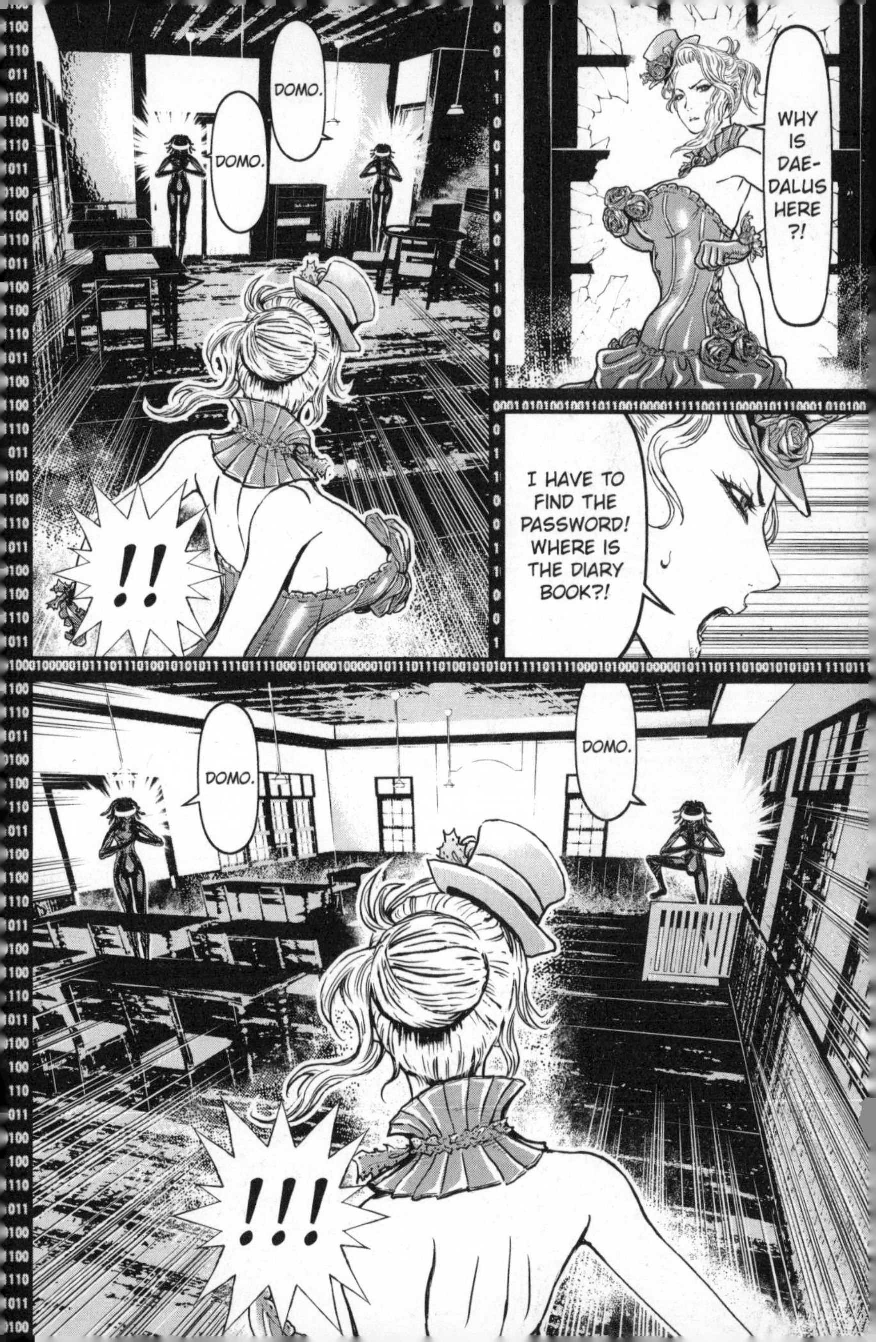
WHY IS DAE-DALUS HERE?!
I HAVE TO FIND THE PASSWORD! WHERE IS THE DIARY BOOK?!
DOMO.
DOMO.
!!
DOMO.
DOMO.
!!!

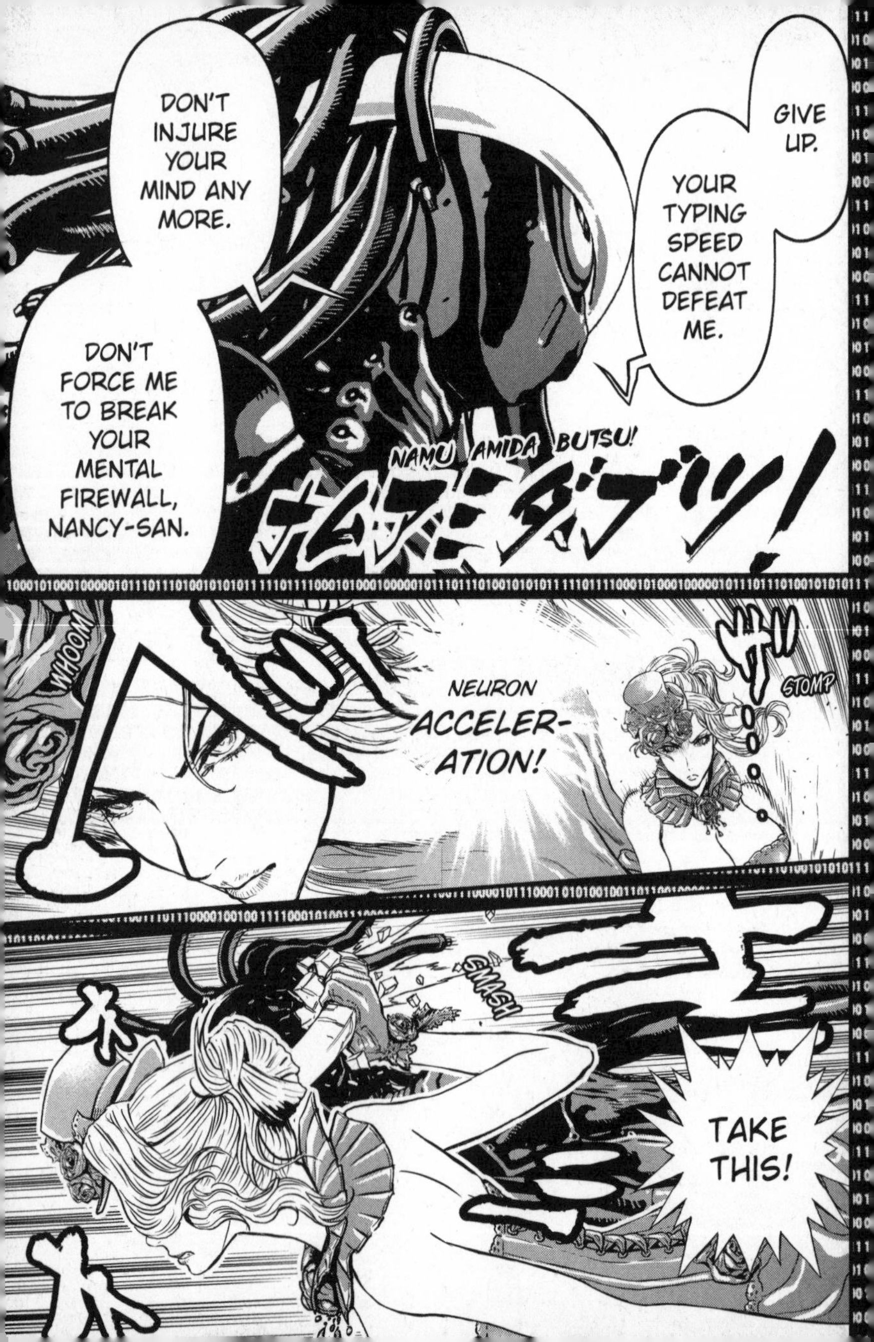
GIVE UP.
YOUR TYPING SPEED CANNOT DEFEAT ME.
DON'T INJURE YOUR MIND ANY MORE.
DON'T FORCE ME TO BREAK YOUR MENTAL FIREWALL, NANCY-SAN.
NAMU AMIDA BUTSU!
STOMP
NEURON ACCELER-ATION!
WHOOM
TAKE THIS!
SMASH

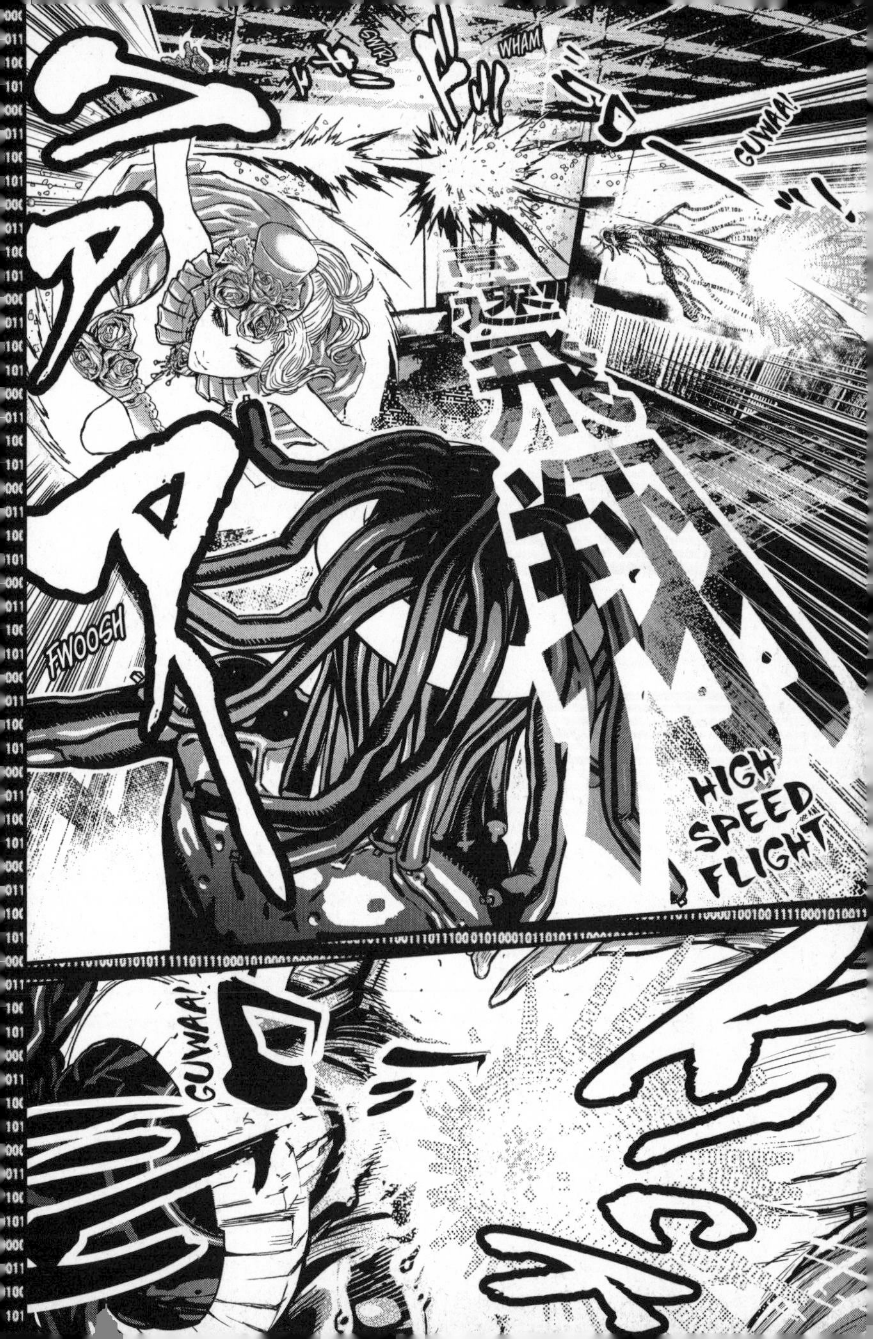
GUWAA!
WHAM
SWIRL
HIGH SPEED FLIGHT
FWOOSH
GUWAA!

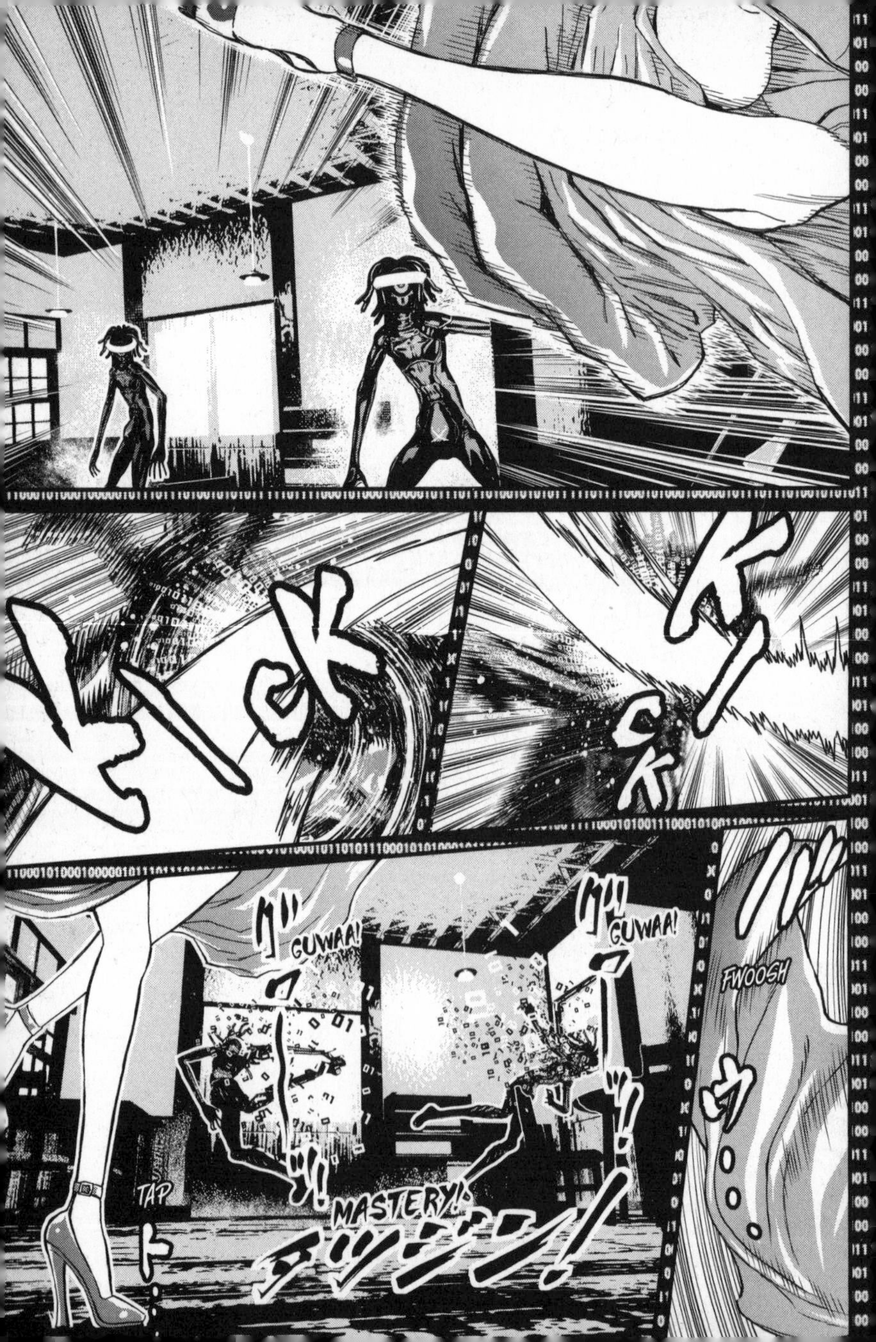
KICK
KICK
FWOOSH
GUWAA!
GUWAA!
MASTERY!
TAP

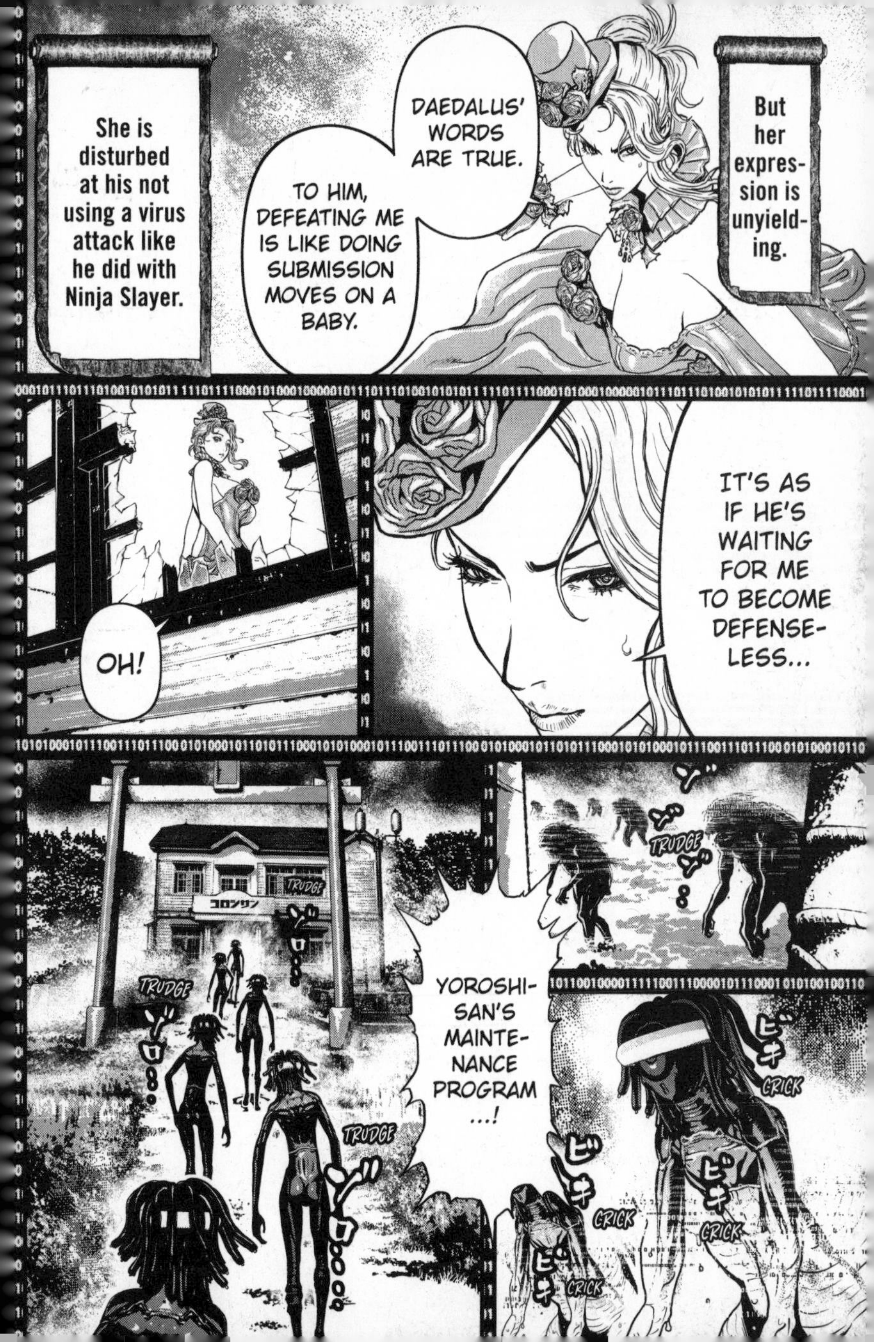

But her expres-sion is unyield-ing.
DAEDALUS' WORDS ARE TRUE.
TO HIM, DEFEATING ME IS LIKE DOING SUBMISSION MOVES ON A BABY.
She is disturbed at his not using a virus attack like he did with Ninja Slayer.
IT'S AS IF HE'S WAITING FOR ME TO BECOME DEFENSE-LESS...
OH!
TRUDGE
CRICK
YOROSHI-SAN'S MAINTE-NANCE PROGRAM ...!
CRICK
CRICK
CRICK
TRUDGE
TRUDGE
TRUDGE

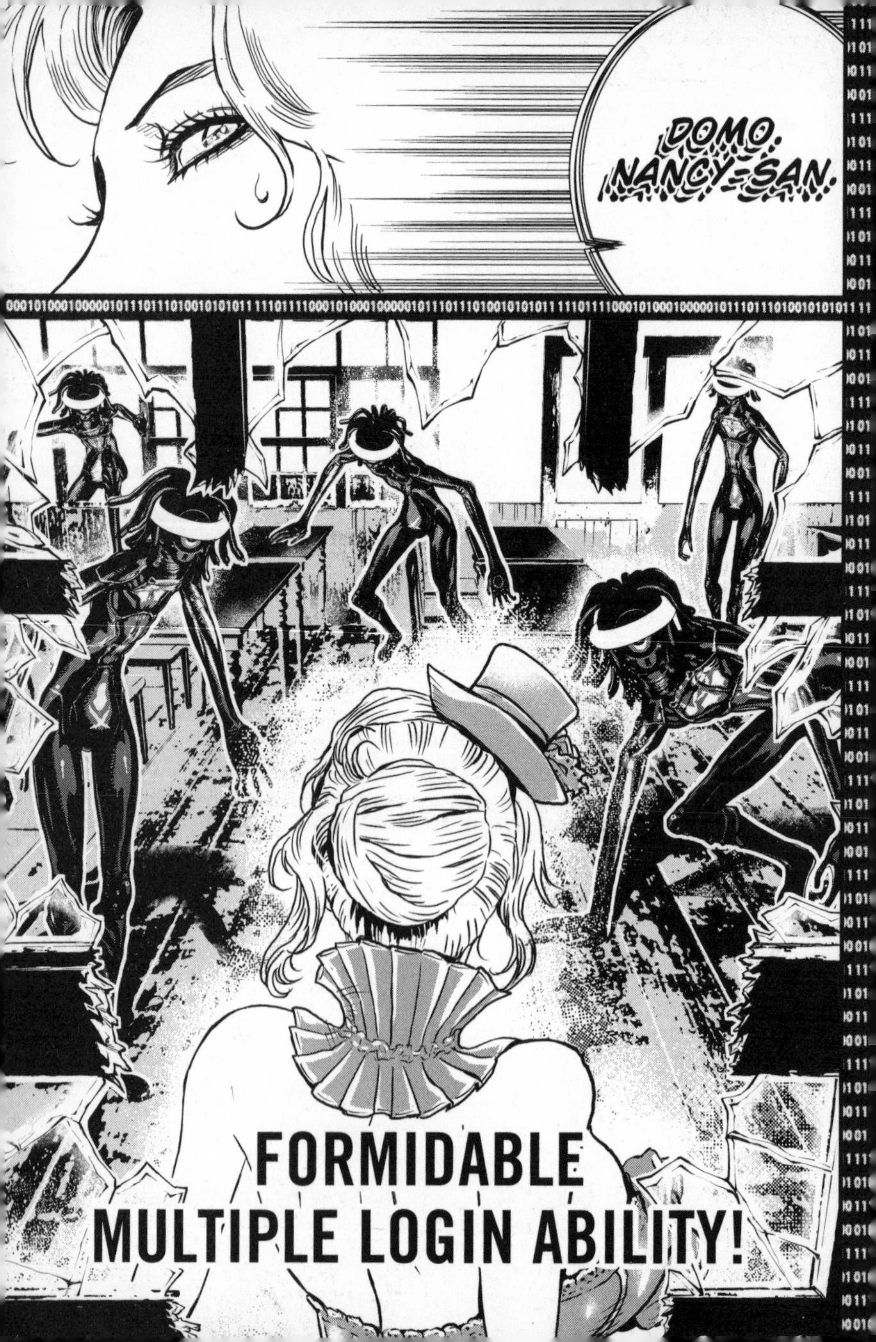
DOMO, NANCY-SAN.
FORMIDABLE MULTIPLE LOGIN ABILITY!

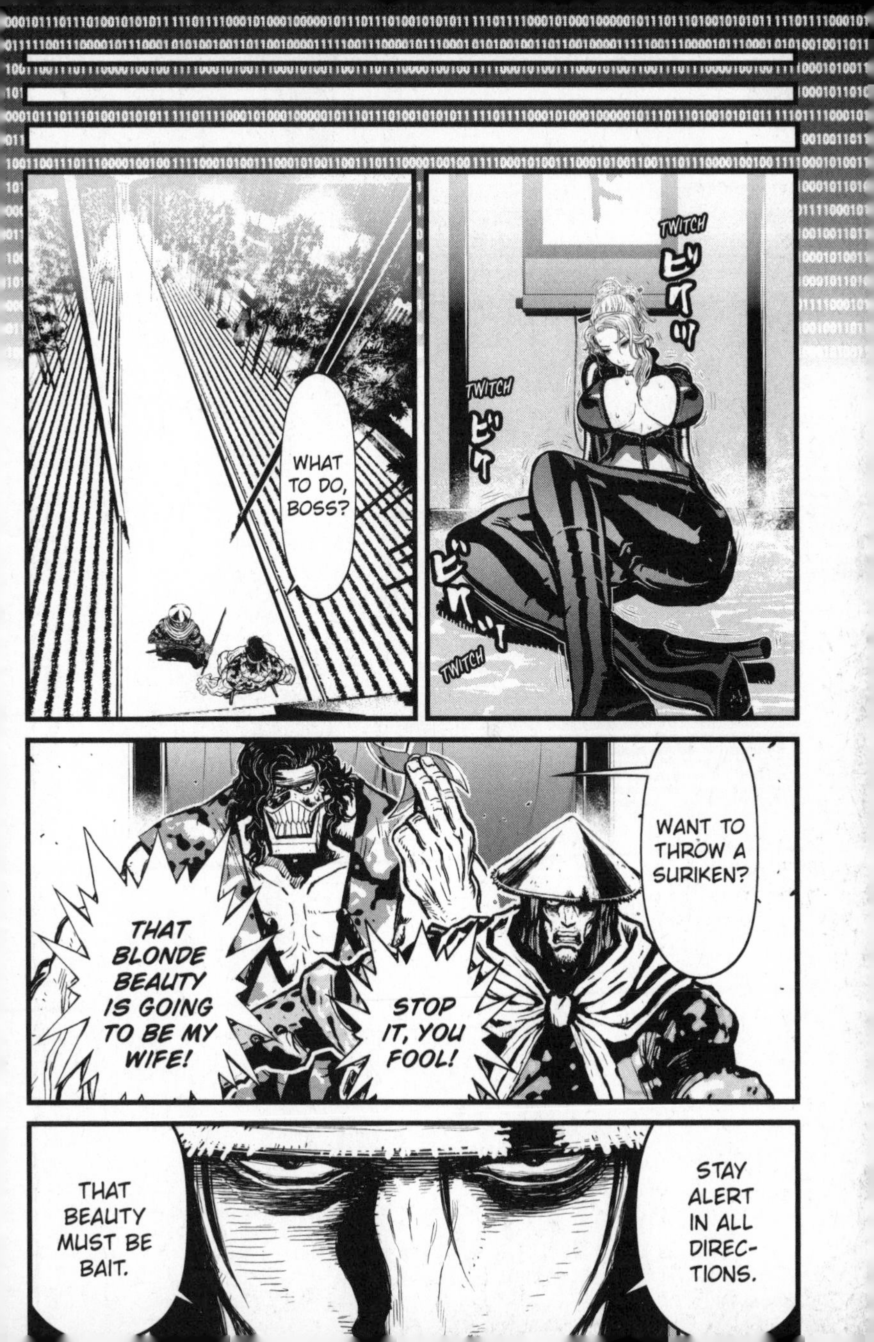
TWITCH
TWITCH
TWITCH
WHAT TO DO, BOSS?
WANT TO THROW A SURIKEN?
STOP IT, YOU FOOL!
THAT BLONDE BEAUTY IS GOING TO BE MY WIFE!
STAY ALERT IN ALL DIREC-TIONS.
THAT BEAUTY MUST BE BAIT.

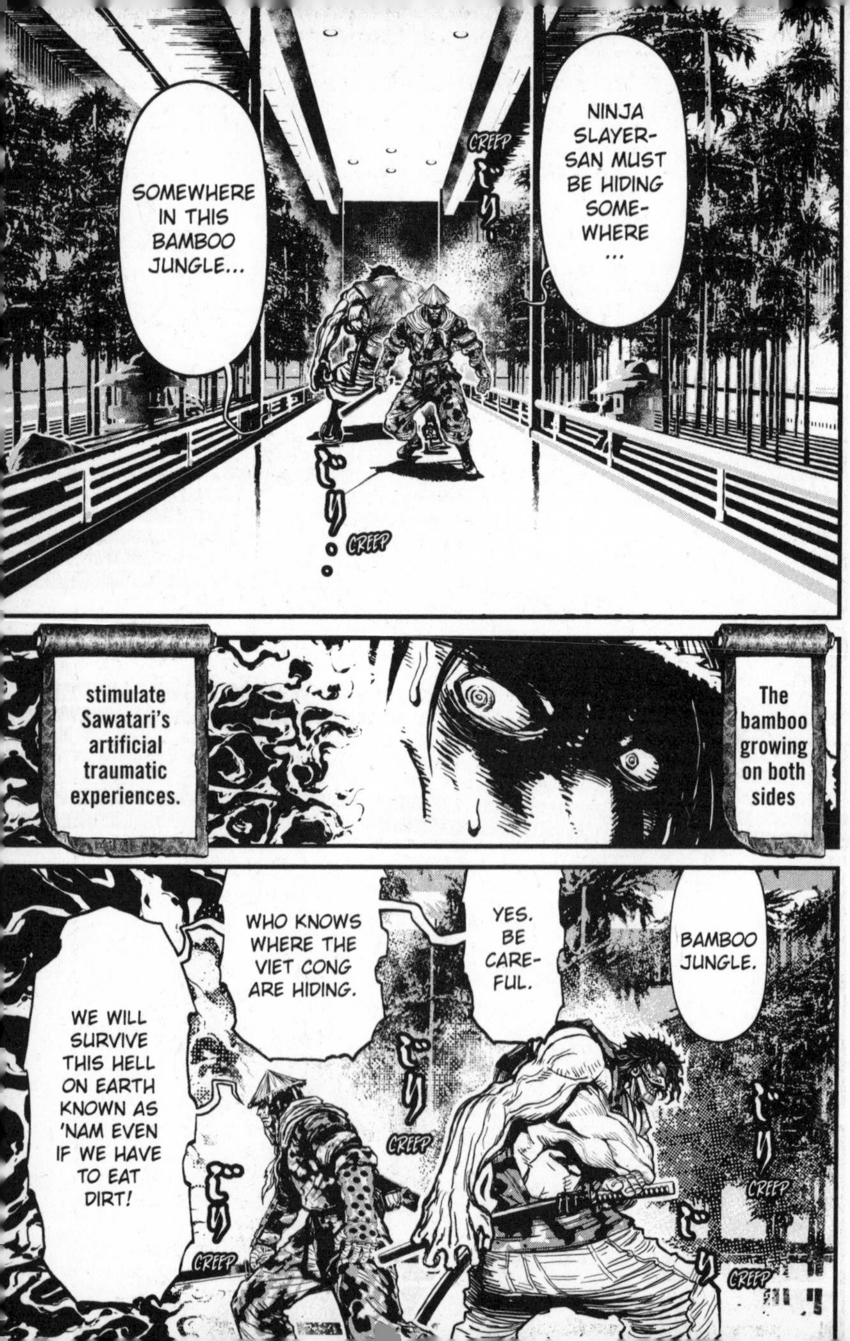
NINJA SLAYER-SAN MUST BE HIDING SOMEWHERE...
CREEP
SOMEWHERE IN THIS BAMBOO JUNGLE...
CREEP
The bamboo growing on both sides
stimulate Sawatari's artificial traumatic experiences.
BAMBOO JUNGLE.
CREEP
CREEP
YES. BE CAREFUL.
CREEP
WHO KNOWS WHERE THE VIET CONG ARE HIDING.
CREEP
WE WILL SURVIVE THIS HELL ON EARTH KNOWN AS 'NAM EVEN IF WE HAVE TO EAT DIRT!

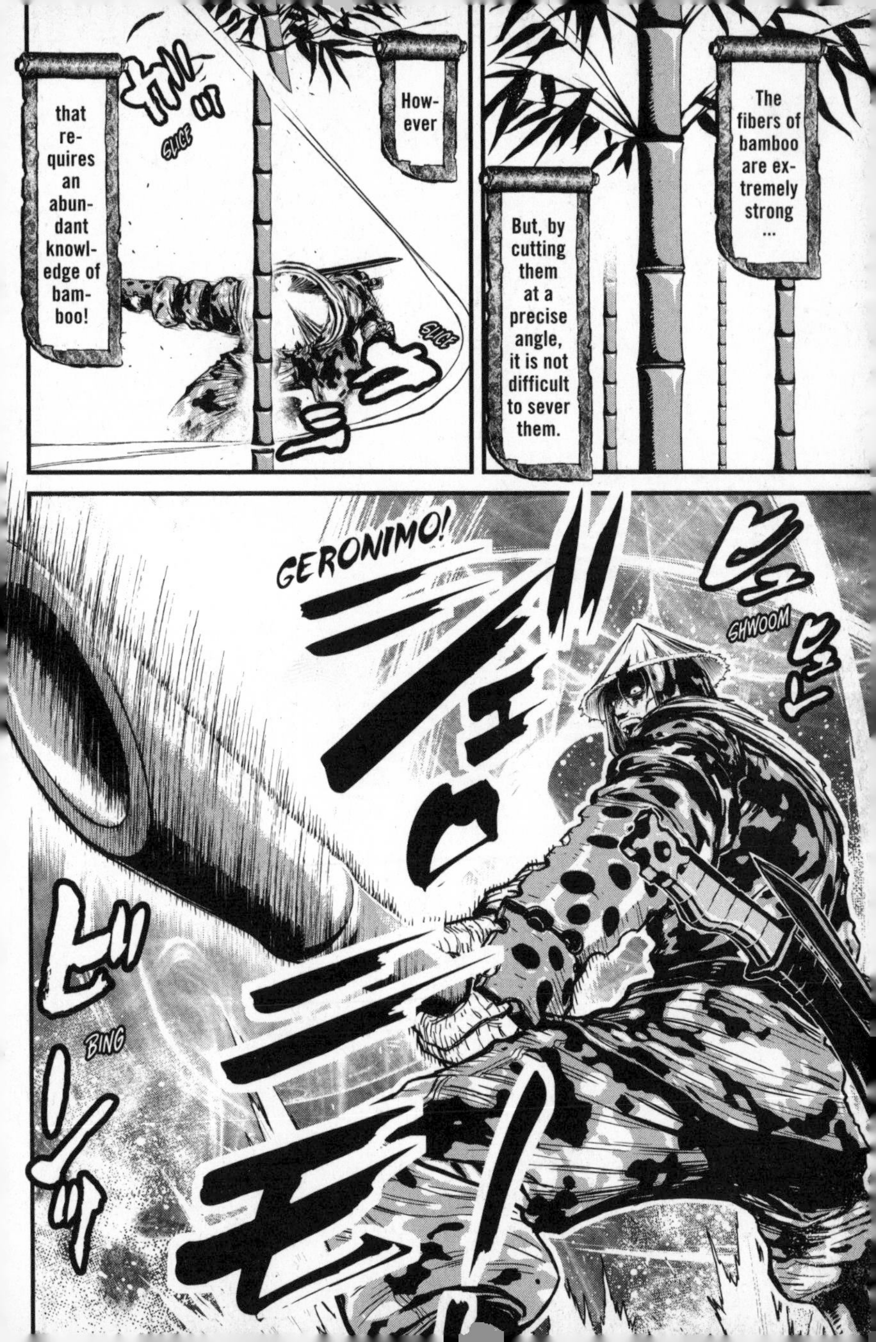
The fibers of bamboo are extremely strong ...
But, by cutting them at a precise angle, it is not difficult to sever them.
However
that requires an abundant knowledge of bamboo!
SLICE
SLICE
SHWOOM
GERONIMO!
BING

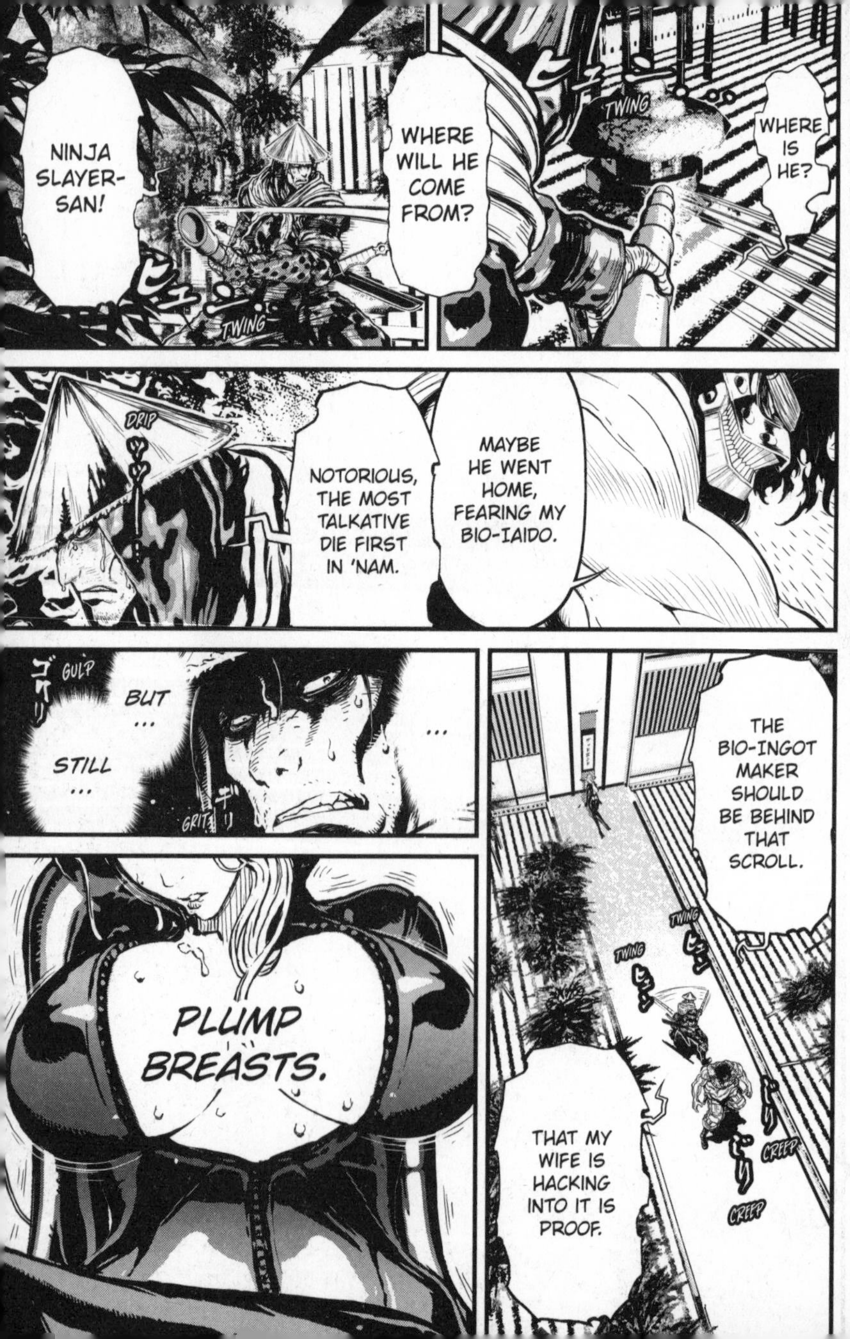
WHERE IS HE?
TWING
WHERE WILL HE COME FROM?
NINJA SLAYER-SAN!
TWING
MAYBE HE WENT HOME, FEARING MY BIO-IAIDO.
NOTORIOUS, THE MOST TALKATIVE DIE FIRST IN 'NAM.
DRIP
THE BIO-INGOT MAKER SHOULD BE BEHIND THAT SCROLL.
TWING
TWING
THAT MY WIFE IS HACKING INTO IT IS PROOF.
CREEP
CREEP
...
BUT ...
STILL ...
GULP
GRIT
PLUMP BREASTS.

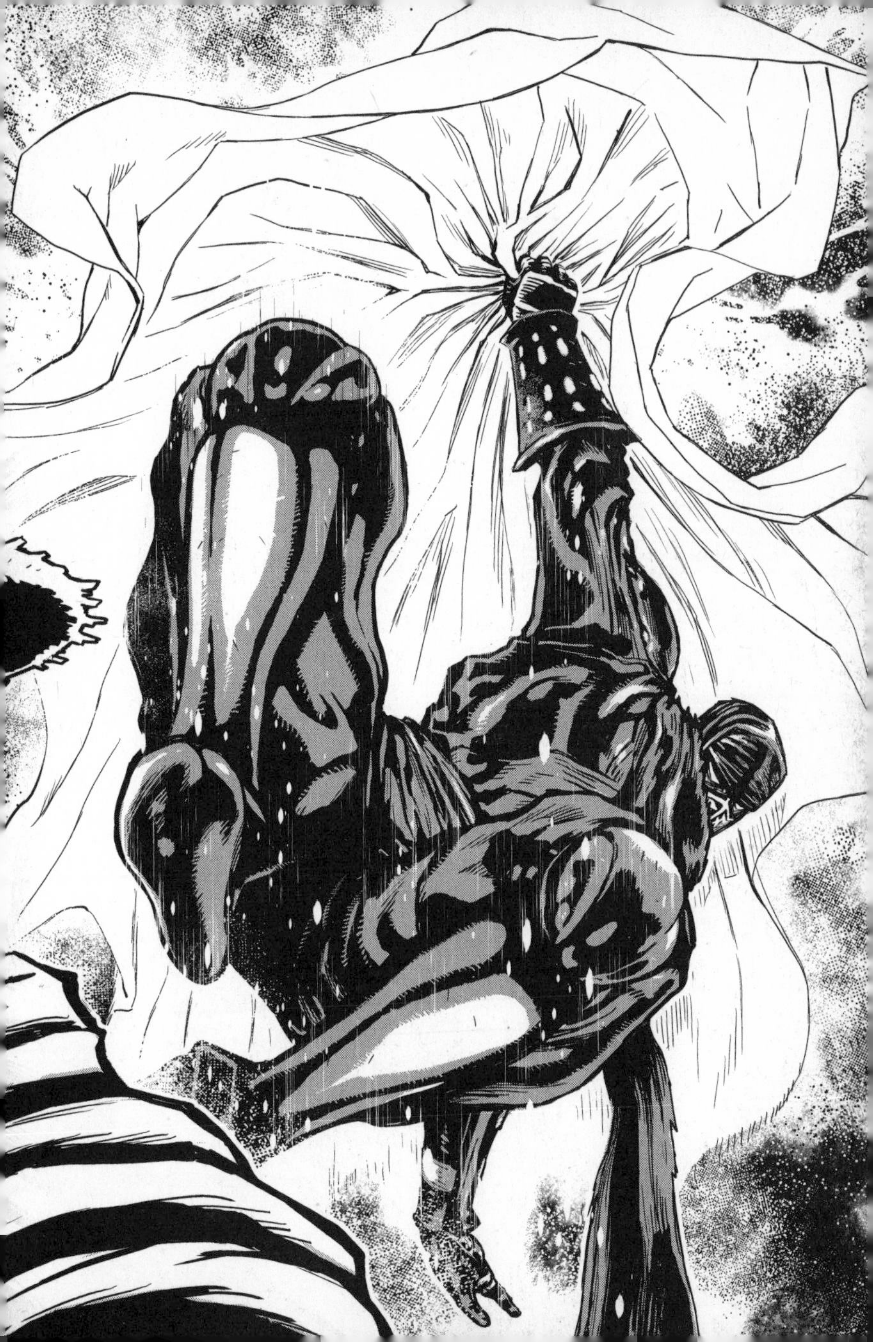

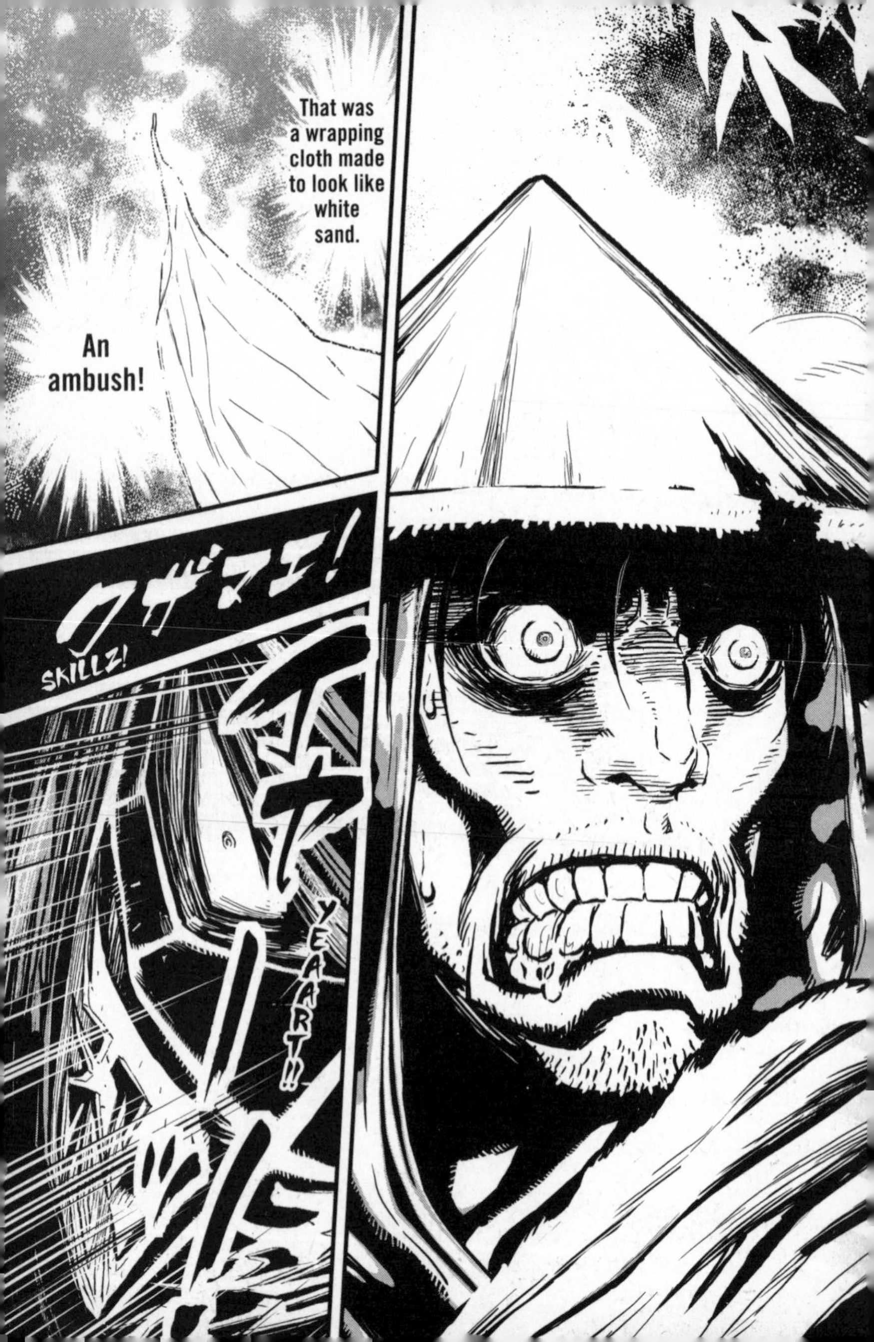
That was a wrapping cloth made to look like white sand.
An ambush!
ワザマエ!
SKILLZ!
YEAAART!!

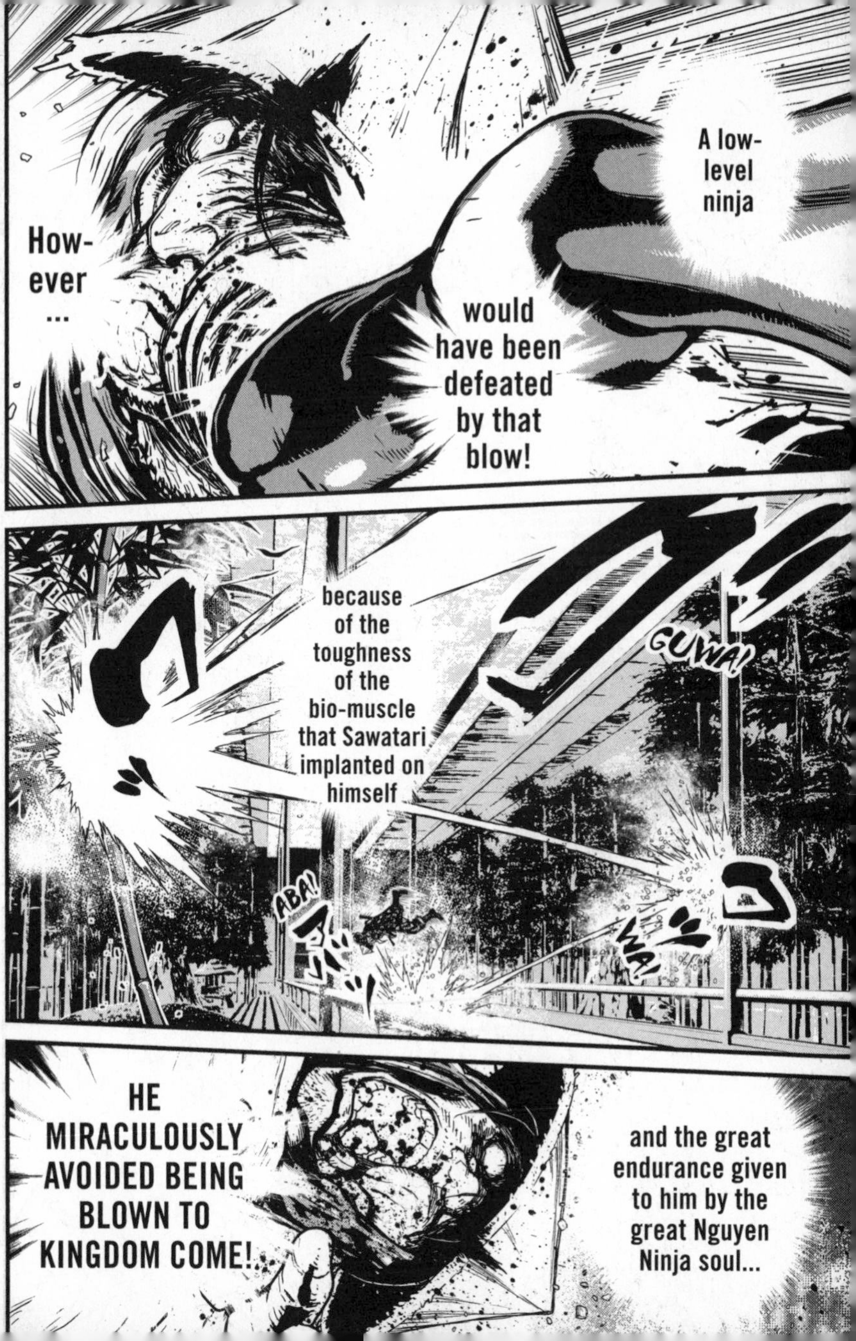
A low-level ninja
would have been defeated by that blow!
However...
GUWA!
because of the toughness of the bio-muscle that Sawatari implanted on himself
WA!
ABA!
and the great endurance given to him by the great Nguyen Ninja soul...
HE MIRACULOUSLY AVOIDED BEING BLOWN TO KINGDOM COME!

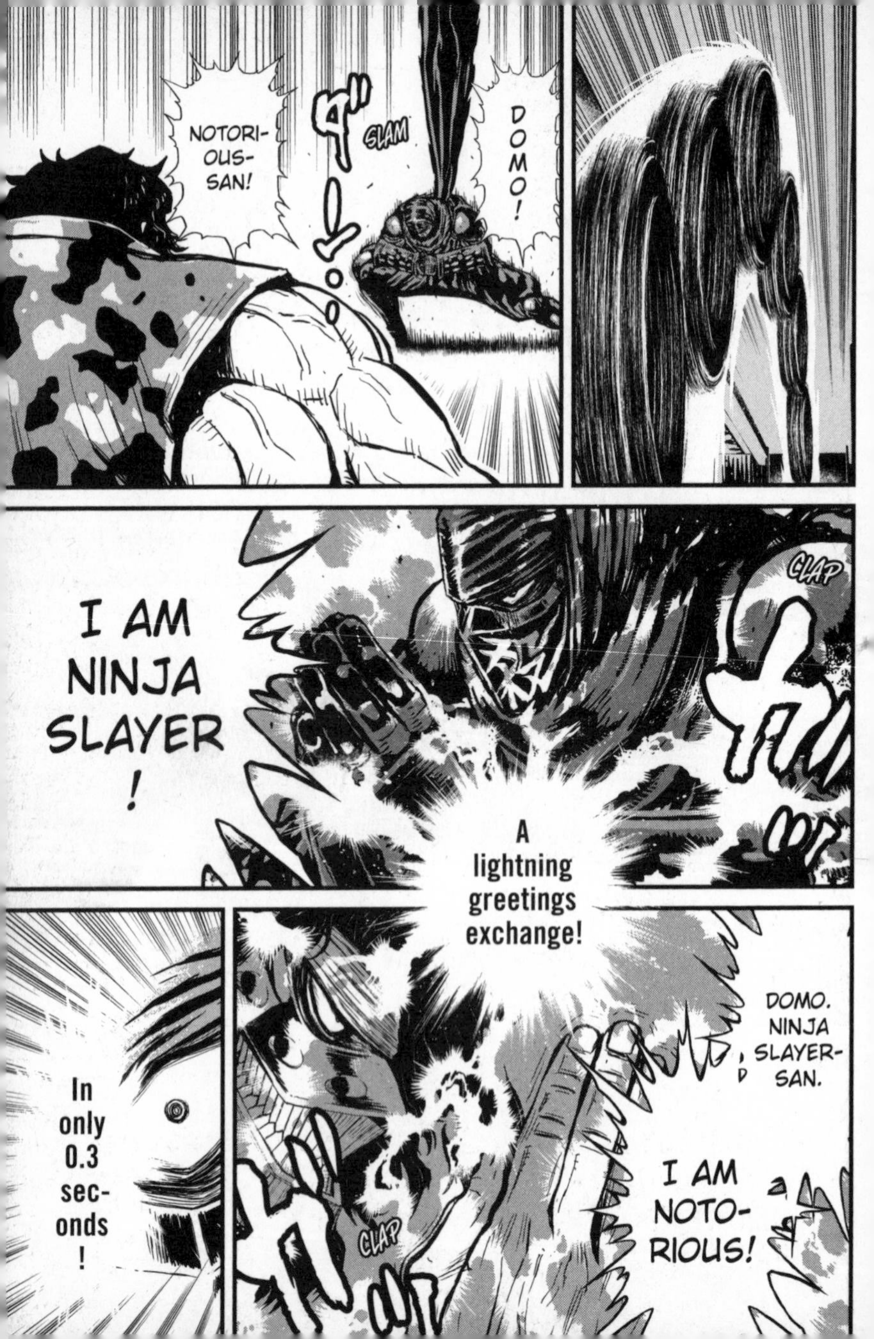
DOMO!
SLAM
NOTORI-OUS-SAN!
CLAP
I AM NINJA SLAYER !
A lightning greetings exchange!
DOMO. NINJA SLAYER-SAN.
I AM NOTO-RIOUS!
CLAP
In only 0.3 sec-onds !

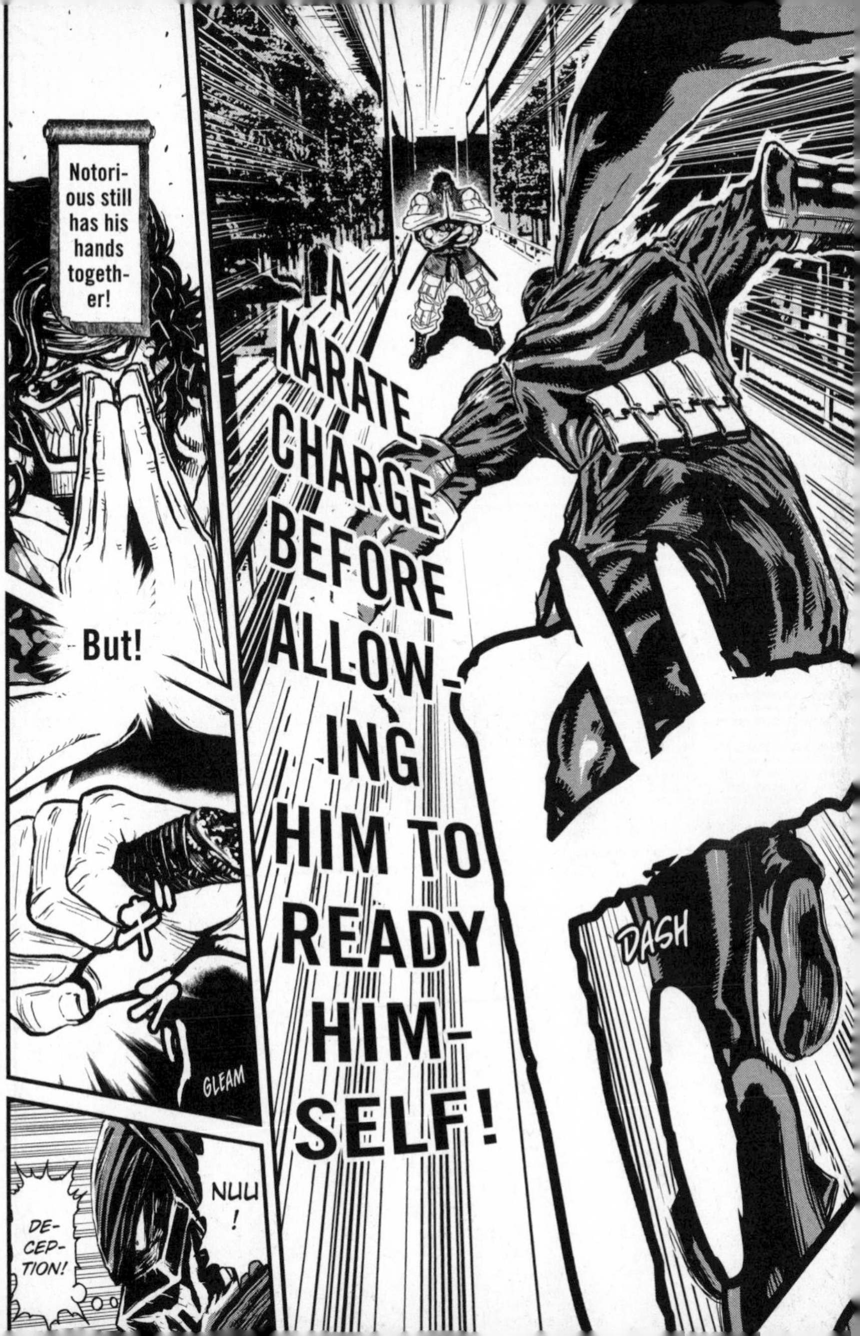
A KARATE CHARGE BEFORE ALLOW-ING HIM TO READY HIM-SELF!
DASH
Notori-ous still has his hands togeth-er!
But!
GLEAM
NUU!
DE-CEP-TION!

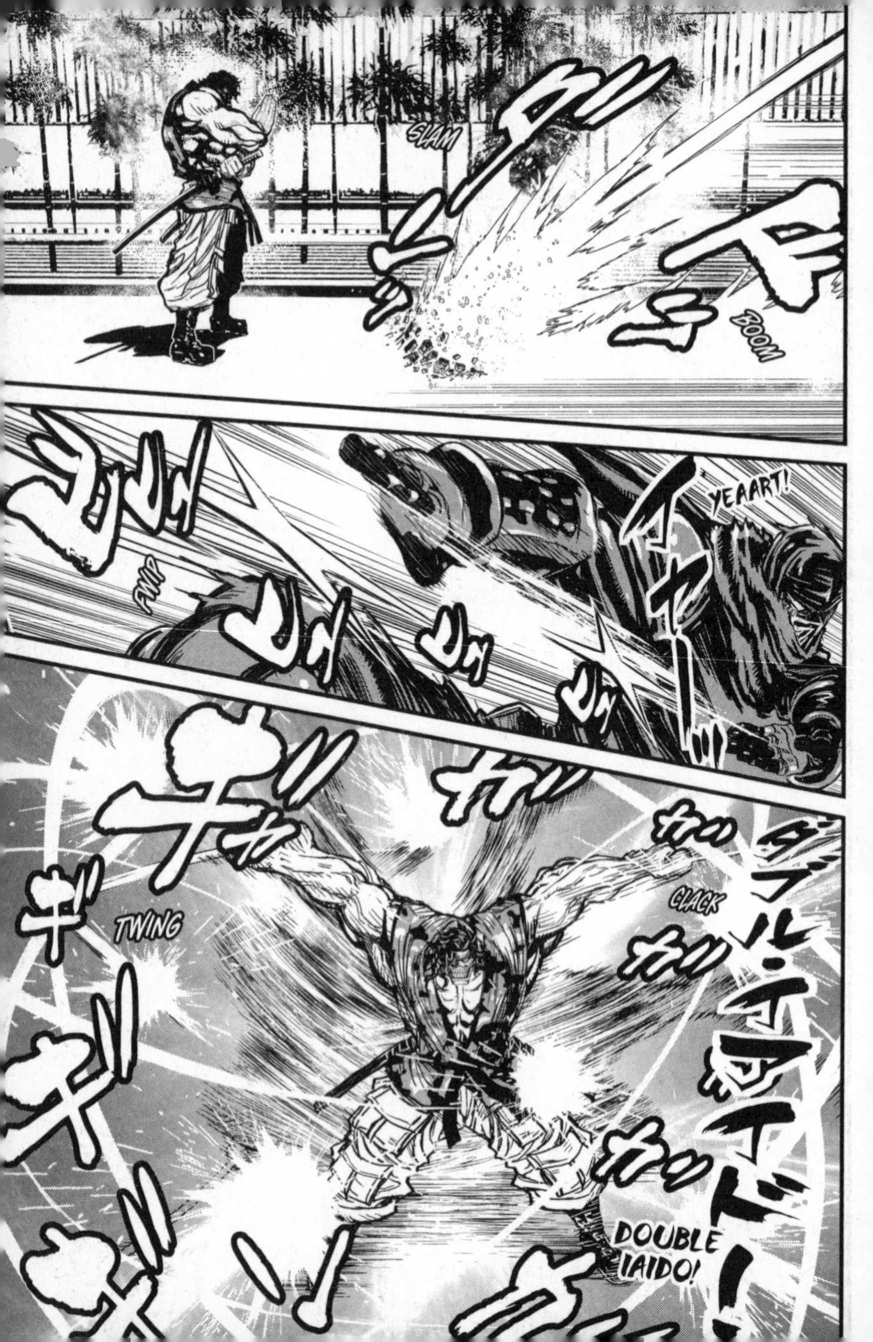
BOOM
SLAM
YEAART!
FWIP
CLACK
DOUBLE IAIDO!
TWING

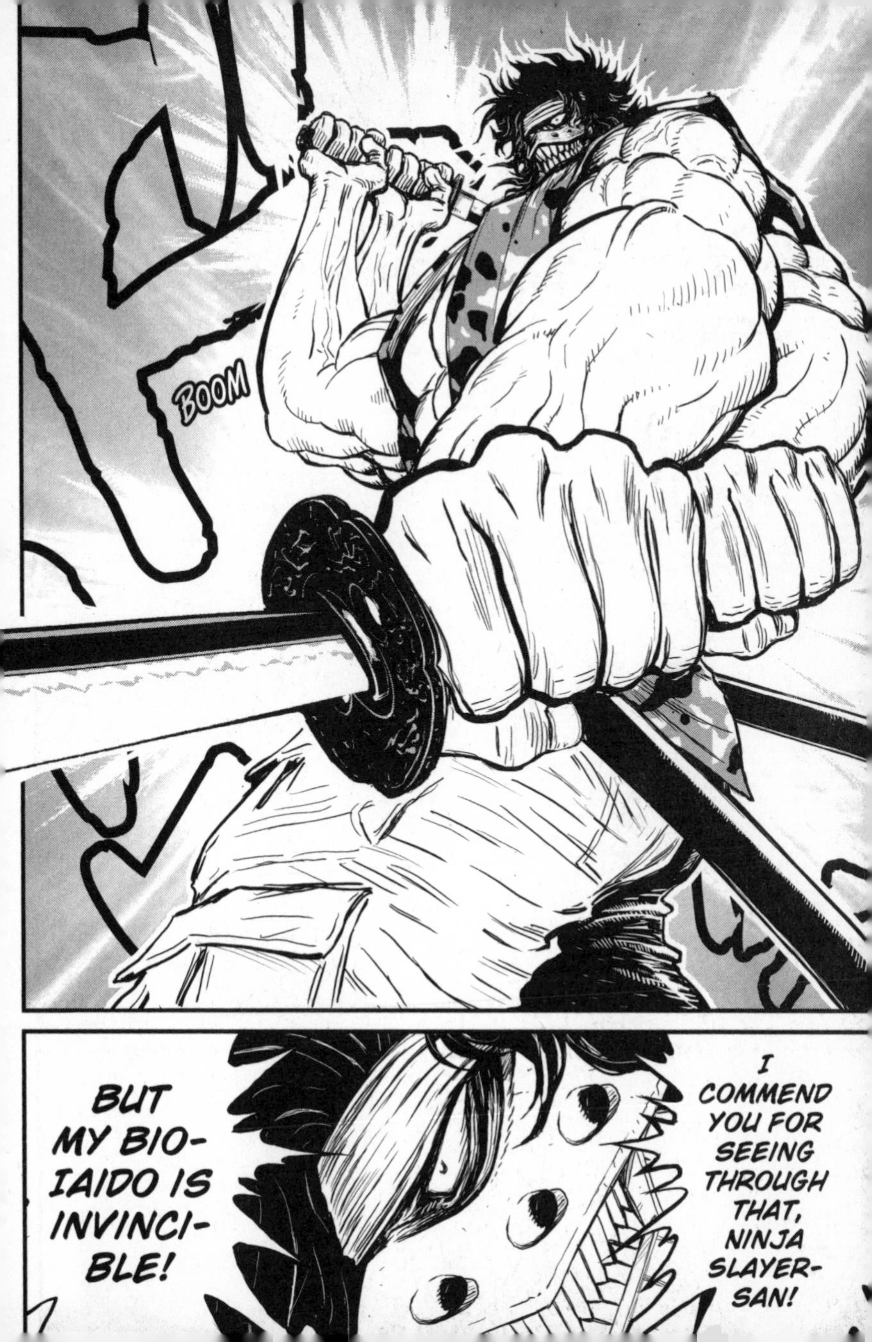
BOOM
I COMMEND YOU FOR SEEING THROUGH THAT, NINJA SLAYER-SAN!
BUT MY BIO-IAIDO IS INVINCIBLE!

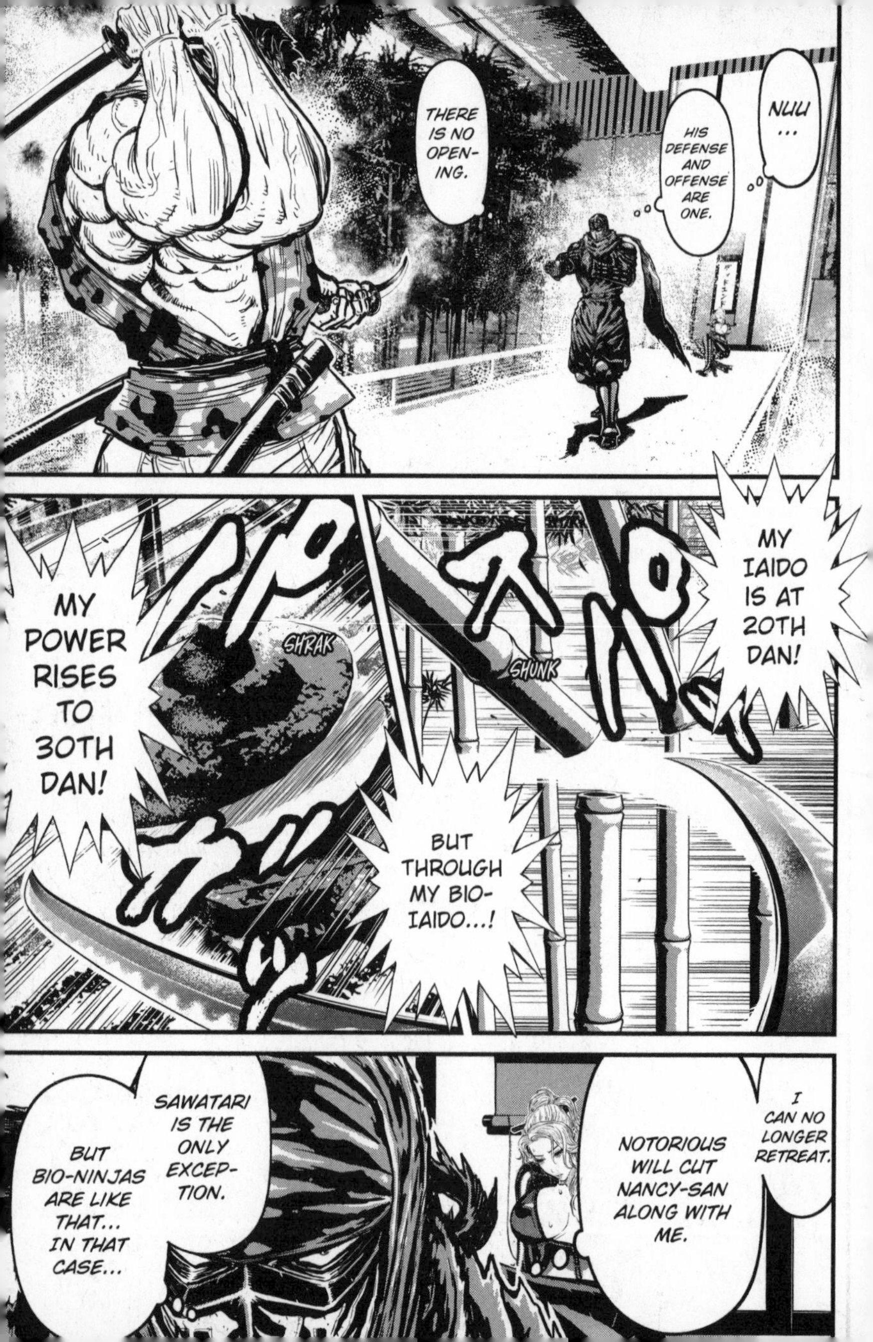
NUU ...
HIS DEFENSE AND OFFENSE ARE ONE.
THERE IS NO OPEN-ING.
MY IAIDO IS AT 20TH DAN!
SHUNK
SHRAK
BUT THROUGH MY BIO-IAIDO...!
MY POWER RISES TO 30TH DAN!
I CAN NO LONGER RETREAT.
NOTORIOUS WILL CUT NANCY-SAN ALONG WITH ME.
SAWATARI IS THE ONLY EXCEP-TION.
BUT BIO-NINJAS ARE LIKE THAT... IN THAT CASE...

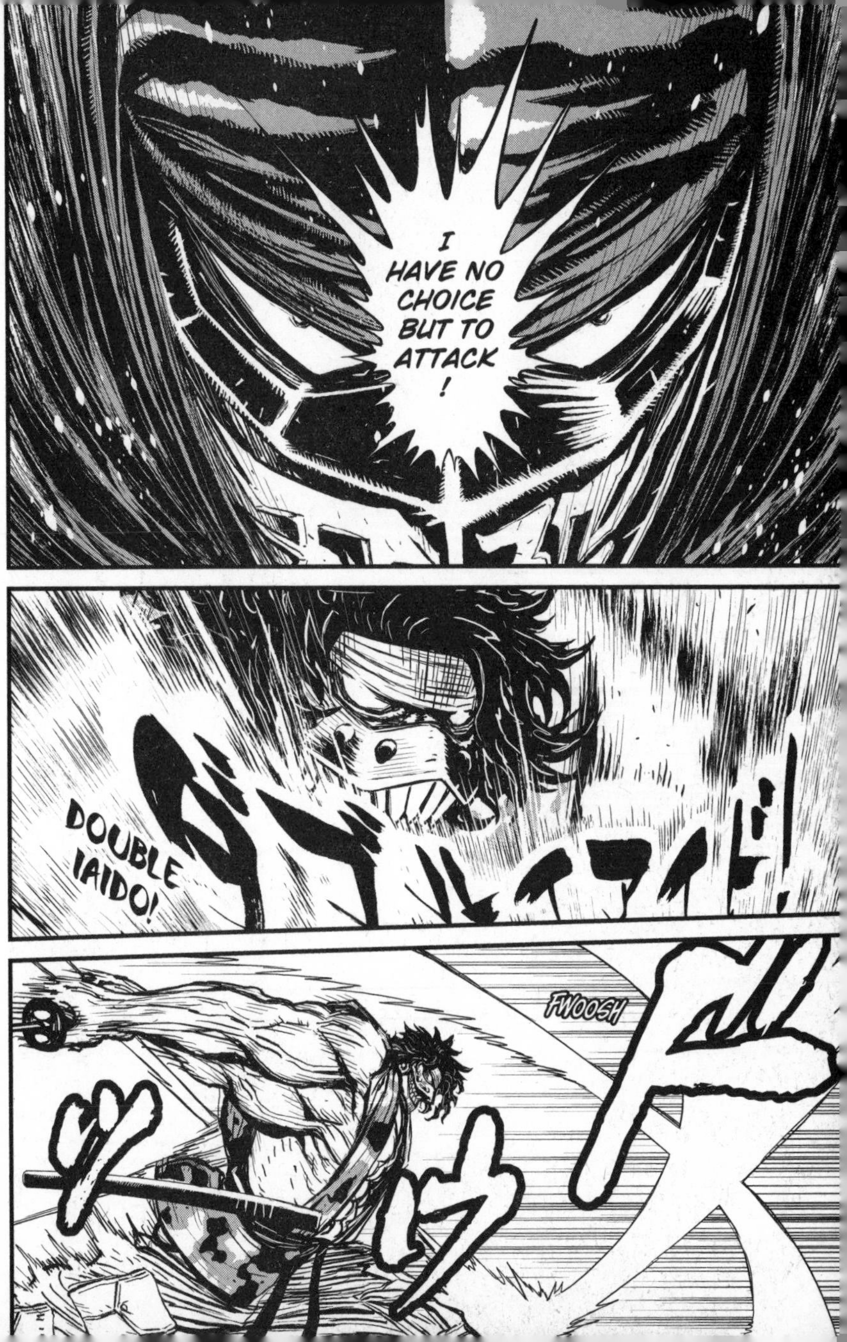
I HAVE NO CHOICE BUT TO ATTACK!
DOUBLE IAIDO!
FWOOSH

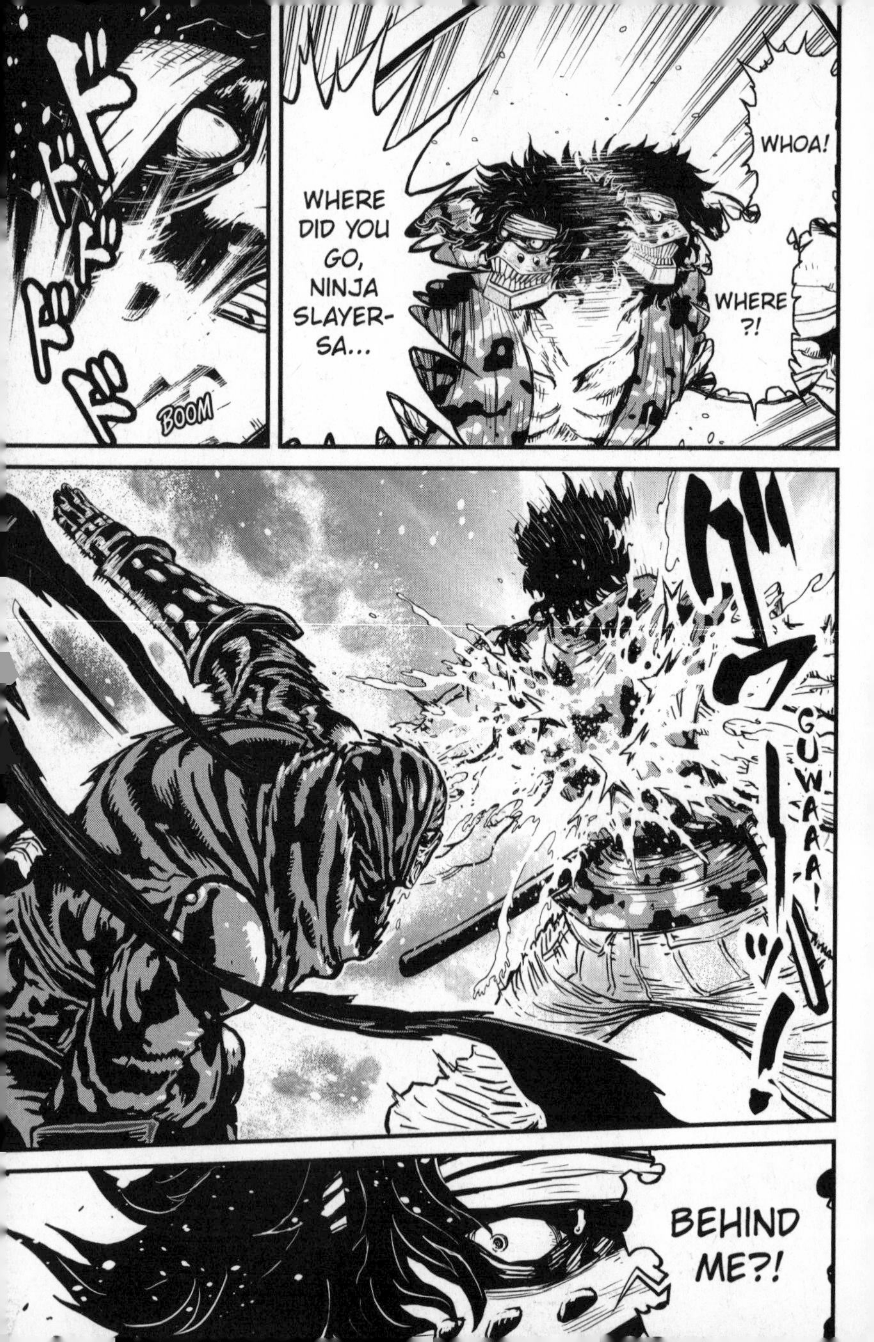
WHOA!
WHERE ?!
WHERE DID YOU GO, NINJA SLAYER-SA...
BOOM
GUWAAAA!!
BEHIND ME?!

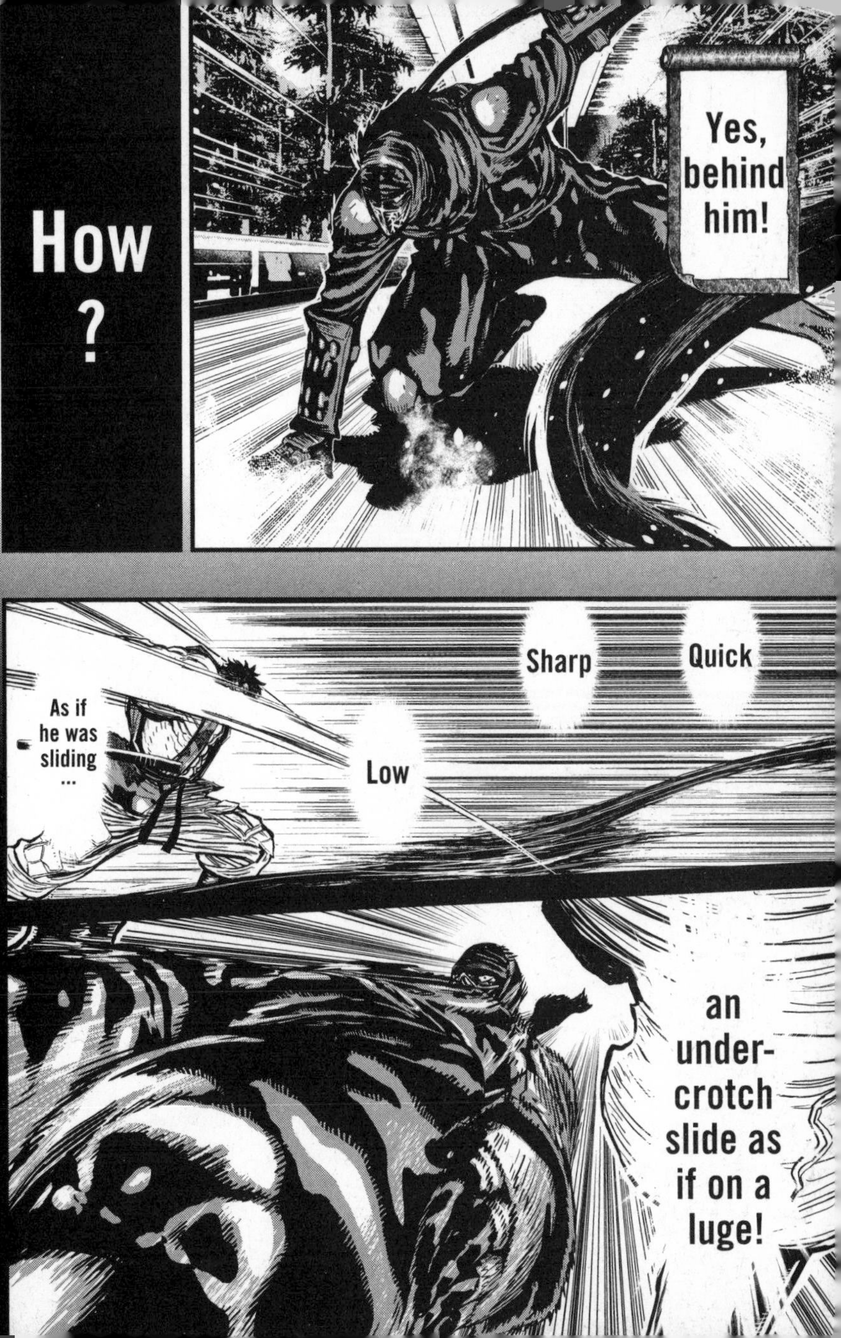
Yes, behind him!
How ?
Quick
Sharp
Low
As if he was sliding ...
an under-crotch slide as if on a luge!

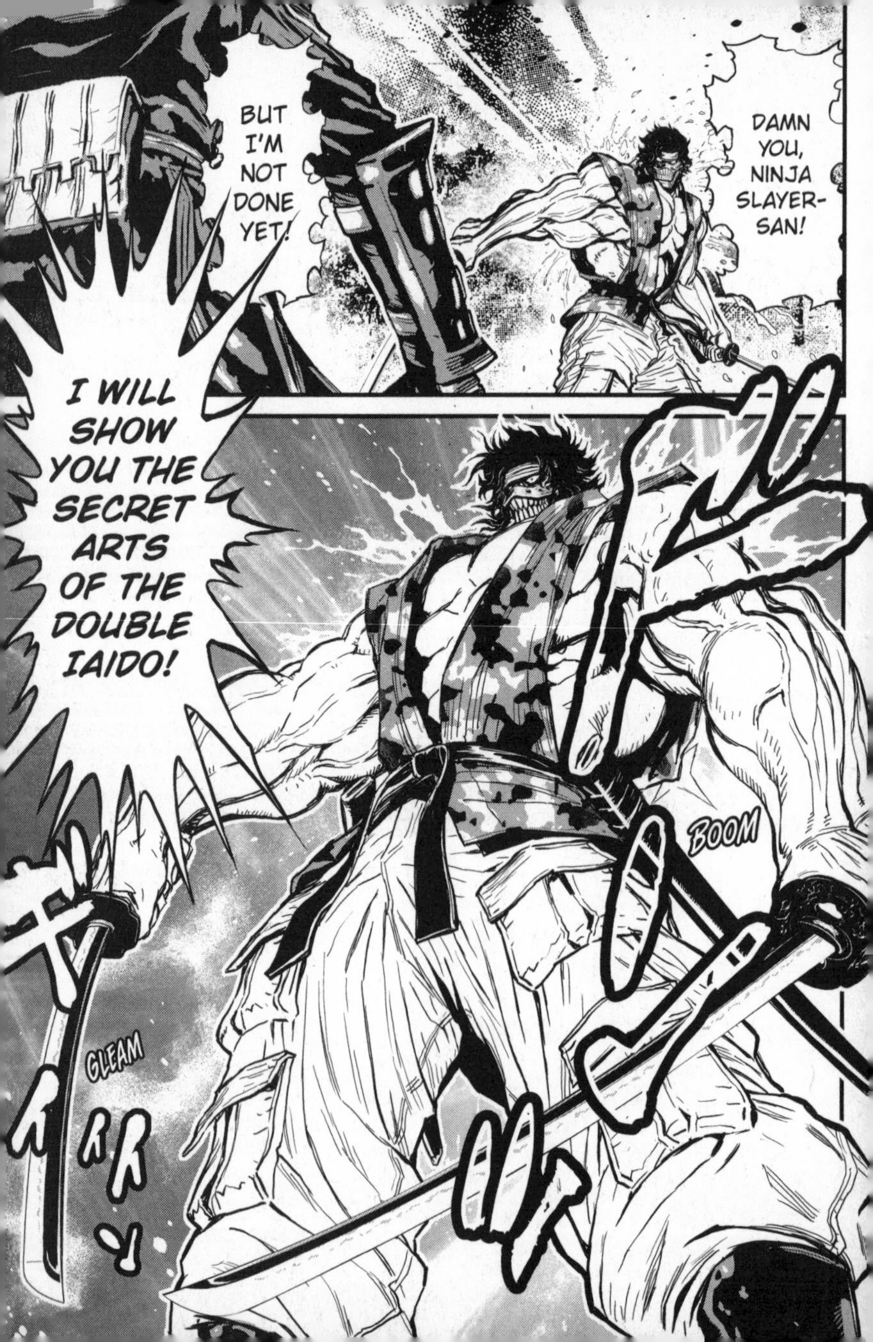
DAMN YOU, NINJA SLAYER-SAN!
BUT I'M NOT DONE YET!
BOOM
I WILL SHOW YOU THE SECRET ARTS OF THE DOUBLE IAIDO!
GLEAM

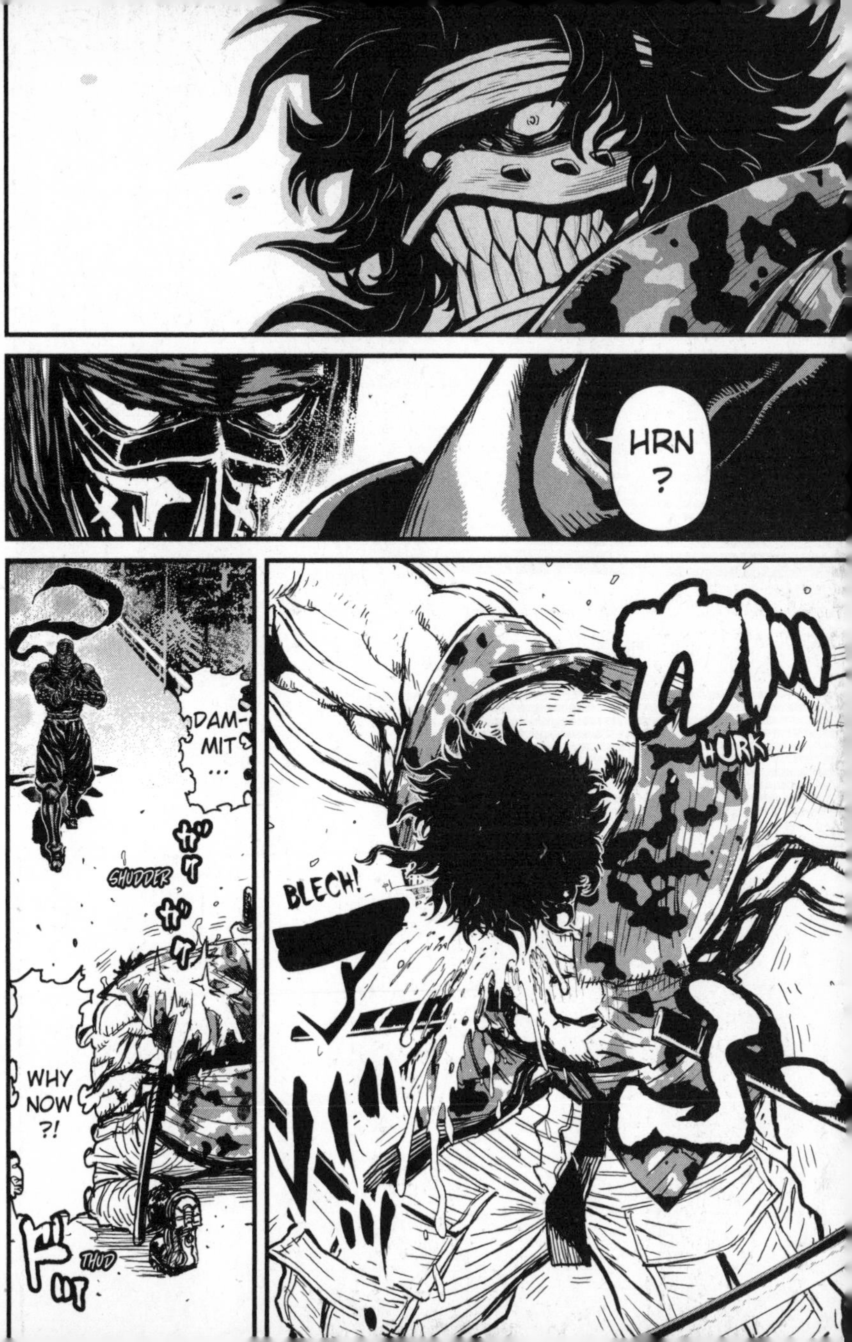
HRN ?
HURK
BLECH!
DAM-MIT ...
SHUDDER
WHY NOW ?!
THUD

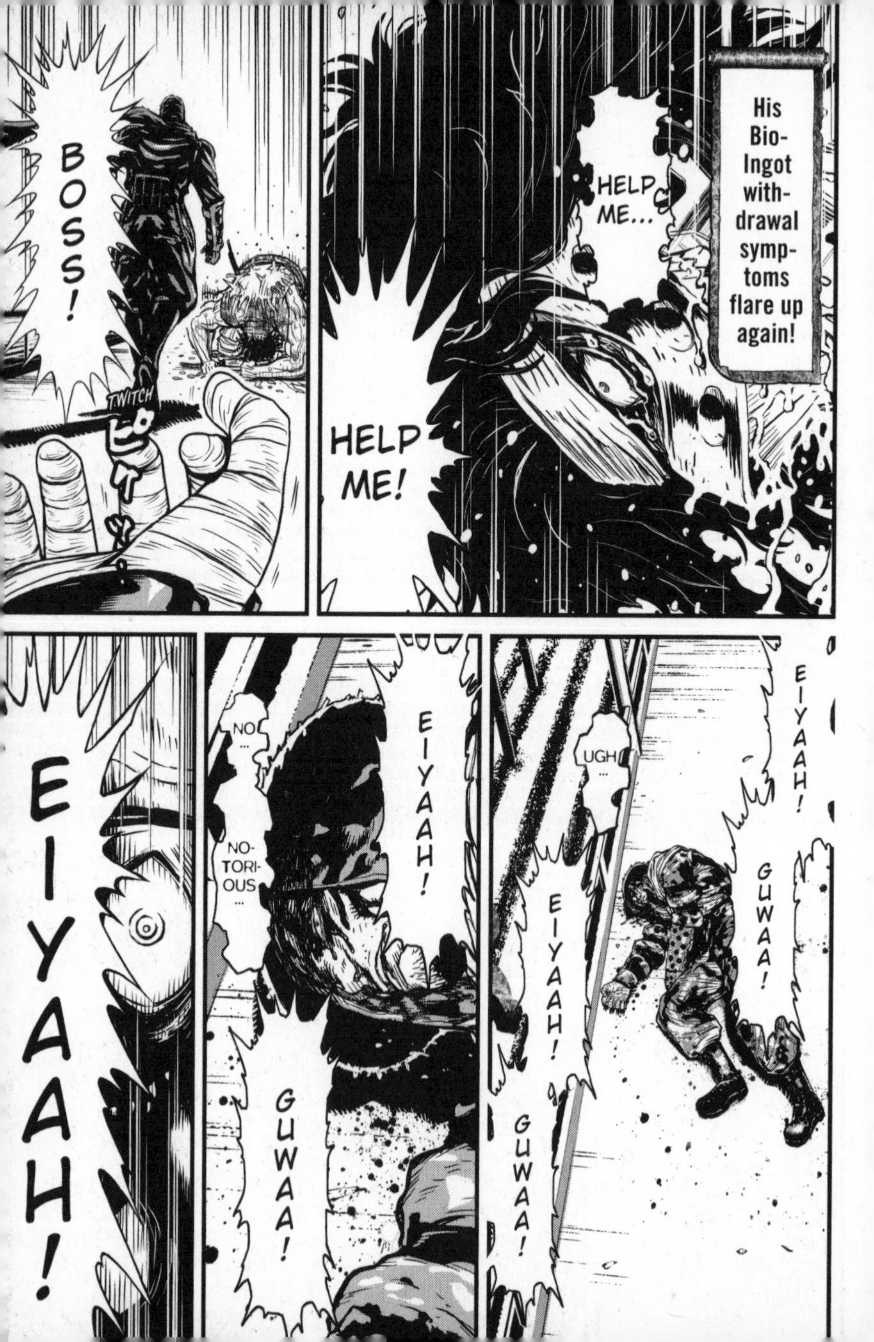
His Bio-Ingot with-drawal symp-toms flare up again!
HELP ME...
HELP ME!
BOSS!
TWITCH
EIYAAH!
UGH...
GUWAAA!
EIYAAH!
GUWAAA!
EIYAAH!
NO...
NO-TORI-OUS...
GUWAAA!
EIYAAH!

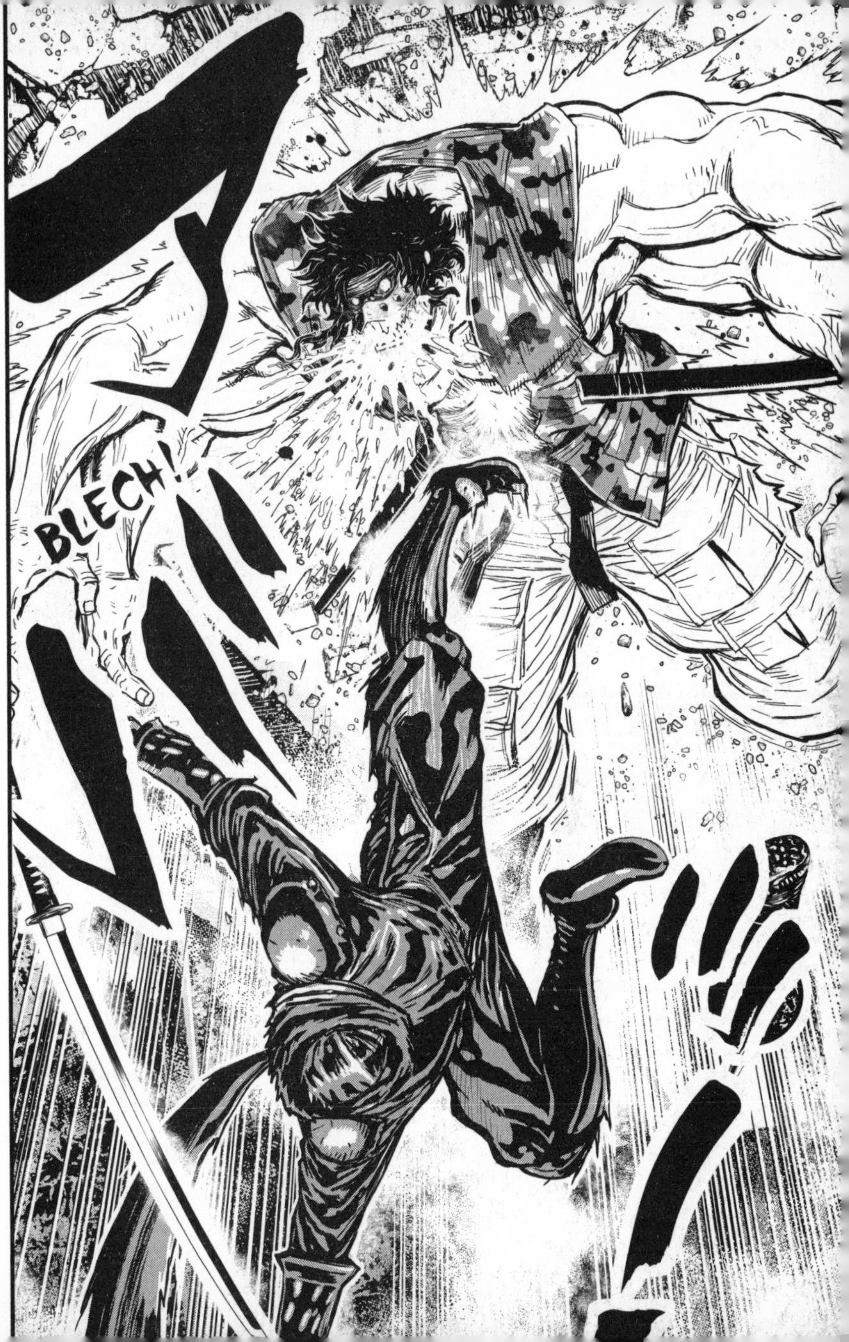
BLECH!

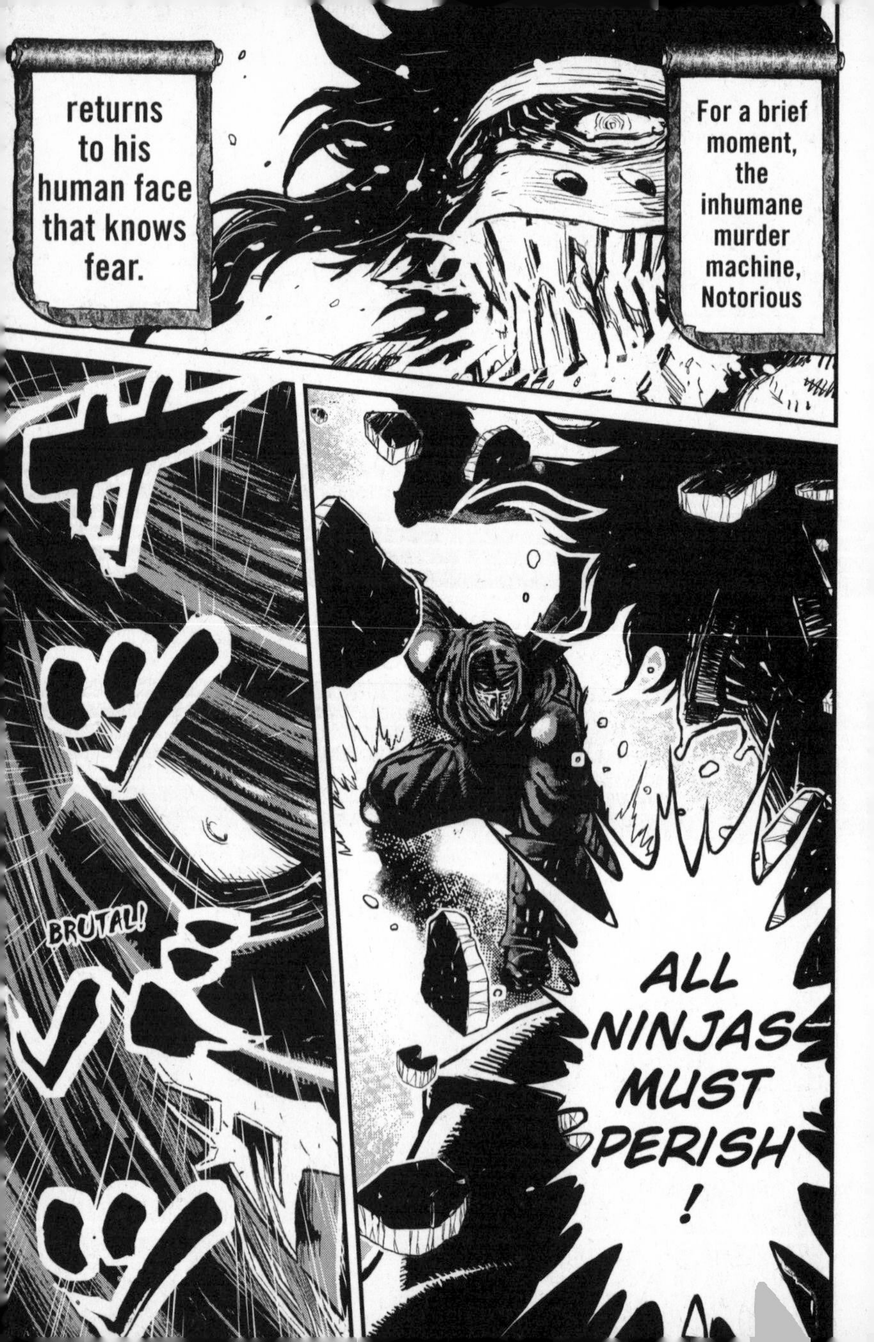
For a brief moment, the inhumane murder machine, Notorious
returns to his human face that knows fear.
ALL NINJAS MUST PERISH!
BRUTAL!

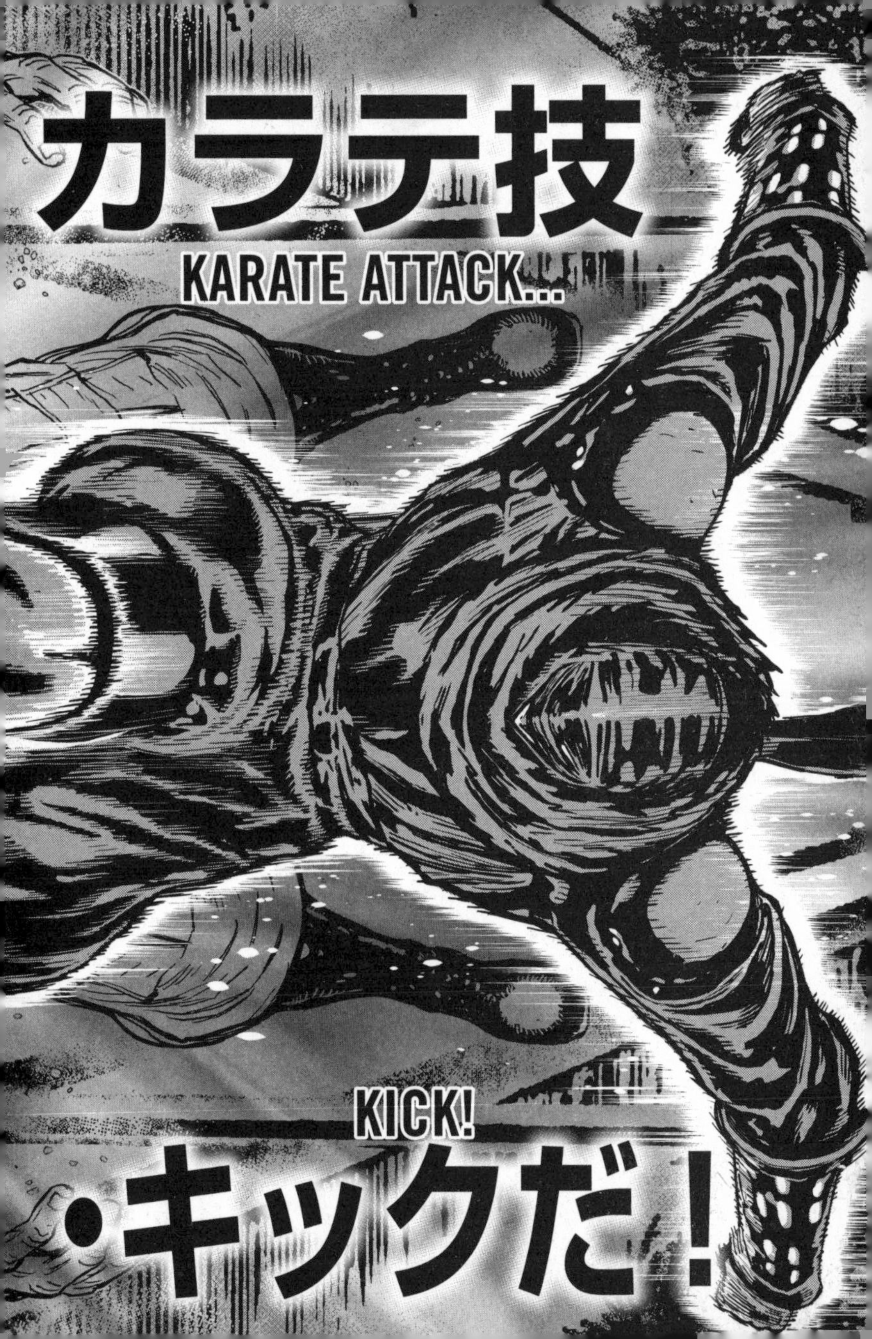

カラテ技
KARATE ATTACK...
KICK!
・キックだ！

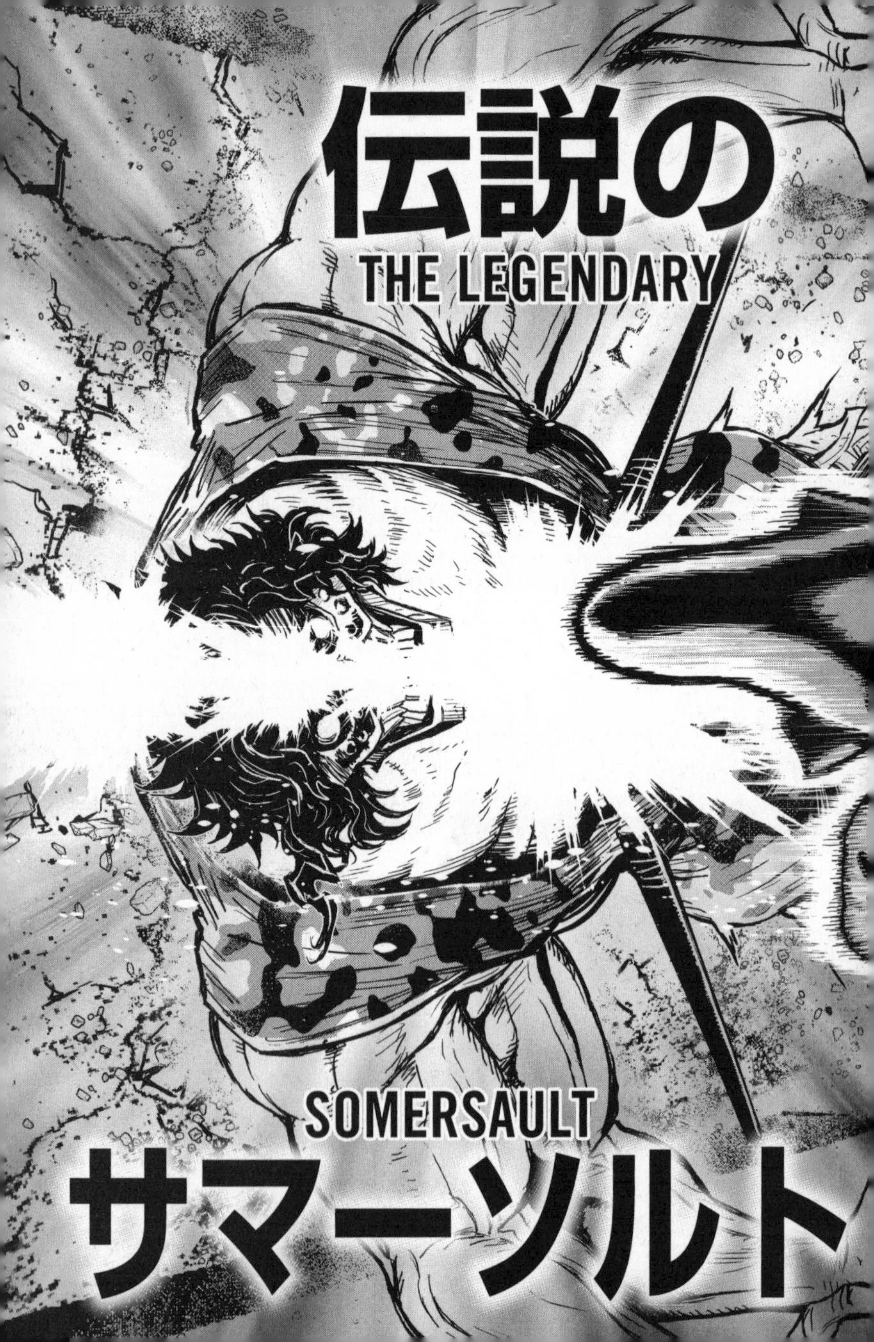
伝説の
THE LEGENDARY
SOMERSAULT
サマーソルト

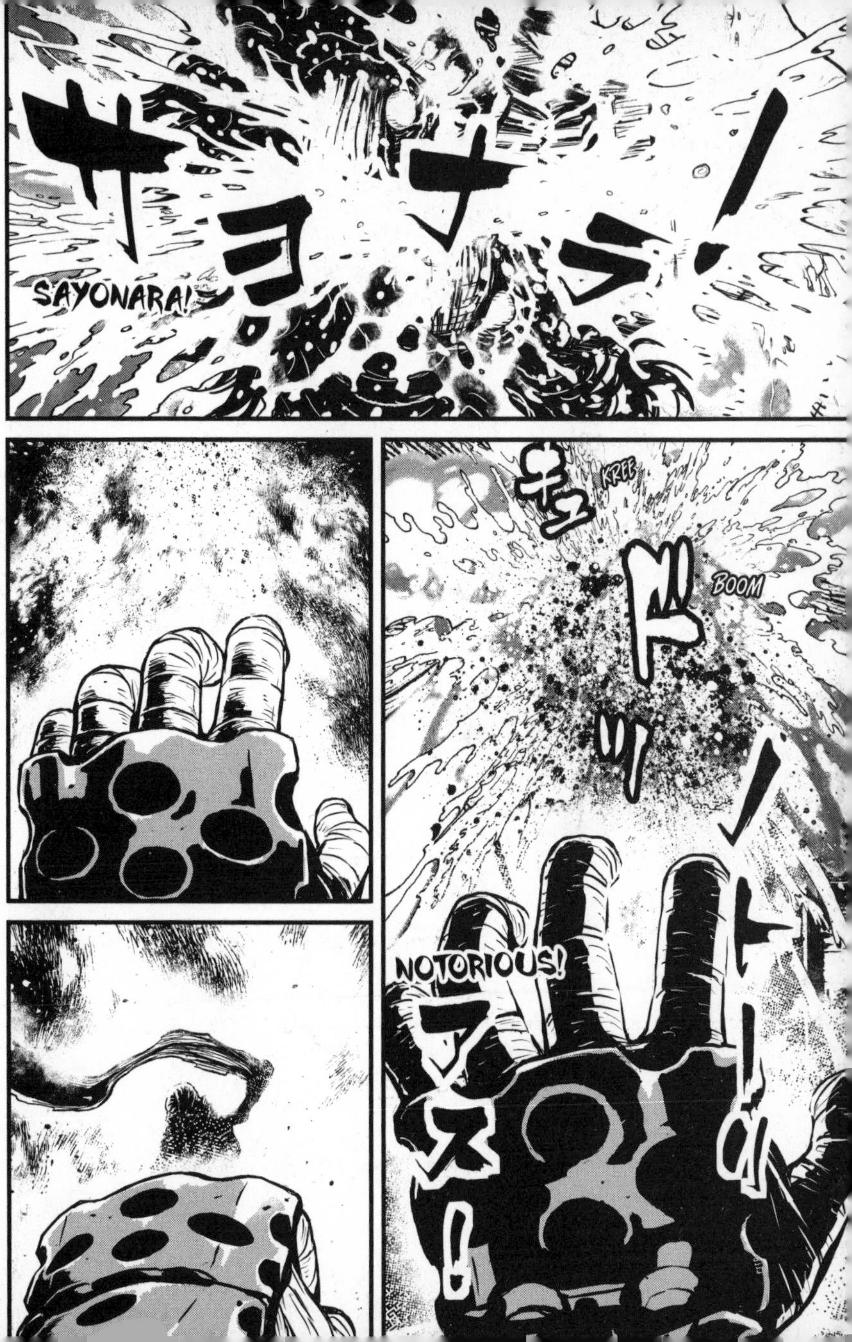
サヨナラ!
SAYONARA!
KREE
BOOM
NOTORIOUS!

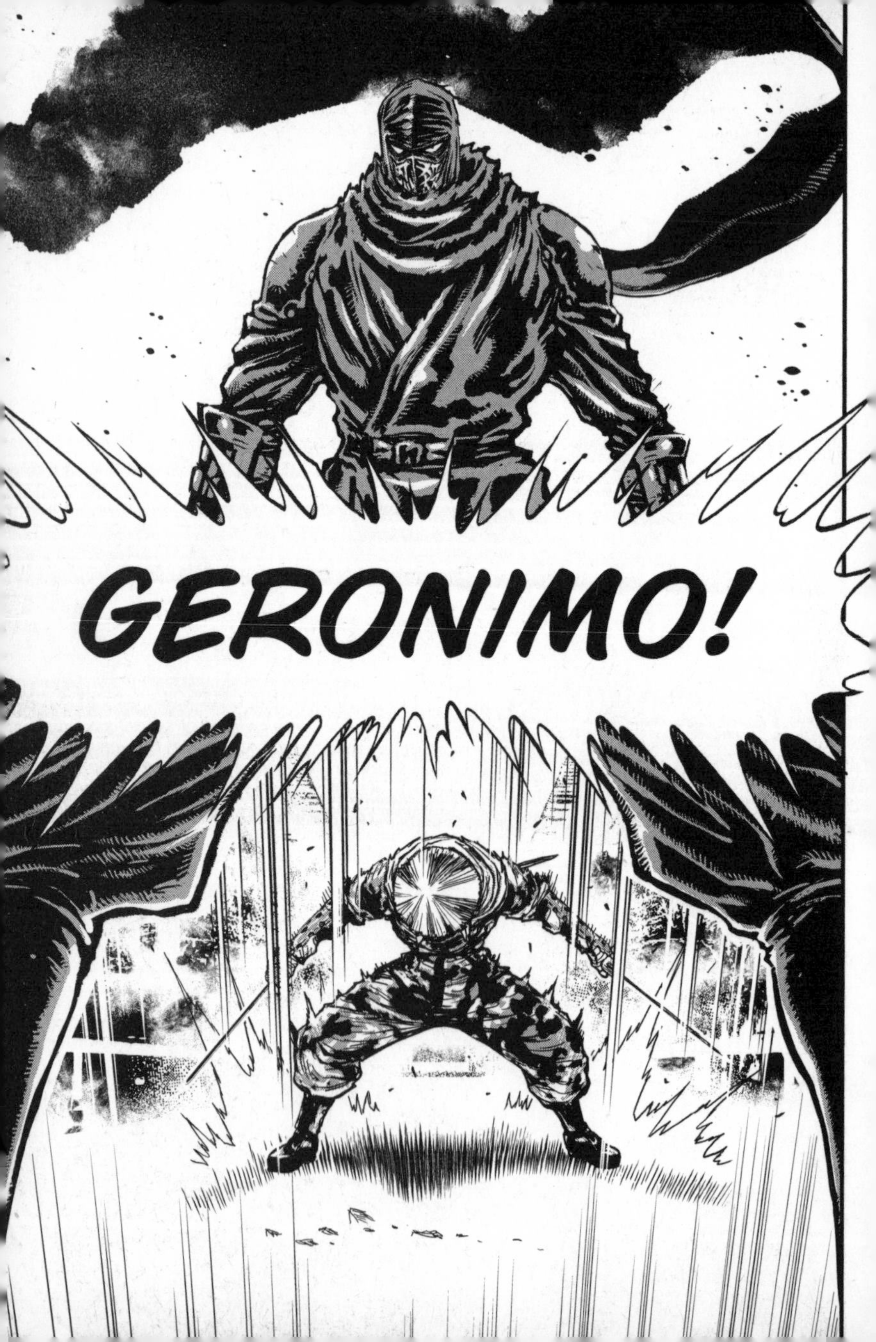
GERONIMO!

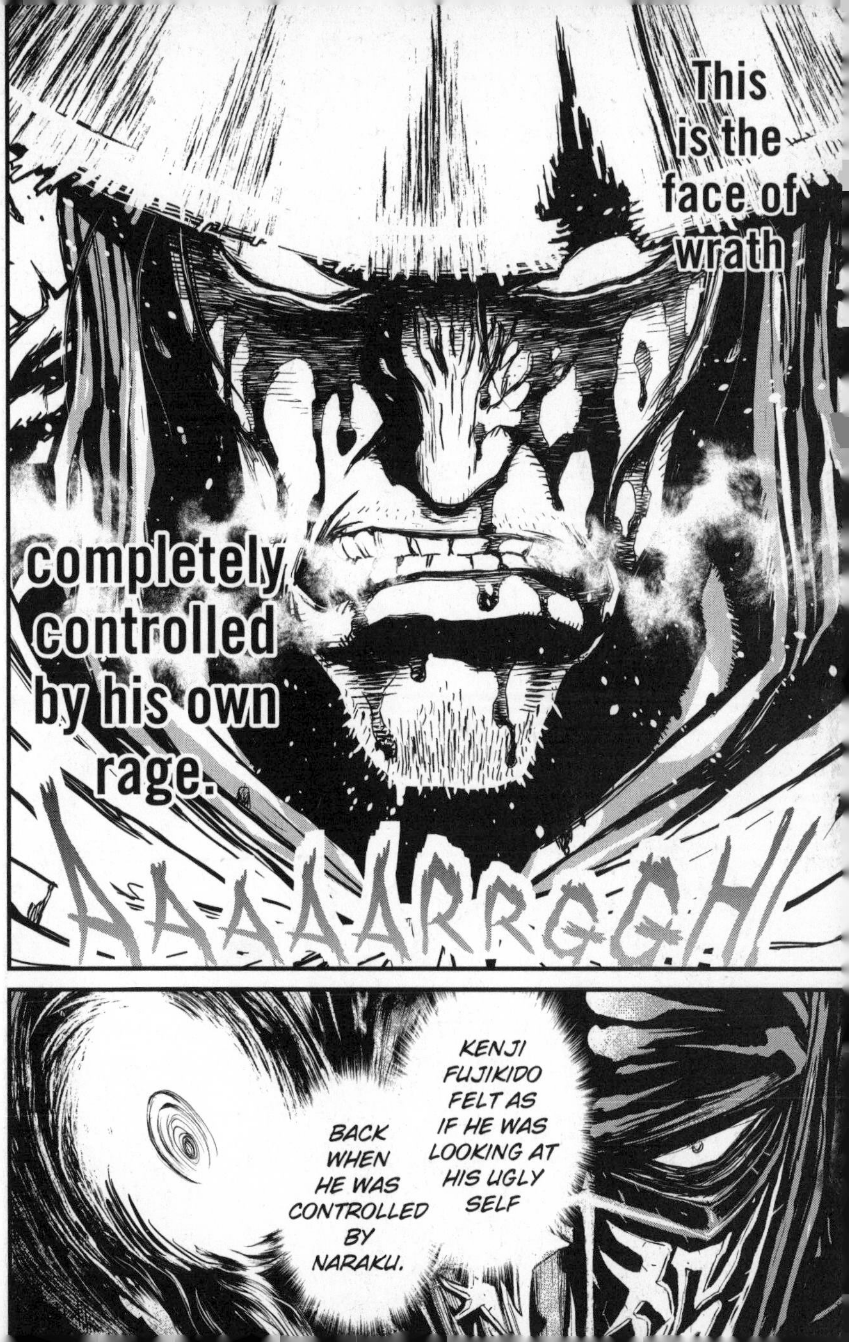
This is the face of wrath
completely controlled by his own rage.
AAAAARRGGH
KENJI FUJIKIDO FELT AS IF HE WAS LOOKING AT HIS UGLY SELF
BACK WHEN HE WAS CONTROLLED BY NARAKU.

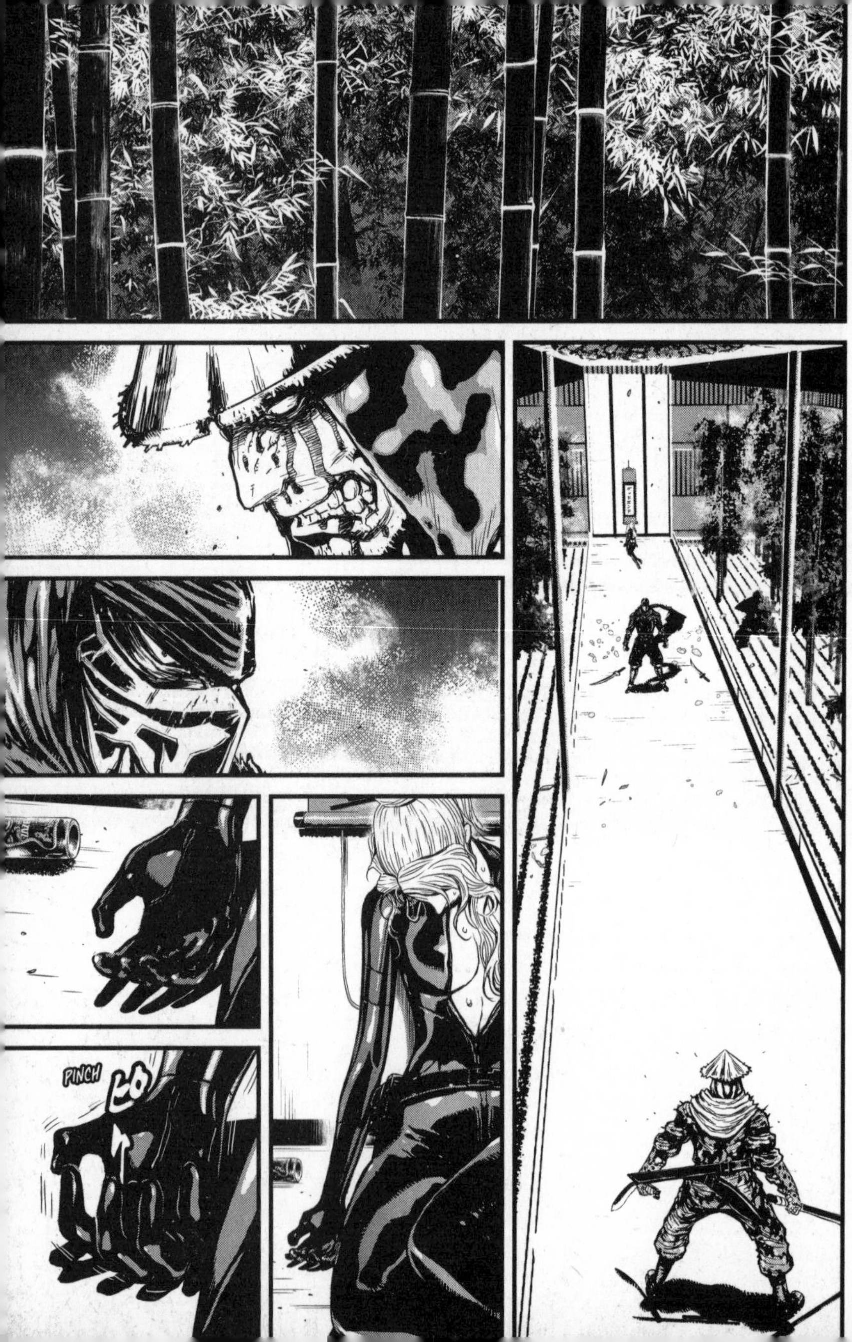
PINCH

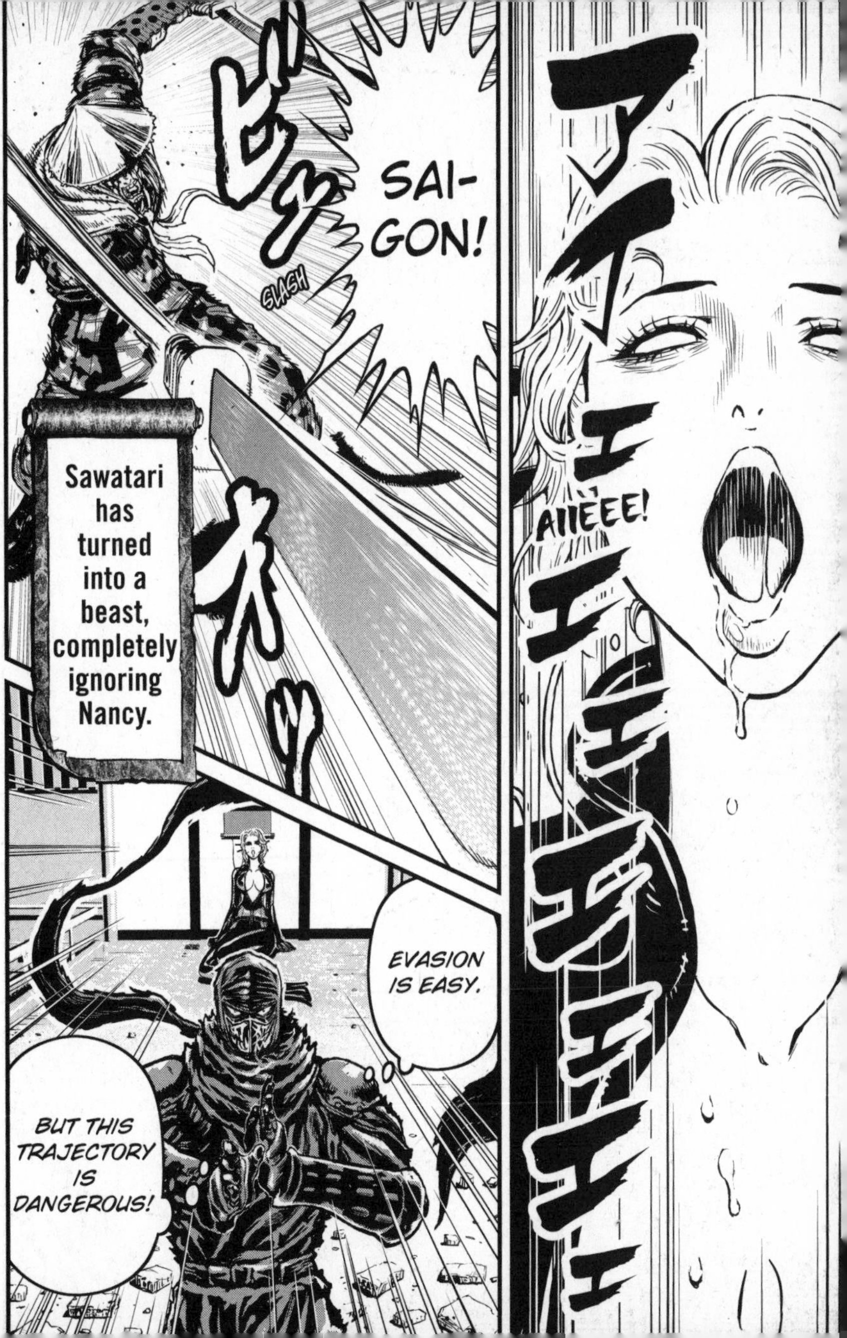
AIIEEE!
SAI-
GON!
SLASH
Sawatari has turned into a beast, completely ignoring Nancy.
EVASION IS EASY.
BUT THIS TRAJECTORY IS DANGEROUS!

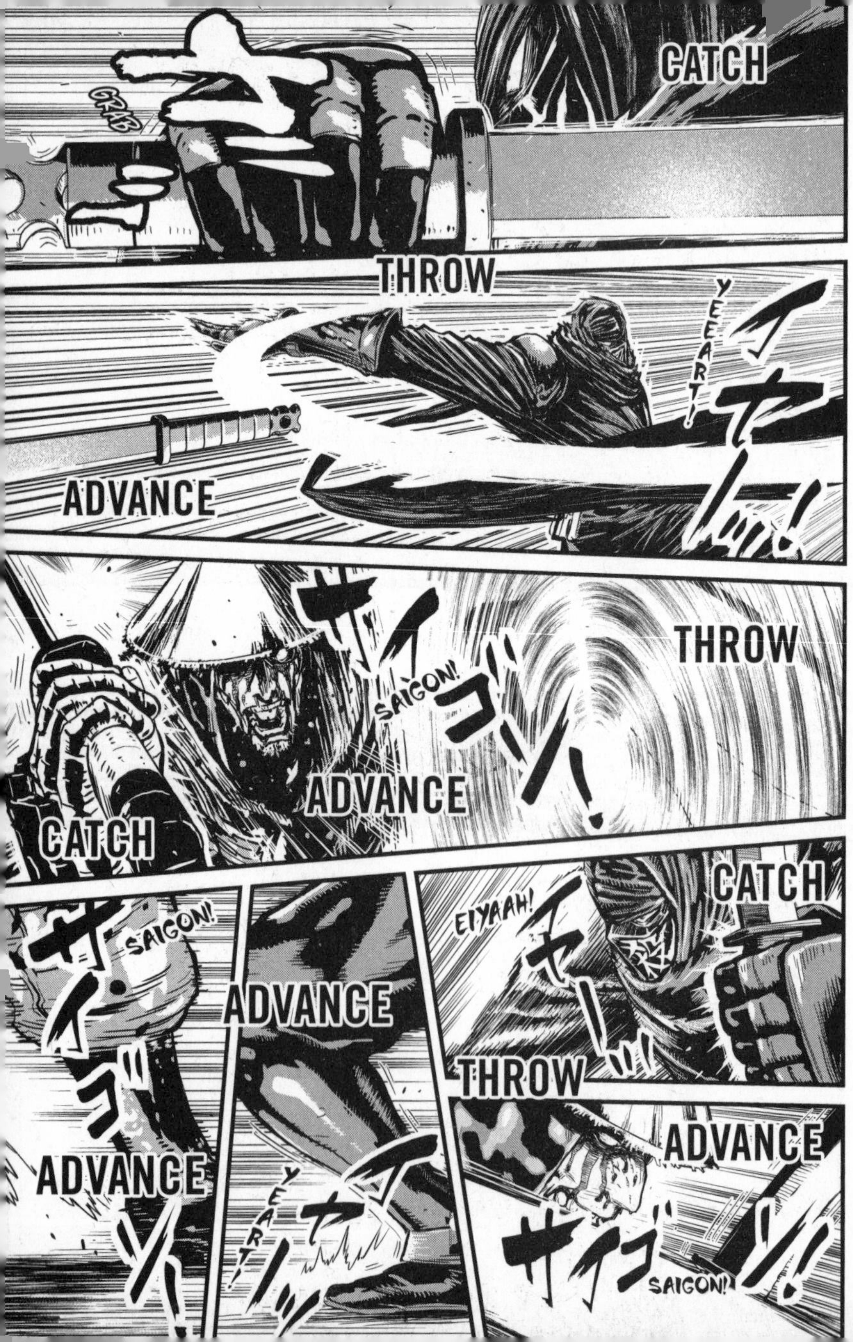

CATCH
GRAB
THROW
YEEART!
ADVANCE
THROW
SAIGON!
ADVANCE
CATCH
CATCH
EIYAAH!
THROW
ADVANCE
SAIGON!
ADVANCE
YEEART!
SAIGON!
ADVANCE

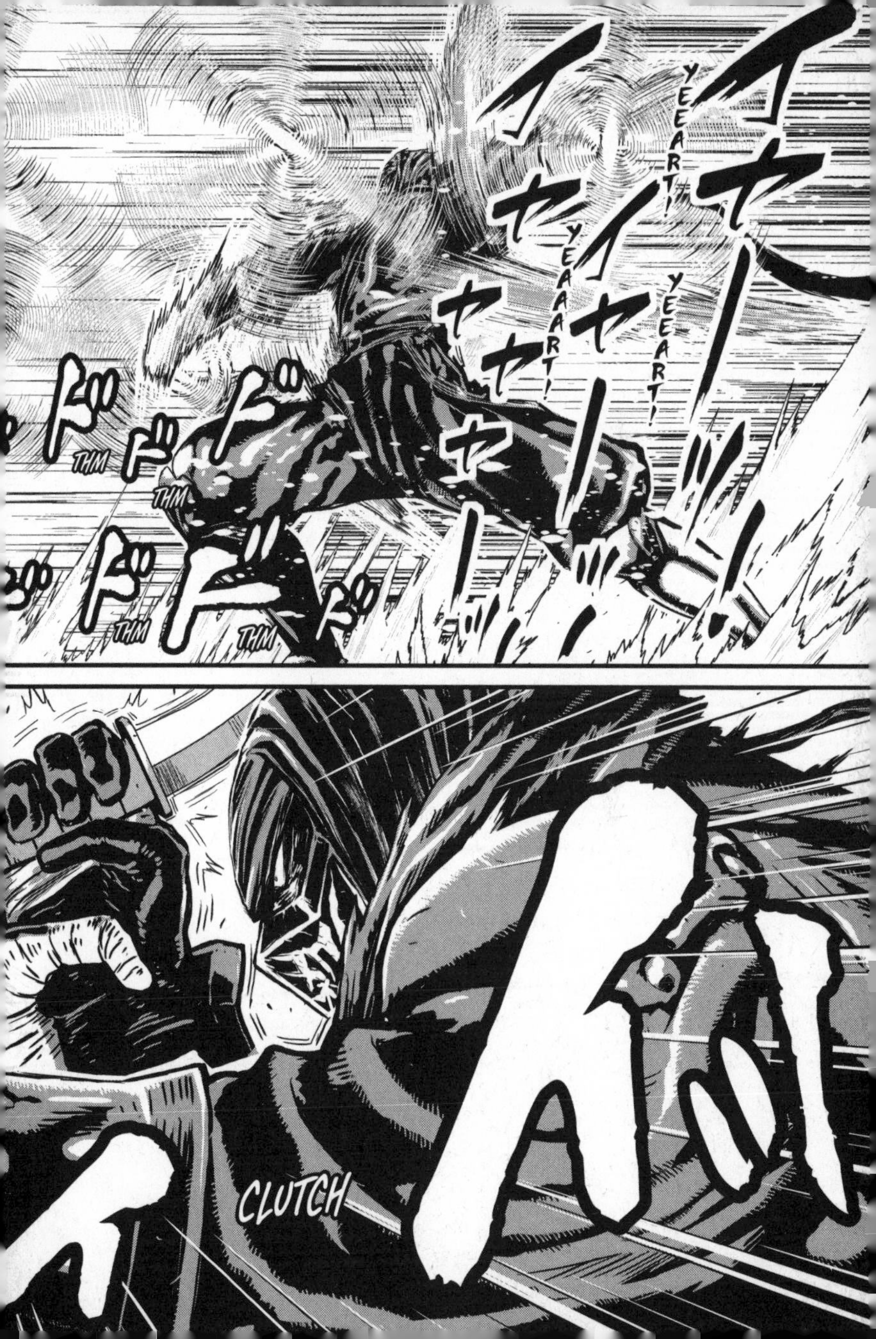
YEEART!
YEEART!
YEAAART!
THM
THM
THM
THM
CLUTCH

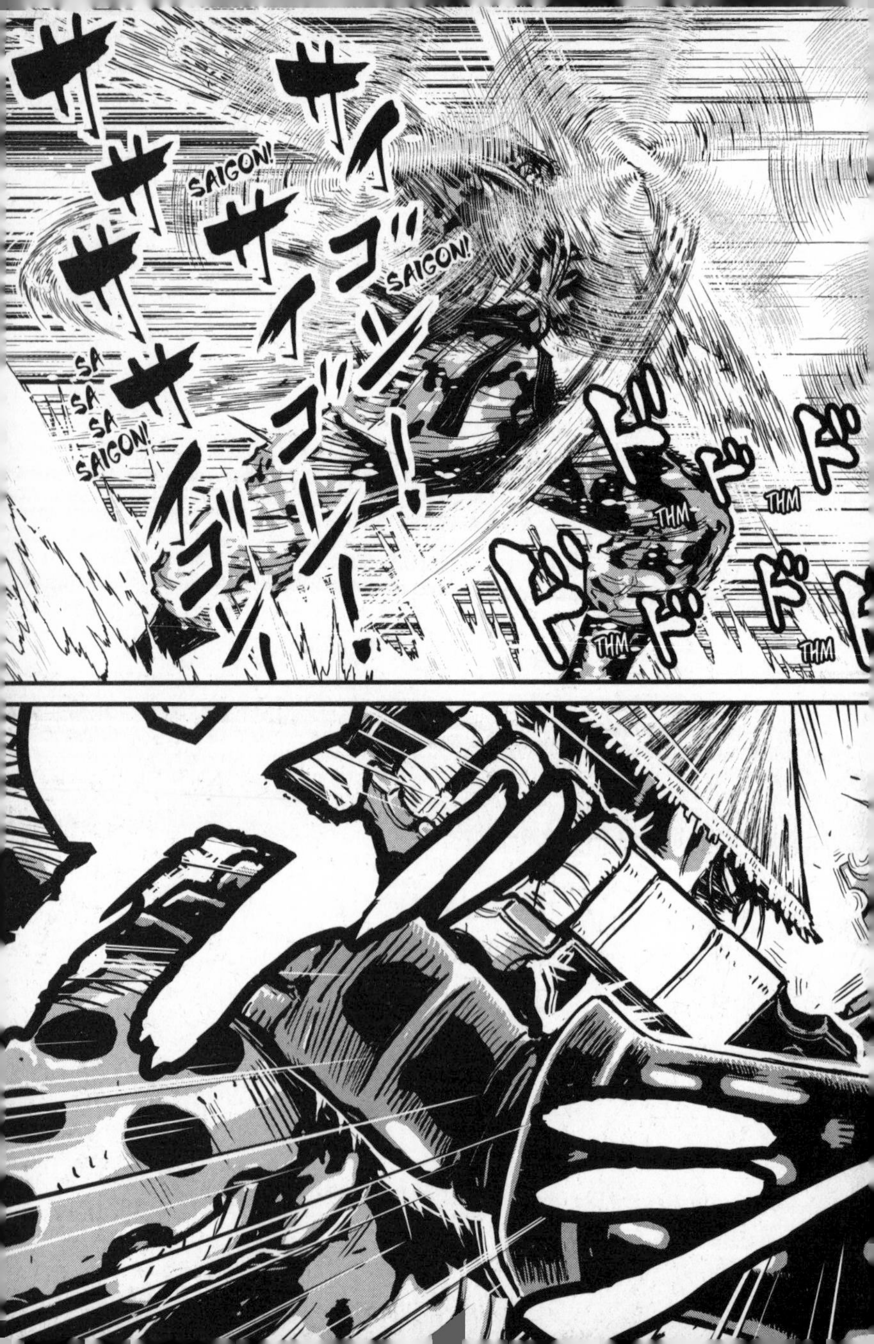
THM
THM
THM
THM
SAIGON!
SAIGON!
SA SA SA SAIGON!

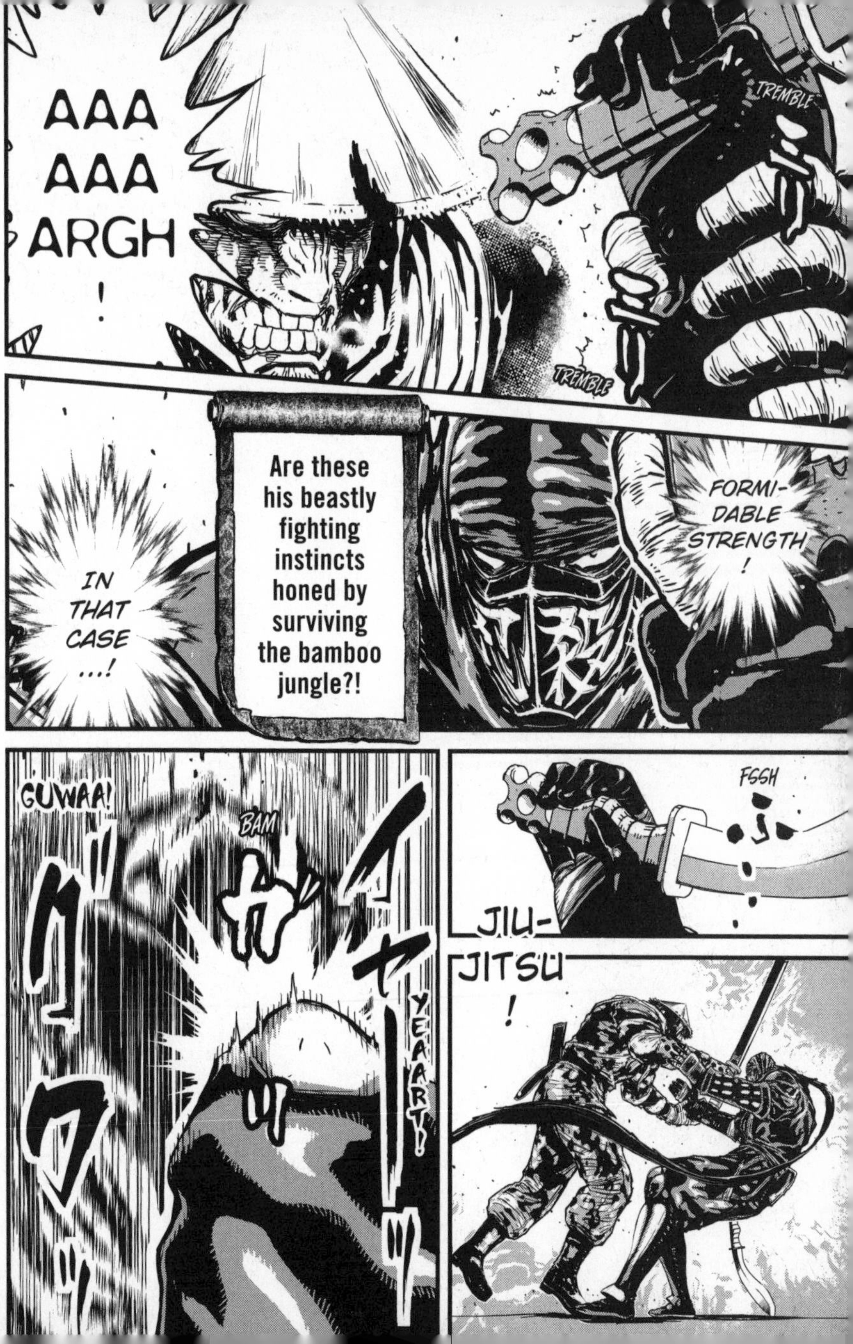
TREMBLE
AAA AAA ARGH !
TREMBLE
FORMI-DABLE STRENGTH !
Are these his beastly fighting instincts honed by surviving the bamboo jungle?!
IN THAT CASE ...!
FSSH
JIU-JITSU !
GUWAA!
BAM
YEAAART!

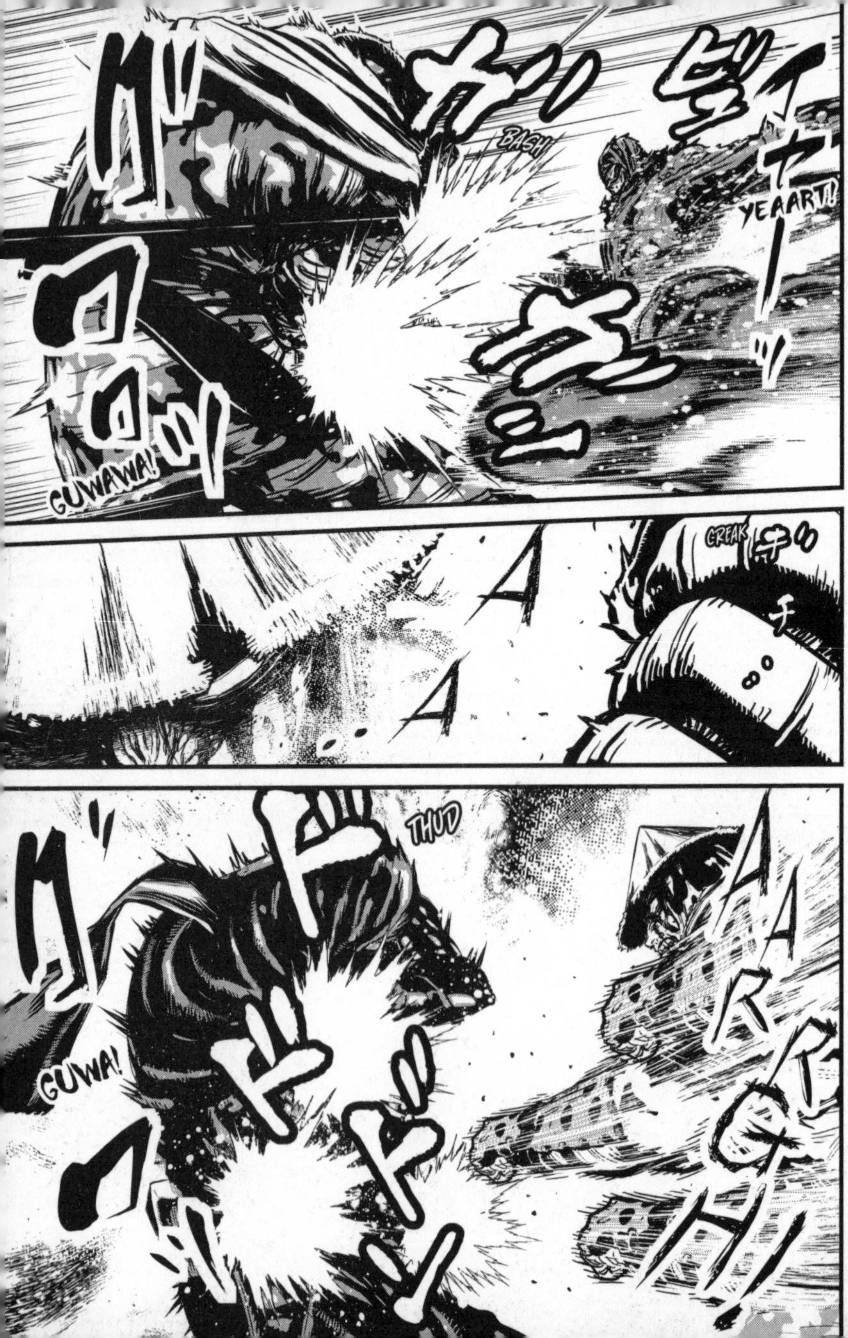
YEAART!!
BASH
GUWAWA!
CREAK
A
A
AAARRGHH!
THUD
GUWA!

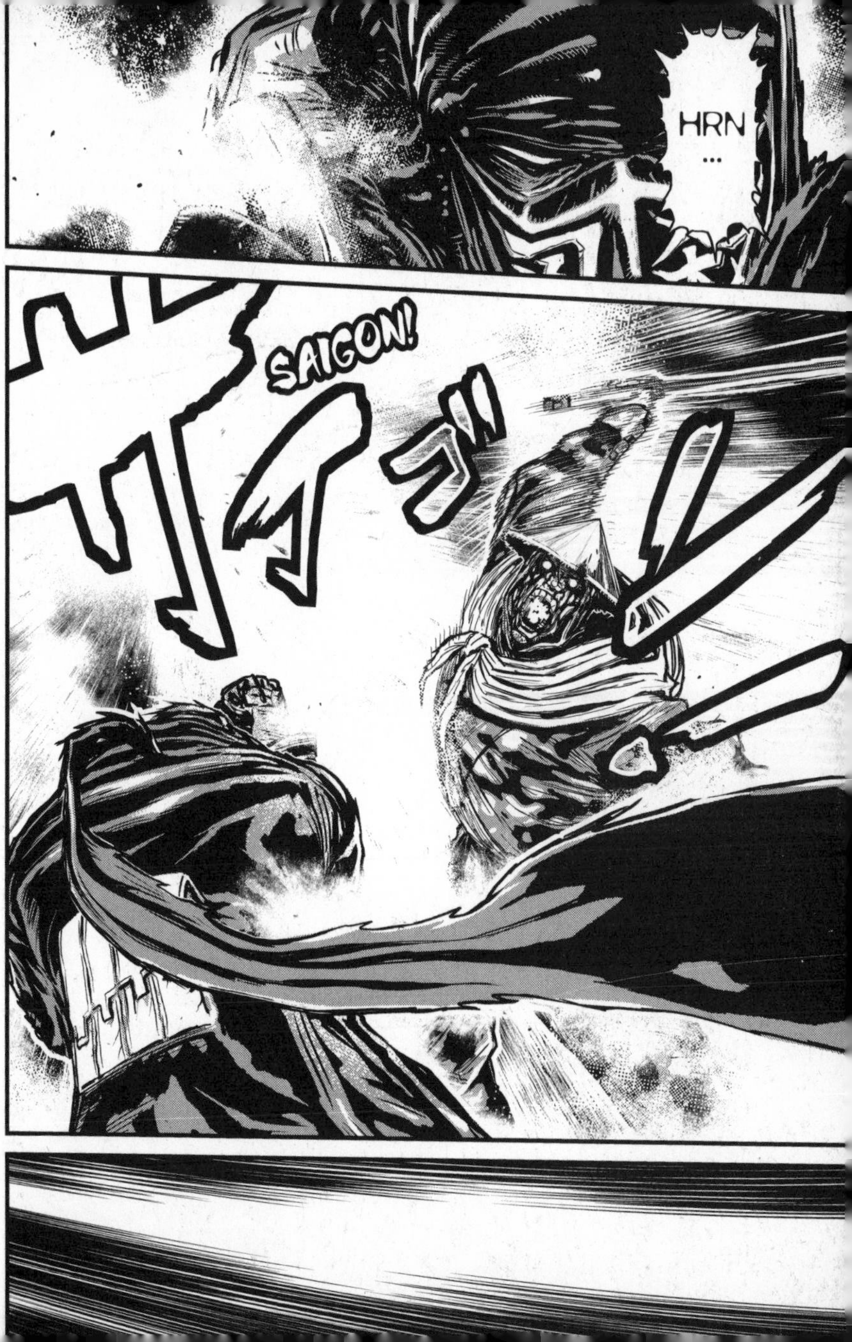
HRN
...
SAIGON!

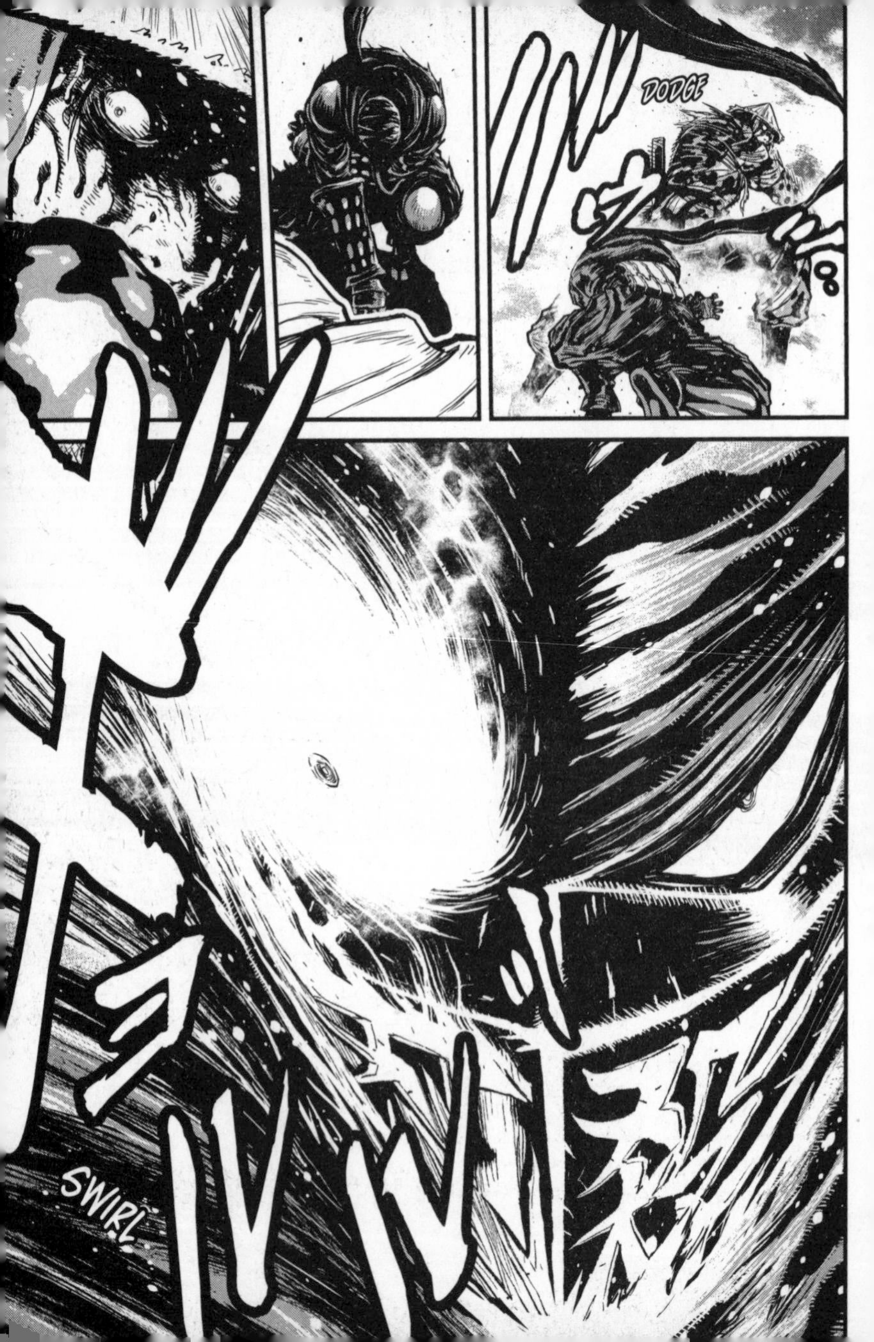
DODGE
SWIRL

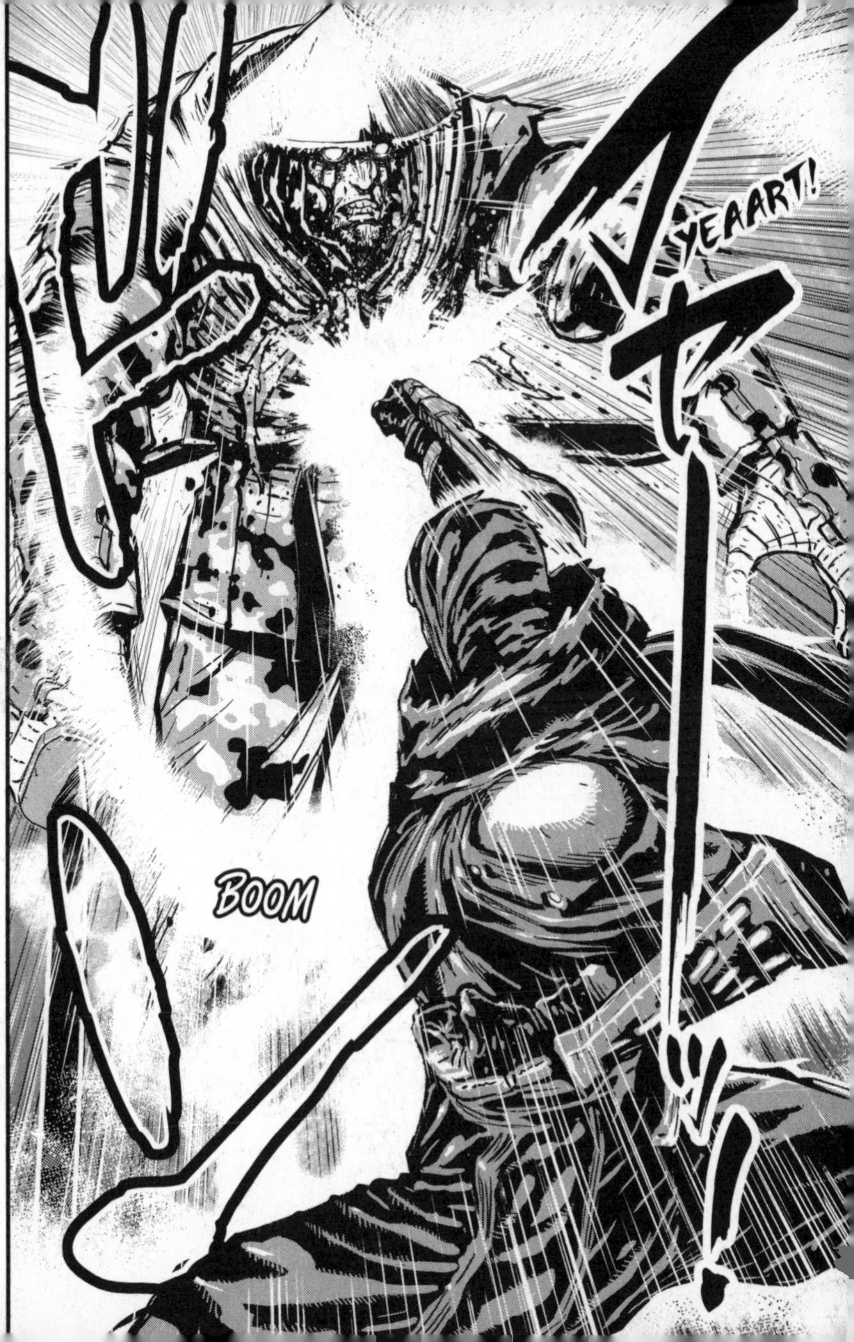
YEAART!
BOOM

THE TECHNIQUE THAT WAS UNLEASHED TOGETHER WITH THE UNEXPECTED ARRIVAL OF THE USHIMITSU HOUR....

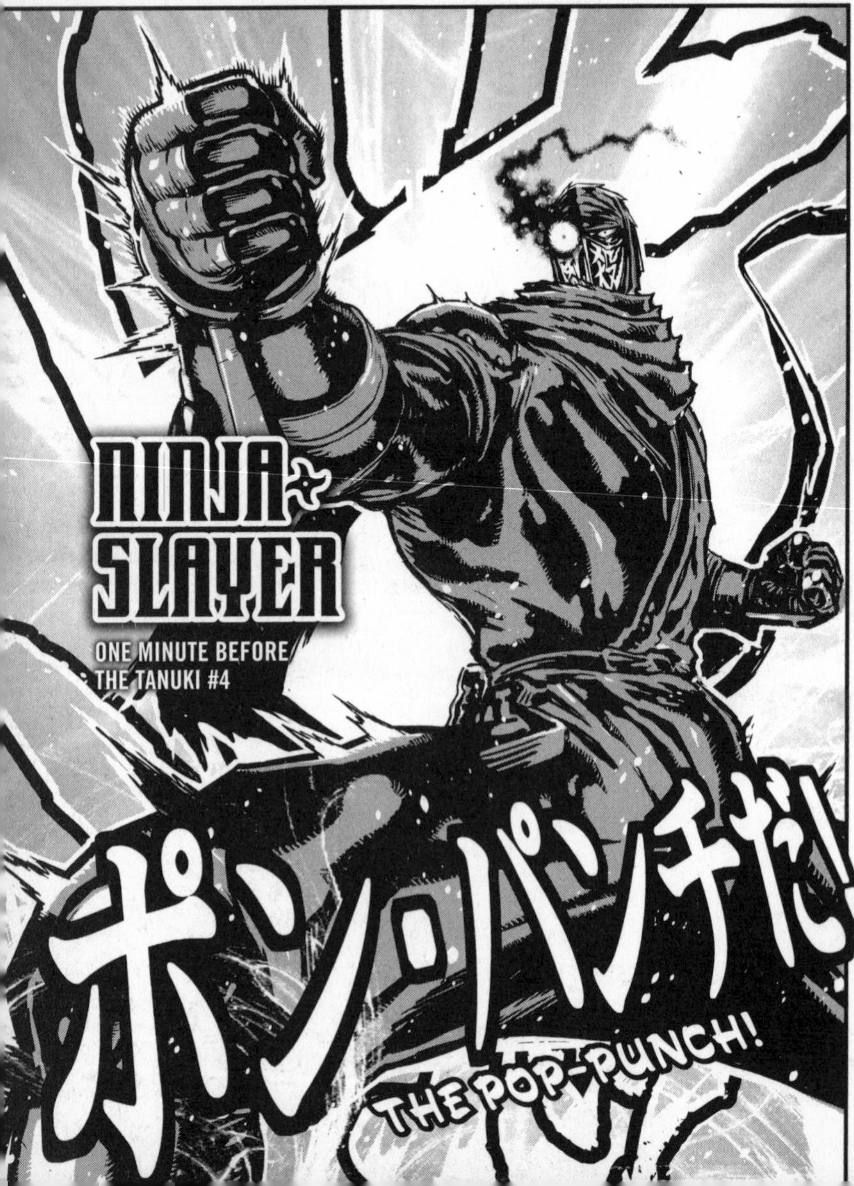
NINJA SLAYER
ONE MINUTE BEFORE THE TANUKI #4
THE POP-PUNCH!

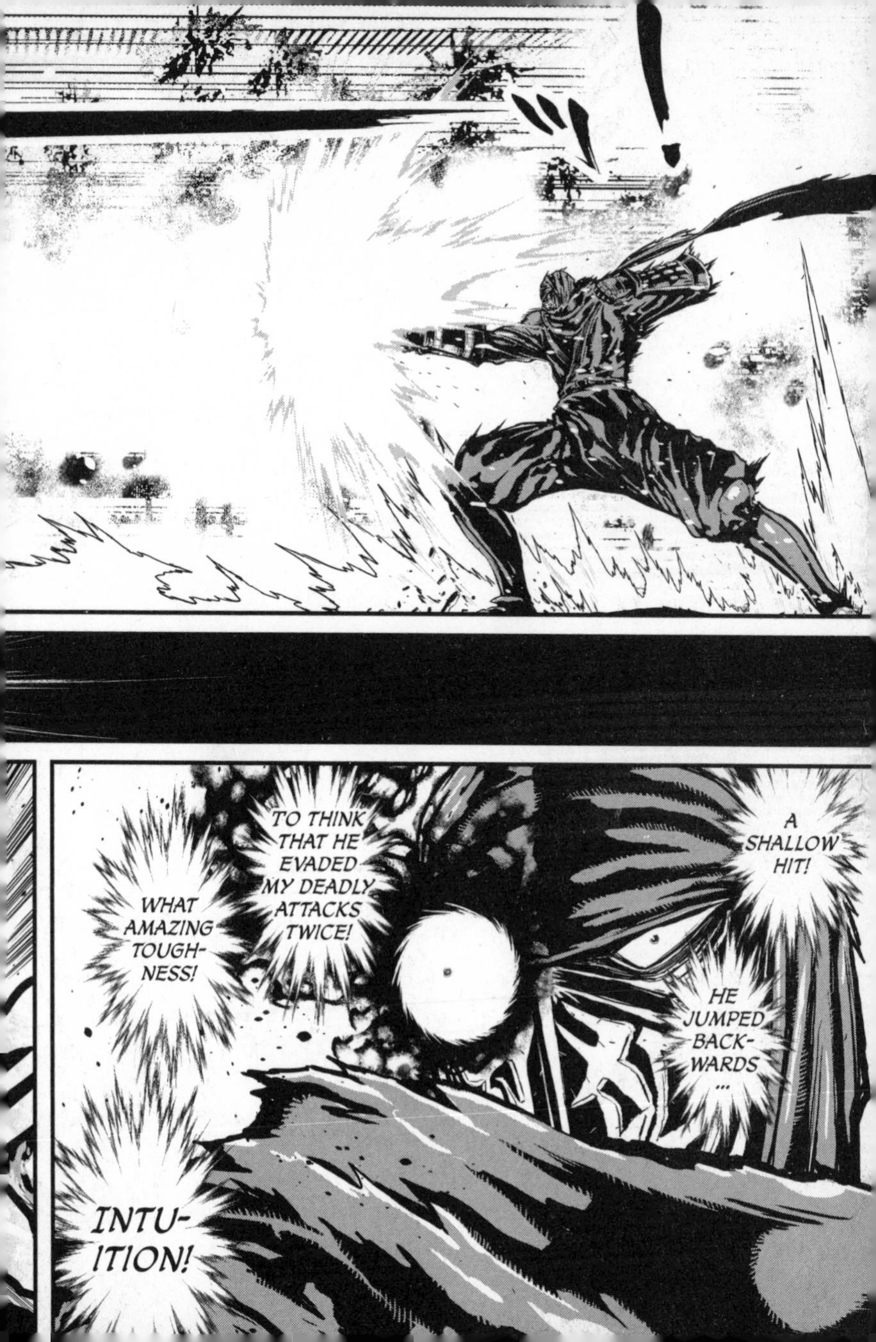
!
A SHALLOW HIT!
HE JUMPED BACKWARDS ...
TO THINK THAT HE EVADED MY DEADLY ATTACKS TWICE!
WHAT AMAZING TOUGHNESS!
INTUITION!

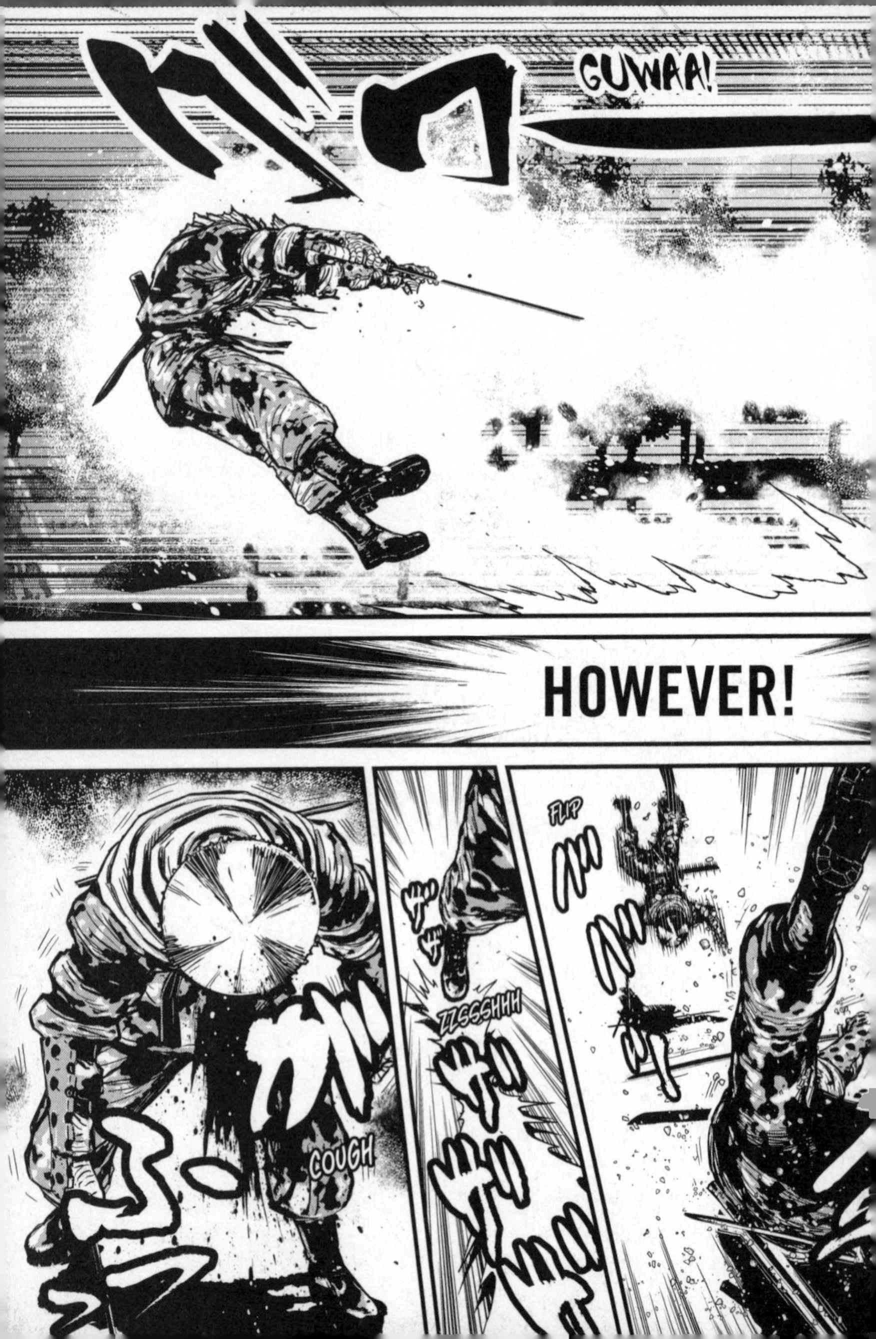
GUWAA!
HOWEVER!
FLIP
ZZSSSHHH
COUGH

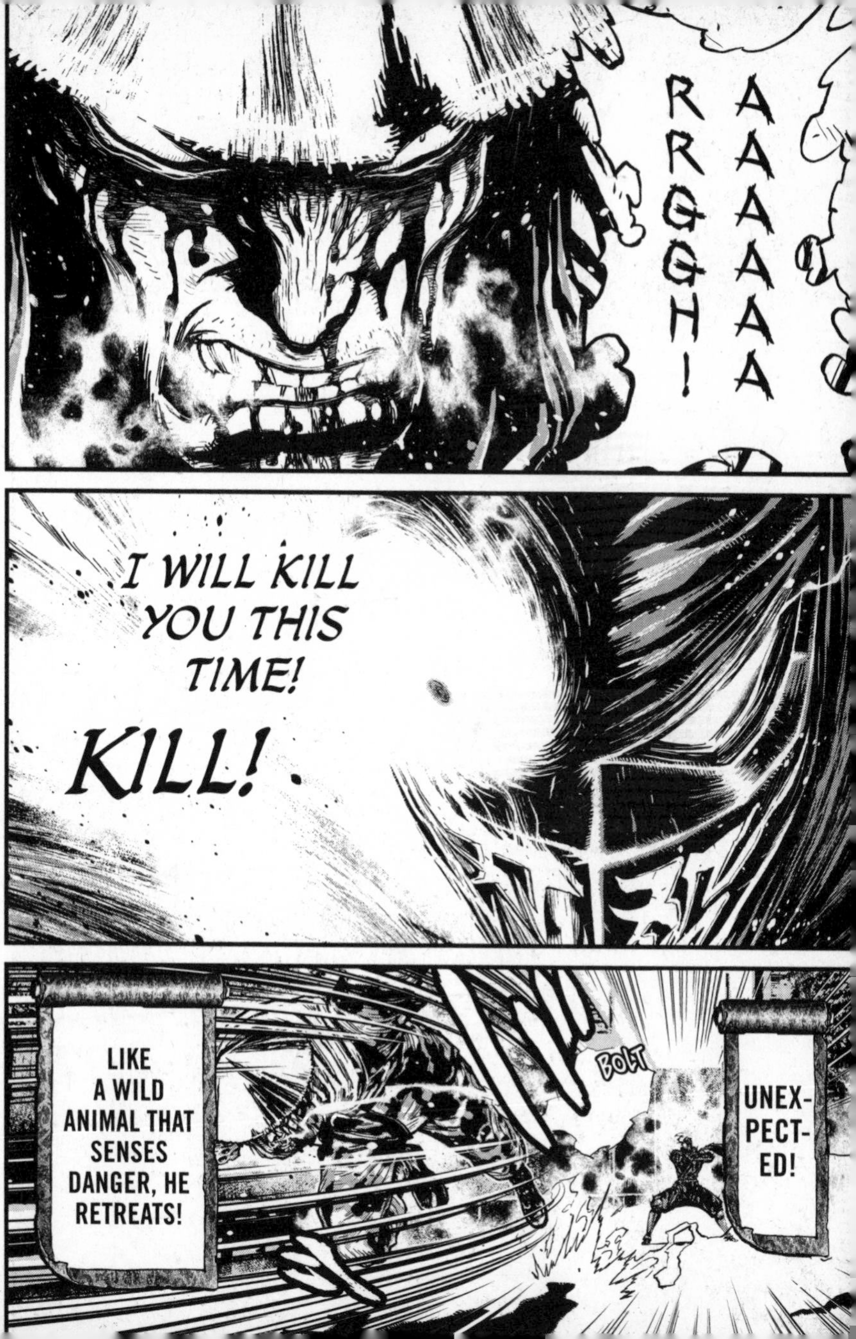

AAAAAAAA
RRGGH!
I WILL KILL YOU THIS TIME!
KILL!
UNEX-PECT-ED!
BOLT
LIKE A WILD ANIMAL THAT SENSES DANGER, HE RETREATS!

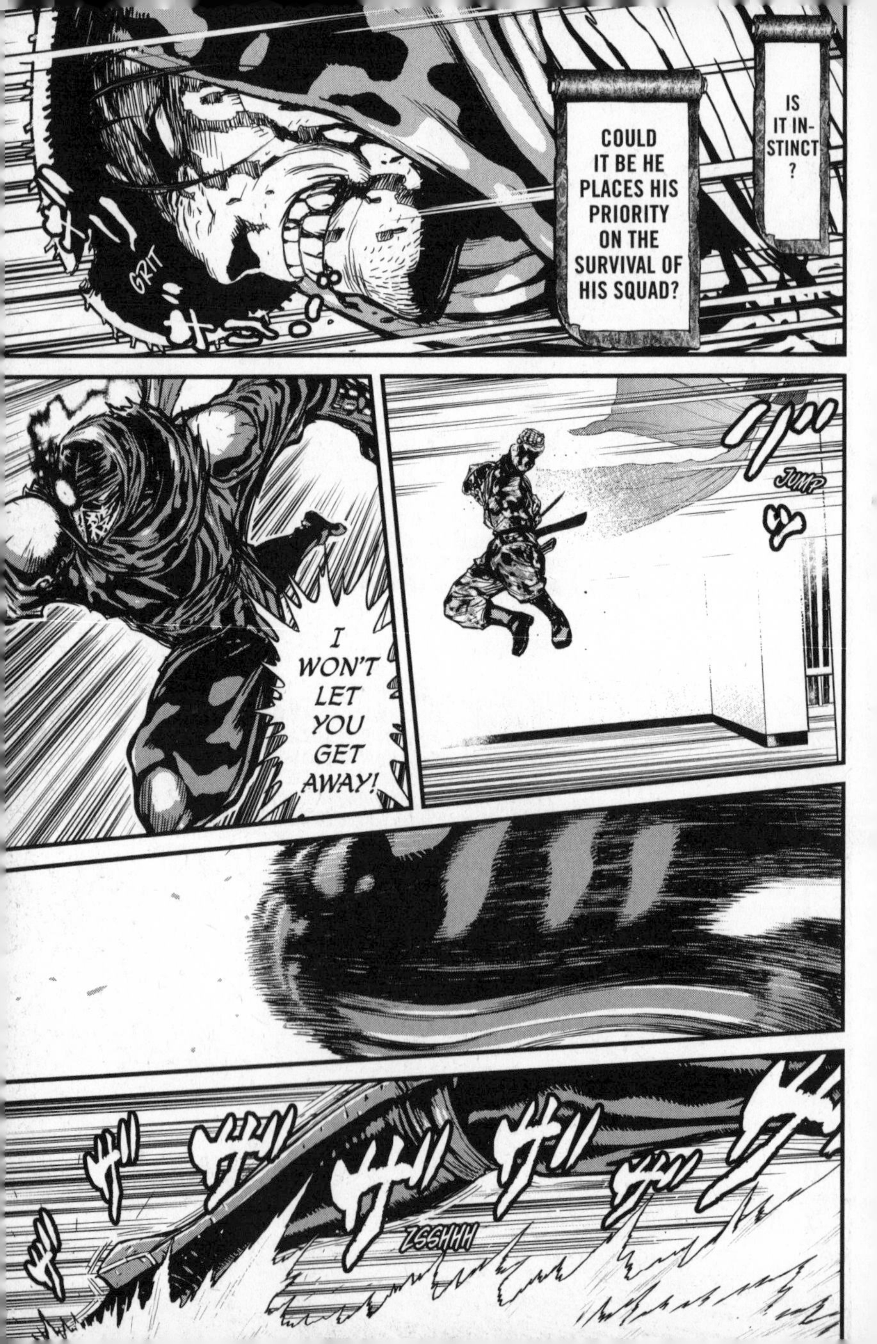
IS IT IN- STINCT ?
COULD IT BE HE PLACES HIS PRIORITY ON THE SURVIVAL OF HIS SQUAD?
GRIT
JUMP
I WON'T LET YOU GET AWAY!
ZSSHHH

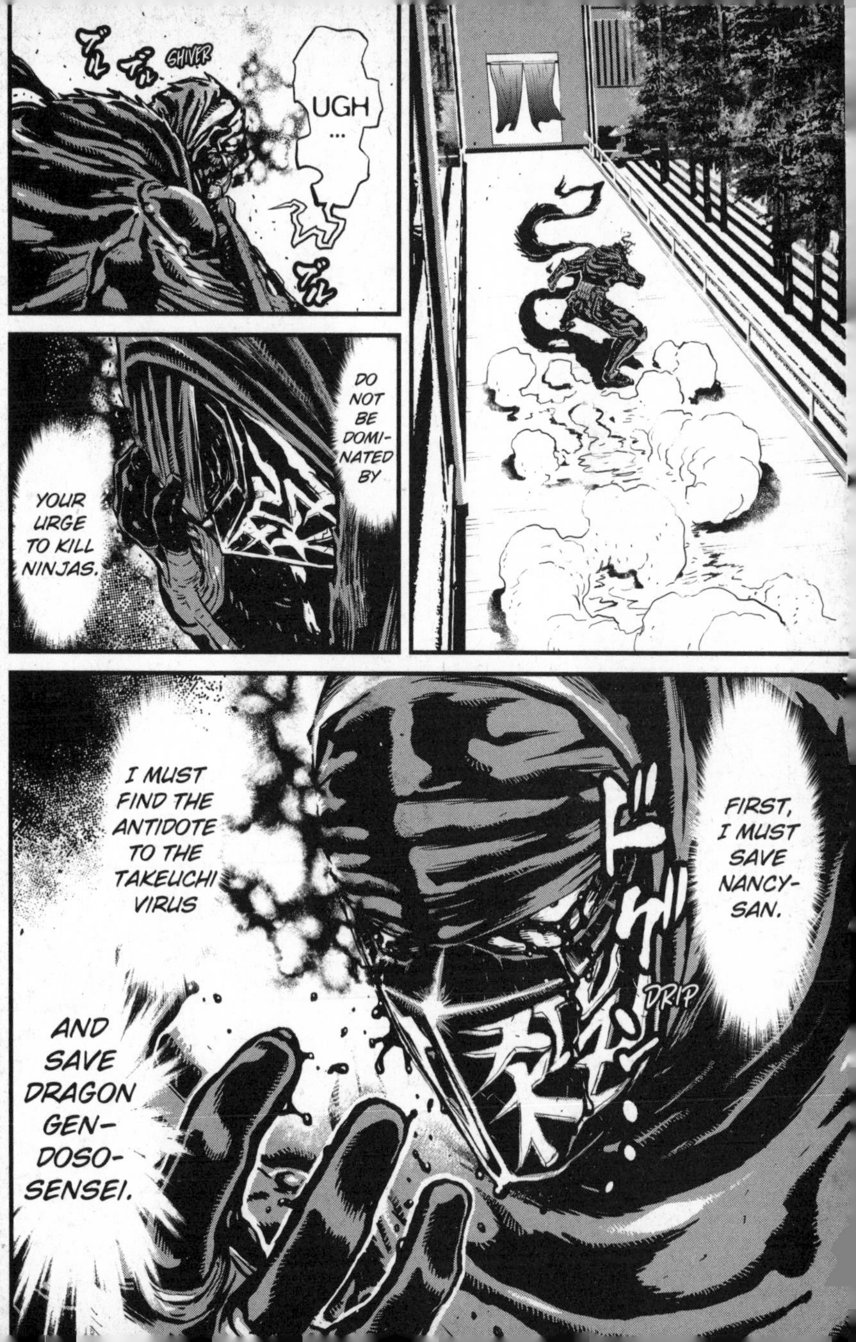
SHIVER
UGH ...
DO NOT BE DOMINATED BY
YOUR URGE TO KILL NINJAS.
FIRST, I MUST SAVE NANCY-SAN.
DRIP
I MUST FIND THE ANTIDOTE TO THE TAKEUCHI VIRUS
AND SAVE DRAGON GEN-DOSO-SENSEI.

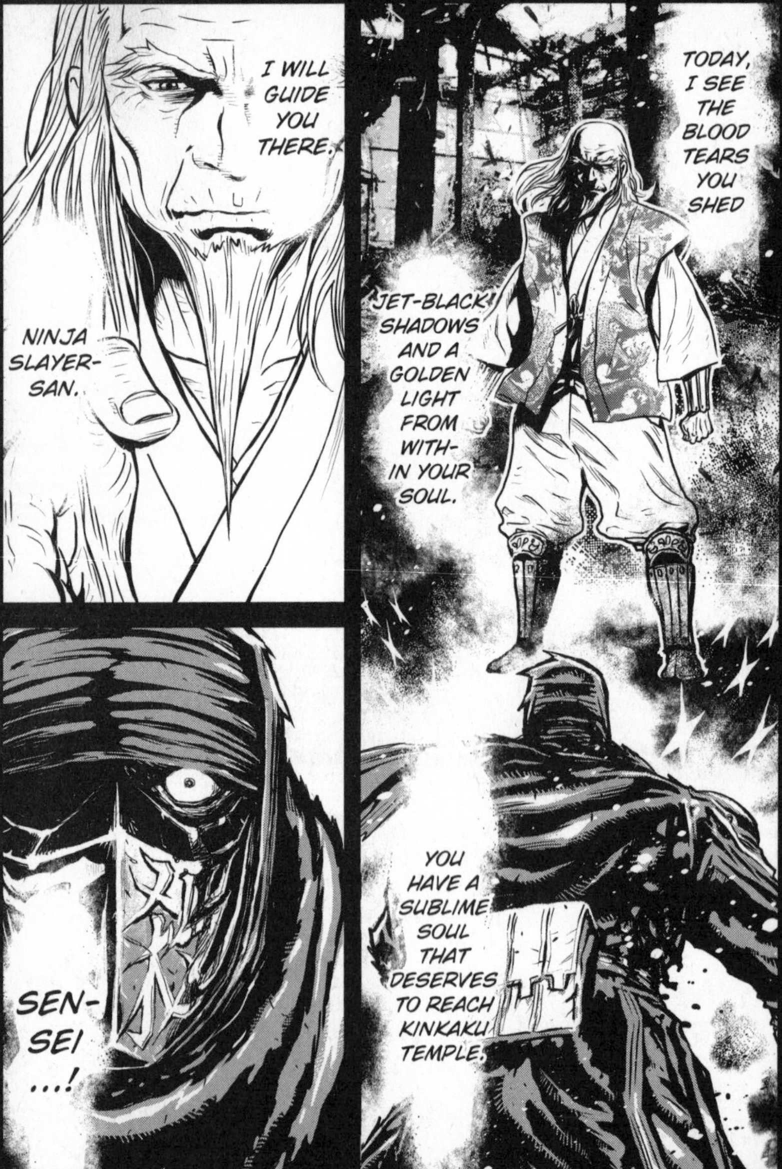
TODAY, I SEE THE BLOOD TEARS YOU SHED
JET-BLACK SHADOWS AND A GOLDEN LIGHT FROM WITHIN YOUR SOUL.
YOU HAVE A SUBLIME SOUL THAT DESERVES TO REACH KINKAKU TEMPLE.
I WILL GUIDE YOU THERE.
NINJA SLAYER-SAN.
SEN-SEI ...!

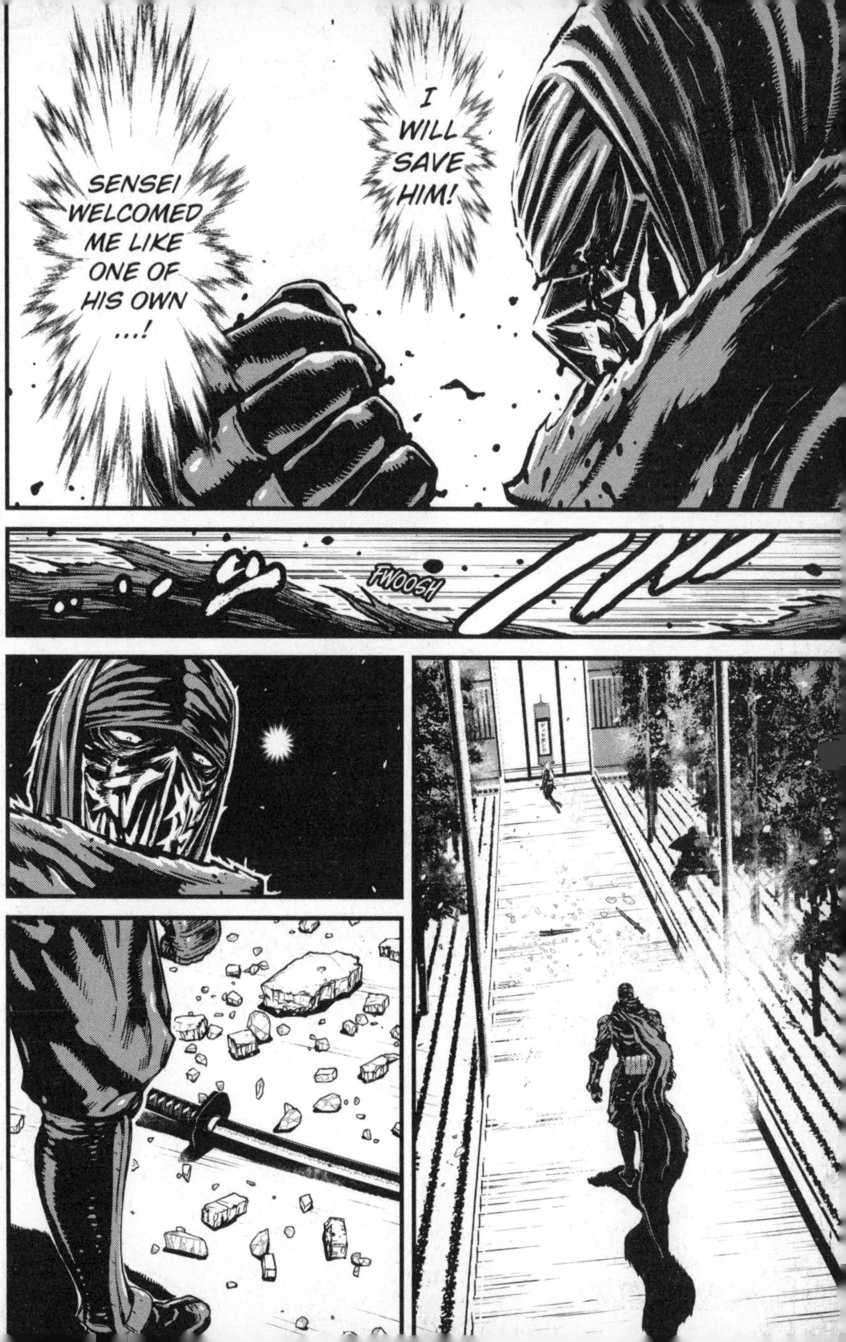
I WILL SAVE HIM!
SENSEI WELCOMED ME LIKE ONE OF HIS OWN ...!
FWOOSH

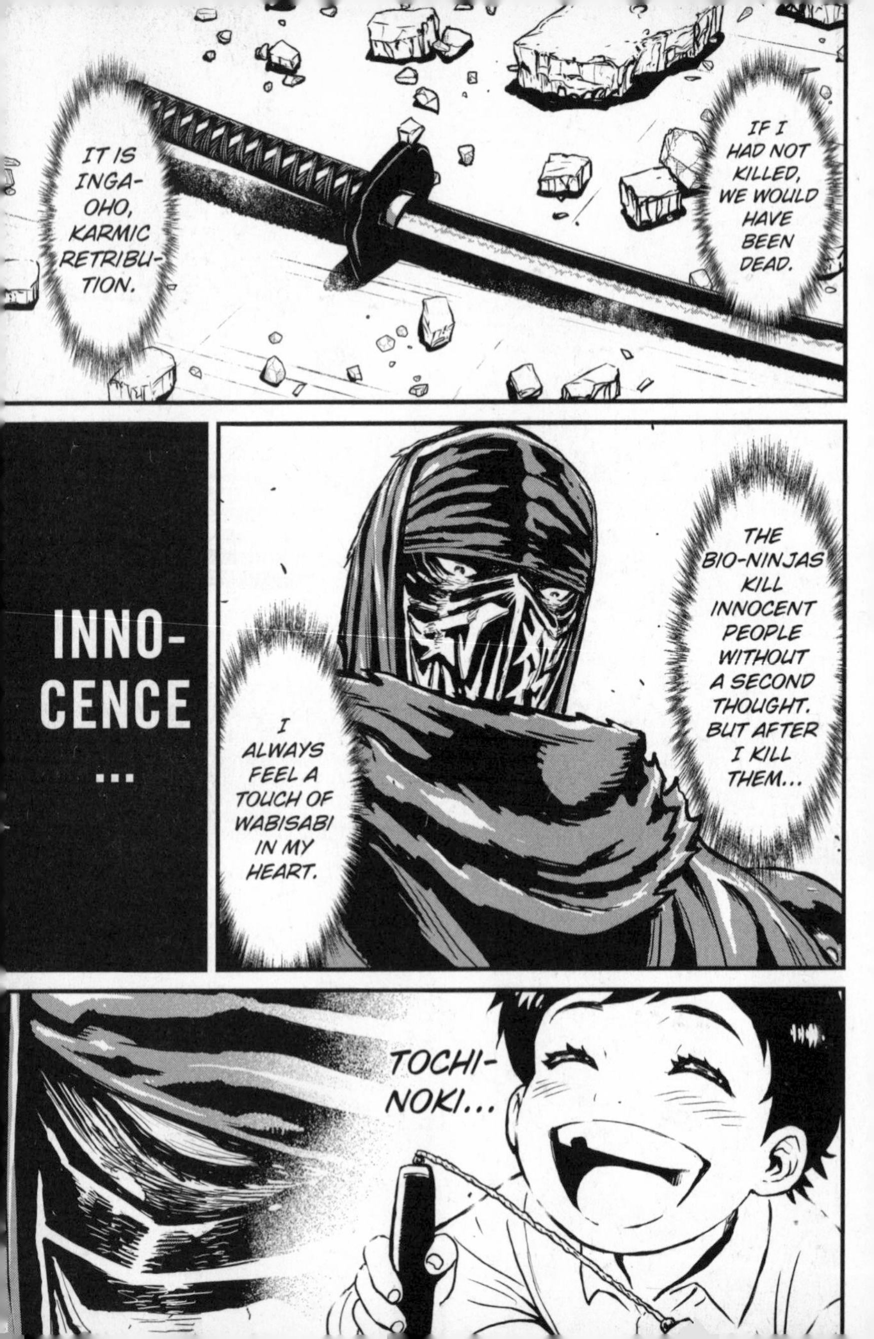
IF I HAD NOT KILLED, WE WOULD HAVE BEEN DEAD.
IT IS INGA-OHO, KARMIC RETRIBU-TION.
THE BIO-NINJAS KILL INNOCENT PEOPLE WITHOUT A SECOND THOUGHT. BUT AFTER I KILL THEM...
I ALWAYS FEEL A TOUCH OF WABISABI IN MY HEART.
INNO-CENCE ...
TOCHI-NOKI...

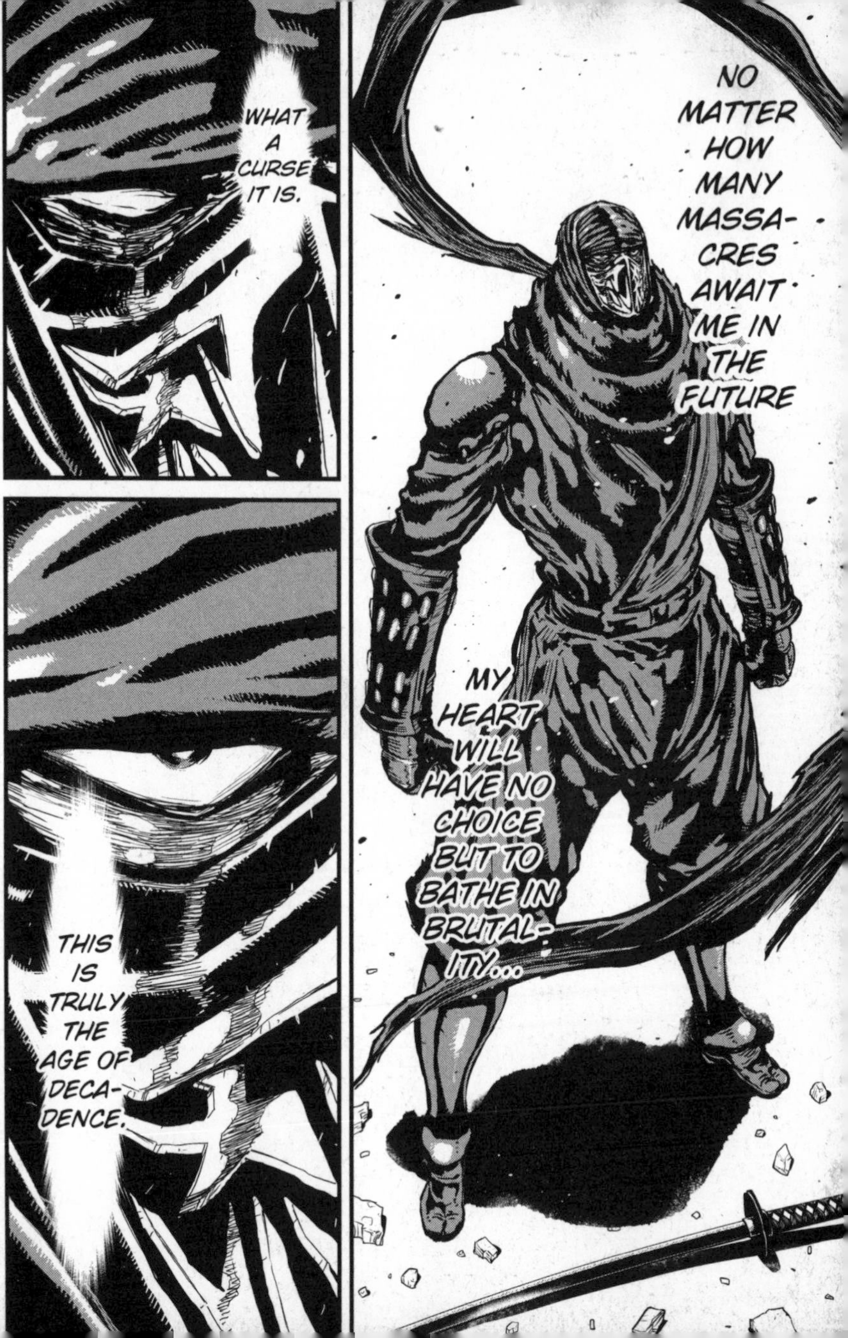
NO MATTER HOW MANY MASSA-CRES AWAIT ME IN THE FUTURE
MY HEART WILL HAVE NO CHOICE BUT TO BATHE IN BRUTAL-ITY...
WHAT A CURSE IT IS.
THIS IS TRULY THE AGE OF DECA-DENCE.

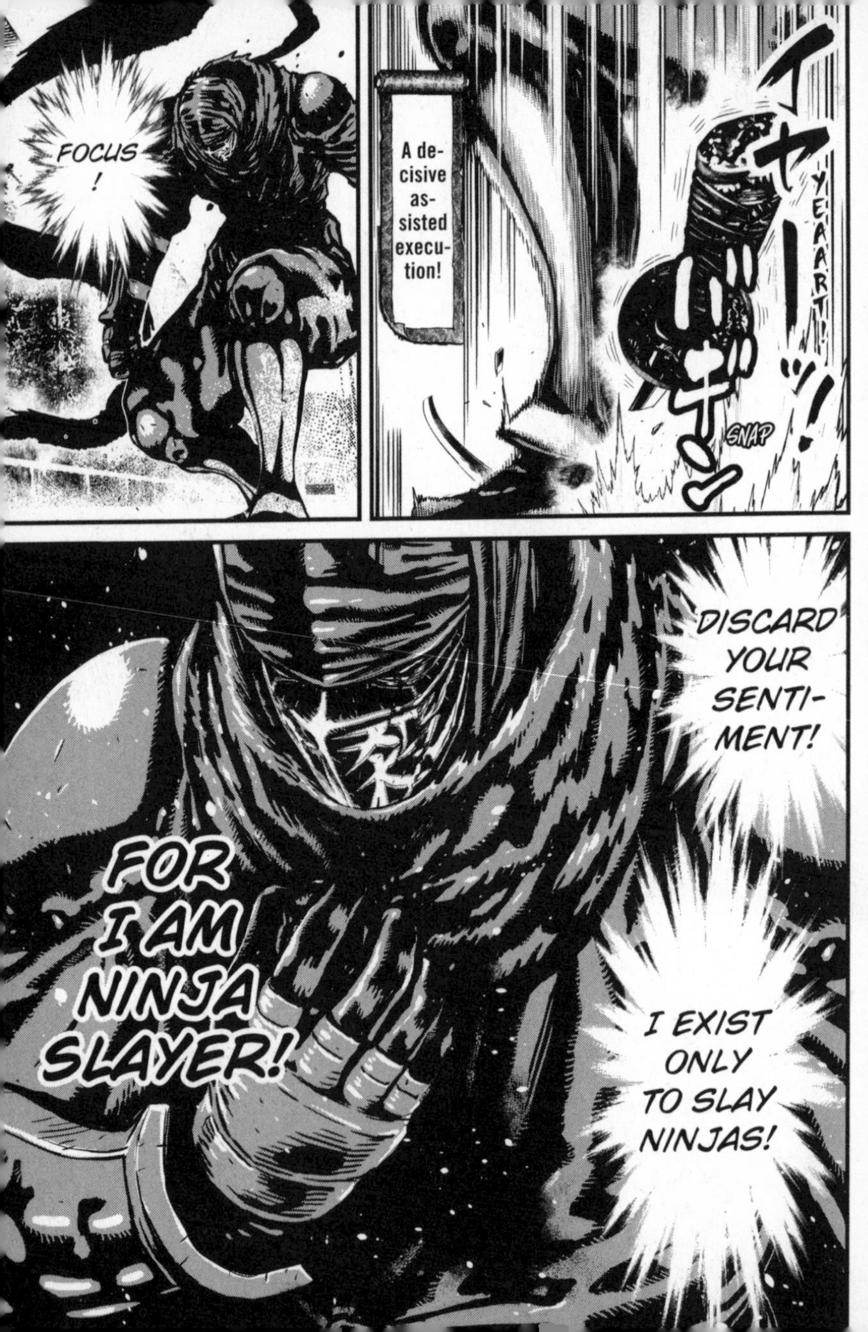
YEAART!
A decisive assisted execution!
SNAP
FOCUS!
DISCARD YOUR SENTIMENT!
I EXIST ONLY TO SLAY NINJAS!
FOR I AM NINJA SLAYER!

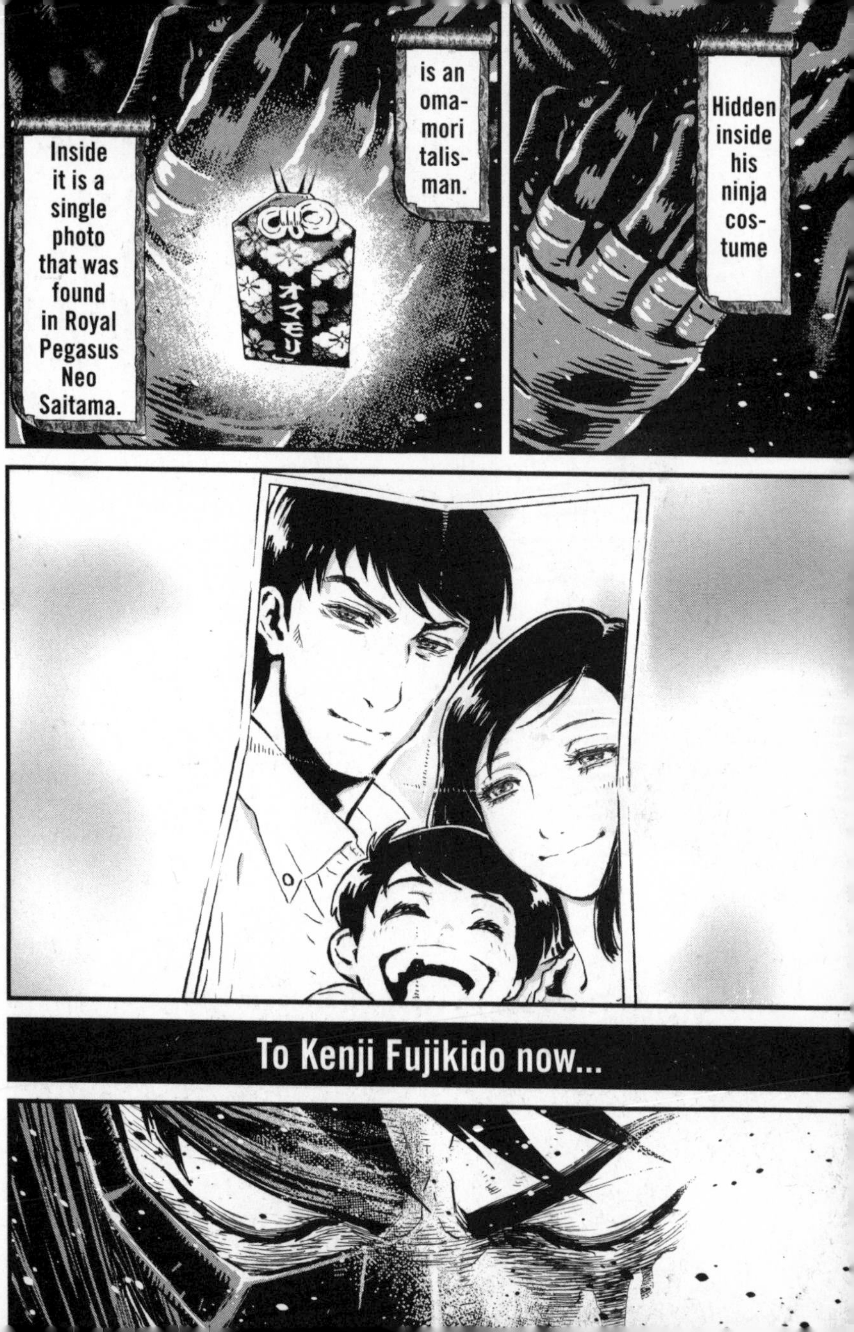
Hidden inside his ninja costume
is an omamori talisman.
Inside it is a single photo that was found in Royal Pegasus Neo Saitama.
オマモリ
To Kenji Fujikido now...

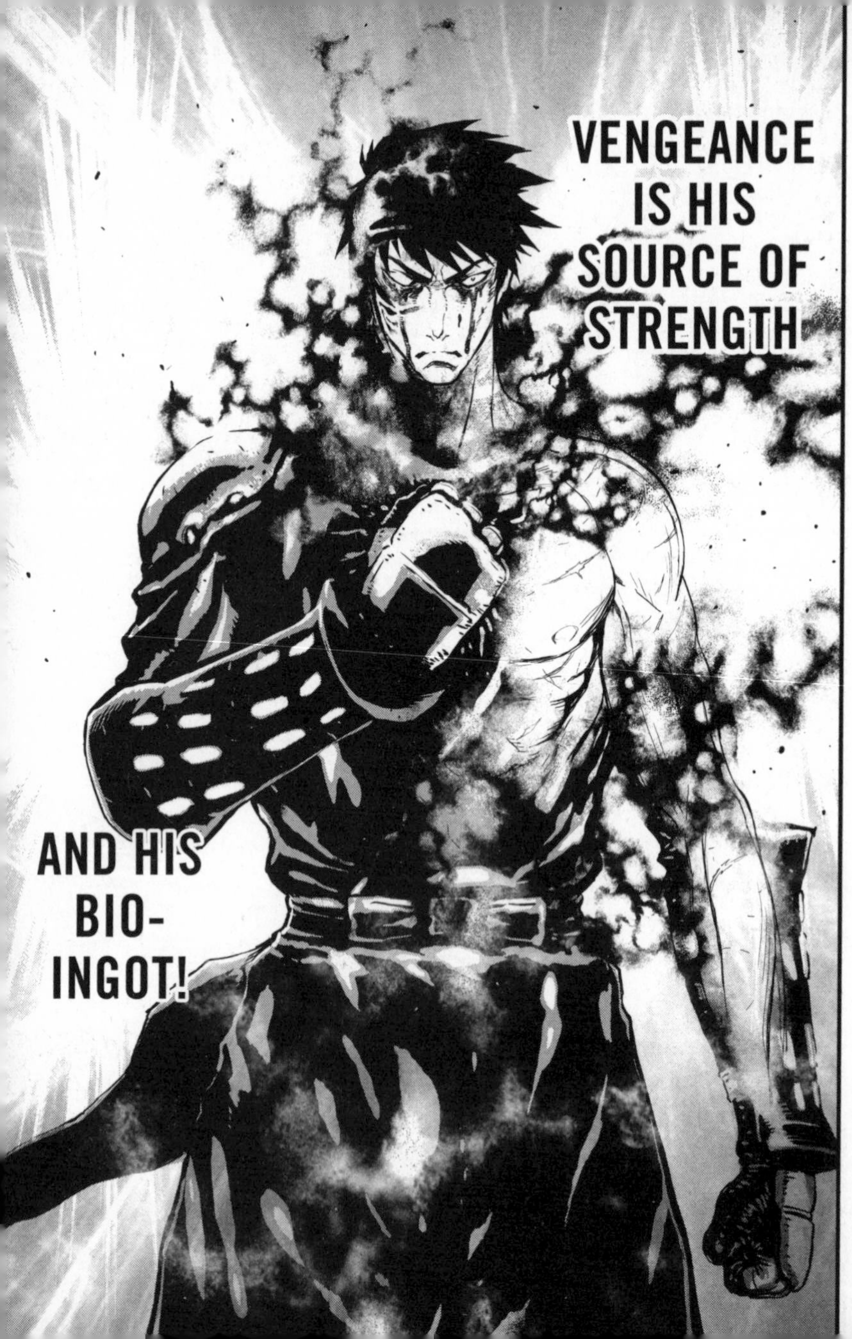
VENGEANCE IS HIS SOURCE OF STRENGTH
AND HIS BIO-INGOT!

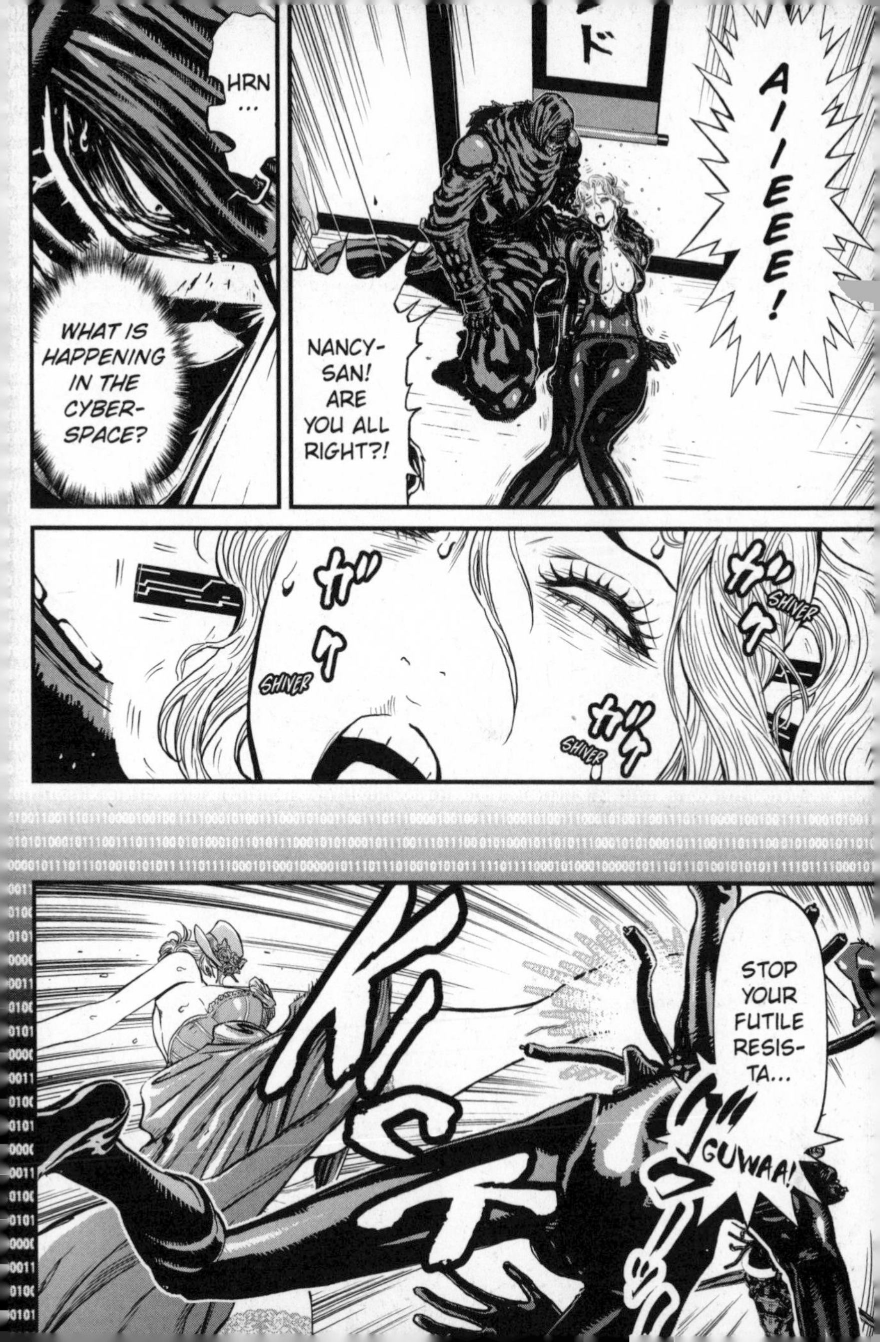
AIIEEE!
NANCY-SAN! ARE YOU ALL RIGHT?!
HRN ...
WHAT IS HAPPENING IN THE CYBER-SPACE?
SHIVER
SHIVER
SHIVER
STOP YOUR FUTILE RESIS-TA...
GUWAA!

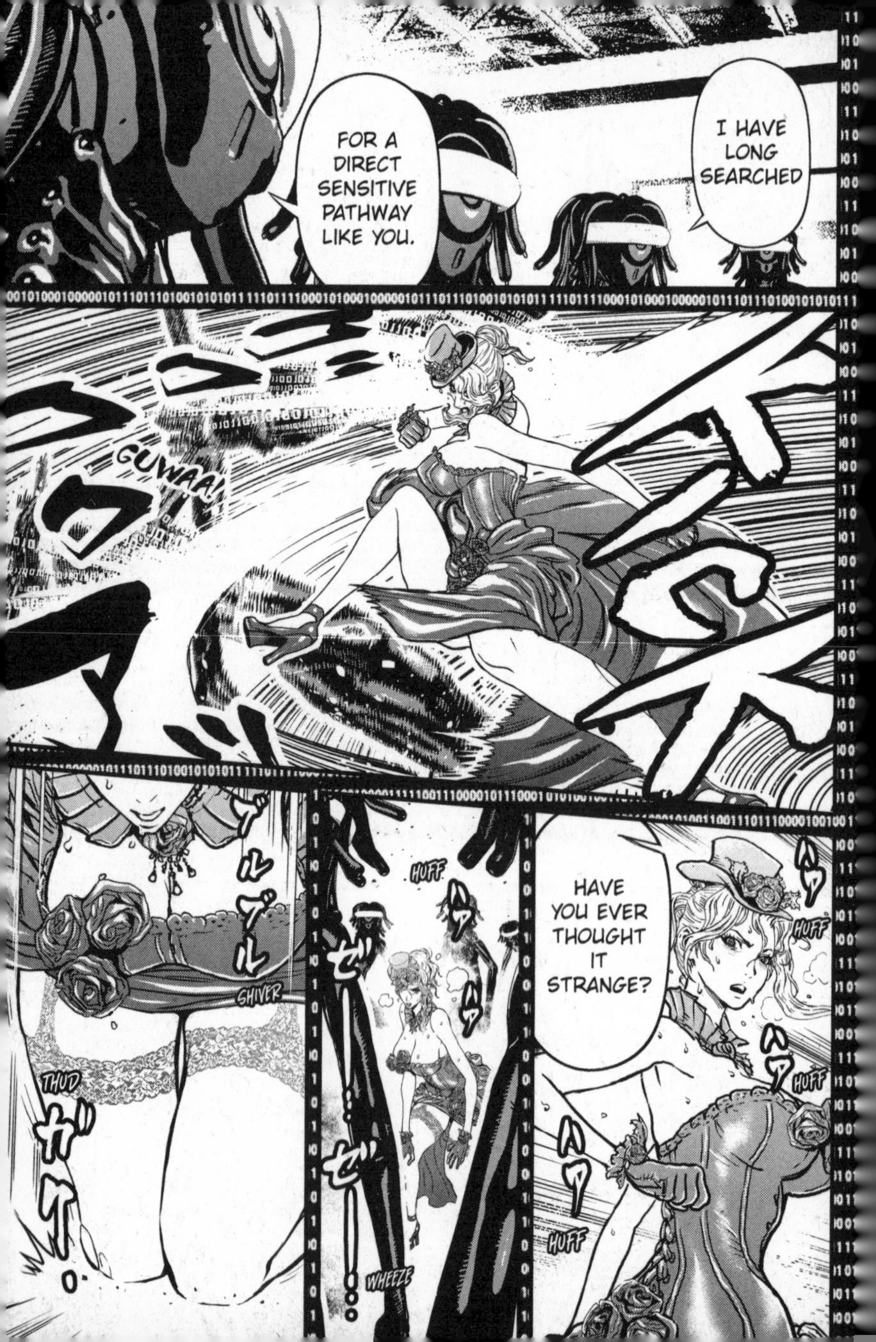
I HAVE LONG SEARCHED
FOR A DIRECT SENSITIVE PATHWAY LIKE YOU.
GUWAA!
HUFF
HAVE YOU EVER THOUGHT IT STRANGE?
HUFF
HUFF
HUFF
HUFF
WHEEZE
SHIVER
THUD

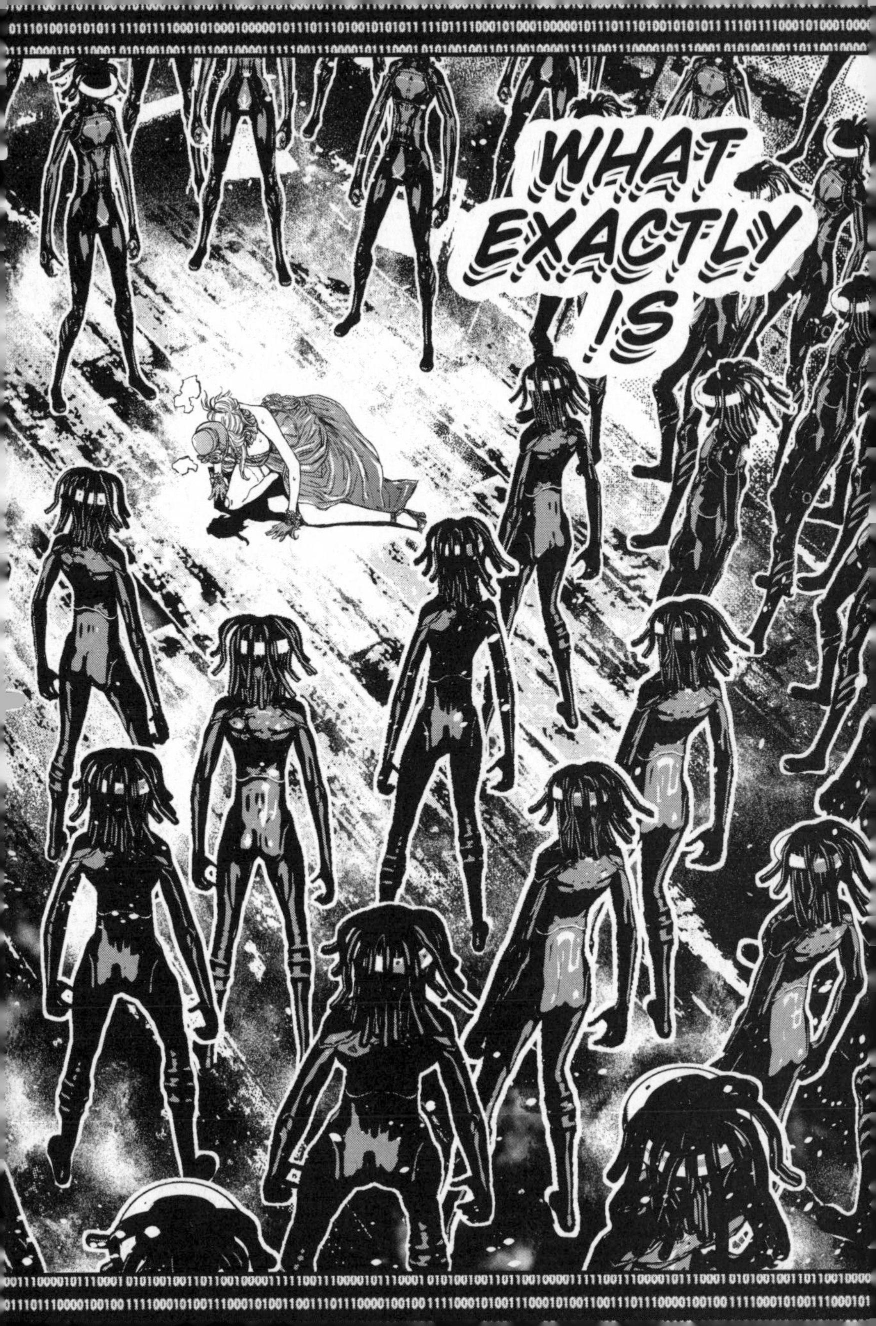
WHAT EXACTLY IS !

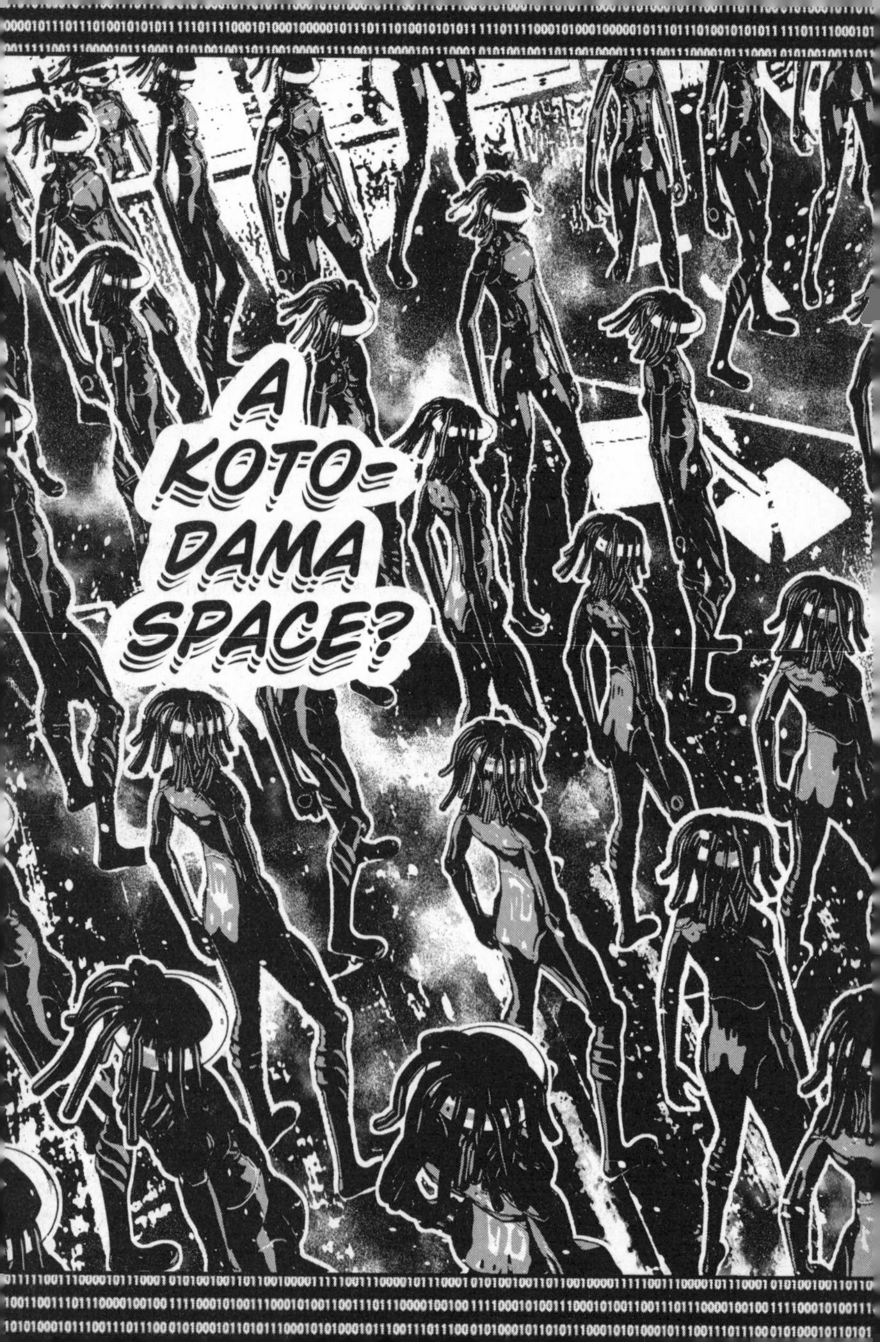
A KOTO-DAMA SPACE?

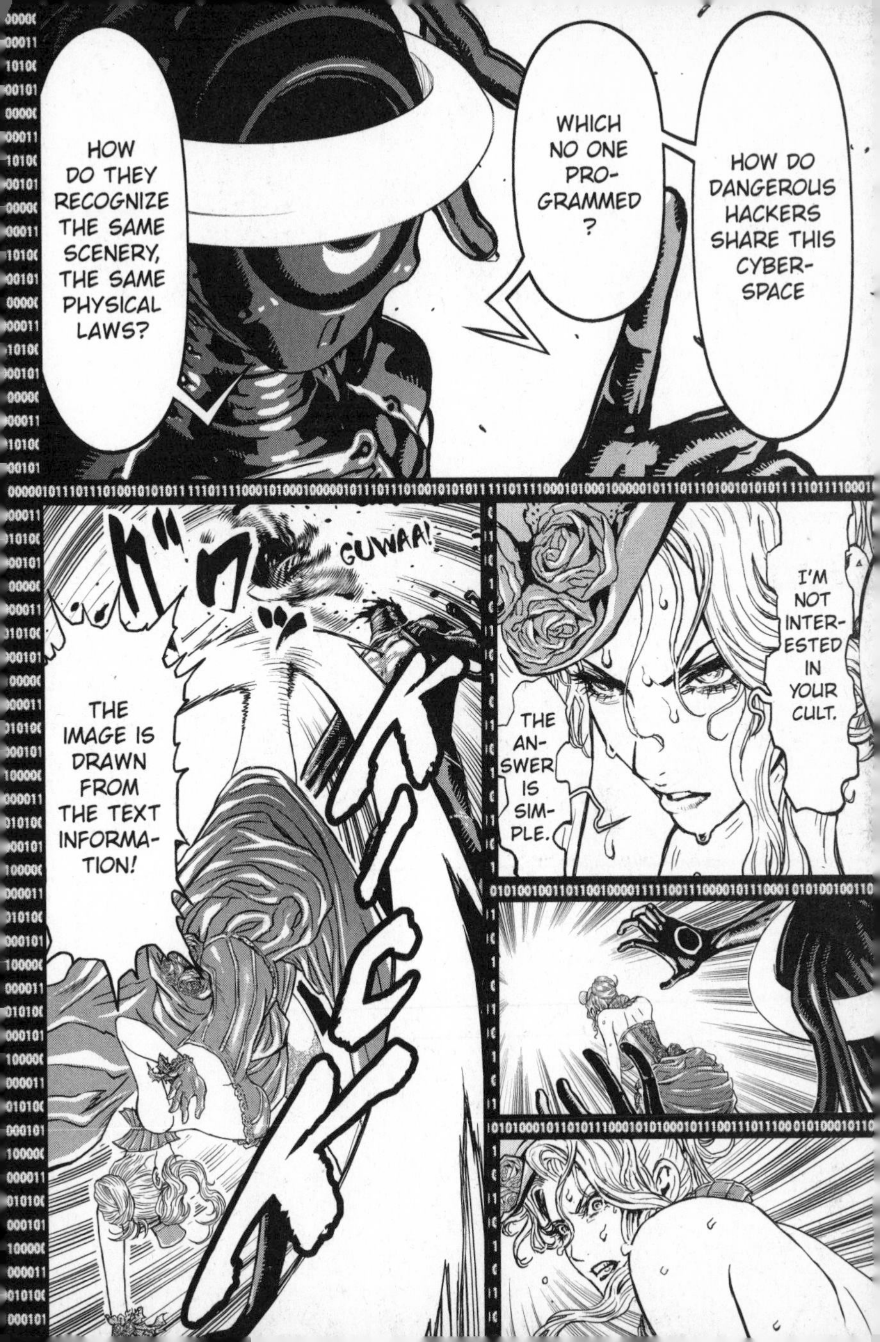
HOW DO DANGEROUS HACKERS SHARE THIS CYBER-SPACE
WHICH NO ONE PRO-GRAMMED ?
HOW DO THEY RECOGNIZE THE SAME SCENERY, THE SAME PHYSICAL LAWS?
I'M NOT INTER-ESTED IN YOUR CULT.
THE AN-SWER IS SIM-PLE.
GUWAA!
THE IMAGE IS DRAWN FROM THE TEXT INFORMA-TION!

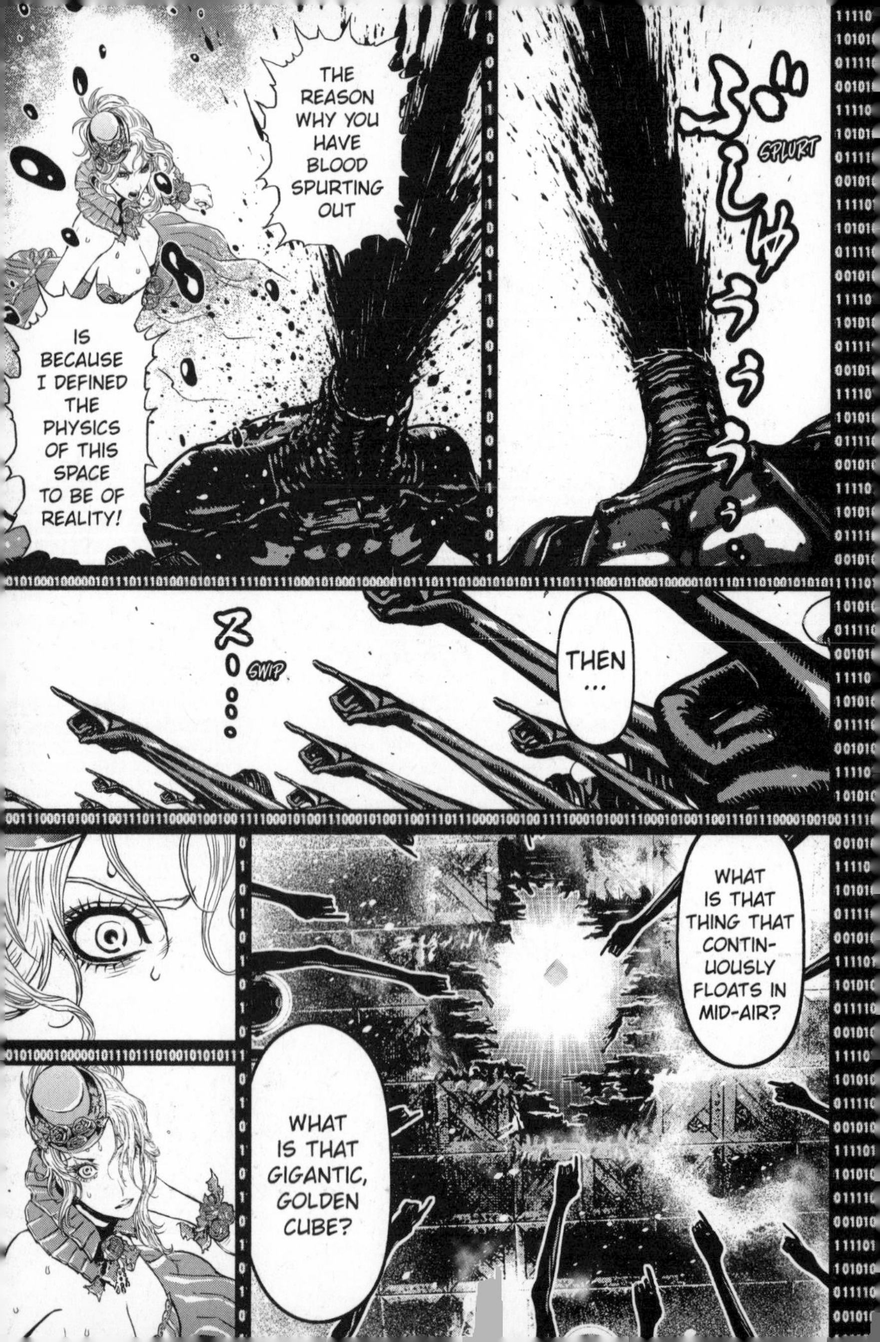
SPLURT
THE REASON WHY YOU HAVE BLOOD SPURTING OUT
IS BECAUSE I DEFINED THE PHYSICS OF THIS SPACE TO BE OF REALITY!
THEN...
SWIP
WHAT IS THAT THING THAT CONTIN-UOUSLY FLOATS IN MID-AIR?
WHAT IS THAT GIGANTIC, GOLDEN CUBE?

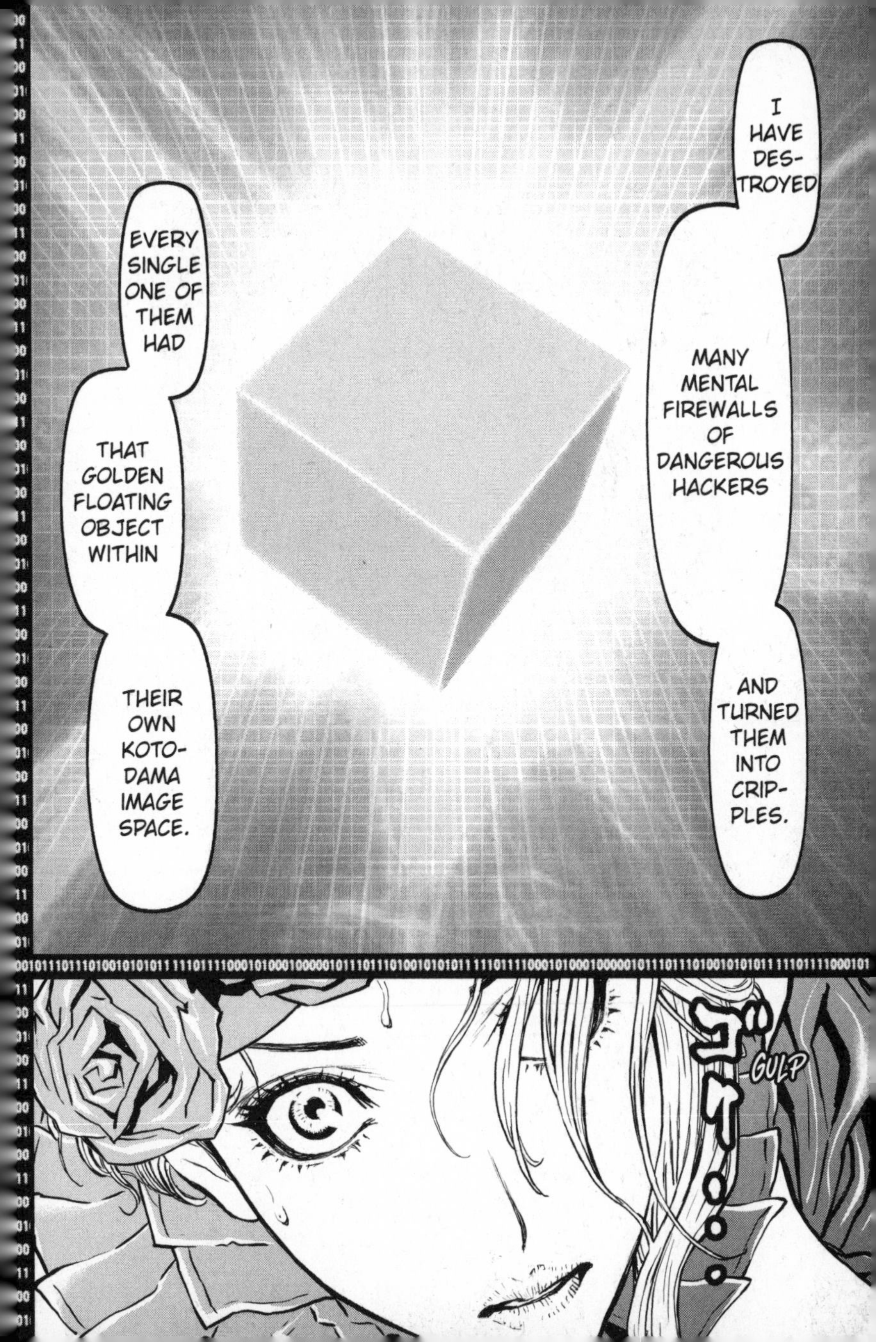
I HAVE DES-TROYED
MANY MENTAL FIREWALLS OF DANGEROUS HACKERS
AND TURNED THEM INTO CRIP-PLES.
EVERY SINGLE ONE OF THEM HAD
THAT GOLDEN FLOATING OBJECT WITHIN
THEIR OWN KOTO-DAMA IMAGE SPACE.
GULP

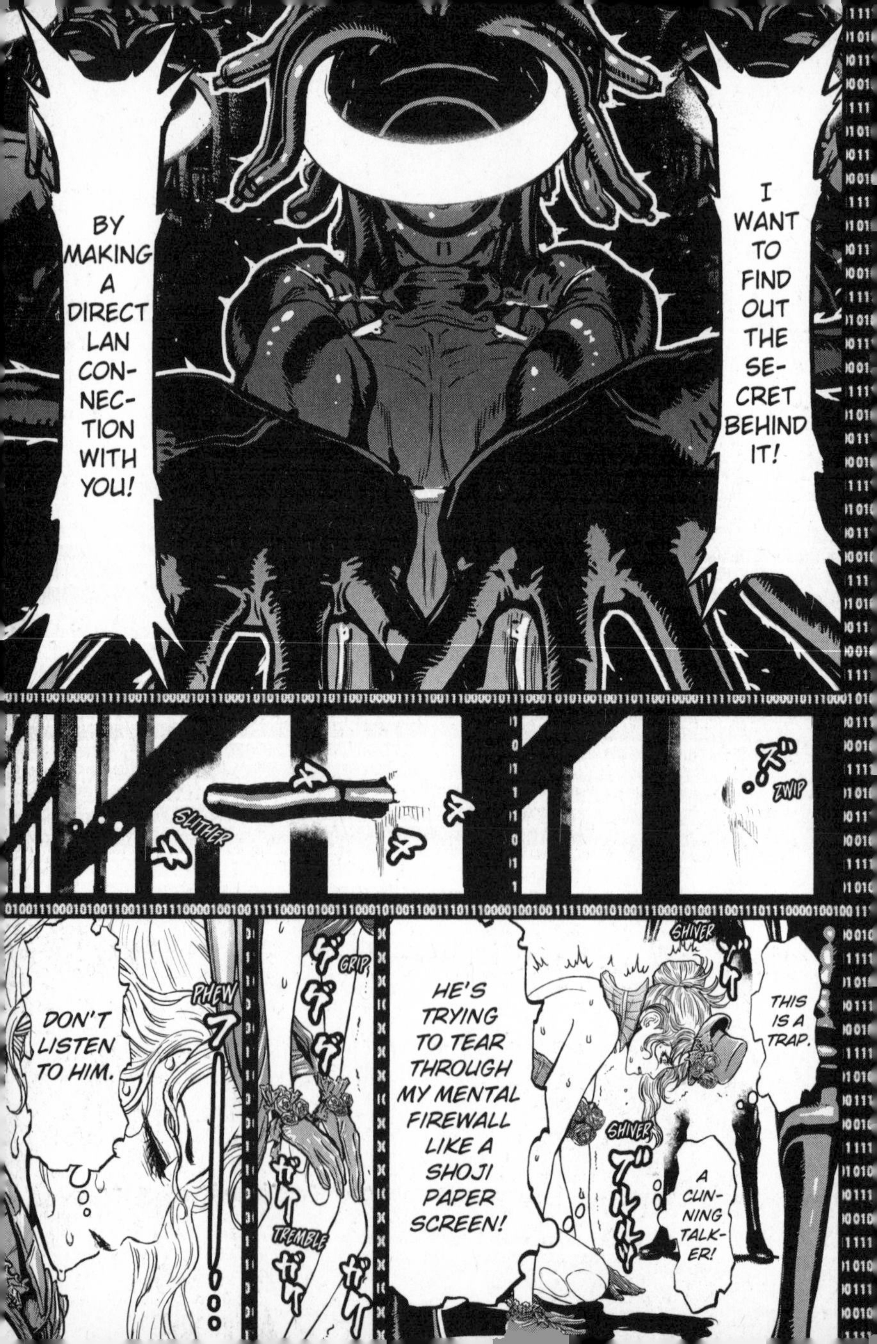
I WANT TO FIND OUT THE SECRET BEHIND IT!
BY MAKING A DIRECT LAN CONNECTION WITH YOU!
ZWIP
SLITHER
SHIVER
THIS IS A TRAP.
A CUNNING TALKER!
SHIVER
HE'S TRYING TO TEAR THROUGH MY MENTAL FIREWALL LIKE A SHOJI PAPER SCREEN!
GRIP
TREMBLE
PHEW
DON'T LISTEN TO HIM.

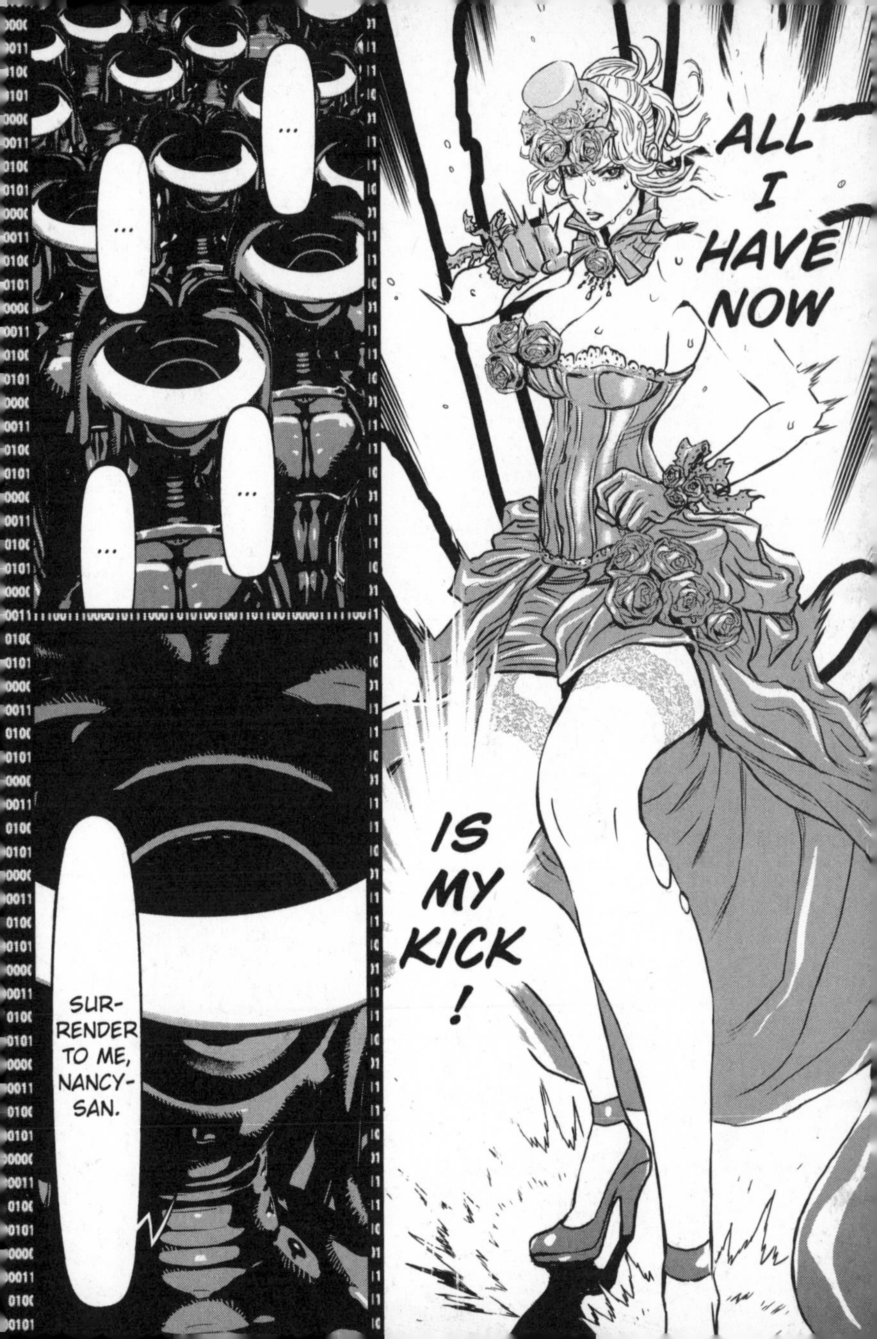
ALL I HAVE NOW
IS MY KICK!
...
...
...
...
SUR-RENDER TO ME, NANCY-SAN.

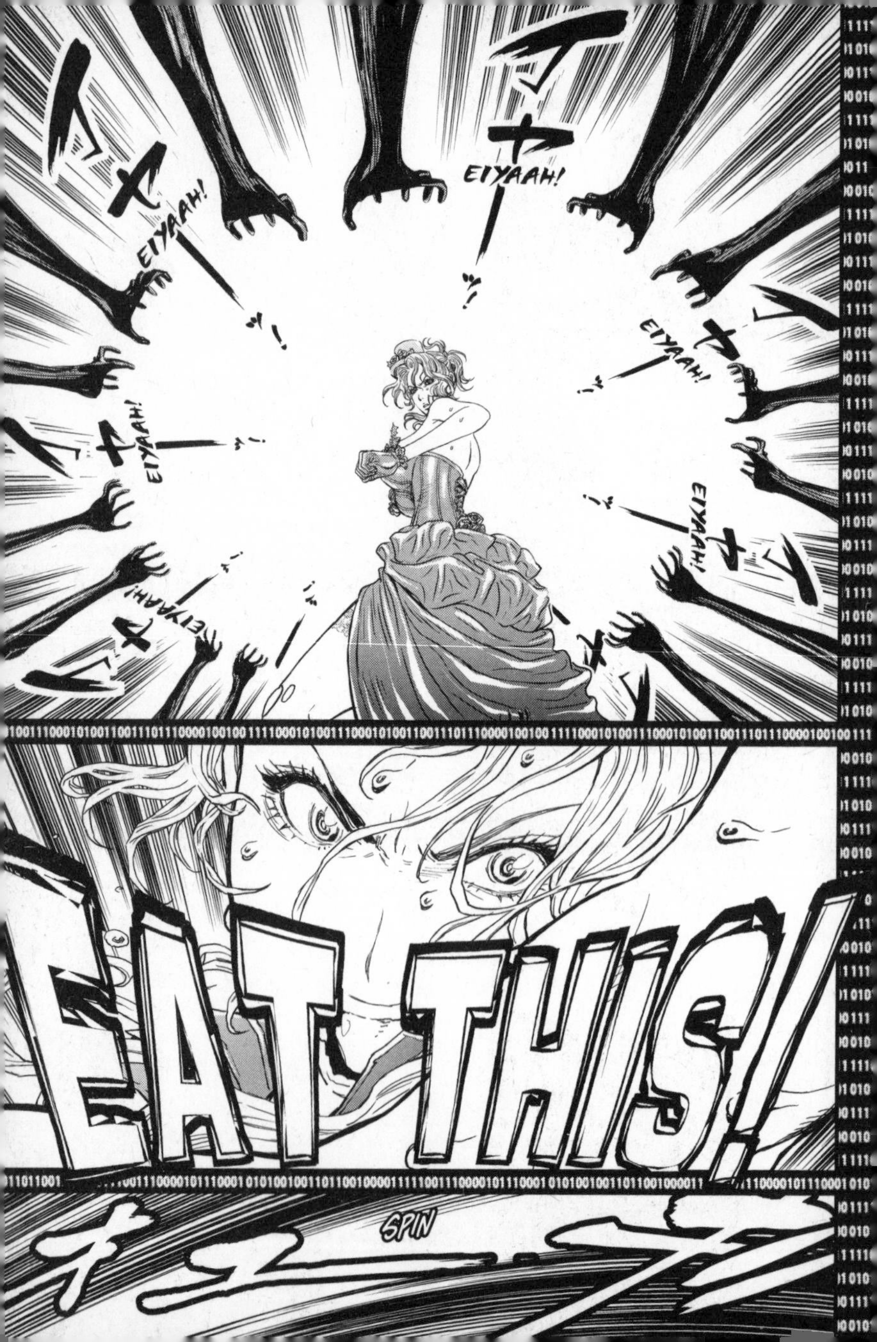

EIYAAH!
EIYAAH!
EIYAAH!
EIYAAH!
EIYAAH!
EIYAAH!
EAT THIS!
SPIN

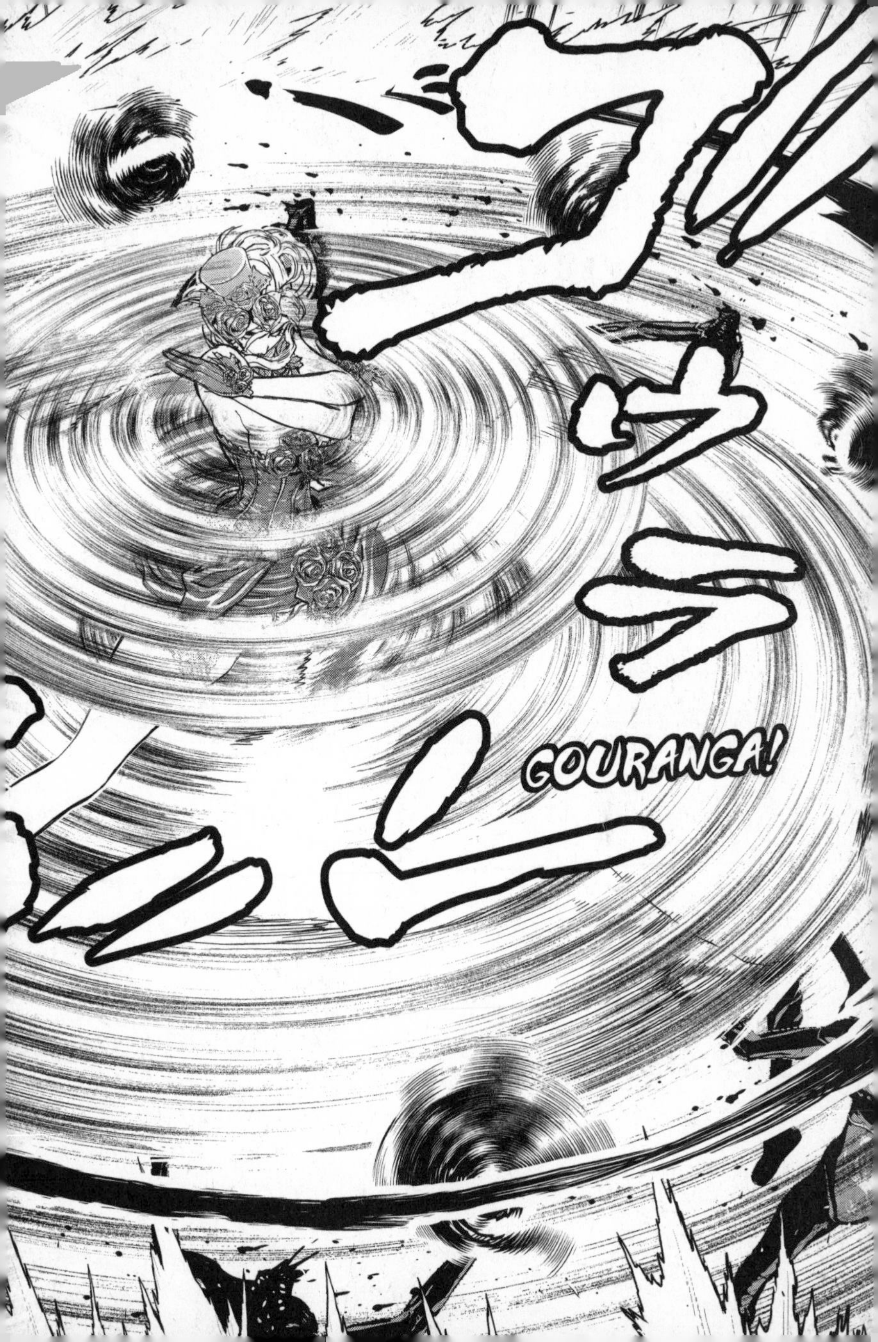
GOURANGA!

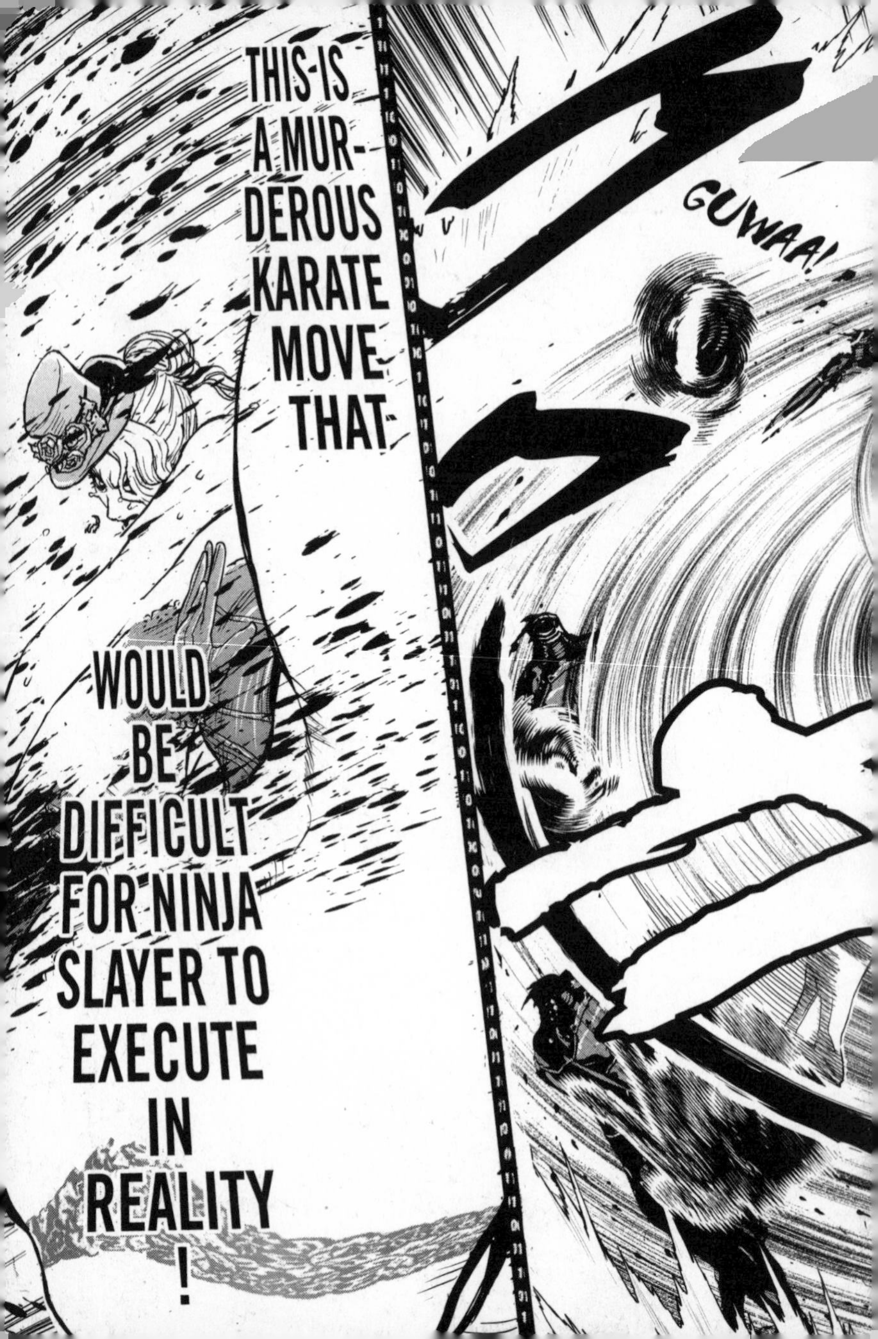
GUWAA!
THIS IS A MURDEROUS KARATE MOVE THAT
WOULD BE DIFFICULT FOR NINJA SLAYER TO EXECUTE IN REALITY!

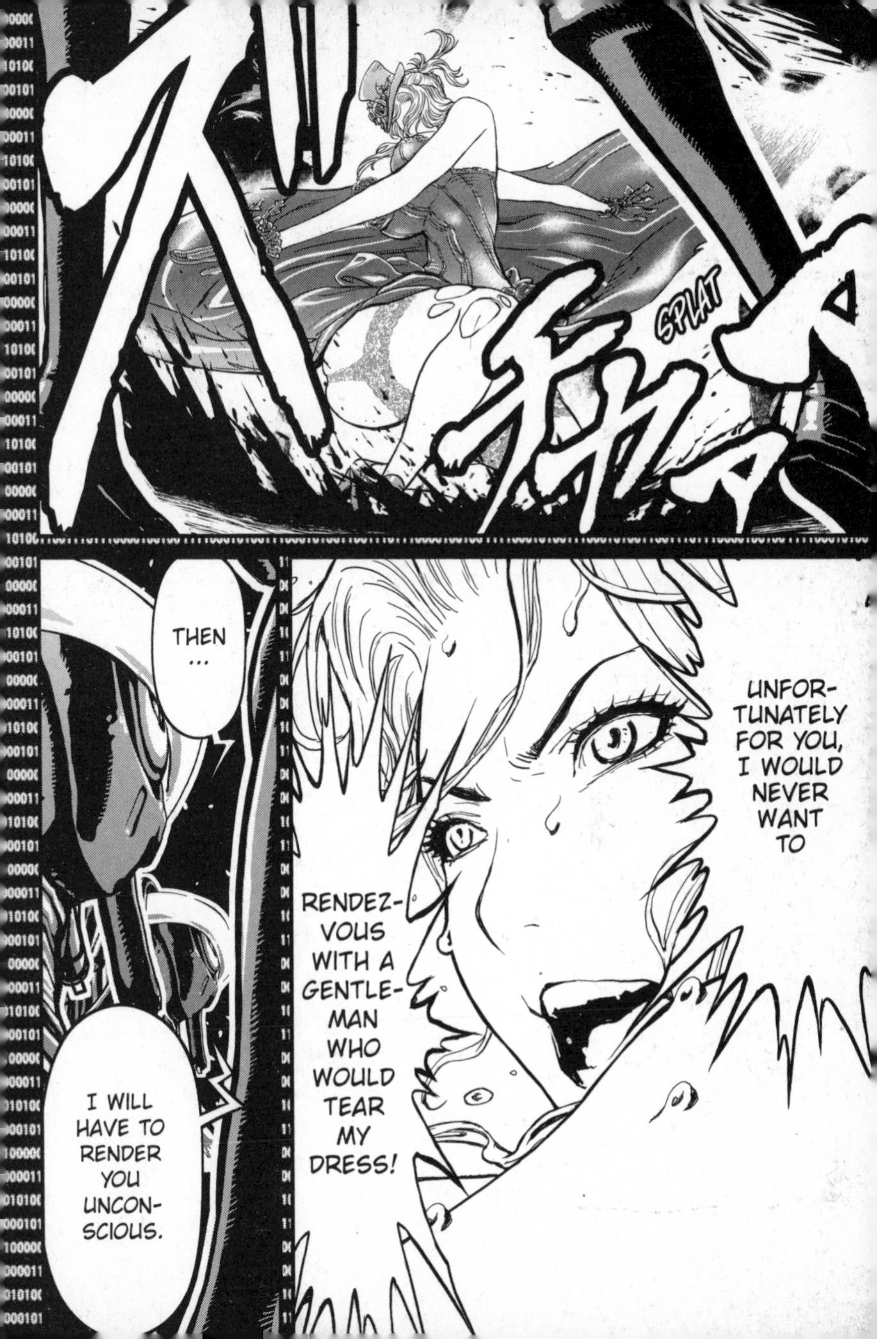
SPLAT
UNFOR-TUNATELY FOR YOU, I WOULD NEVER WANT TO
RENDEZ-VOUS WITH A GENTLE-MAN WHO WOULD TEAR MY DRESS!
THEN ...
I WILL HAVE TO RENDER YOU UNCON-SCIOUS.

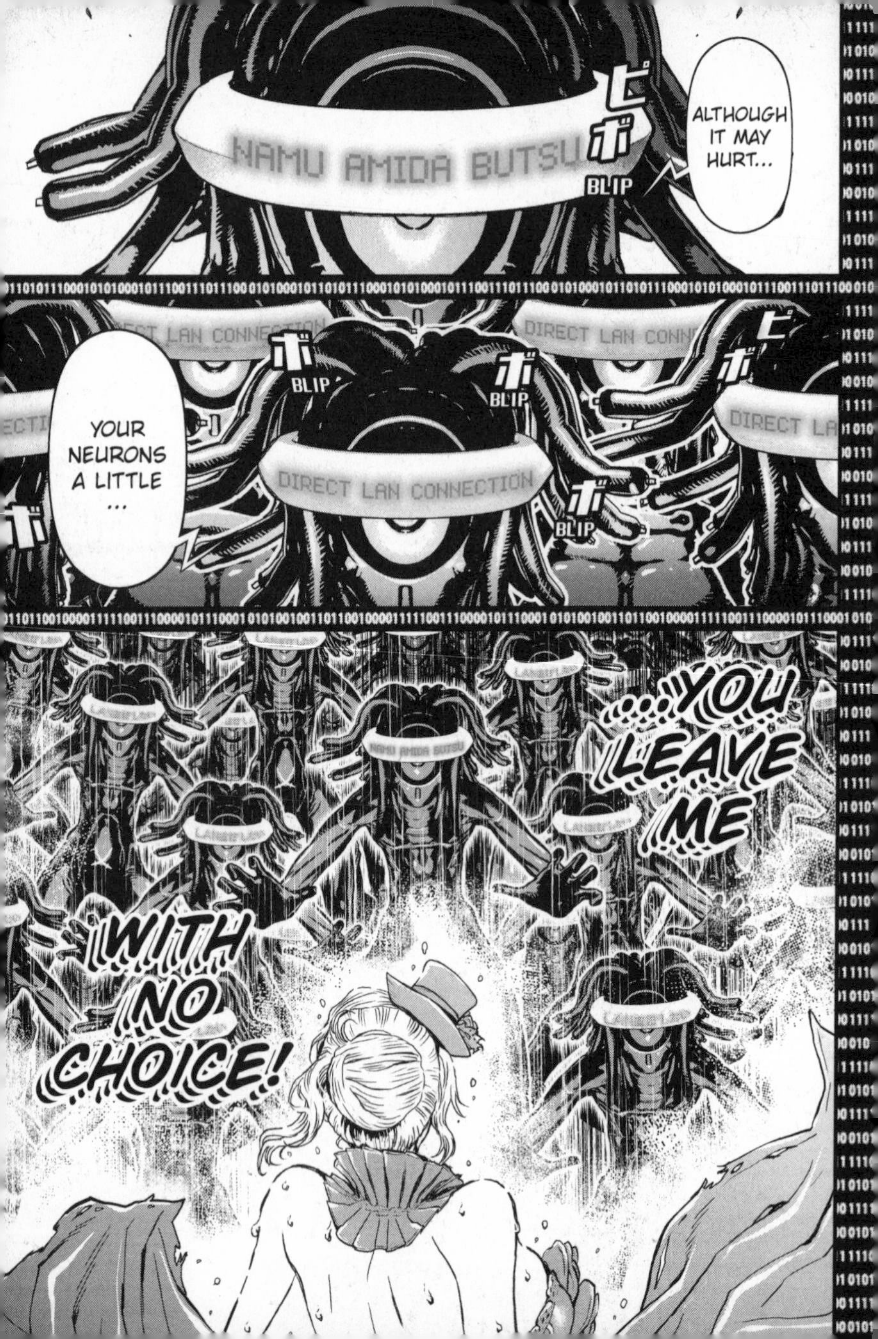
ALTHOUGH IT MAY HURT...
ピポ
BLIP
NAMU AMIDA BUTSU
ピ
ボ
BLIP
DIRECT LAN CONNECTION
YOUR NEURONS A LITTLE ...
...YOU LEAVE ME
WITH NO CHOICE!

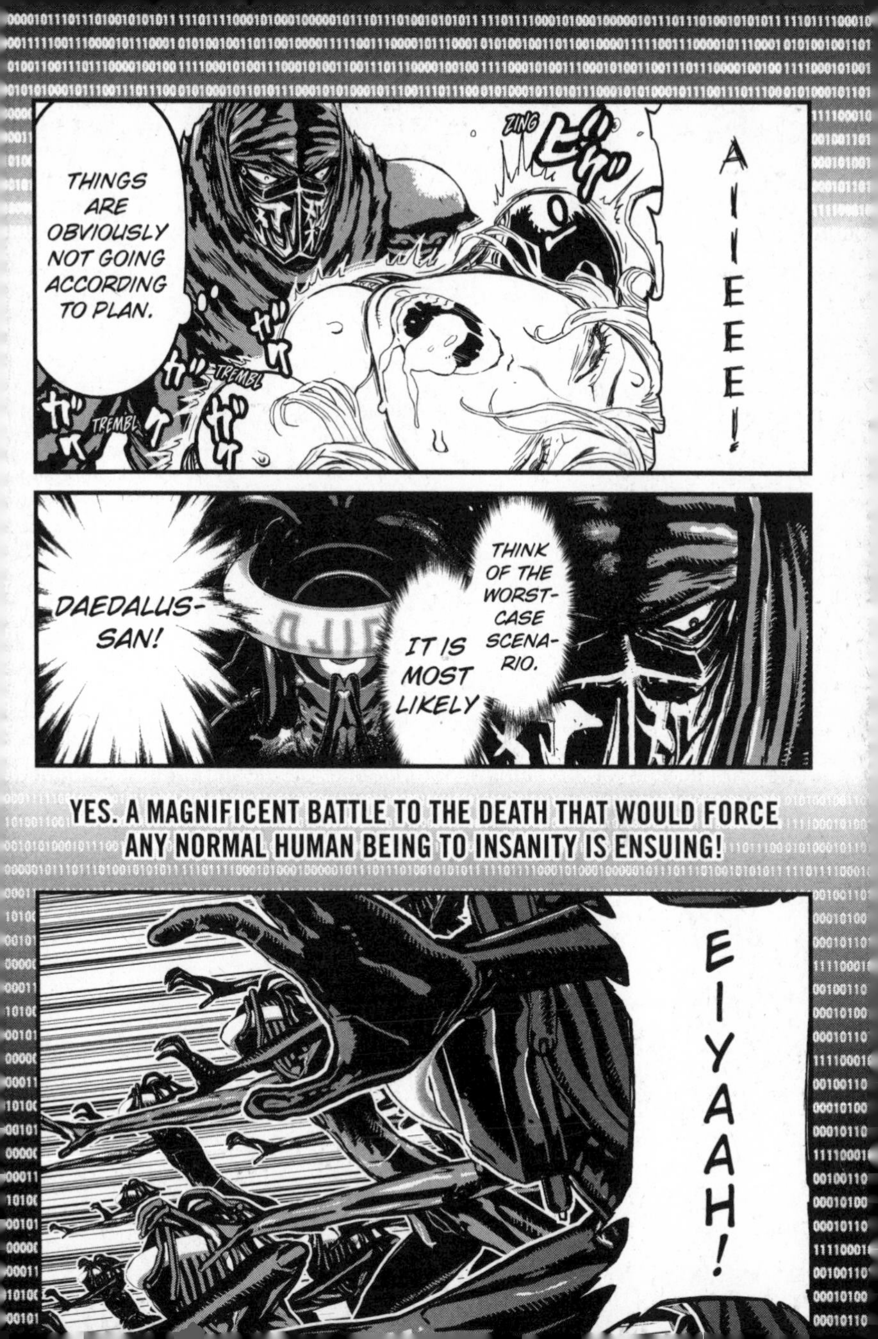

ZING
AIIEEE!
THINGS ARE OBVIOUSLY NOT GOING ACCORDING TO PLAN.
TREMBL
TREMBL
THINK OF THE WORST-CASE SCENA-RIO.
IT IS MOST LIKELY
DAEDALUS-SAN!
YES. A MAGNIFICENT BATTLE TO THE DEATH THAT WOULD FORCE ANY NORMAL HUMAN BEING TO INSANITY IS ENSUING!
EIYAAH!

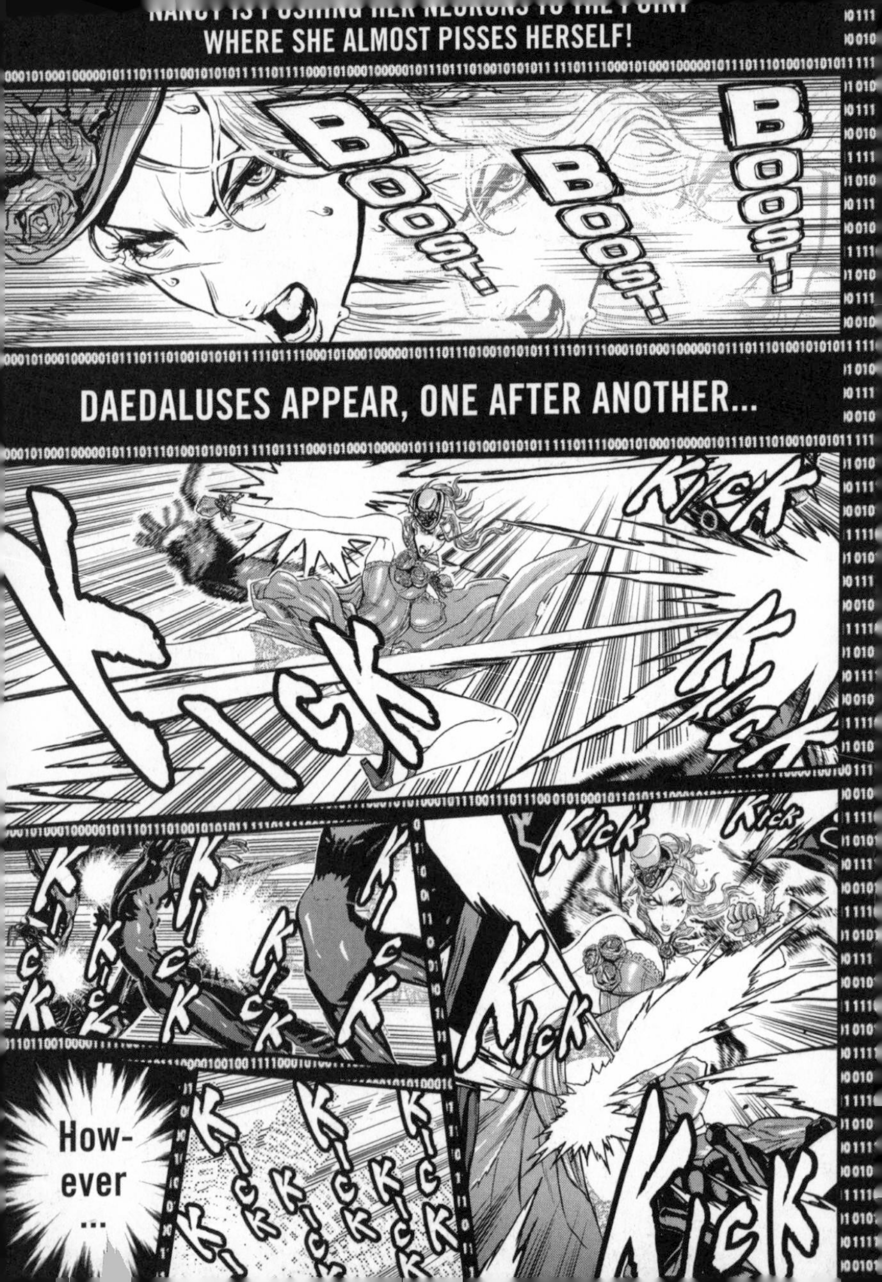
NANCY IS PUSHING HER NEURONS TO THE POINT
WHERE SHE ALMOST PISSES HERSELF!
BOOST!!
BOOST!!
BOOST!!
DAEDALUSES APPEAR, ONE AFTER ANOTHER...
KICK
KICK
KICK
KICK
KICK
KICK
KICK
KICK
KICK KICK
KICK KICK
KICK KICK
How-ever...

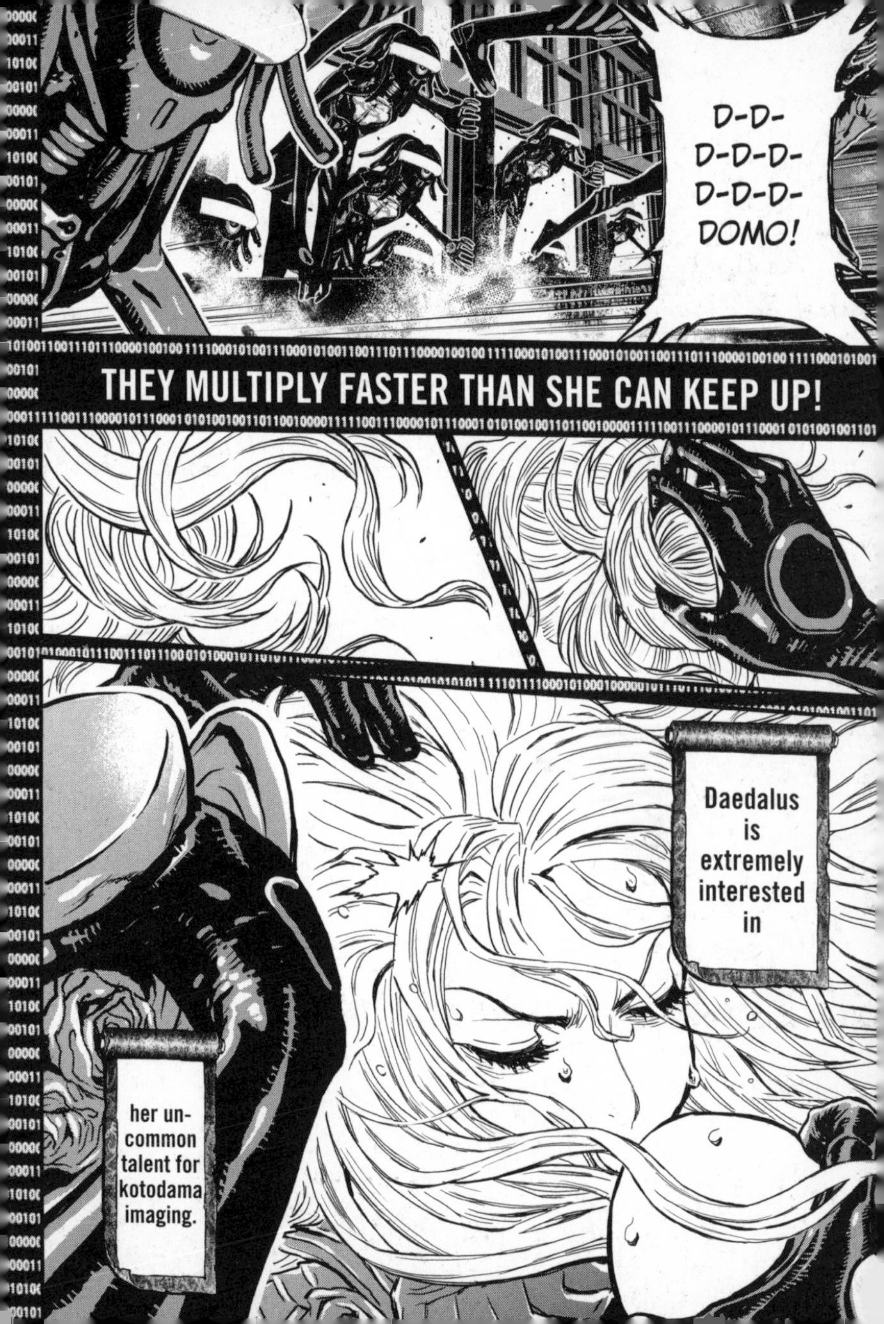
D-D-
D-D-D-
D-D-D-
DOMO!
THEY MULTIPLY FASTER THAN SHE CAN KEEP UP!
Daedalus is extremely interested in
her un-common talent for kotodama imaging.

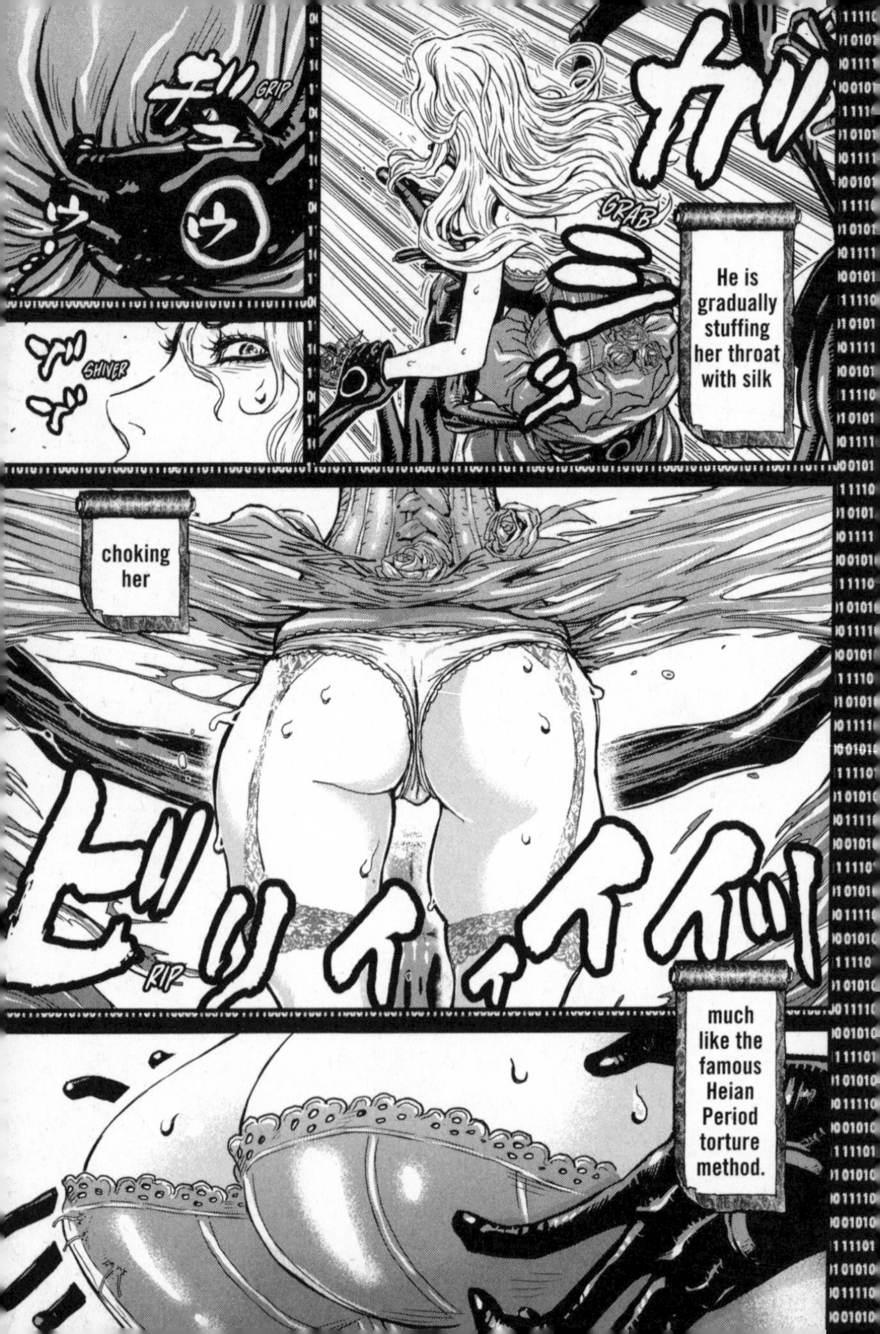
GRAB
He is gradually stuffing her throat with silk
GRIP
SHIVER
choking her
RIP
much like the famous Heian Period torture method.

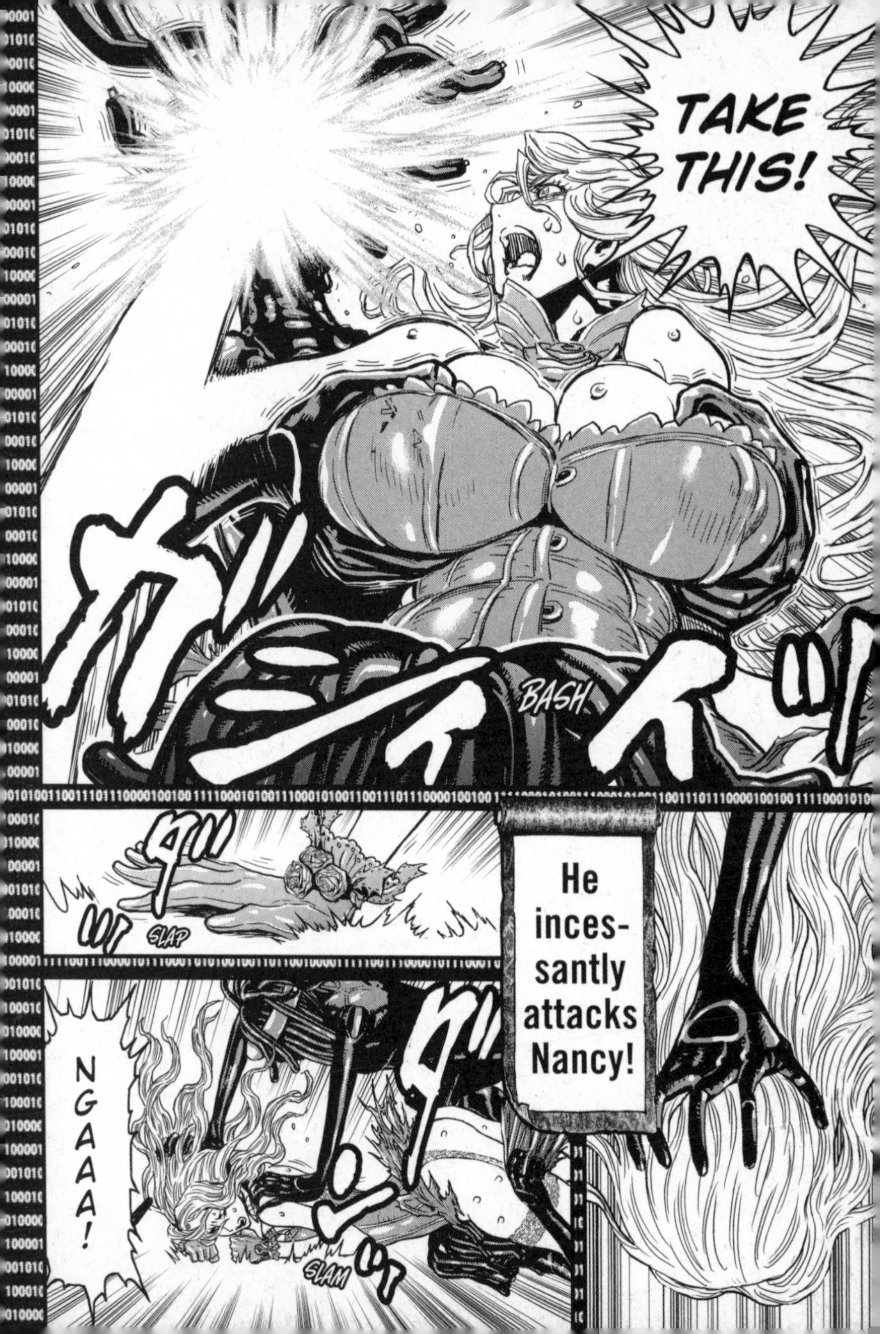
TAKE THIS!
BASH
He incessantly attacks Nancy!
SLAP
NGAAAA!
SLAM

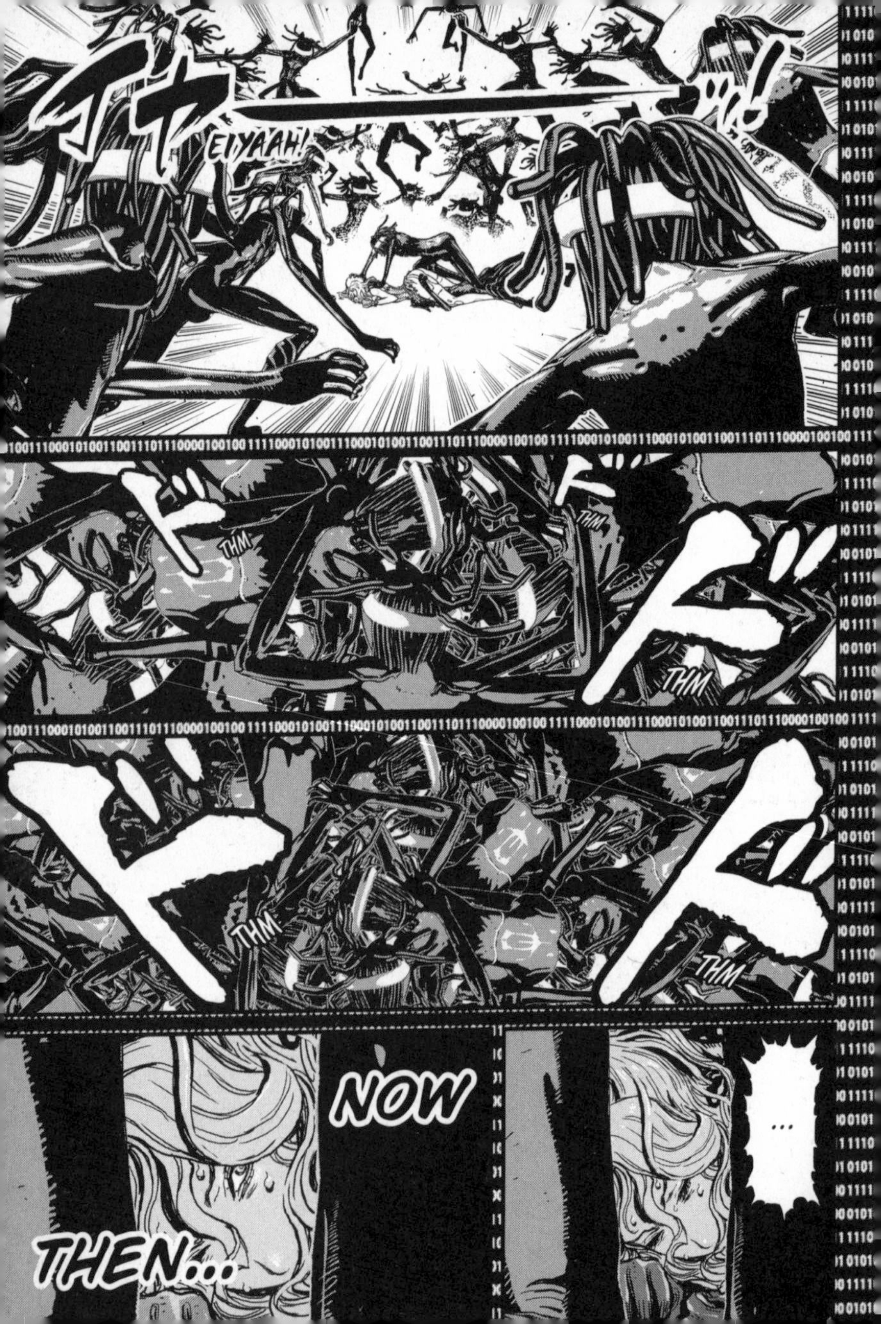
EIYAAH!
THM
THM
THM
THM
THM
THM
...
NOW
THEN...

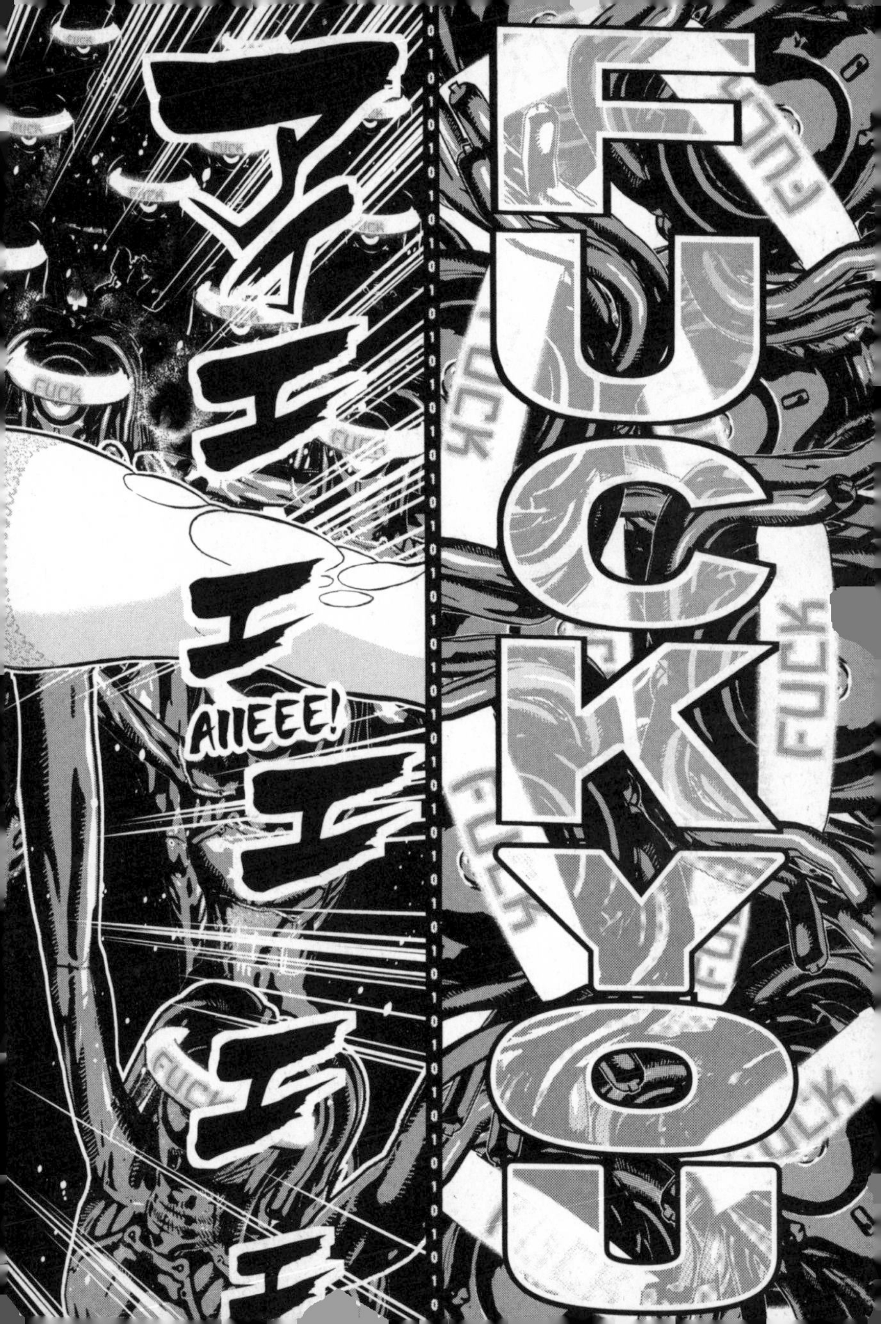
FUCK YOU
AIIEEE!

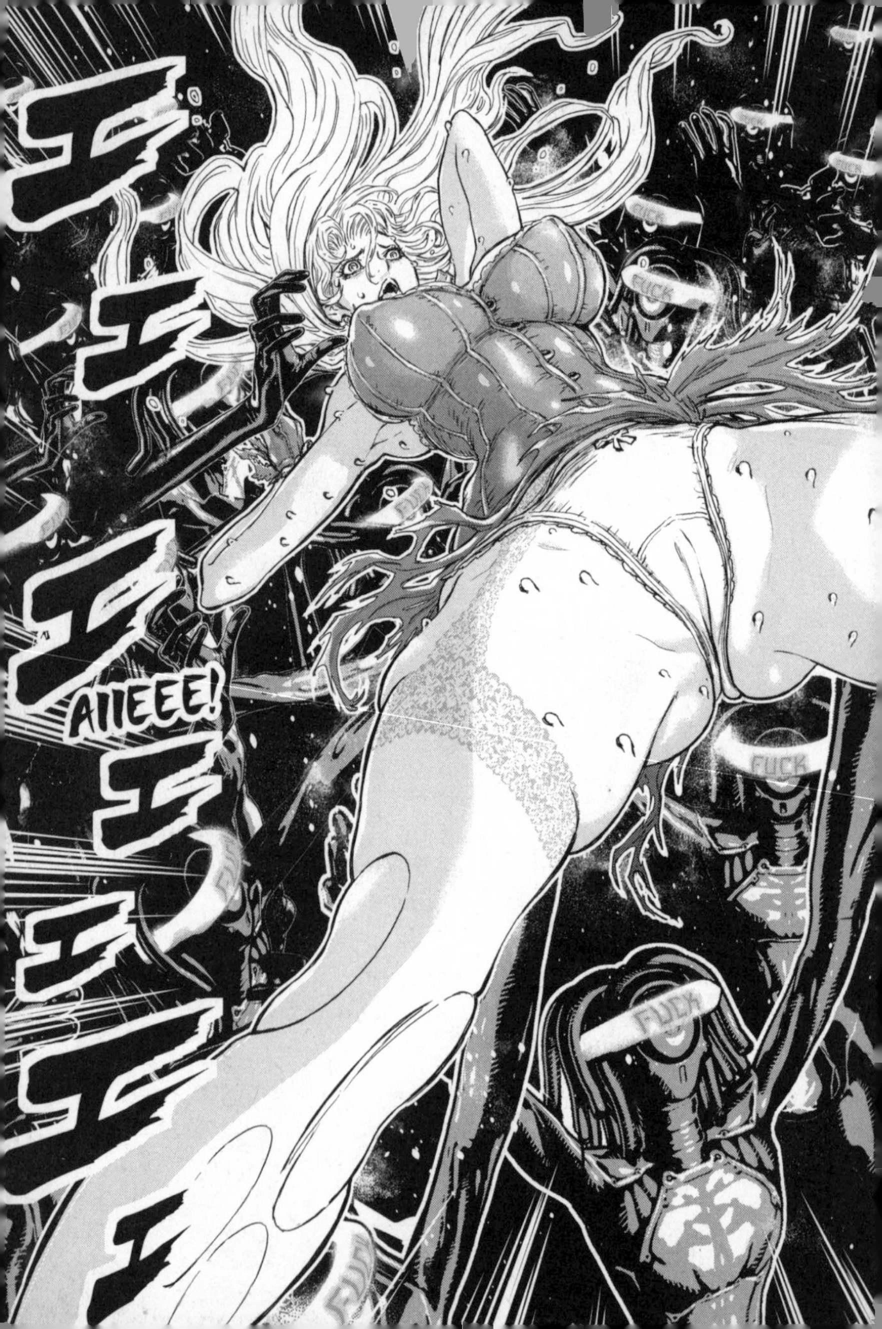
AIIEEE!
FUCK

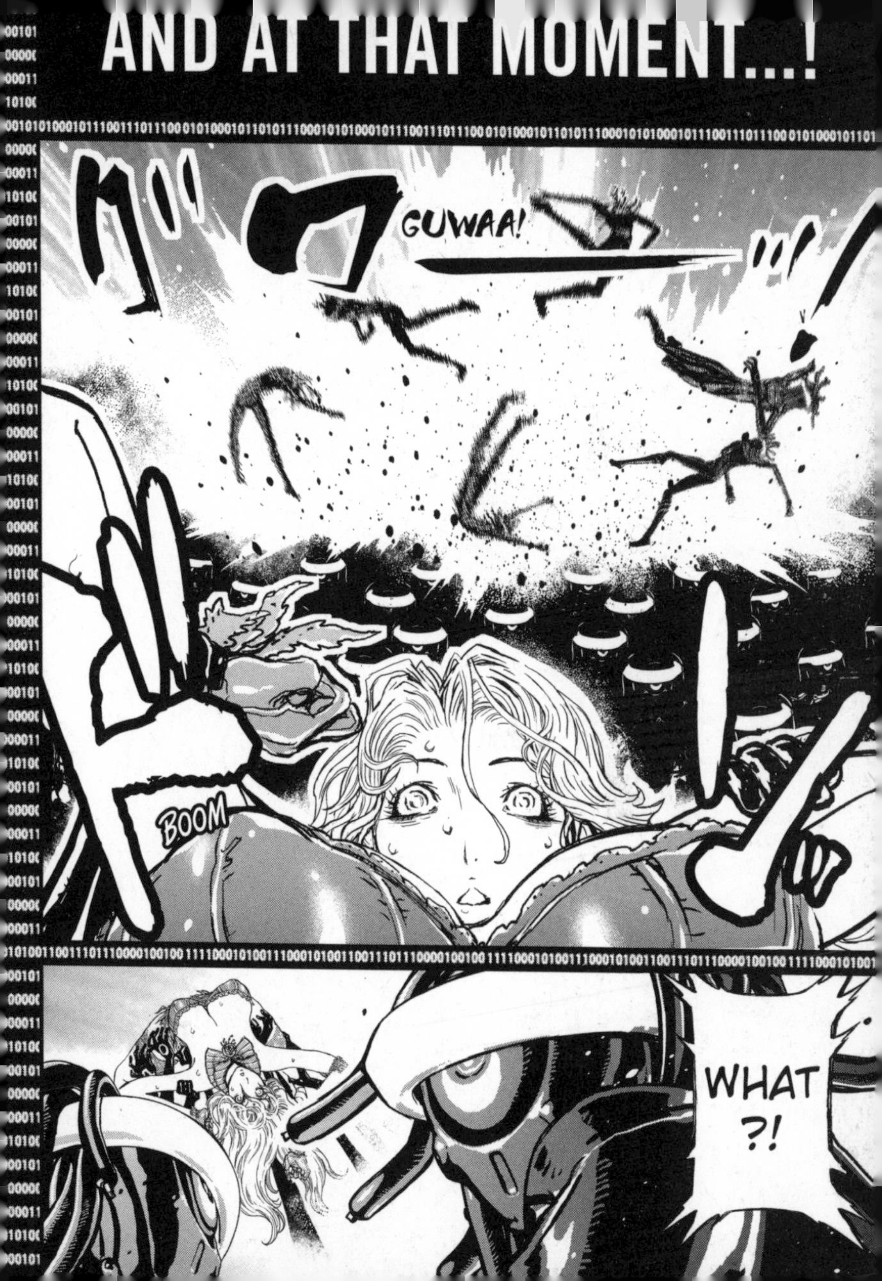
AND AT THAT MOMENT...!
GUWAA!
BOOM
WHAT ?!

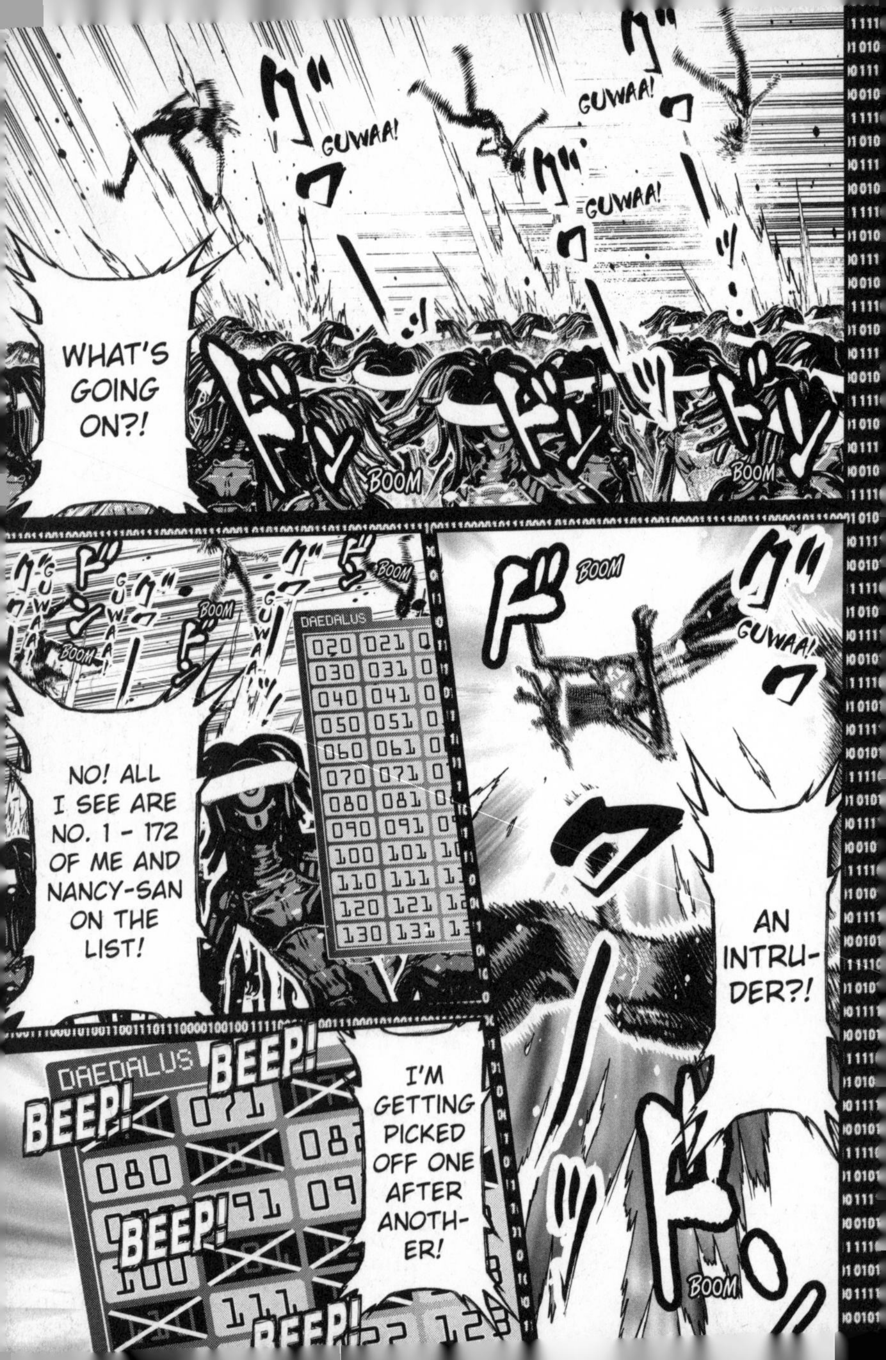
GUWAA!
GUWAA!
GUWAA!
WHAT'S GOING ON?!
BOOM
BOOM
BOOM
GUWAA!
AN INTRUDER?!
BOOM
BOOM
GUWAA!
GUWAA!
GUWAA!
BOOM
BOOM
DAEDALUS
NO! ALL I SEE ARE NO. 1 - 172 OF ME AND NANCY-SAN ON THE LIST!
BEEP!
BEEP!
DAEDALUS
I'M GETTING PICKED OFF ONE AFTER ANOTHER!
BEEP!

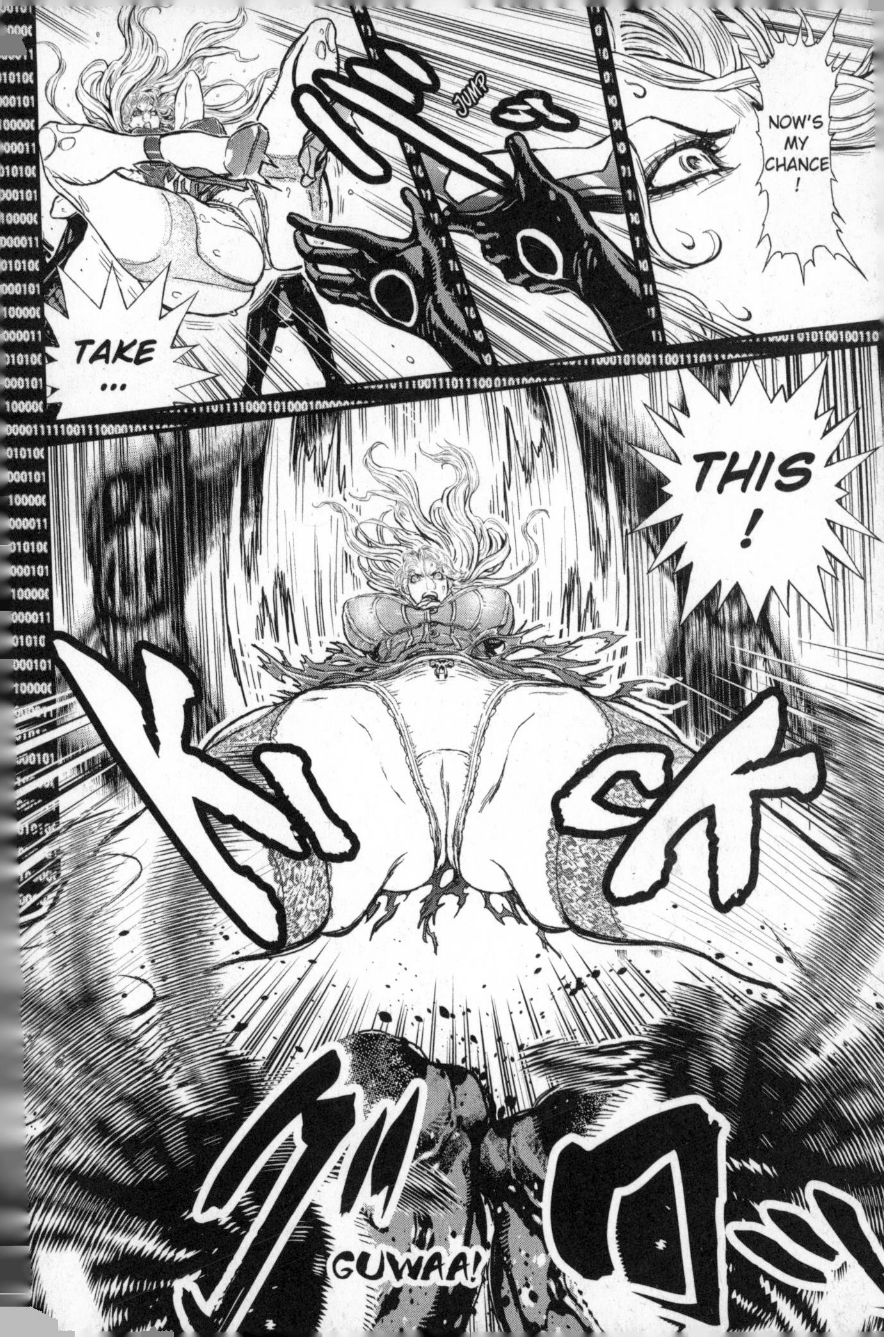
NOW'S MY CHANCE!
JUMP
TAKE ...
THIS!
GUWAA!

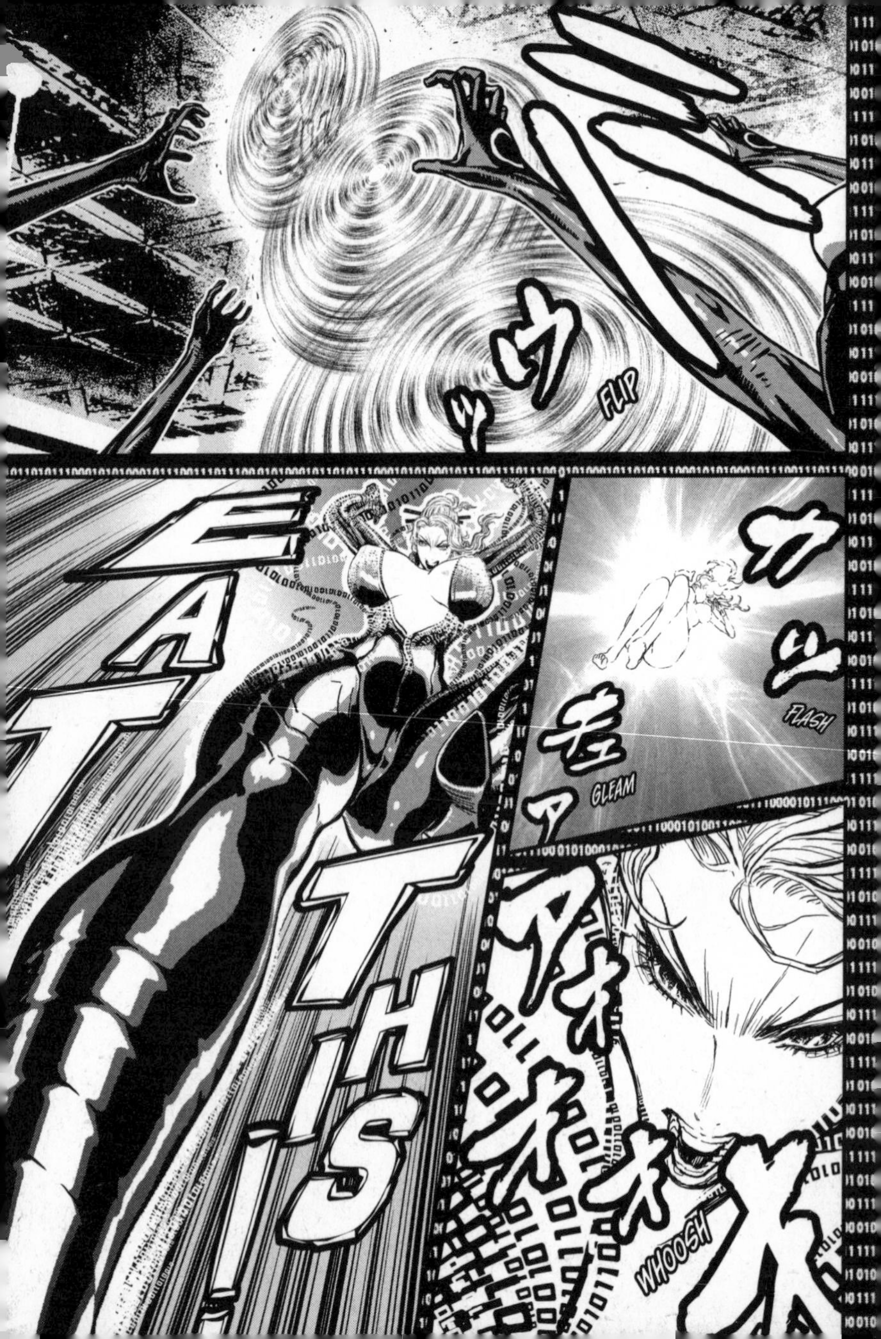
FLIP
FLASH
GLEAM
WHOOSH
EAT
THIS

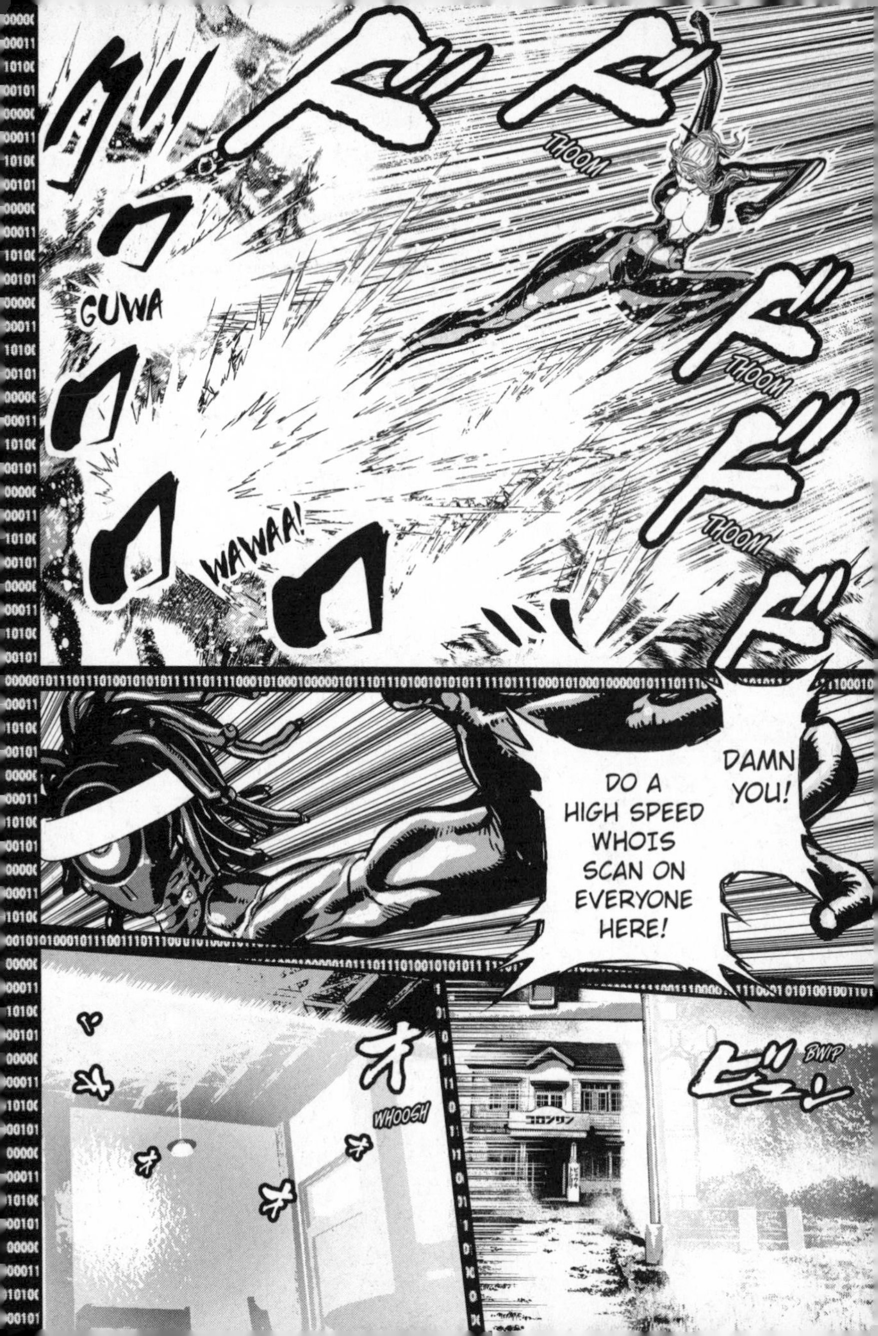

THOOM
THOOM
THOOM
WAWAA!
GUWA
DAMN YOU!
DO A HIGH SPEED WHOIS SCAN ON EVERYONE HERE!
BWIP
WHOOSH

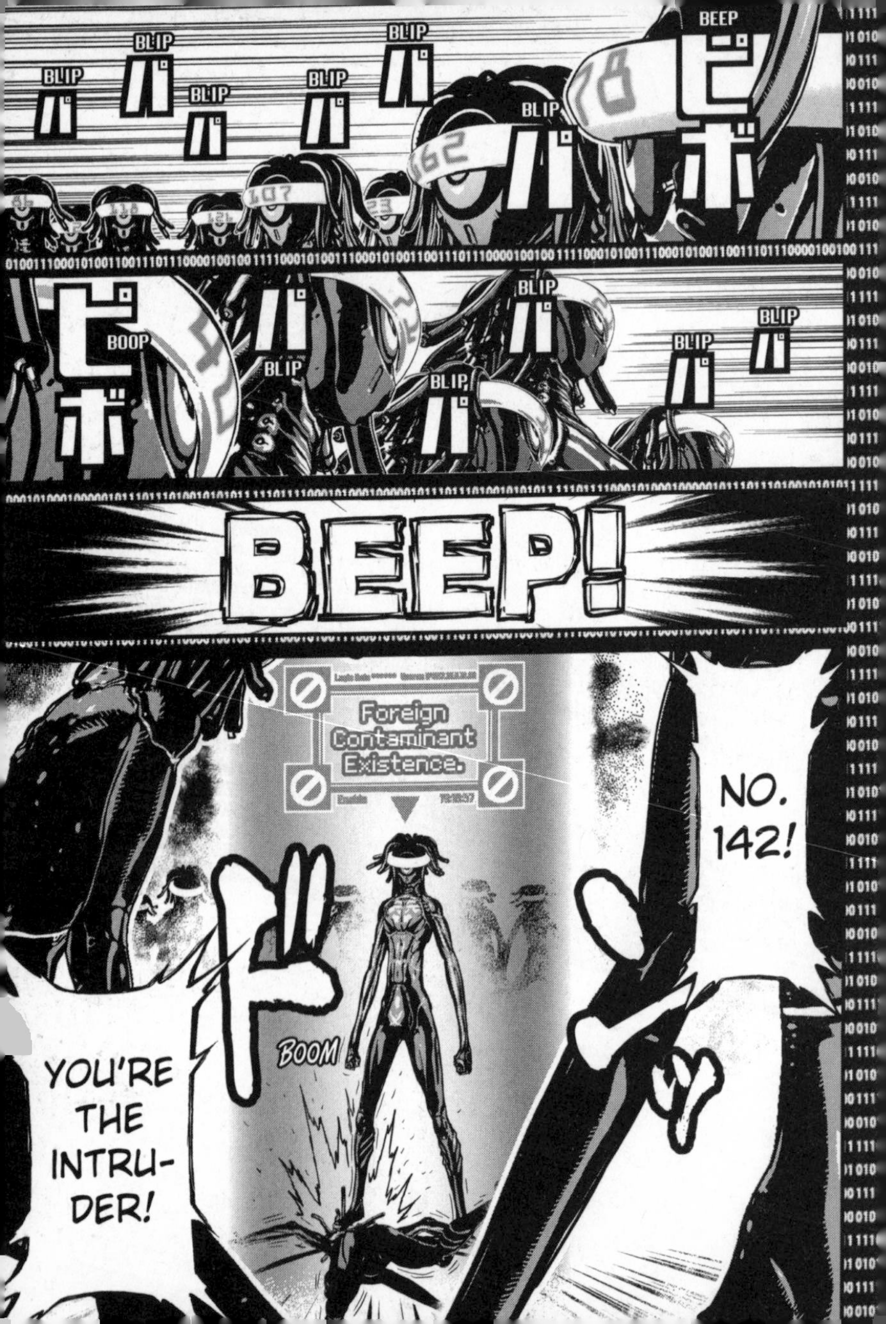
BEEP
ピボ
BLIP
パ
BLIP
パ
BLIP
パ
BLIP
パ
BLIP
パ
BLIP
パ
BLIP
パ
BLIP
パ
BLIP
パ
BLIP
パ
BLIP
パ
BOOP
ピボ
BEEP!
NO. 142!
Foreign Contaminant Existence.
ド
BOOM
YOU'RE THE INTRU-DER!

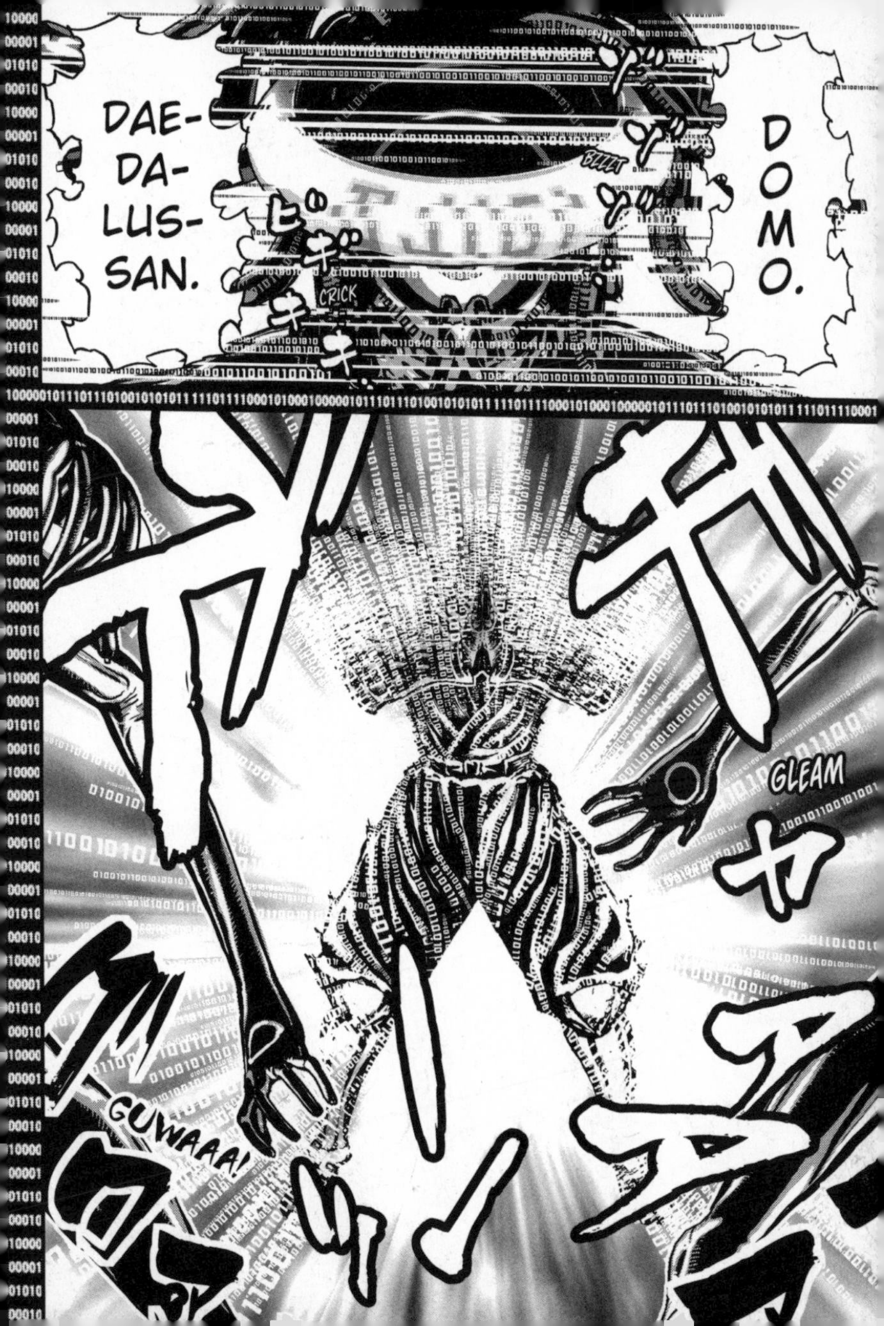
DOMO.
BZZZT
DAE-DA-LUS-SAN.
CRICK
GLEAM
GUWAAA!

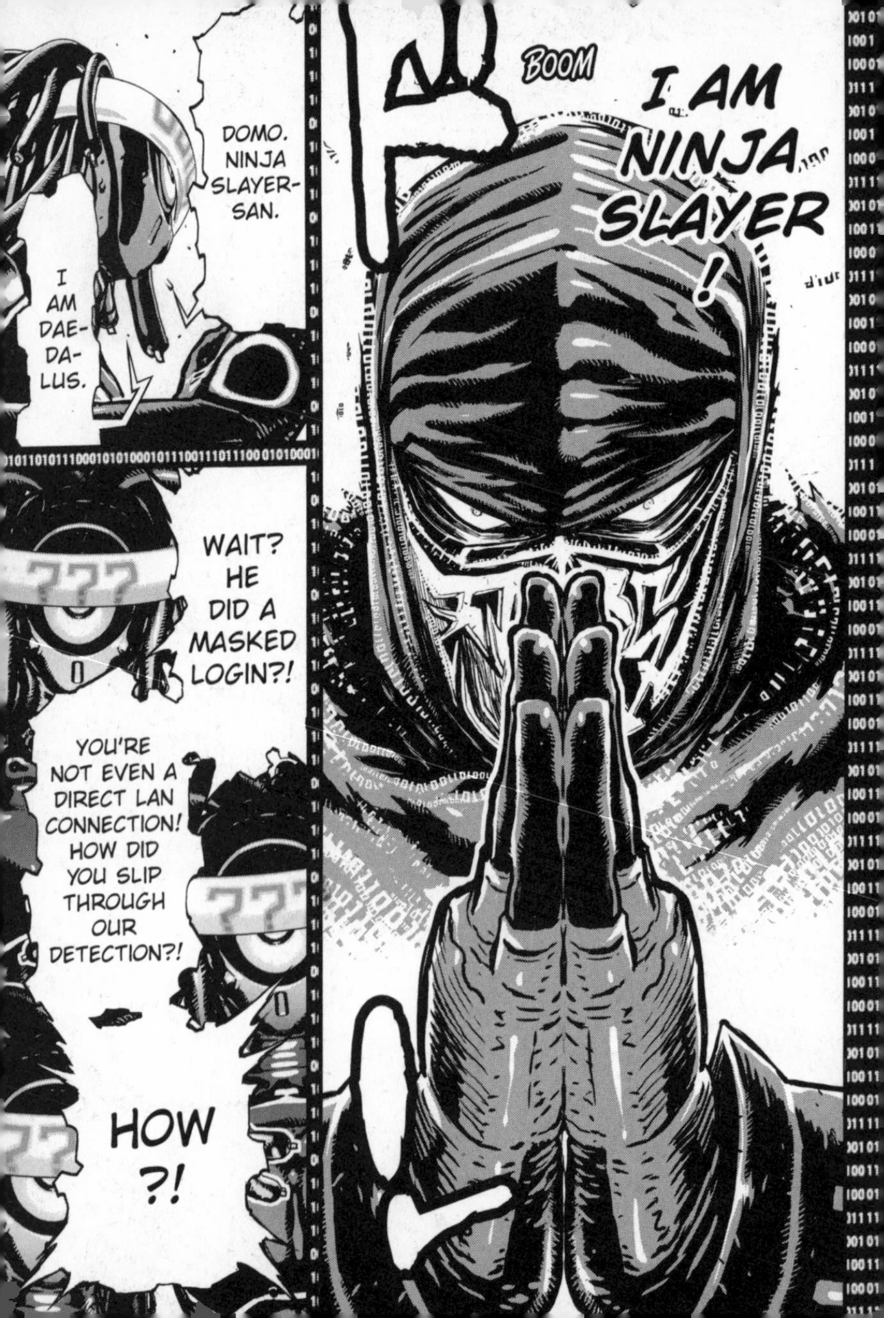
BOOM
I AM NINJA SLAYER!
DOMO. NINJA SLAYER-SAN.
I AM DAEDALUS.
WAIT? HE DID A MASKED LOGIN?!
YOU'RE NOT EVEN A DIRECT LAN CONNECTION! HOW DID YOU SLIP THROUGH OUR DETECTION?!
HOW?!

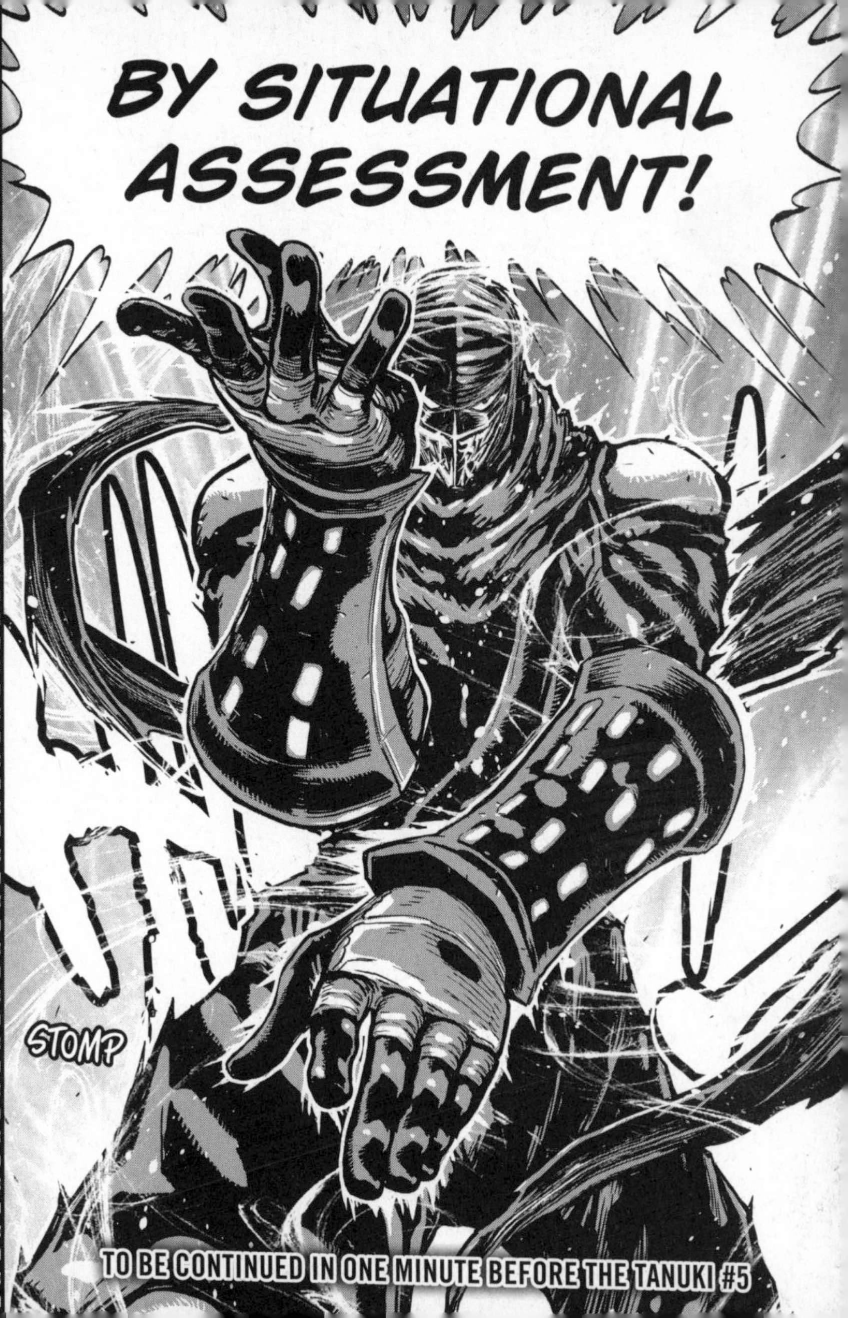
BY SITUATIONAL ASSESSMENT!
STOMP
TO BE CONTINUED IN ONE MINUTE BEFORE THE TANUKI #5

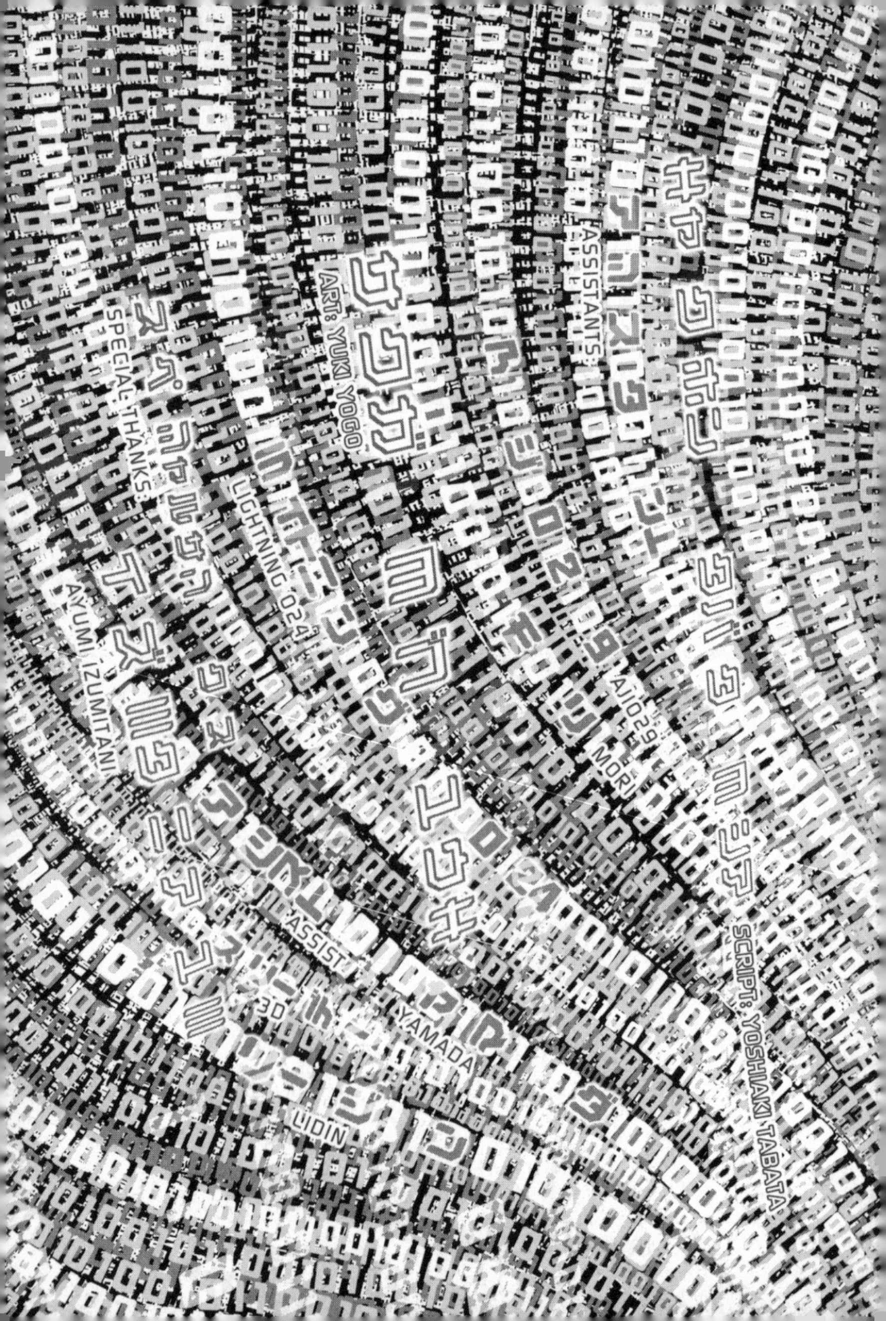
SCRIPT: YOSHIAKI TABATA
ASSISTANTS: AJIO29
MORI
ART: YUKI YOGO
ASSIST
3D
YAMADA
LIDIN
LIGHTNING 024
SPECIAL THANKS:
AYUMI IZUMITANI

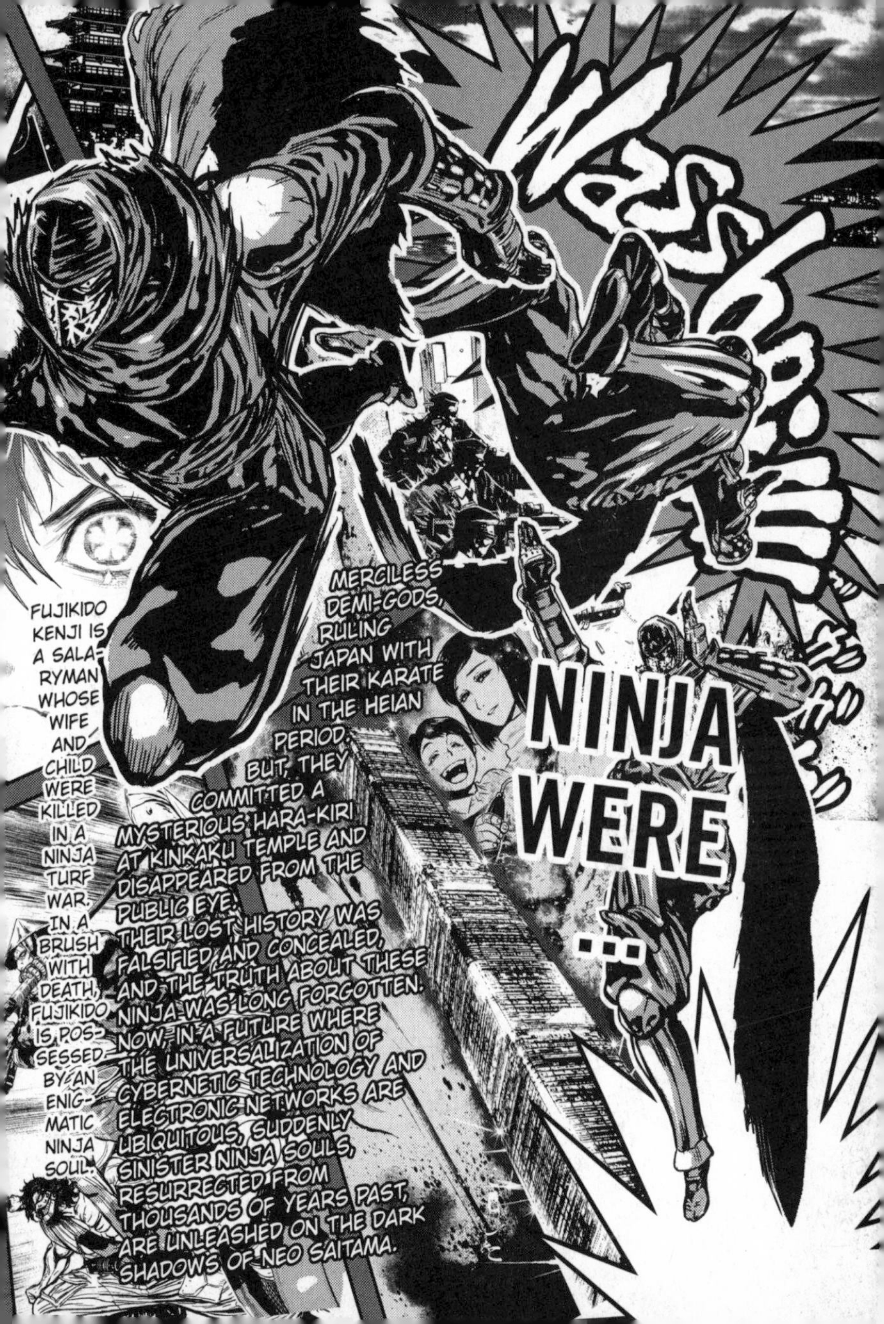
NINJA WERE ...
MERCILESS DEMI-GODS, RULING JAPAN WITH THEIR KARATE IN THE HEIAN PERIOD. BUT, THEY COMMITTED A MYSTERIOUS HARA-KIRI AT KINKAKU TEMPLE AND DISAPPEARED FROM THE PUBLIC EYE. THEIR LOST HISTORY WAS FALSIFIED AND CONCEALED, AND THE TRUTH ABOUT THESE NINJA WAS LONG FORGOTTEN. NOW, IN A FUTURE WHERE THE UNIVERSALIZATION OF CYBERNETIC TECHNOLOGY AND ELECTRONIC NETWORKS ARE UBIQUITOUS, SUDDENLY SINISTER NINJA SOULS, RESURRECTED FROM THOUSANDS OF YEARS PAST, ARE UNLEASHED ON THE DARK SHADOWS OF NEO SAITAMA.
FUJIKIDO KENJI IS A SALARYMAN WHOSE WIFE AND CHILD WERE KILLED IN A NINJA TURF WAR. IN A BRUSH WITH DEATH, FUJIKIDO IS POSSESSED BY AN ENIGMATIC NINJA SOUL.

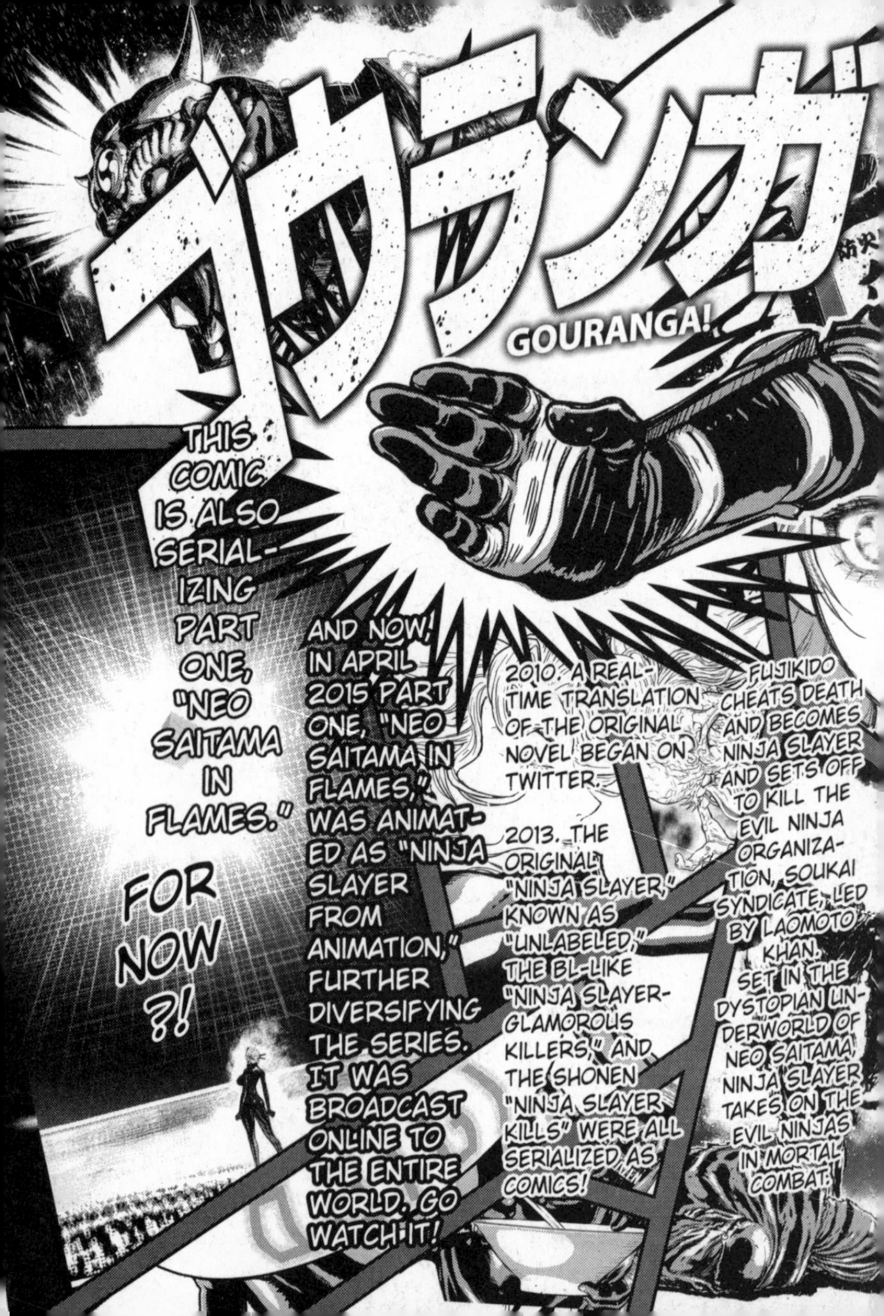
ゴウランガ
GOURANGA!
FUJIKIDO CHEATS DEATH AND BECOMES NINJA SLAYER AND SETS OFF TO KILL THE EVIL NINJA ORGANIZATION, SOUKAI SYNDICATE, LED BY LAOMOTO KHAN. SET IN THE DYSTOPIAN UNDERWORLD OF NEO SAITAMA, NINJA SLAYER TAKES ON THE EVIL NINJAS IN MORTAL COMBAT.
2010. A REAL-TIME TRANSLATION OF THE ORIGINAL NOVEL BEGAN ON TWITTER.
2013. THE ORIGINAL "NINJA SLAYER," KNOWN AS "UNLABELED," THE BL-LIKE "NINJA SLAYER-GLAMOROUS KILLERS," AND THE SHONEN "NINJA SLAYER KILLS" WERE ALL SERIALIZED AS COMICS!
AND NOW, IN APRIL 2015 PART ONE, "NEO SAITAMA IN FLAMES," WAS ANIMATED AS "NINJA SLAYER FROM ANIMATION," FURTHER DIVERSIFYING THE SERIES. IT WAS BROADCAST ONLINE TO THE ENTIRE WORLD. GO WATCH IT!
THIS COMIC IS ALSO SERIALIZING PART ONE, "NEO SAITAMA IN FLAMES."
FOR NOW ?!

NINJA SLAYER Volume 5
~ONE MINUTE BEFORE THE TANUKI~

A Vertical Comics Edition

Translation: Christian Storms and HCL
Original Production: Keiran O'Leary

First published in Japan in 2015 by KADOKAWA CORPORATION, Tokyo.
English translation rights arranged with KADOKAWA CORPORATION, Tokyo
through TUTTLE-MORI AGENCY, INC., Tokyo.

Published by Vertical Comics, an imprint of Vertical, Inc., New York

Originally published in Japanese as *Ninja Sureiyaa~Wan Minitto Bifoa Za Tanuki~*
by Kadokawa
Ninja Sureiyaa first serialized in *Comptiq*, Kadokawa, 2013-

Ninja Slayer was created based on contents from the original *Ninja Slayer* novels and
some details, including time periods, the order of events, and character settings have
been changed with the consent of the original authors.

This is a work of fiction.

ISBN: 978-1-942993-55-1

Manufactured in Canada

First Edition

Vertical, Inc.
451 Park Avenue South
7th Floor
New York, NY 10016
www.vertical-inc.com

Vertical books are distributed through Penguin-Random House Publisher Services.